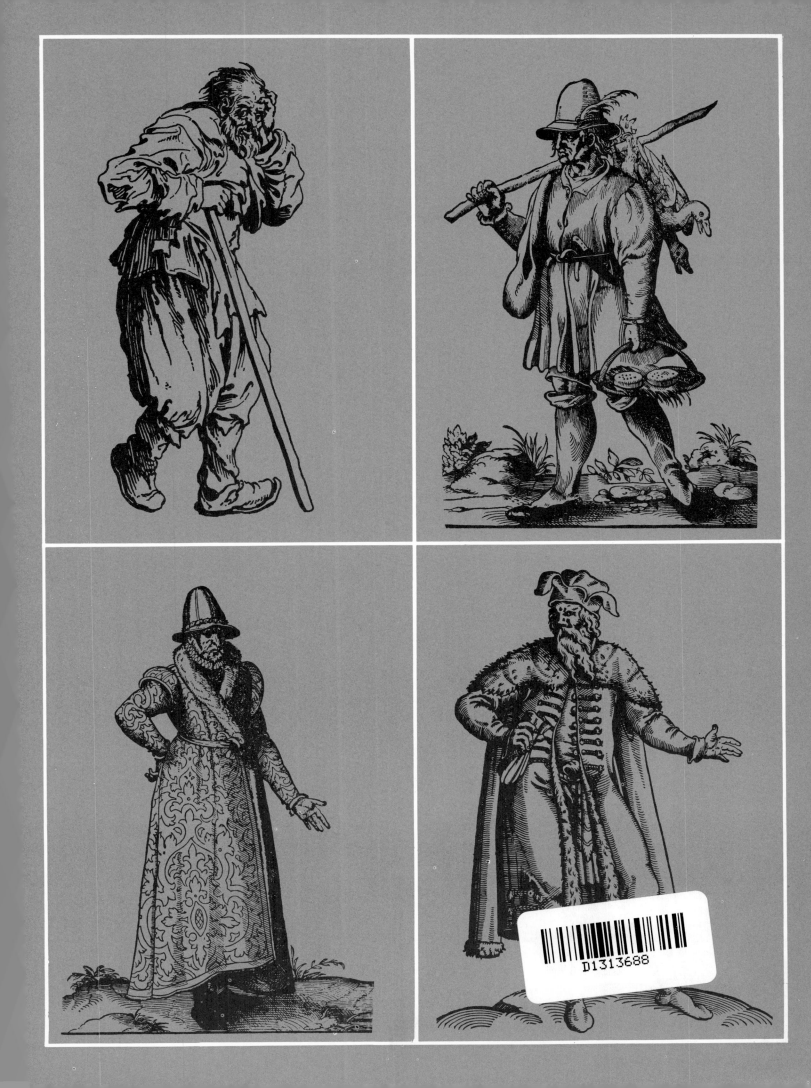

The Golden Age of Europe

With 279 illustrations
69 in color
210 photographs, engravings,
drawings and maps

EDITED BY
HUGH TREVOR-ROPER

The Golden Age
of Europe

FROM ELIZABETH I TO THE SUN KING

Texts by

HUGH TREVOR-ROPER

HENRY KAMEN CHARLES WILSON

CLAUS-PETER CLASEN H.G.KOENIGSBERGER

MENNA PRESTWICH G.E.AYLMER

HENRY WILLETTS

BONANZA BOOKS
New York

Endpapers: engravings from Palestrina's *Missarum Liber Primus*; Hans Weigel's *Trachtenbuch*; and Jacques Callot's *Beggers*.
Titlepage: Joost Amman, *German Burgher*, c. 1560 (British Museum).

This 1987 edition published by Bonanza Books, distributed by
Crown Publishers, Inc.,
225 Park Avenue South,
New York, New York 10003

Printed in Yugoslavia
h g f e d c b a

Contents

Acknowledgments

The illustrations-sections have been the responsibility of the publishers, who would like to thank all the authors for their patient advice on the wording of the captions. Generous help has been received from many individuals and institutions, particularly:

His Majesty the King of Sweden; the Marquess of Bath; Professor C. R. Boxer; the Duke of Buccleuch and Queensberry; J. O. Flatter, Esq.; Miss Beatrice Harris of Petworth House, Sussex; Dr H. Hartgerink of Martinus Nijhoff, The Hague; Dr H. Hornung of Staatsbibliothek der Stiftung Preussischer Kulturbesitz, Tübingen; Dobrosław Kobielski of CAF, Warsaw; Dr Richard Lane; E. J. Laws, Esq., of the City of Nottingham Museum and Art Gallery; Denis Mahon, Esq.; Miss Margaret Medley of the Percival David Foundation of Chinese Art, London; the Duke of Norfolk; Lord Primrose; H. Russell Robinson, Esq., of the Armouries, Tower of London; the Marquess of Salisbury; Dr K.-F. Schweiger; Dr Oskar Thulin of the Lutherhalle, Wittenberg; Dr J. H. van der Meer of the Germanisches Nationalmuseum, Nuremberg; the Earl of Verulam; S. C. Welch, Esq.; T. S. Wragg, Esq., of the Devonshire Collections, Chatsworth; Rijksbureau voor Kunsthistorische Documentatie, The Hague; British Museum (Departments of Maps, Oriental Antiquities, Oriental Printed Books and Manuscripts, and Prints and Drawings), Society of Antiquaries of London, Victoria and Albert Museum (Indian Section), London.

FOREWORD

HUGH TREVOR-ROPER

THE SERIES to which this volume belongs seeks to illustrate as well as to describe the history of civilization, and by its illustrations not merely to enliven but to deepen the study and understanding of that history. History, we would now generally agree, is multi-dimensional. We no longer see it as political history only, as the register of mere political action: legislation, institutions, war. Of course it is still—it always must be—the record of man: but it is the record of man in society, not merely in politics; and society conditions, or is conditioned by, a whole range of non-political activities, from the apparently impersonal forces of geography or economics to the individual achievements of science and art. This widened range of history cannot, without insufferable congestion, be expressed through one medium only. In this series we seek to express it, or at least to adumbrate it, in several. Faced by the vast expansion of our field, we have called in the new world of photographic reproduction, which informs through the eyes, to redress the imbalance of the old purely literary method, channelled exclusively through the mind.

This is not to claim any outrageously novel interpretation. In the past generation many novel historical theories have been advanced, and novel methods of teaching it have been recommended. But when these new ideas have been digested or rejected, the old truths remain. History may have become multi-dimensional, but politics cannot be altogether excluded from it. Politics give it its form and direction. History without politics is history without its essential mechanism. Even purely social history is conditioned by politics. How can we understand the development of society if we ignore the pressure of legal institutions, the political framework of trade, or the impact of war? G. M. Trevelyan's statement that social history is history with the politics left out is a dangerous half-truth.

In this volume the politics are not left out; but since we recognize that politics are inseparable from the physical and intellectual structure of society, and cannot be explained without reference to that structure, we have sought, while describing political change, to illustrate this wider context within which it took place, and to illustrate it with all the resources which modern methods of reproduction have made available to us. It is our hope that the text of this book will be read for its scholarship, and that the illustrations will be found to give a fuller understanding of the text.

The 16th century marks a new awareness on the part of Europeans of what lay beyond their horizons. In the Middle Ages, the world was divided into separate compartments, and the dwellers in one compartment were, for the most part, uninformed, even incurious, about the others. But in the 15th century the Europeans at least became curious, and by the mid-16th century exploration and discovery was in full swing. In the following hundred years, the various civilizations of the world, which for so long had ignored each other, were in contact. It was no longer a contact of individuals—of Viking adventurers penetrating to Greenland and beyond, of Nestorian or Franciscan missionaries or Venetian merchants finding their way to China. It was a contact of states, of societies. When the ancient, famous states of Europe were destroyed or threatened by the armies of 'the Grand Turk', there was need of regular relations with his eastern enemy, the 'Sophy' of Persia. The settlement of a whole continent by Spain, the seizure of a world-wide commercial empire by Portugal, forced other governments to join in a competition which so formidably augmented the wealth and power of rival states. And the process, once begun, could not be reversed. The old almost water-tight compartments between ancient, mutually exclusive civilizations, were breached and Europeans, who broke up, with such ease, the primitive civilizations of America, began to recognize, and be impressed by, the majestic, antique culture of China.

But if, in the 16th century, the great civilizations came closer together, it was Europe which brought them together. It was not Chinese or Japanese or

9

Indians or Persians who came to Lisbon or London: it was Europeans who went out to them. World-history, moreover, was Europocentric. Each civilization might be equal in the eyes of God. The empire of the Ming or the Moghuls might be greater, richer, more magnificent than the kingdom of England or the United Provinces of Holland. But when we look at them together, when we look at history as a process, as a form of change, we see that Europe is the dynamic element. It provides the motor of the process. It makes—as it will continue to make for another three centuries—the pace of change.

By 1559 we find a Europe dominated by the two branches of the house of Habsburg, whose rivalry will be the motive force of the whole century. That rivalry involves us in the Netherlands, the citadel of resistance to Spain which also became, through its resistance, a world-wide commercial power, the heir of Portugal, and in Germany, that amorphous system of states which refused to be ruled centrally from Vienna. This resistance, this refusal, led ultimately to a European conflagration, and we have devoted a chapter to it: to the Thirty Years' War which not only created a new balance of power but a new mental climate in Europe. Then we turn to the other powers of Europe, which were less directly involved in that absorbent struggle: to France which intervened late, to profit from the exhaustion of its old rivals; to England, distracted by its own internal revolution; and finally to Poland and the new, as yet weak state of Russia, only marginally concerned with the conflicts of the West.

In such a scheme much has been necessarily sacrificed, and some subjects may accidentally have slipped out. But we cannot afford to be too ambitious. Our aim is to present not a complete record but an intelligible picture of a century in which Europe was itself radically transformed and, by its expansion, began to transform the rest of the world too.

1 INTRODUCTION

The Baroque Century

HUGH TREVOR-ROPER

'I cannot but be raised to this persuasion,

that this third period of time will far surpass that of

the Grecian and Roman learning, only if men will

know their own strength and weakness both, and take one from the other

light of invention, and not fire of contradiction.'

SIR FRANCIS BACON, Advancement of learning, BOOK II, 1605

The decisive event

of the early 16th century had been the Reformation, which split Europe into two ideological camps. It transformed the intellectual climate, making it impossible for Erasmian humanism and reasonableness to survive, and the most systematic attempt at Catholic reform, the Council of Trent, ended by making the break irreparable.

The Catholic Church, however, was itself transformed in the process. It became more unified but less tolerant, more intense but less comprehensive. The Jesuit Order had been founded in 1540, laying stress on external discipline, inner spirituality, and evangelism. Among laymen as well as among priests and theologians there was a new emphasis on the mystical and personal elements of Christianity. The end of the century brought renewed confidence, for it was then becoming clear that the Reformation had been contained. Italy, Spain, France, Bavaria, Austria and Poland had been saved for the old faith. The task was now one of consolidation and further reconquest. New saints—St Ignatius Loyola, St Teresa of Avila, St Philip Neri, St Francis Xavier, St Charles Borromeo—attracted the devotion of the people, leading to the building of new churches and the creation of a new iconography.

The ambiguities of Mannerism now gave way to the untrammelled energy of Baroque. Rome became a Baroque city, replanned by Sixtus V (1585–90), as a series of linked monumental spaces enriched with fountains, obelisks and church façades calculated to overwhelm the faithful from all over the world. The basilica of St Peter was completed by Carlo Maderna and (under Urban VIII) furnished by Bernini with his two flamboyant masterpieces—the great bronze *baldacchino* over the high altar and the *Cathedra Petri* (opposite) beyond it. Bernini was the perfect Counter-Reformation artist. In the *Cathedra* he utilized every means at his disposal— marble, gilded bronze, stucco, light itself—to achieve a single dynamic effect. The papal throne floats upon golden clouds. SS Peter and Paul, Ambrose and Augustine present it to mankind while cherubs hold the keys and the tiara over it. Above, amidst the yellow rays of the sun projected into the realm of sculpture as sharp lines of bronze, the dove of the Holy Ghost spreads its wings, surrounded by tumultuous *putti* and angels. This represents everything that the Reformers hated most, yet, on its own terms, is undeniably a success. It is both a mystical vision made palpable and a precise statement of doctrine.

The heart of Christendom was to be the new St Peter's (*above*), which took almost exactly a hundred years to complete. In 1655 Bernini was commissioned by Alexander VII to build the piazza in front of it. He designed an oval colonnade of huge Tuscan columns leading to a shallow flight of steps which gently fan out towards the top. In the centre stands an Egyptian obelisk. The whole sequence of spaces is typical of Baroque planning, with its flair for the dramatic.

In a brief pontificate of five years, Sixtus V began the grandiose scheme that made Rome basically the city that it is today. The work continued for decades after his death, but it embodied what were in origin his ideas. Points of special emphasis were connected by straight roads opening up long vistas and bringing into prominence the churches and palaces of the new Rome. *Left:* S. Ivo, with its unique dome by Borromini, Bernini's rival in architecture. *Right:* the Piazza Navona, built on the site of an ancient race-course. The fountain is Bernini's, the church partly by Borromini.

While the popes created a new Rome, increasing numbers of travellers were drawn to the ruins of the old. The forum – known as the *Campo Vaccino* (cowfield) – was still a rural backwater, and ancient monuments continued to be plundered for building material, but the appeal of such paintings as Paul Brill's in the mid 16th century (*right*) was already partly antiquarian. Italy as a whole was at peace, though the price of peace was domination by Spain. Economically the country was in a decline.

Venice alone was able to maintain its freedom, though it was losing both its territorial conquests overseas and its commercial leadership. By the middle of the century it had assumed something of that air of decadent gaiety that was to make it the 'pleasure city' of Europe for the next 150 years. This painting of a Venetian carnival in the mid 17th century is by Joseph Heintz the Younger.

The setting for worship reflected the doctrines of the separated churches. The Jesuits adopted a style that used every resource of art, drama and music to the full. Their headquarters at Rome, the Gesù (*left*), designed by Vignola, soon became the model for Jesuit churches all over the world. In this painting Pope Urban VIII is seen visiting it; the building is finished and lavishly hung with decoration, but the famous frescoes of the vault have not yet been carried out.

The Jesuit style in Flanders: the church of St Michael at Louvain (*right*), designed in 1650 by the Jesuit architect and preacher Willem van Hees, in the full tide of the Flemish Counter-Reformation.

For the total rejection of art and imagery we must turn to the Calvinists. Their churches (*below*) were plain bare rooms centred not on the altar but on the pulpit, a sign that the sermon had replaced the mass as the heart of the service.

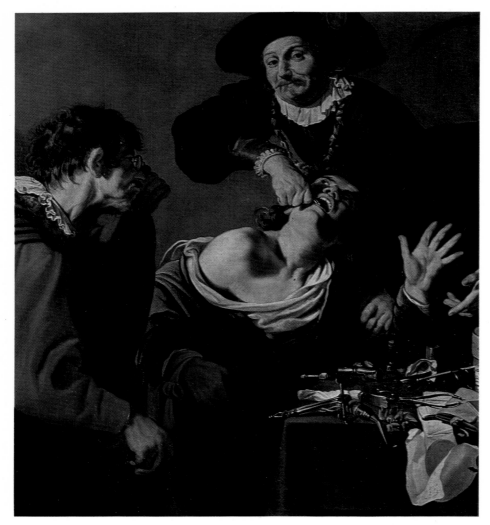

Medical science made advances in the 17th century, but more in research than in practice. Although physicians had to be men of education with degrees from a university, surgery, midwifery and pharmacology were commonly left to men who had simply received a practical training. The dentist had an array of instruments for his use, as this painting by Rombouts shows. The main treatment, however, was to extract the decaying tooth, an operation for which little skill was thought to be needed.

Anatomy, as an academic study, was arousing wider interest after the pioneer work of Vesalius. *Right:* Rembrandt's painting of Nicolas Tulp demonstrating the dissection of the left arm. The body is that of a hanged criminal. Tulp was a leading citizen of Amsterdam, a magistrate and member of the city council. *Below:* an Italian anatomical figure made of ivory and dating from the late 16th century. The organs are revealed by taking off the front of the torso; the two other parts lying below it are the intestines and the wall of the womb.

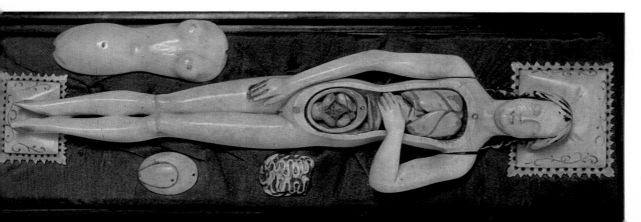

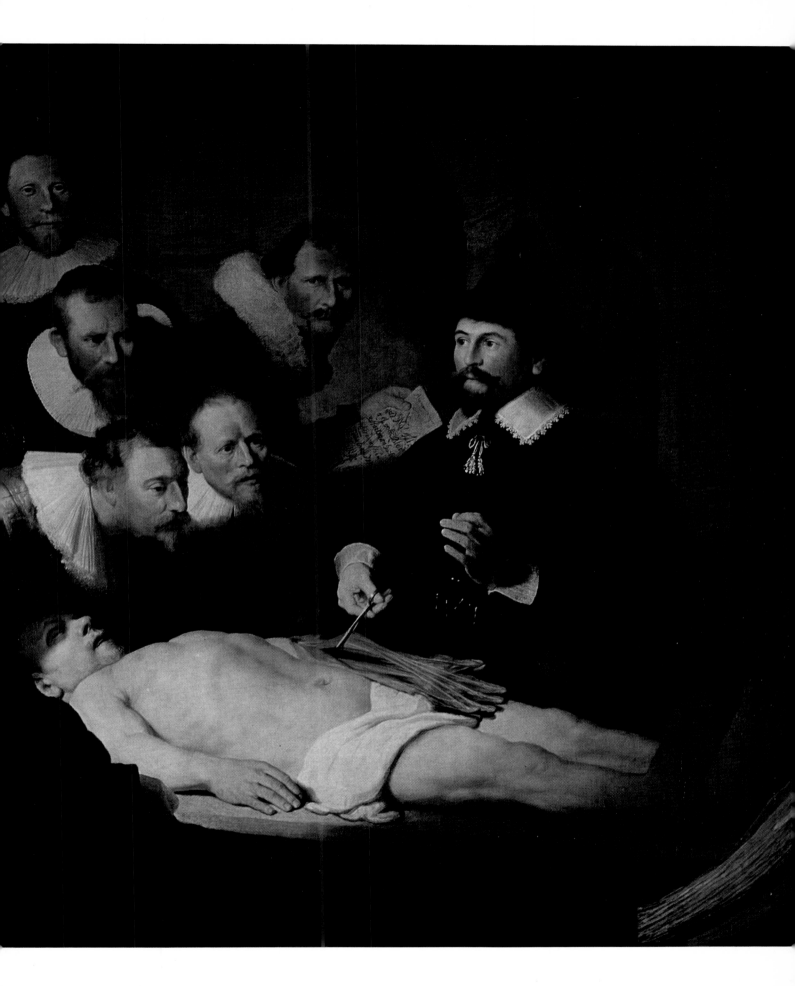

Mathematics and astronomy are the two sciences with which the 17th century is particularly associated. The Renaissance scientists, in spite of their boldness in speculation, had been relatively uninterested in experiment, observation and proof, but the rise of a genuinely scientific method had to contend with the renewed bigotry of the churches, suspicious of all new ideas. Galileo (*left*) was the most famous sufferer. The condemnation of his astronomical system in 1633 inevitably discouraged scientific work in Catholic countries.

A quadrant to measure the elevation of stars (*right*) was constructed by the Danzig astronomer Hevelius (Johann Höwelcke). Hevelius made numerous discoveries relating to sun-spots, comets and fixed stars, and published the first moon map with any claim to accuracy in 1647.

An early adding machine (*below*) was invented by Blaise Pascal in about 1644. It consists of eight wheels, each with ten cogs corresponding to the digits 0–9. Each wheel moves one unit for every complete turn of the wheel on its right – forward for addition, backward for subtraction. This model is dedicated to Chancellor Séguier.

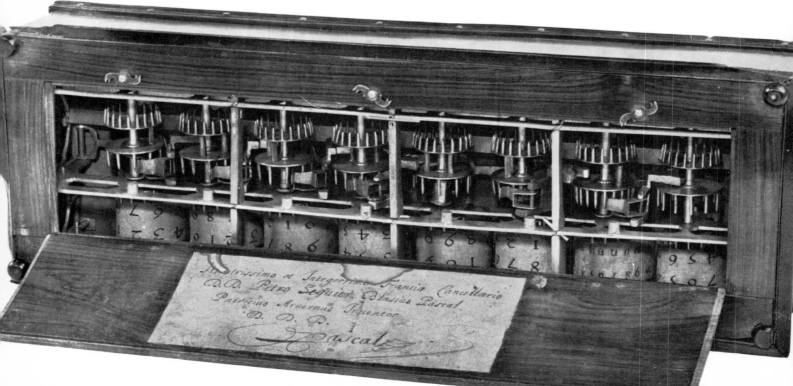

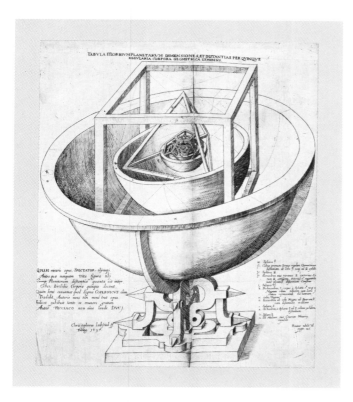

The amassing of facts and the search for harmony that would make sense of those facts were the twin preoccupations of the early astronomers. Johann Kepler (1571–1630) was the greatest of the theoreticians. Using the statistical data assembled by Tycho Brahe (*above right*) he tried various theories – including the idea that the intervals between the planets corresponded with the five regular solids (*above left*) – before reaching those orbital laws which in conjunction with Galileo's laws of motion, enabled Newton to give an almost definitive picture of the solar system. Tycho Brahe was born in Denmark in 1546. His wealth enabled him to begin, and the generosity of two royal patrons to continue, a vast methodical record of planetary movements. On the island of Hveen he built himself two beautifully equipped observatories – Uraniborg begun in 1576, and Stellaborg (*below*), 1584. At the latter the instruments were placed in underground rooms. Tycho lived at Hveen for twenty years. The death of Frederick II of Denmark caused him to leave in 1597; but two years later he found another patron in the Emperor Rudolf II and established himself near Prague, with Kepler as his chief assistant.

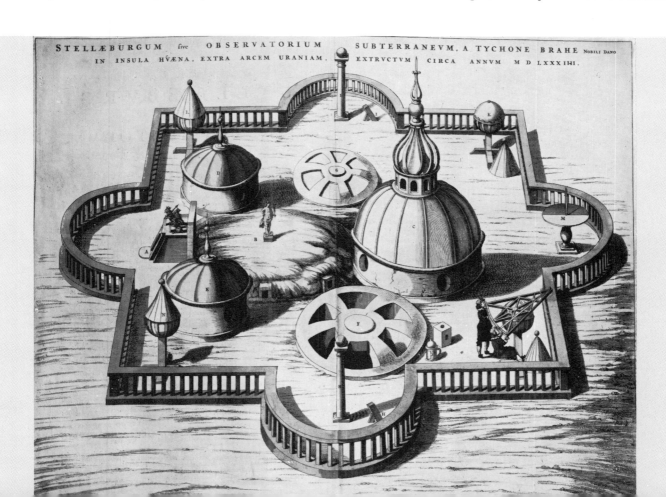

The Baroque Century

HUGH TREVOR-ROPER

The middle years of the 17th century saw almost the whole of Europe engaged in warfare, made worse by the development of artillery and the bitterness of the religious quarrel. This engraving from a book of moral precepts by Daniel Sudermann was published in 1628.

THE CENTURY 1559–1660 is no more homogeneous than any other century, no more constant in development, no more submissive to an easy label. How can we define it? A century of progress? But is not every century, to some extent, progressive, and can this century outbid that of the Renaissance, which preceded it, or that of the Enlightenment, which followed? A century of Revolution? Some historians would say so; but the greatest of European revolutions—the Protestant Reformation and the French Revolution—both lie outside it, and the Asiatic revolutions of our time are still far in the future. The century of expansion then? That would be a possibility, and certainly it is no more false than the others; but it is well to begin by admitting its imperfection. In a finite world expansion here means contraction there. It is Europe only which expands. Nor is even that expansion continuous, at an even rate.

Expansion and Contraction

Certainly in the first fifty years Christendom is aggressively extrovert. The Spaniards are colonizing the vast continent of America and reaching out across the Pacific Ocean. In 1583 the Spanish governor of the Philippine Islands would assure his master than with 12 or 13 galleons and 8000 Spaniards he could conquer the whole empire of China. The Portuguese are mobilizing the slave labour of Africa to work the sugar-mills of Brazil: next to the Baltic corn-fleets, their Brazilian sugar-fleets would be the largest trade-fleets in the world. Through Macao and Nagasaki they would also press on the riches of China and Japan. The French are establishing themselves in Florida and Canada. The English are feeling their way in Virginia and Massachusetts, probing new routes to Russia and Persia, knocking at the gates of Isfahan and Agra. The Dutch, most aggressive of all, are breaking into all the oceans and establishing, in Indonesia, the centre of an East Asiatic Empire which lasted to our time.

The New World had been regarded during most of the 16th century as a field for conquest and profit. During the 17th it also became a refuge from political and religious persecution. Small groups of settlers emigrated from western Europe, tempted by the prospect of liberty, good farm-land and trade; but they found obstacles in Indian tribes, harsh conditions and each other. Jean Ribaut landed in Florida in 1562 and erected a column, brought from France for the purpose. The colony failed and was abandoned after a year. In 1564 another expedition arrived and its leader, René de Laudonnière, was taken by an Indian chief to see Ribaut's column (above), now adopted as a totem by the local tribe. Living red Indians, brought back from the east coast of America, were arousing great public interest. Princess Pocahontas married an Englishman and came to London in 1616. The young man shown here may be one of her servants; he was drawn in St James's Park in the album of a Dutch visitor. The far north was explored early in an attempt to discover a north-west passage to the Far East. This coloured drawing, after John White, was made about 1610 and probably shows an incident in Martin Frobisher's second voyage of 1577.

But neither the pace nor the confidence is sustained at an even rate. Shortly after the turn of the century, the expansion is halted, or slowed up. After 1610, first here, then there, the economy of the European states mysteriously trembles. There are complaints of a general contraction, a 'decay of trade'. The cause of that contraction is still disputed. Was it purely economic or even financial? Was it social, the result of a growing burden of administrative centralization? Or was it created, and not merely aggravated, by the renewal of general war? We do not know. All we can say is that economic crisis and foreign war came close together. From 1618 the energies of Europe are turned inwards, to be consumed in the long, destructive contest of the Thirty Years' War.

So, in the last part of our century, the spectacular European expansion of the 16th century is not altogether halted, but it is not continued at the same rate. Colonization and settlement are slowed up. If the 16th century was the century of the rapid conquest, evangelization, organization of America, the 17th is its 'century of depression'. Such advances as are made by the European powers are now made at each other's expense—often as the result of European battles. Sometimes the advance of earlier years is even reversed. After the great victory of Lepanto in 1571, which seemed the end of Turkish sea power in the Mediterranean, Don John of Austria had dreamed of liberating Greece and establishing there a Christian kingdom. In the next century, for all the internal decay of Turkey, how vain that dream appeared! The first half of the 17th century was the great age of the Barbary pirates; the second half saw the Turkish revival. A century after Lepanto, Turkish fleets would wrest from the Christians the last relic of Greece—the island of Crete, which had been, under Venetian rule, the centre of a Greek Renaissance. Turkish armies would threaten Lvov and besiege Vienna. Further east, the Portuguese would lose Hormuz to the Persians in 1622. By 1640 they would be expelled from their foothold in Japan, which would become, for two centuries, 'the Closed Country'. The E glish East India Company, after its flying start, would mark time, and Cromwell would be prepared to wind it up altogether, to surrender all English interests in Asia to the Dutch. Even the Dutch, who alone remained in contact with Japan, would suffer a reverse in the Far East, losing their stations in Formosa to the Chinese exile and patriot, the last defender of the fallen Ming dynasty, the founder of a new island dynasty, Koxinga.

This relative European contraction which began in the second decade of the 17th century is not merely economic, a collapse of prices; or political, a failure of peace. It is general. We see it in thought, in art, in manners. The expansion of the 16th century had been reflected in its literature. Its greatest writers, from Ariosto to Shakespeare breathe an air of confidence: the world is theirs to conquer and enjoy. In the 17th century, this changes.

As the genial, expansive art of the Renaissance is gradually transformed into the narrower attitudes of Mannerism and the strained postures and anguished faces of later Baroque, so the mind of Europe is turned gradually inwards from the endless adventure to the tragic predicament of man. In Spain, the crusading, conquering saint, Santiago Matamoros, the Moor-killer, is suddenly replaced by the agonized image of St Teresa—not the real St Teresa, that voluble, efficient 'gadabout nun', but the ecstatic mystical *beata* of Baroque art. It is not only *Don Quixote*, that incomparable expression of national disillusion, it is a change of generation that kills the extrovert romances of chivalry. In England and France, Shakespeare and Ronsard were conformists who took the outer world for granted and hardly troubled themselves with religion. There is not a trace of religious feeling in Shakespeare, and Ronsard, though a priest, wore his soutane very lightly. How different are Milton and Pascal! A new spirit of pessimism infuses the literature of 17th century Europe, clothed in renewed religious forms: in English Puritanism, French Jansenism, German mysticism: the religion of the individual conscience, turned in on itself, distrustful of all institutional mediation, no longer sure even of the benevolence of God.

Of course this change was not sudden: no historical change ever is. Even the sharpest political or economic crisis is distorted in its human effects, for it has to pass through the slowening medium of human generations. A general shock may thus take half a generation to express itself in public life, as a mood of the time; and sometimes the accident of survival—the survival of a small group of men, or even of one overpowering personality, in positions of power or patronage—can prolong an obsolescent mental climate beyond its natural term. But this accident of the human life-cycle, which can diffract or postpone the impact of events, can also concentrate the moment of change. It is to such a concentration that we may ascribe some of the obvious 'watersheds' of history, those moments of sharp transition about which historians, for all their scholarly reservations, are obliged to agree. Just as the survival of a small group of men may artificially prolong a public mood, so their simultaneous death may suddenly terminate it, revealing the new mood which more recent events have generated beneath it. Such sudden transitions in fact occurred both at the beginning and at the end of our century, and we may therefore begin by observing them: for it is they which justify us in treating it as a self-contained historical 'period'.

Watersheds

Let us glance at the beginning. In the years 1558–60 there was an epidemic of death among great European rulers: the Emperor Charles V and Mary Tudor in 1558, Pope Paul IV and Henri II in 1559, Gustav Vasa of Sweden and Mary of Lorraine, regent of Scotland, in 1560. These had been the generation of Reform, the last generation of 'Erasmian' humanism, who had fought the battles of the New Learning and had, too often, become soured in the struggle. Their passing brought a new generation suddenly to the fore. After a decade of repression—the decade of the Placards of Flanders, the Chambre Ardente of Paris, the Smithfield fires, the new Index and the revived Roman Inquisition—a group of tense, embittered, backward-looking rulers left the stage to their heirs: Philip II, Catherine de Médicis, Eric XIV, Queen Elizabeth and the new Popes of the Counter-Reformation. Many of these rulers, or their successors, would afterwards sink, disillusioned, into the ways of their predecessors; but in 1560 they were still untried, still hopeful, eager to tackle and prepared to solve the problems of their time.

As at the beginning, so at the end of our century, a whole generation seems to go at once. In 1657–61 there is another epidemic of death among the great: the Emperor Ferdinand III in 1657, Oliver Cromwell in 1658, Charles Gustavus of Sweden in 1660, Cardinal Mazarin in 1661. These were not vulgar deaths: they carried away the leaders of a generation; and that generation was the generation of the Thirty Years' War, whose minds had been scarred by the crisis of the 1620s. With them a whole *Weltanschauung* passed away. Their successors would look very differently on the world which they had inherited.

But if our century has a clear beginning and a clear end, it is not therefore without internal breaks, for it embraces three clear generations, and one generation at least is very different from the other two. It is the central generation, the generation that came to maturity in the 1580s and 1590s and ruled at the beginning of the 17th century; and we may pause for a moment on it, not only because it is exceptional but because it represented the high point of our century: the last summer flowering of a culture and a way of life which had been growing up for years past and which, in the years after 1620, was to wither finally away. Looking at the century as a whole, we see Philip IV resuming wearily the wars of Philip II, Oliver Cromwell harking back to Queen Elizabeth; but the intervening generation, the generation of Philip III and James I is very different. It may not look forward, but it does not look back: it enjoys a golden present.

First of all it is a generation of peace. In the 1590s men appreciated the value of peace. All over Europe those were years of famine and plague, social unrest and economic bankruptcy. In the end, the bankruptcy—as in the 1550s—forced statesmen to make peace; and once again, death helped. The aggression of Philip II was halted by Philip III, the motor of European resistance died with Queen Elizabeth. But to the new generation, peace was not only a necessity, it was also desirable in itself: it could be enjoyed. The princes of the time gloried in peace as their predecessors had gloried in war. *Beati Pacifici*, blessed are the peacemakers, was their motto. Philip III was the king of *Las Pazes*, 'the Peaces': his reign was *Pax Hispanica*. James I was *Rex Pacificus*, the professional pacifier of Europe. Marie de Médicis in France, 'the Archdukes' in the Netherlands, sang the same tune. And all vied with each other in advertizing the blessings and patronizing the arts of peace.

Some of their offerings to the goddess of Peace were evanescent: elaborate pageants, magnificent 'progresses', brilliant masques, costly feasts. Some were more solid: Paris rebuilt by Henri IV, Baroque churches rising in devastated Antwerp, the palaces of Spanish viceroys in Europe crammed with the artistic spoils of Italy, the 'houses like Nebuchadnezzar's' with which Jacobean courtiers in England advertized their mushroom prosperity. The greatest of artists was also the propagandist of these dazzling, spendthrift courts. Rubens decorated the new churches of Flanders, painted the triumphs of Henri IV and Marie de Médicis for the new *Palais du Luxembourg* and the apotheosis of King James for the new banqueting hall of Whitehall, and would have proudly inscribed on his tomb that he was the friend and ambassador of kings.

But this carefree generation, on which its grimmer successors would look back with such puritan disapproval, was not entirely *insouciante*. It was also one of the greatest generations in the history of European thought. Peace restored the Republic of Letters which the long war had dislocated. Scholars and thinkers, scientists, historians, philosophers, *virtuosi*, engaged in international correspondence. It was a correspondence which took little account of ideological frontiers—at least north of the Pyrenees. Rubens himself, the greatest propagandist of the Counter-Reformation, corresponded freely with Protestants, visited England, basked in the warmth of its Protestant court, and marvelled to see such Italian elegance in a northern capital. Rubens' friend Nicolas Fabri de Peiresc, 'the prince of erudition', was the dynamo which drove the machine of intellectual discussion throughout the Continent. From his house in Aix-en-Provence he organized the correspondence of the élite of Europe: Jacques-Auguste de Thou, greatest of French historians; Paolo Sarpi, historian of the Council of Trent and champion of Venetian liberty against the Counter-Reformation; Tomaso Campanella, utopian and rebel, victim and theorist of the same Counter-Reformation; William Camden, the father of English 'civil history'; Francis Bacon, the prophet of the scientific revolution; Hugo Grotius, the philosopher of Natural Law; Pierre Gassendi, the 'mechanical philosopher', who would also become his biographer; John Barclay, the most famous of émigré Scottish Catholic writers; Joseph Justus Scaliger, the undisputed prince of scholars; Justus Lipsius, the Tacitus of his age; Isaac Casaubon, Selden, Gruter, Salmasius, and a hundred other once famous

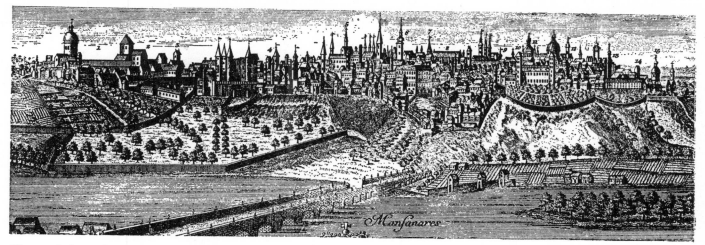

The growth of capital cities is a feature which Europe shares at this period with the Islamic Empires. Madrid (above), created capital and 'only court' of Spain by Philip II in 1560, mushroomed in the years between 1530 and 1597 from 5,000 inhabitants to 60,000. The population of Paris and London also increased hugely, thanks largely to the attraction of the court.

names. This scholarly International would never be entirely broken, although the Thirty Years' War and the English Revolution would reduce and fragment it. It would continue in Richelieu's Paris, where the scientific friar, Marin Mersenne, would be the heir of Peiresc, bringing together the French émigré Descartes and the English émigré Hobbes. There would be Protestant circles too, animated by the refugees of central Europe, imagining a universal enlightenment still to come. Then, when the period of revolution was over, the 'Republic of Letters' would be restored in full and Peiresc would find his real and greater heir in the universal genius of Leibniz.

Unity—by accident and by force

Three generations then, two of war and one of peace, span our 'century of expansion'. So far, we have spoken of external expansion only: of Europe's contact with, and conquest of, the other continents. But there was internal expansion too: the expansion of central government, the absorption of outlying provinces or independent kingdoms, the unification of the great European 'nation-states'. This process too had been continuous throughout the 16th century; but it too, after 1620, was slowed down and changed its quality.

At first this unification had seemed almost accidental. It was dynastic accidents that had united Castile and Aragon in Spain, as they would unite Spain and the Netherlands in 1517, Spain and Portugal in 1580, France and Navarre in 1589, England and Scotland in 1603. In every instance, the 'liberties' of the smaller society were at first guaranteed, the union was personal only, a union of crowns. But inevitably, in that monarchical, 'bureaucratic' age, the greater courts gradually subsumed the smaller and the residence of the prince grew while old, deserted capitals, unless they were sustained by new commerce or industry, sank into provincial cities. In Spain, Philip II made himself a new capital at Madrid which, without any other cause, quickly grew into a great, magnetic city, drawing to it the aristocracy, the talent and the wealth of the other kingdoms of Spain. The growth of London, as a centre of government and consumption, drew constant complaints from the provinces, especially after 1600: this 'dropsical' city, it was said, was sucking the life out of the country; and the Stuart Kings vainly ordered the immigrants back to their counties. Among the immigrants, of course, was an army of Scottish adventurers, 'beggarly bluecaps' who from 1603 would follow the golden road to London. Paris similarly grew, and became, under Henri IV, as it has remained ever since, almost a substitute for France. This growth of capital cities gave great opportunities to the entrepreneur, the architect, the town-planner; for law-courts, colleges, the palaces of courtiers, all tended to rise around the residence of the prince.

But if the chosen capital prospered, the abandoned capital sank often into decay and disaffection. Many of the political revolts of

our century were provoked, at least in part, by the loss of the court and its patronage. Philip II's removal of the Burgundian court, once the most magnificent in Europe, from Brussels to Madrid fired the revolt of the Burgundian nobility which would develop into the 'eighty years' war' of the Netherlands. The departure of the Stuart Kings from Edinburgh to London fomented the mutiny of the Scotch nobility which would lead to the Puritan Revolution in England. And the migration of the Habsburg court from Prague to Vienna would be followed by the revolt of the Bohemian nobility and the Thirty Years' War.

Such consequences could be foreseen. How then could they be avoided when princes found themselves rulers of more than one kingdom? One method was rotation of residence. The Emperor Charles V had moved continually from capital to capital of his vast empire, and his great minister, Cardinal Granvelle, constantly urged his son, Philip II, to do the same. But Philip had not—who had?—the energy of his father; and without that energy, some other, and more modern method was needed. One such method was a more centralized administration. Philip II thought to centralize the government of the Netherlands. Zygmunt August turned the personal union of Poland and Lithuania into a political fusion in 1569. James I similarly aspired to a 'more perfect union' of his kingdoms: he wished to be not King of England, King of Ireland, King of Scotland, but King of 'Great Britain'. Olivares advised Philip IV to cease to be King of Castile, King of Aragon, King of Portugal, Count of Barcelona, etc. and become 'King of Spain'. But such centralization was a direct affront to those ancient rights and liberties which had often been expressly guaranteed at the time of union. Consequently, it often led to trouble. In the 1640s Olivares' schemes of unity led to the revolt of Catalonia and Portugal, those of Charles I to revolution in both Scotland and Ireland. The union both of Spain and of Britain, which seemed so near in 1620 was not achieved till after 1700. Where such centralized union was imposed, it always required force. Louis XIII destroyed the independence of Navarre by force. Bohemia, after its revolt, was crushed: its native nobility was destroyed and replaced by a new, imported ruling class. Cromwell's brief union of Britain was achieved by the sword. In Scotland it failed; in Ireland, as in Bohemia, it was made permanent by the destruction of the native or naturalized ruling class, and the imposition of a foreign 'ascendancy'.

These clashes of nations within expanding political systems led to a new force, or at least a new outbreak of an old force: nationalism. Spanish centralization produced Dutch nationalism. English centralization produced Scottish and Irish nationalism; and the revolt of Scotland and Ireland in their turn produced English nationalism. Since this nationalism clothed itself in religious forms, religion itself became nationalized. In 1620 it seemed that all Britain might gradually accept an established

'Anglican' episcopacy. By 1660 that prospect was over. 'Anglicanism' was now the badge of English domination. Consequently Scotland became irredeemably Calvinist, Ireland irredeemably Catholic, and England—witness the 'Clarendon Code' of 1661/5—more Anglican than ever. At the other end of Europe, Sweden, which during the Thirty Years' War had patronized a pan-Protestant 'syncretist' movement in Germany, now assumed a narrow and intolerant Lutheranism; Poland, almost swamped by Lutheran Swedes and Orthodox Russians, took refuge in fanatical Catholicism; and Transylvania, wedged between Catholic Austria and Poland and the infidel Turk, sustained itself by a defiant, eccentric Calvinism.

Thus 'nationality' resisted under the banner of religion. Equally, when nationalism was crushed, religion had to be crushed too. To unite France Louis XIII had to crush the Huguenotism of the south. To hold Bohemia, the Emperor had to destroy its historic Protestantism. By such struggles, religion, which in 1560 had seemed so cosmopolitan, became by 1660 everywhere a department of state. The day of international ideologies was over—for a time.

The 'New Monarchy' of the Counter-Reformation

The rise and fall of the great ideological systems is one of the most striking events of our century. In 1560 two international Churches stood ready for battle. For the next century they competed throughout the world. They drew their strength from many different sources—political and social as well as spiritual. Let us consider them in turn, beginning with what at first seemed the weaker: the Church of Rome.

In 1560 the Roman Church seemed everywhere on the defensive. All Europe north of the Alps and the Pyrenees was either lost or in danger. Scandinavia, England, Scotland, Bohemia, most of Germany had gone. Poland, Austria, Bavaria, France, the Netherlands were, it seemed, going: their princes uncertain, their nobility Protestant, their clergy failing. But by 1563, when the Council of Trent concluded its last session, the means of reconquest had been devised, the campaign prepared. The next 70 years were to see it nearly victorious.

As so often in history, the result of the Council of Trent was very different from its original intention. When it had first met, in 1545, summoned by the Emperor, its purpose had been to reunite and purify the Church and also to reverse the monarchical tendency in it: the absolutism of the Pope was to be corrected by the greater autonomy of national churches and the higher claims of General Councils. The effect was otherwise. As Paolo Sarpi would write, instead of reuniting the Church, the Council made the split permanent; instead of reforming abuses it introduced 'the greatest corruption since the name of Christian was first heard'; instead of restoring authority to the bishops, 'it ended by taking away from them such little authority as they had kept and reconciling them to their own slavery'. This strange reversal had three main causes: the patronage of the court of Rome which enabled it to divide and control; the new balance of power in Italy; and the new spiritual strength, missionary fervour and political skill of the Jesuits.

The growth of the papal court—the *monarchia romana* as Sarpi called it—was no doubt inevitable in itself in this age of centralization; but the heavy patronage of Spain, the model of all such courts, guaranteed the process. For the Treaty of Cateau-Cambrésis of 1559 fastened the hold of Spain over all Italy and made Rome, for almost a century, a satellite of Madrid. Individual popes might wriggle—Pius V, an enthroned friar, austere and fanatical, both wriggled and squealed—but circumstances were too strong for them. They therefore made the best of them. It was thanks to Spanish arms that Catholicism triumphed in Europe and America. Spanish power protected Italy itself against the Turkish threat. On the other hand the King of Spain jealously preserved his monopoly of Church patronage throughout his dominions (which soon included those of Portugal); the Pope could not even protect the archbishop of Seville from disgrace and imprisonment through the intrigues of his Spanish enemies; and his attempts to forbid Spanish bull-fights were completely defeated. In vain the popes looked to France as a counter-weight to

Spain. France, throughout the reign of Philip II, was hamstrung by civil dissension; and although the conversion of Henri IV (a triumph of papal diplomacy) roused hopes of independence, they soon subsided. Only Spain, the master of Milan and Naples, could be effective in Italian politics. Only Spain could support Paul V against the obstinate republic of Venice. Only the Habsburgs could sustain the Catholic reconquest in Germany. Henri IV might be a good Catholic, Richelieu might be a cardinal, but in politics, they were, necessarily, the patrons of Protestants.

But if Spain provided the military force of the Catholic reconquest, the spiritual force came from the Jesuits. At first these two forces had not been united. The early Jesuits, though of Spanish foundation, had been unpopular in Spain: their spirituality seemed dangerously close to the 'Erasmianism' which the Spanish Church had crushed in the 1530s. But gradually, as Spanish policy became more aggressive, it made use of these daring spiritual aggressors. It was thanks to the Portuguese Jesuits that Philip II won the crown of Portugal in 1580, and soon they were promising to bring him the crowns of France and England too. By the end of the century the Jesuits were seen as the agents of Spain throughout the world. English Jesuits took their orders from Philip II before setting out to their dangerous mission in England. Spanish ambitions lurked behind the Jesuits who penetrated Lutheran Sweden and Orthodox Russia. It was as Spanish agents that the Italian Jesuits would be expelled from Japan. And Spanish imperialists watched with interest the mathematical triumphs of the Jesuit Matteo Ricci at the imperial court of Peking.

But the alliance of Pope and Spain was not only a political and religious alliance. It was also an alliance of social philosophy. In its struggle to recover lost ground, the Catholic Church identified itself increasingly with particular social forms. Pre-Reformation Catholicism had been applicable equally to a monarchy or to a city-state, a commune. Counter-Reformation Catholicism was the religion of princely courts and bureaucratic, hierarchical societies. By 1580 this was clear. Some northern princes might still seek to harness and ride the storm of religious radicalism, but with the failure of Mary Stuart and Catherine de Médicis before their eyes, most princes preferred to insure their hierarchical courts with a hierarchical Church. Henri IV thought Paris worth a mass. His daughter, Queen Henrietta Maria of England, never ceased to recommend her husband to preserve London in the same way. Popery, it was said, was the only guarantee of monarchy; and the model for both was generalized in Europe by the power and example of Spain.

If the great courts accepted the ideology of Rome, equally Rome accepted the social character of the great courts. As secular rulers, the popes too centralized their government, increased indirect taxes, multiplied and sold offices, squeezed out private capitalists, suppressed provincial independence. They also replanned, rebuilt, redecorated their capital. Sixtus V, in particular, laid his mark on the city and government of Rome. He tamed the great Roman families by patronage, broke rural banditry by force, built aqueducts, laid out streets and *piazze*, planted obelisks and fountains, set 600 men to work night and day on the dome of St Peter's, and, 'for the glory of God and the Church', zealously destroyed the monuments of antiquity which his humanist predecessors had zealously preserved. He demolished the Septizonium of Severus and used its columns for the church of St Peter's, threatened to destroy the Capitol unless its pagan statues were removed; and he converted the columns of Trajan and Antoninus into props of orthodoxy.

Sixtus V's furious rebuilding of Rome was continued, with a finer taste, by his successors: in particular by Paul V and his magnificent nephew Scipione Borghese and by Urban VIII and his nephew Francesco Barberini. Between Sixtus, the austere, plebeian friar, and Urban, the opulent worldly *virtuoso* there was little personal resemblance; but in their architectural energy they were equally matched. Once again, during the reign of the Barberini, the Romans saw the monuments of antiquity destroyed to make way, or material, for new magnificence: '*quod non fecere barbari*', they observed, as they surveyed the new sack of the imperial city, '*fecere Barberini*'. But besides their own palaces, the Barberini

Music, like the other arts, was coloured by the demands of the Counter-Reformation. The greatest of the 16th century composers was Giovanni Pierluigi da Palestrina, whose new style subordinated the elaborate polyphony of his predecessors to an emphatic liturgical content. His career in the papal service began in 1551 when he was appointed 'maestro di capella' by Pope Julius III. This illustration shows him presenting his first book of masses to the Pope in 1554.

built for the city too. It was they who completed St Peter's; and by their patronage of the most prolific and eloquent of all Baroque sculptors, Gianlorenzo Bernini, they gave to papal Rome its decisive, unique and permanent architectural character.

Thus the Counter-Reformation popes, like the secular princes, built up and advertized their 'new monarchy' as a political and social model. But Rome, the capital of Catholicism, could not be only a secular model: it was also, once again, an aggressive evangelical centre. The worldly popes of the Renaissance had fostered the humane sciences. They had cultivated pagan letters, adopted pagan cults, admired pagan arts. The arts and sciences, it could be said, had then become divorced from religion. The boldest works of innovation—the 'civil history' and secular political theory of Machiavelli, the new, unbiblical astronomy of Copernicus—had been dedicated to popes; and the dedication had been accepted. Now all this was reversed. By deliberate decisions of the Council of Trent all arts, all sciences, were subjected again to the Church. Like the old pagan monuments, they were either destroyed or converted into new supports of orthodoxy. The elegant latinity and exact scholarship of the humanists, which had led so many of them into heresy, were recovered by the Jesuits. Their pagan stoicism was made Christian and Catholic. The political theory of Machiavelli was converted into the 'reason of state' of Botero, his 'civil history' submerged in the lucid, emphatic, scholarly but orthodox annals of Baronius. The astronomy of Copernicus was first manipulated towards orthodoxy, then, when it resisted—when Galileo would not pay the lip-service demanded by Urban VIII—condemned. Music was brought to order in 1565 when, the Council of Trent having condemned the elaborate, sensuous Flemish counterpoint, Pius IV installed Palestrina as Composer to the Pontifical Choir. From then on, the new music illustrated the glory and majesty of the Church. The control of painting was shown in 1573 when Paolo Veronese was haled before the Inquisition in Venice and questioned on the symbolic detail of his work. Here again the Jesuits were the agents of conformity. Their scholars mastered all the sciences in order to bend them in the right direction. Their schools formed the princes and courtiers of the Counter-Reformation. They taught the new icono-

graphy which the painters and sculptors expressed. The new style of the Counter-Reformation, the style of their great church in Rome, the *Gesù*, was not invented by them; but they were the patrons of its dissemination, and it was not unreasonably baptized *le style jésuite*.

The Catholic Counter-Reformation, which was formally launched in 1563, reached its apogee in 1630. If we compare the religious situation in Europe at those two dates we can measure the extent of its triumph. In 1563 Catholicism had been driven back to the Mediterranean. Its only solid bases seemed to be Italy and Spain. By 1630, the position was changed indeed. Bavaria, Poland, Austria, France and half the Netherlands—what had been the richest, most highly developed half—had been recovered. In 1621 Rome had celebrated with a solemn procession, and a new church—the church of Sta Maria della Vittoria—the destruction of Bohemian Protestantism, the most ancient in Europe. In 1629 the last Huguenot citadel of France had been reduced. In the same year the Jesuits advanced eastward along the Baltic and the imperial Edict of Restitution seemed to turn back the reformation of Luther in Germany. Nor were these victories won at the expense of Protestantism only. In eastern Europe, in the 1590s, the founding of the 'Uniate' Church detached a portion of the Greek Orthodox Church in South Russia; and Catholic missionaries counted their converts among the Red Indians of Canada, the war-like *daimyos* of Japan, and even—they thought—the Confucian mandarins of China.

However protected or backed by secular power, the architects of these great victories were, above all, the Jesuits. In every country they had been the agents of the Catholic restoration, where it had succeeded, its martyrs where it had failed. In the reign of Urban VIII they too enjoyed their triumph. The Pope was their protector, his great artist Bernini their artist. Urban blessed their new churches, extolled their martyrs, and struck down their enemies, even his old friend Galileo himself. In 1640, the centenary year of their foundation, two Belgian Jesuits published a commemorative volume, *Imago primi saeculi*. It was the record of a hundred years of heroism and triumph that had restored the Church. Ironically, it was published at the beginning of a new century of decline.

The Calvinist Diaspora

Meanwhile what of the Protestants? The extraordinary revival of the Roman Church had not stimulated a similar effort in Lutheranism. In Germany and Scandinavia the princes had taken over the machinery of the Church, expropriated the monastic orders, secularized the monasteries. But they had not created a new model of society: indeed, in some ways, they imitated the Catholic courts—especially in northern Europe, where Frederick III of Denmark built himself lavish palaces, and where flamboyant Baroque pulpits and organs invaded the churches of the Baltic. The real antithesis to Catholicism, in the days of its recovery, was supplied not by Lutheranism but by Calvinism. For whereas Lutheranism was essentially a German, Calvinism was essentially a Latin revolt: therefore it was better able to confront Catholicism on its own ground. It was also, on that ground, the expression of an alternative form of society. Unlike Lutheranism, which rejected so much of the mediation of the Church and left discipline to the secular authority, Calvinism had a discipline of its own, hard, clear and effective. To Calvin, as to his Catholic adversaries, the Church was not merely spiritual: it was visible, militant, articulated, international. To him the church of Rome was a false Church: the great worldly Babylon which the true Church, from small beginnings—the saints, the élite—must conquer, destroy and totally replace. For that purpose his own Church could not be content with mere local or national success. The revolution was indivisible. The Lutherans in Germany might accept the principle *cuius regio eius religio*. The Calvinists could not.

Calvinism thus began with ecumenical claims. In many ways it began as a derivation from Erasmian reform: for Erasmus too had been ecumenical and had preached an undivided, purified, 'apostolic' Church. But the hardening of Catholicism in face of the Lutheran threat had destroyed that possibility, and the next generation of Erasmists, if they were to continue the struggle, were forced into a harder posture and a narrower path. Many of the early Calvinists had begun as Erasmian humanists: Calvin himself; his successor Theodore de Bèze, or Beza; the Scotsman George Buchanan; the great French Huguenots Languet, Hotman, Duplessis-Mornay; Dousa and Heinsius, Lingelsheim and Camerarius, the scholar-statesmen of Holland and Heidelberg. But as Catholicism re-established itself as the religion of hierarchical society, so Calvinism was forced back on to a narrower social basis. It became the religion of urban republics, of those commercial city-states out of which Erasmianism itself had been born. From that base it reached out for support in other social classes, and found it sometimes among the lesser princes, struggling for independence against the great centralizing courts, sometimes among turbulent magnates, happy to exploit a ready-made political party, sometimes among backwood gentry or the urban poor. In some places, as in rural Scotland or Gelderland, these secondary allies would distort and transform the original character of Calvinism; but basically it would remain urban and at least semi-republican. Its local centres would not be self-contained, highly developed nation-states but either commercial city-states or petty principalities on the fringes of the great kingdoms. The great princes, whether Catholic or Lutheran, looked askance at them as nurseries of sedition.

Being weak and severed, these little Calvinist centres needed common defence. Politically and diplomatically they acted together. The Calvinist International, ideologically united by constant consultation and firm internal discipline, was a sensitive system strung across Europe. The Synod of Dordt, in 1617, was the Calvinist equivalent of the Catholic Council of Trent. It also skilfully exploited the interests of the great powers. Through it, any threat to a Calvinist city or prince could raise the alarm through Protestant Europe, and interest of state might bring in the support of Lutheran Germany, Erasmian England, even Catholic Venice or France.

The ideological capital of Calvinism was of course Calvin's own chosen city, Geneva. Once established there, Calvin had uttered his message to Christendom. The princes were to establish the true Church, instead of the false, in their dominions. The faithful among their subjects were to lend their support. If the princes failed, the subjects were not to rebel; they were to endure.

If they were persecuted beyond endurance, they were to seek a 'refuge' abroad. In the 1550s they were so persecuted, and they took refuge in Geneva. In the 1560s, when a new race of princes seemed to offer hope of toleration, they returned home. Geneva, from the 'refuge', became the 'school of Christ', the seminary of a new generation of revolutionary apostles. John Knox and Christopher Goodman, the makers of the Scottish revolution, were Geneva-trained. So were several of the 'Marian exiles' who returned to Elizabethan England. So were almost all the new pastors who poured into the Netherlands and France. At first, these men sought to convert their princes. When they failed, the doctrine of Geneva hardened. Calvin's successor, Beza, openly advocated the deposition of the persecutors. The Scottish revolution of 1567, the Massacre of St Bartholomew of 1572, showed that co-existence was at an end. Two international parties faced each other in ideological war. The Jesuits took over the Calvinist doctrine of deposition. The Calvinist International was faced by the international order of Loyola, the Huguenots of France by the *Sainte Ligue*, the Calvinist-directed Protestant Union in Germany by the Catholic League.

In this ideological war, victory as we have seen, went mainly to the Catholics—at least until 1630. But the Catholic victory, in one respect at least, was pyrrhic. For in the hour of struggle, or of victory, the Catholic princes expelled the Calvinists whom they despaired of assimilating. Since the earliest strongholds of Calvinism were the old 'Erasmian' cities of western Europe, this expulsion entailed the break-up of urban structures and the loss of urban talent, sometimes to other more tolerant cities, sometimes to more backward areas. New 'refuges' were found; and the refugees, by their dynamism, sometimes converted them into new power-houses. The industrial heart of Europe was displaced. Alba's Tribunal of Blood drove the clothiers and miners of the southern Netherlands north and east to the Rhine. The Massacre of St Bartholomew sent French silk-workers from Lyons across the Jura. The capture of Antwerp by Alexander Farnese in 1585 dispersed the entrepreneurs of the economic capital of the world. In the next century, the Catholic reconquest would scatter the Calvinists of Bohemia, the Palatinate and the Baltic. Fifty years later still, the French Huguenots, expelled by Louis XIV, would similarly carry their crafts to enrich more hospitable lands.

And what were the main catchment areas of this great Calvinist dispersion? Holland and Zeeland received the rejected talent of Flanders and Brabant. Amsterdam inherited the prosperity of Antwerp, Leiden the cloth-industry of Hondschoote. The cities of the North Sea—Hamburg, Bremen, Emden—and the cities of the Rhineland—Wesel, Hanau, Frankfurt—were all enriched from the shattered urban life of the southern Netherlands. The Rhenish Palatinate and Alsace drew in the Calvinists expelled by the King of France and the prince-bishops of Germany. Switzerland was the reservoir into which France, Germany and Italy discharged their refugees. Many a minuscule city or insignificant duchy, thanks to the accident of a Calvinist ruler, suddenly benefited from this transfusion of vitality. Sedan, thanks to its Huguenot dukes, became a great clothing centre; Herborn, because it was an outlying property of the Dukes of Nassau, became the seat of an international academy. On the Atlantic coast, La Rochelle grew into an independent mercantile republic on the coast of France. In the east, Transylvania received the refugees of Germany and Bohemia and became, for a brief period, a landlocked island of western culture under the protection of the Turks, a branch of the Calvinist International beyond the Habsburg Reich.

This injection of Calvinist immigrants into disconnected areas of Europe inevitably caused a hardening of attitudes, and of frontiers, around them. If the northern Netherlands, the Palatinate, parts of Alsace and western Switzerland became centres of militant émigré Calvinism, the southern Netherlands, Lorraine, Franch-Comté and Savoy became, by opposition, strongholds of Catholicism. Württemberg, penned between Catholic Bavaria and Calvinist Alsace, became defiantly Lutheran. In Switzerland the division between Protestant and Catholic cantons was sharpened. Philip II made a separate treaty with the Catholic cantons for the passage of his armies; and the Protestant Grisons oppressed their Catholic colony in the crucial mountain pass of the Valtelline.

The economic consequences of the Calvinist diaspora in the Rhine valley are very important. The political consequences were no less important. For this same area—the old trade-route from Flanders to Italy, studded with factories and fairs—was also both the exposed eastern frontier of France and the military life-line of the Spanish empire in Europe, the well-trodden route whereby the invincible Spanish *tercios* moved from Milan to the Low Countries. The conversion of this geographical area into a complex of inflamed and antithetical ideologies inevitably sharpened international tension. The uncertainties of an ecclesiastical election, or a princely succession, the conversion, or the marriage, of a wayward ruler, in that jig-saw puzzle of clerical and lay lordships, might convulse the trembling balance of power throughout the Continent. The conversion to Protestantism of the Elector of Cologne caused the Cologne War of 1583; the death of the Duke of Cleve in 1609 would have plunged Europe in war but for the timely assassination of the King of France; and in 1618 the mobilization of the Calvinist International by the Elector Palatine, and his election as Calvinist King of Bohemia, was to precipitate the second and final stage in the war for Habsburg domination in Europe.

The Thirty Years' War was a war, or rather a complex of wars, of rival imperialisms: of Spanish ambitions in Europe, of Saxon ambitions in Germany, of Swedish ambitions in the Baltic, and of all the fears and secondary ambitions which they excited. It was also, at the beginning, a war of ideologies: of the Counter-Reformation against the Calvinist International. As such, it overflowed mere political frontiers. The Protestants of the West called for help to the Protestants of the East, seeking an ideological second front in Transylvania, and contending with their Jesuit enemies even in the Turkish Empire. One of the strangest episodes in that great struggle is the career of the Cretan, Cyril Lucaris, Patriarch of Constantinople. In his youth, in South Russia, Cyril had been outraged by the Jesuit intrigues which had led to the creation of the 'Uniate' Church. As Patriarch, he took his revenge by joining the Protestant International. He worked with the emissaries of Calvinist Geneva and Holland (and also Catholic but antipapal Venice), corresponded with the Archbishop of Canterbury, and the King of Sweden and the Calvinist Prince of Transylvania. He even put forth or at least avowed a Calvinist confession of faith for his own Greek Church. But this attempt at a Calvinist Reformation of the Greek Church was defeated. The ablest of Greek clerical statesmen was undermined by his Greek rivals, who in turn, were mobilized and manipulated by Rome. Four times deposed and restored by the Sultan, Cyril was ultimately strangled on his orders. His party was ruined; his 'Calvinist' Confession was denounced by successive Councils of his Church; and his closest disciple, Nathaniel Conopius, fleeing to Balliol College, Oxford, introduced into England the Turkish habit of drinking coffee.

The End of a World Picture

Ideological wars are also social wars, and from the beginning men recognized that the Habsburg bid for conquest war also an attempt to generalize the social form of the Counter-Reformation state. Ironically, even at the beginning, this form of society was already seen to be economically bankrupt: it had expelled its most productive subjects and had to be sustained by foreign colonies or foreign conquest. When the Spanish Council of State in 1621 debated the renewal of the war, speaker after speaker admitted the fact. In peace time, Spain had been the model for Europe, but the real beneficiaries of the peace had not been the Spaniards. They had been the irreducible 'rebels' and the expelled 'heretics': the exiled Antwerp Calvinists who now directed the aggressive West India Company in Amsterdam; the exiled Moriscos who now manned the fleets of the predatory 'Sallee rovers'. Only war, it now seemed, could nourish a system which, by its nature, regularly consumed more than it generated. It was to be a cannibal war: the great spaniolized courts meant to destroy the heretics and suck from them the sustenance which they could not create for themselves. The Austrian Habsburgs would devour Bohemia, Bavaria, the Upper Palatinate—as, on the other side, Lutheran Saxony would absorb Lusatia, and Lutheran Sweden the German cities of the Baltic.

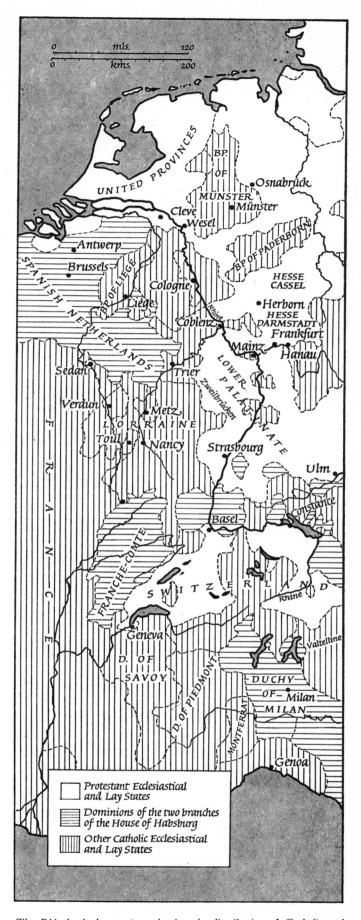

The Rhineland about 1620, showing the distribution of Catholic and Protestant states along the river, which was also the essential Spanish military route between Milan and the Spanish Netherlands.

The cannibalism of the great courts in their last struggle is vividly illustrated in that field in which they advertized their magnificence. In the years of peace, the princes had vied with each other as ostentatious builders and munificent patrons of art. Now they rifled each other's collections without pity. The Emperor Rudolf II had built up a splendid collection in Prague. When the Swedes took Prague in 1649, the entire collection was sent off to Stockholm to give lustre to an upstart dynasty (it did not stay there long: a few years later Queen Christina abdicated and took it with her to Rome). If the most famous collection of Europe, that of the Dukes of Mantua, escaped the sack of Mantua in 1630, that was only because two years earlier it had been secretly bought from the half-bankrupt duke by Charles I of England. Twenty years later the court of Charles I, 'the last Renaissance court in Europe', would itself be sold up and, in Clarendon's words, the other kings of Europe would come as buyers 'to get shares in the spoils of a murdered monarch'. Calvinist princes, of course, were less inclined to collect pictures (though there were rogue Calvinists, like Prince John Maurice of Nassau in Holland); but they gloried in their literacy and their libraries. The most famous of all was the Palatine Library at Heidelberg. When the Bavarians took Heidelberg, their duke—who, being Catholic, collected pictures, not books—sent it off as a present to the Pope who was at least a censor of literature; and a long trail of loaded mules lumbered southward over the Alps, each one with a label round its neck, *fero bibliothecam Principis Palatini*, 'I carry the library of the Prince Palatine'.

When all was over, who had gained, who lost? Politically, it is easy to make up the account. The Spanish Empire in Europe was broken. The Habsburg Reich was a shadow of itself. Saxony and Bavaria were independent powers in Germany. Sweden was the great power of the Baltic. Above all, France had a firm government, clear frontiers, influence in Germany, the initiative everywhere. But politics is only part of the account. The Thirty Years' War destroyed far more than the Spanish hegemony in Europe. It destroyed a whole system, the synthesis of a century. The Counter-Reformation State, the Calvinist International, both went down in the struggle and were never afterwards the same. So indeed did a whole philosophy. The Thirty Years' War saw the end of a *Weltanschauung*: of a world picture which had been inherited from the Middle Ages, which the great Catholic doctors had elevated into a universal system, and which neither the Lutherans nor the Calvinists, for all their ideological radicalism, had really challenged.

Battlefields of the Mind

That philosophy was the 'Aristotelean'—or rather pseudo-Aristotelean—synthesis of the Middle Ages, the grand, elaborate concept of a hierarchical Nature which gave cosmological justification to a hierarchical society and a hierarchical Church. The great schoolmen of the 13th and 14th centuries had constructed and explained and refined this system, sustaining it at every point by theories of physics and metaphysics, until the whole synthesis seemed self-explanatory and self-contained. The philosophers of the Italian Renaissance had questioned it, but they had not broken it, and with the Reformation and the Counter-Reformation it had been repaired and positively strengthened. For neither Reformation nor Counter-Reformation were, in the intellectual field, progressive movements, though both absorbed certain detached elements of progressive thought. Luther and Calvin might reject the superficial 'corruptions', 'mechanical devotions' and superstitious usages of medieval Christianity; but they accepted the fundamental synthesis of the medieval Church. Their encyclopaedists reasserted its principles, their historians operated within its framework. The Calvinists might reduce it to a bare, functional system, while the Catholics of the Counter-Reformation regilded and redecorated it and blew into it a warm air of new devotion; but Protestant or Catholic in name, intellectual or aesthetic in appeal, it was still basically the same system, positively fortified for the ideological struggle of the next hundred years.

Indeed, as that struggle continued, both Churches became, in intellectual matters, more reactionary, more fundamentalist. The Protestants became less critical of the Bible, the Catholics of the

Interpreting the Apocalypse (Book of Revelation) occupied some of the best talents of Europe in the early 17th century. Above: the Beast, ridden by the Whore of Babylon, from the second edition of Matthieu de la Cottière's 'Expositio' published in Sedan in 1625.

legends of the saints. The scepticism of Erasmus was repudiated on both sides. One aspect of this fundamentalism is illustrated by the new interest in the prophetic books of the Bible and their application to history. The historians of the Renaissance had repudiated the old theory of the Five Monarchies, derived from the Book of Daniel. The Protestants revived it, and by the early 17th century the Catholics spoke the same language. The authenticity of the Apocalypse had been doubted by Erasmus. Calvin himself refused to discuss it and regarded the calculation of the Millennium as a barren exercise. But by the early 17th century, interpretation of the Apocalypse had become a major industry on both sides, and the greatest of scholars and mathematicians found themselves involved in it. Joseph Justus Scaliger's great chronometrical work, *De emendatione temporum*, which coincided with the Gregorian reform of the calendar, and the astronomical observations of Tycho Brahe, were used to quicken the calculation of the last days. John Napier, the Scotsman who invented logarithms, devoted his mathematical genius to the same unpromising exercise. And in the 1640s a chorus of enlightened investigators hailed, as the greatest discovery of the century, the interpretation by a Fellow of Trinity College, Oxford, of the Number of the Beast.

The same increasing fundamentalism of both Churches is illustrated by the growth of witch-trials. The schoolmen, and especially St Thomas Aquinas, had fitted witch-beliefs into their 'Aristotelean' cosmology and elaborated them within it. With the weakening of that cosmology at the Renaissance, scepticism had been expressed; but the bigots of Catholicism stood fast and the Reformers—Luther and Calvin alike—reasserted the old doctrines and demanded the extirpation of witches as the allies of their religious enemies. The century from 1560 to 1660 was probably the worst century in history for the persecution of witches; and in that century the years of ideological war were the worst years, with Calvinists and Jesuits preaching persecution from either side. As long as the Aristotelean cosmology held firm, witch beliefs were 'rational' and the most learned and 'enlightened' scholars of the time buried themselves in the 'science' and fostered the persecution. But at the close of the Thirty Years' War the cosmology was found to be devalued; Jesuits and Calvinists were devalued with it; and in the new intellectual atmosphere the belief in witches, like that in the Five Monarchies and the historical application of the Apocalypse, simply withered away.

How did the Aristotelean cosmology collapse? Of course it did not happen suddenly. All through our century, behind the formal struggle of obscurantist, increasingly national Churches, new philosophies were fermenting, which took little account of such narrow frontiers. In some ways the doctrinal struggle, by discrediting the exclusive claims of each side, positively forwarded the process of fermentation. Sometimes the established orthodoxy, while appearing solid without, was quietly transformed within. Sometimes the critics worked from outside the establishment, as open heretics. Above all, there was a new cosmology which, though still bizarre and formless, could be the embryo, or the envelope, of a new world picture, indeed of a new understanding of the world.

The established orthodoxies were weakened from within by scepticism. Scepticism—'pyrrhonism' as it was called, the suspension of belief—had been launched, in the 16th century, by Erasmus, whose doubting spirit and suggestive use of language had been one of the gravest charges brought against him by believers on both sides. After his death, Erasmus had been condemned by his own Church, and Calvin and Loyola had alike rejected even the possibility of doubt. But as they could not agree on the obligatory truth, scepticism could not be altogether exorcized. What, men asked, was the ultimate canon of truth? Where was one to begin to reason? In the later 16th century the pyrrhonists produced their greatest figure in Michel de Montaigne who, like Erasmus, combined formal orthodoxy and seductive elegance of style with a permanent scepticism. In the early 17th century, many a young scholar found himself entangled in the 'troublesome labyrinths' of the pyrrhonists before settling for one of the comfortable orthodoxies. And it was 'pour esbranler les pyrrhoniens' that the greatest architect of the new cosmology, René Descartes, elaborated his new philosophy, basing a new rationalism not on any revealed axiom but on the irreducible canon of truth, *cogito ergo sum*.

Descartes' secular rationalism could be used—he intended it to be used—to support Catholic orthodoxy. It was to be the modern equivalent of Thomism: a self-contained, irrefutable intellectual system which would explain both the natural and the supernatural world; and its 'empirical' critics rejected it explicitly as a new scholasticism. But meanwhile other less ambitious forms of 'rationalism' were effectively undermining the orthodoxies. Once again, the impulse was given by Erasmus, who had insisted on applying the same critical standards to Christian doctrine as to secular problems. In consequence, Erasmus had suggested—though he was careful not to state—that the central doctrine of the Trinity had no basis in Scripture. The suggestion was taken up by his successors who, from the Italian Fausto Sozzini, were known as Socinians and were sharply condemned by the orthodox of all parties. Technically, the Socinians were Unitarians; in common usage they were all who applied human reason in religious matters; and they were noted especially for their belief in toleration. Persecuted in western Europe, they withdrew, in the later 16th century, to Poland and Transylvania. But the movement could never be crushed, and 'Socinian' ideas were always being detected, and repressed, in intellectual centres. In the early 17th century, as the Counter-Reformation prevailed in Poland, the headquarters of the movement was transferred to Holland and the ideas became merged with 'Arminianism', the Erasmian doctrine of free will. The Socinians, narrowly defined, were always few; but those whom their enemies called Socinians —believers in rational theology and toleration, undoubtedly influenced by Socinian writers—were many and they exercised a profound, transforming influence within the Churches. Hugo Grotius in Holland, William Chillingworth in England, are but two of the greatest of them: they smoothed the way from the fundamentalism of the Churches to the century of the Enlightenment.

'Pyrrhonism', 'Socinianism', weakened the 'Aristotelean' synthesis from within; but they did not create an alternative synthesis. That was the work, above all, of the 'Platonists'—that is, of the neo-Platonists of the Renaissance, who to the surviving neo-Platonic mysticism of the Middle Ages and the revived Platonism of the humanists added the strange 'Hermetic' doctrines of Roman Alexandria: doctrines which pretended to emanate from Hermes Trismegistus, an Egyptian sage contemporary with Moses and Zoroaster and other *prisci theologi*, forerunners of Plato. The reception of these doctrines in Renaissance

Europe, and the fortune which they made throughout the 16th century, is a subject in itself. For our purposes it is enough to say that, involved though they were in a bizarre, mystical demonology, they nevertheless provided the embryo of a new cosmology, the whirling, incandescent nebula which would ultimately condense into the orderly solar system of Galileo and Newton. For instead of the hierarchical, static Nature of the Aristoteleans, in which every element had its value and sought its place, and all change was by means of contact, the Platonists conceived of a dynamic Nature, moved indeed by spirits and demons, shot through indeed by 'influences', responding indeed to arcane numerological formulae, but self-contained, self-regulating, and intelligible by direct observation. The early expressions of this Hermetic pantheism, seem to us very grotesque; but, 'drained of its animism', it could become the new 'natural philosophy'. Paracelsus, for all his bombast, would be the father of modern chemistry; Giordano Bruno, for all his 'Egyptian' megalomania, would look forward to the new astronomy; and Kepler, for all his mathematical mysticism, would discover the laws of planetary motion, while the sane, civilized Aristotelean rationalists were compiling encyclopaedias of dead knowledge, or defending weakened religious postures, or interpreting the Apocalypse, or burning witches. What Miss Frances Yates has called 'the hermetic core of Renaissance Platonism' inspired, in different ways, most of the makers of the new science. Even Francis Bacon, that lucid intellect, the founder of a scientific spirit more fertile than the scholasticism of Descartes, drew on the ideas of the *magi* which he wished to disseminate rather than, like them, to reserve to himself; and Isaac Newton seemed to Lord Keynes not so much the first scientist as 'the last magician.'

The Search for Utopia

In the second of our three generations, the generation of peace, the great generation of Bacon and Grotius and Galileo, many men thought that, with this new knowledge, or possibility of knowledge, a better human society could also be constructed. But how could they begin? Everywhere around them they found

The 17th century saw numerous messianic and millenarian movements, both Christian and Jewish. In 1648 Zabbatai Zevi (1626–76), a Jew of Smyrna, declared himself the Messiah and attracted a host of disciples in the Jewries of Europe. This woodcut from an English account published in 1685 shows him receiving converts in his native city, which is imagined as a typical English town with minarets added.

the old social structures firm, rigid and repressive. Even the new universities which princes or city councils had founded, largely for their own glory, seemed closed to new ideas. Therefore such men met together in little societies—societies of *virtuosi*, like the *Accademia dei Lincei* in Italy of which Galileo and the future Pope Urban VIII were members, or the Academia Parisiensis of Marin Mersenne in France, or the *Fruchtbringende Gesellschaft* founded at Weimar in 1617; societies of idealist reformers, like the German Rosicrucians. As the political horizon darkened, these men often took refuge in 'utopias'. Faced by the solid-seeming structure of society, with its vested interests, they saw little chance of reform from above and so, like the early Christians in the Roman Empire, they dreamed of building up their new society from beneath, from simple cells which might yet provide a model for the future. Campanella's *City of the Sun* and Bacon's *New Atlantis* are but the most famous of the 'utopias' written at that time. About 1618 Valentin Andreae, the founder of the Rosicrucians, established an idealist society in south Germany, and although it was soon broken up by the wars, he and his followers never ceased to plan its revival. During the Thirty Years' War, displaced scholars and reformers, claiming to be disciples of Bacon or Campanella, regularly published blueprints of such societies: *Christianopolis, Macaria, Antilia* etc. The exiled Baltic reformer, Samuel Hartlib, devoted his life to 'the building of Christian societies in small models'. The exiled Bohemian Comenius imagined a 'pansophic' society as the means of enlightening all Protestant Europe; and in Puritan London, Robert Boyle conceived an 'invisible college' and James Harrington and his friends a 'Rota' to devise 'airy models' of a new commonwealth.

These utopian projects which pullulated in Europe in the early 17th century were an indication of malaise—but also

vitality. Campanella—a Platonist *enragé*—had been crushed by the viceregal court of Naples and the papal court in Rome: his utopia was conceived in the dungeons in which he would spend thirty years of his life. Bacon wrote at the court of King James: he hoped, in vain, to convert the learned Aristotelean on the throne. The German idealists looked hopefully to lesser princes as patrons—generally to Calvinist or crypto-Calvinist enemies of the great Catholic or Lutheran courts. Frustrated, they turned aside, often, into messianism. Campanella lost himself in messianic speculations. Comenius listened to half-cracked central European prophets. The social projects of Hartlib were entangled in millenarian fantasies. During the Thirty Years' War, most of these schemes of social and intellectual improvement were fused with religious enthusiasm. But the religious enthusiasm was generated by the war, and would disappear with the war; the ideas of progress were independent of it and would continue. The English Royal Society and its foreign imitators would be the realization, in a new generation of ideological peace, of the 'utopian' projects of the Thirty Years' War.

So when the wars and revolutions of forty years were wound up in 1660 a whole age, as it seemed, was swept away. The great courts were no longer the same: their vast systems of patronage, their swollen bureaucracies, their parasitic economy were broken. The international Churches were broken too: the Catholic Church had destroyed the Calvinist International only itself to founder in defeat. The Aristotelean cosmology itself had collapsed with the political and intellectual system of which it had been the product and which it had sustained. The new forms which had germinated beneath it would now show themselves through the broken crust. With a new generation in power, Europe, from 1660, would look forward again. In this sense at least we can describe the century 1560–1660 as a century of expansion.

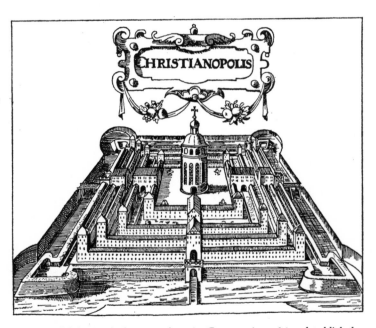

Johann Valentin Andreae was born in Germany in 1586 and published his 'Christianopolis' (above) in 1619, on the eve of the Thirty Years' War. Such blueprints for an ideal society reflected disillusion with the real world; but Andreae's imaginary community dedicated to Christian learning has its place in the idealist movement behind the foundation of the Royal Society in London.

II SPAIN'S DOMINION

Problems and Policies of a World Power

HENRY KAMEN

'I sailed through climates, saw new constellations,

Reconnoitred unnavegable gulfs,

Extending, Sire, the glory of your Crown

Even to the lands of southern ice!

What days by land and sea your standards led

To Italy, to Augsburg, Flanders, England . . .'

ALONSO DE ERCILLA TO PHILIP II

Spain's miraculous golden age

came in the century after the conquest of Mexico and Peru. Rapidly she became by far the richest country in Europe, the arbiter of the world. From the Netherlands to the eastern Mediterranean her authority was respected and her armies feared. Yet within fifty years of Charles V's death the sun was setting. The economy of Spain had proved unequal to the strain imposed upon it. Her wealth, instead of nourishing home resources, fatally competed with them. Inflation halted initiative and caused commercial stagnation. Abroad, as the revolt in the Netherlands assumed the proportions of a long and costly war, her commitments began to eat up first her overseas profits, then her internal revenue. Society, lacking the strong bourgeois element that was already powerful in other countries, froze into a rigid hierarchy of classes. The rich became richer, the poor poorer. National unity, in a state torn between so many racial and regional loyalties, could only be preserved by obedience to the king and to the church. Both were made absolute. Spain

became the fanatic of Europe, and even the figure of Philip II, *el rey prudente*, may be seen as the focus of twin fanaticisms—of rank and of faith.

The background to El Greco's *Dream of Philip II* is thus a complicated one. In the sky shines the monogram of Christ, IHS. The ranks of the angels encircle it in adoration. 'At the name of Jesus' wrote St Paul in the *Letter to the Philippians* (the allusion to the king was not lost), 'every knee should bow, of things in heaven and things on earth and things in hell'. On earth, with St Paul, king Philip kneels in the centre, a sombre figure in black, next to the Pope and the Doge of Venice: the very alliance which achieved victory at Lepanto. On the right, hell-mouth gapes. El Greco, in a composition of superb Mannerist bravura, has indeed brought into one canvas earth, heaven and hell, this world and the world to come, temporal politics and eternal truth, united—as perhaps they could only be in this country and at this moment—in a transfiguring blaze of mystical illumination.

Cervantes mocked the death of the chivalric ideal, but with such nostalgia and affection that it remained permanently part of the Spanish spirit. *Don Quixote* was published in 1605 and immediately became popular with all ranks and classes.

Lope de Vega, the greatest dramatist of the period, took the traditional 'cloak and dagger' play and made it material for both comedy and high drama. He was immensely prolific, writing over a thousand plays.

The Escorial – palace, monastery and church – was an image of Philip II's own character. It was his refuge from the stresses of empire and the tomb destined for himself, his father and his successors. 'We saw tears flow from his eyes,' said a contemporary – 'such were the devout feelings with which he meditated his lofty plans'. Dedicated to St Lawrence, it is built entirely of granite, and the plan, following the king's own wish, was based on the gridiron upon which the saint was martyred.

Philip's son, Philip III, came to the throne when he was twenty and occupied it for twenty-three years. He proved to be everything his father was not. Irresponsible, lazy, pleasure-loving and of limited intelligence, he could not provide the leadership that Spain more than ever needed.

High taxes and debased currency reduced large parts of Spain to misery. At this tax-gatherer's table the king's authority is represented by the grandee; a clerk, in cap and spectacles, records the sums in a ledger. When taxation failed Lerma tried reducing the real value of coins, and finally, in 1599, issuing coinage of copper, the first in Europe.

'The greatest occasion that past or present ages have seen or that future ones can hope to see.' So Cervantes, who lost an arm at Lepanto serving in the ship of his admiral, Don John of Austria, described the battle which freed Europe from the threat, at least the immediate threat, of Turkish expansion. It was an international enterprise. The fleets of Spain, Venice and the Papal States – over 200 ships – assembled at Messina and on October 7th 1571 met the Turkish fleet in the Gulf of Lepanto, off the Greek coast. The battle (shown *above* in Vicentino's painting in the Ducal Palace at Venice) was a brutal affair of hand-to-hand fighting between boarding parties (unlike the English strategy against the Armada some years later) and resulted in a complete Christian victory. Most of the advantages, however, were lost in subsequent quarrels between the allies and Turkish power was not materially diminished.

Against England, Spain's bitterness was more recent. The Catholic Queen, Mary Tudor, had married Philip II as his second wife in 1554; he even considered marrying the Protestant Elizabeth when she in turn came to the throne. But hostility mounted over English support for the Dutch rebels and over attacks on Spanish shipping in America. In 1588, after Elizabeth's excommunication, the Armada (*right*) sailed up the Channel to ferry Alba's army across from the Netherlands for the conquest of heretical England.

Spanish orthodoxy and the fervour of the Spanish faith had its roots in the past. Christianity in Spain had always been a crusade. It was **St Ignatius of Loyola** (*above left*), the crippled and disillusioned soldier, who saw that spiritual battles too could be won by military discipline. In 1534 he and a few companions started what was to become the Society of Jesus, a tightly knit order of dedicated militant priests. **St Francis Xavier** (*centre*) carried the faith to the Far East. Born in 1506, he met St Ignatius in 1529 and was among the first members of the new order. In 1541 he left Europe, visiting India, Ceylon, Malacca, the East Indian islands and in 1549, Japan (this portrait is by a Japanese convert). Spanish missionaries penetrated to every corner of the world, often meeting martyrdom in the process. **St Teresa of Avila** (*above right*) (1515–82) was the grand-daughter of a Jew – an interesting sidelight on the religious background. She joined the Carmelites at the age of twenty. Her autobiography and the poems of her friend and sympathizer St John of the Cross are the two most powerful spiritual documents to have come out of the Counter-Reformation. She was canonized in 1622.

Mass deportation was Lerma's answer to the problem of the Moriscos, the 300,000 Moors who remained in Spain nominally Christian but mostly still at heart Muslim, and potentially, in Spanish eyes, part of a conspiracy with their Muslim enemies, the Turks. In 1609, came the decree for the expulsion of the whole Moorish population to North Africa, bringing destitution to the Moriscos and unintended bankruptcy to parts of Spain.

The religious life kept its tenacious hold on Spain, where a vast army of priests, monks and nuns – mostly economically unproductive – added to the country's problems. This quiet picture of a Carthusian refectory by Zurbarán, illustrates a miracle in the life of the founder, St Hugo. The Carthusian order, the strictest of monastic orders, each monk living alone in his own house, made a deep appeal to the austere and mystical side of the Spanish character. Zurbarán's subtle art catches perfectly its combination of tranquillity and strength.

Upon Judaism and Islam Spanish Christianity imposed total submission, yet it learned much from both. *Left:* the Alcázar, Seville, meeting place of Islamic and Renaissance art. *Right:* Sta Maria la Blanca at Toledo – built by Jews as a synagogue in the Moorish style in the 13th century, converted into a Christian church in 1405.

The Grand Inquisitor (*left*) – Cardinal Fernando Niño de Guevara, Bishop of Toledo – painted about 1600 by El Greco. Born in 1541, he was created cardinal when he was fifty-five, Inquisitor four years later and, for the last eight years of his life (1601–09), Archbishop of Seville.

The Inquisition itself had been introduced in Spain by Ferdinand and Isabella as a means of ensuring political unity. During the reign of Philip II and his successors it was used both against Jews and Muslims whose conversion was suspect and against Protestant heretics. Philip extended its powers – often against the wishes of the regional councils – and the Spanish Dominicans (more fanatically Catholic in this respect than the Pope) initiated a reign of terror in the name of orthodoxy. The *autos-de-fé* ('acts of faith') continued with little abatement throughout the reigns of Philip III, Philip IV and Charles II. In the panorama of which a detail is shown opposite a great *auto-de-fé* is about to take place in the Plaza Mayor at Madrid in 1680. On the dais at the back sit Charles II, his Queen and the Queen Mother (note on the king's right the court dwarfs and jesters). In the centre several episodes are shown together, including the passing of sentence and preaching of sermons. The plaza is full of spectators, sitting on benches or lining the galleries behind. One of the victims in penitential garb is led past the king by two friars. Others, both men and women, in various parts of the picture, are shown pleading, recanting or resisting; they bear placards relating their crimes.

Christ's sufferings are more real in Spanish art than in any other. Every device of naturalism is used. The eyes run with tears, the red blood seems hardly dry on the side, the mouth is half open in a groan of agony. This figure by Gregorio Fernández was commissioned by Philip III and presented to the Capuchin monastery of El Pardo.

In its closed world, the court, rigidly proud, led a charmed life, immune to the crises that shook the country as a whole. *Above:* a stag-hunt arranged for the ladies of Aranjuez, a royal park outside Madrid. The animals are driven into the trap to be butchered underneath the platform where ladies of the court, and even nuns, have gathered to enjoy the sport.

The royal children were immortalized in their pathetic, premature dignity by Velázquez. *Right:* the little infanta Margarita-Teresa, aged five, part of Velázquez' great painting *Las Meniñas.*

Don Baltasar Carlos, eldest son of Philip IV, died aged fourteen, a victim, it seems, of the vices to which court life exposed him. He is seen here at the Madrid Riding School. This was the beginning of Spain's decline – a decline brought about, paradoxically, by the enormous wealth flooding in from America, which undermined the stability of the home economy. The court, nevertheless, retained its standards of ceremony and display.

The regional centres retained a measure of power, varying from province to province. *Below left:* two members of the Cortes of Valencia, the *administrador* and the *contador*. *Below right:* the councillors of Barcelona, sitting in church, as was their privilege, without removing their hats.

The Twelve Years' Truce signed with the United Provinces in 1609 came to an end in 1621. War began again, this time as part of the larger European struggle. Ambrosio de Spinola, a rich Genoese who had risen to fame in 1604 with the capture of Ostende, laid siege to the town of Breda, an ancestral possession of the house of Nassau. In 1624 it fell – a relatively minor incident made famous by Velázquez' commemorative painting ten years later. Justin of Nassau delivers the keys of the city to Spinola, who seems to greet and comfort him by his chivalrous gesture of the right hand.

The 'Count-Duke' of Olivares (*left*), favourite and first minister of Philip IV, virtually ruled Spain for twenty-two years. Velázquez, as usual, manages to flatter his sitter by his technique and composition but at the same time to convey something of his vanity and self-importance. One of Olivares' titles at this time (1634) was 'General of the Cavalry of Spain', and it is in this rôle that he is portrayed, though in fact he never commanded troops in the field. He died disgraced eleven years later.

Problems and policies
of a world power

HENRY KAMEN

The publication of 'Don Quixote de la Mancha' in 1605 brought immediate fame to its author Miguel de Cervantes. Ostensibly a satire on the current taste for tales of chivalry, it had a deeper, more universal appeal in its portrayal of human idealism and frailty. Above, the titlepage of the first Portuguese edition (Portugal was then part of the Spanish dominions). It shows the knight riding his horse Rosinante, preceded by his 'squire' Sancho Panza.

IN 1492, when the Catholic monarchs Ferdinand and Isabella expelled their Jewish population and destroyed the last Moorish stronghold of Granada, they claimed to have established a Christian Spain. The Moors and Jews, however, continued to play a fundamental part in Spanish history. Moorish language, art and culture remained part of the Spanish heritage; the converted Moors, known as *Moriscos*, remained a considerable part of the population until their expulsion over a century later; and the tradition of battle against the Moors, which had inspired the medieval Reconquest of Christian territory, continued to inspire the soldiers of Castile in their search for empire under the early Habsburgs. Those Jews who stayed and accepted baptism in 1492 likewise made their contribution, above all in the world of science and creativity: in medicine, philosophy, and theological writing. The fusion of these three racial cultures—the Christian, the Moorish and the Jewish—promised a continuation of the triumphs of medieval Spanish civilization.

Culture and Conquest

But the unity so achieved was, in a way, an illusion. The *Moriscos* were never treated as social equals; the converted Jews—*conversos*—were never fully accepted into the Christian community and continued to be the prime target of the Spanish Inquisition, which began functioning in 1480. Both races were eventually hounded down into virtual extinction. Racial disunity was matched by the political fragmentation of Spain. Castile and Aragon had remained completely independent of each other under the Catholic monarchs, and continued so throughout the two centuries of Habsburg rule that commenced with the accession of Charles of Burgundy in 1516. Navarre was an ancient kingdom with its own institutions; the Basque provinces had their *fueros* or provincial liberties which excluded the laws of Castile; and Portugal, unwilling to throw in its lot with that of Spain, remained an independent sovereign state save for the 'sixty years' captivity' from 1580 to 1640 when it was occupied by Castilian troops.

This inherent disunity of history, race and government has remained into modern times a heavy liability on Spanish internal development. Looked at from the outside, the liability was not so obvious in 1559, the year when Philip II officially inherited the crown from his father Charles V. Spain at this date was a world power without equal. 'His empire embraced the whole face of the earth', wrote one biographer of Philip, 'and he had subjects and vassals in all the four corners of the world, Asia, Africa, Europe and America. When he sailed in his fleets and armadas, it was as lord of all the seas, from pole to pole, and his captains and men bore his royal banner from the Antarctic to the Arctic'.

The Spanish urge to empire had been visibly influenced by the resumption, at the end of the 15th century, of the old 'Reconquest' campaign against Granada. The success of that campaign had in turn revived the dream of a crusade against Islam, into North Africa and beyond. The discovery of America occurred opportunely to divert this enthusiasm into more profitable channels. Political theorists of the time, notably the great jurist Francisco de Vitoria, found themselves employed in justifying a vast programme of imperialist expansion that was to alter the outlook of Castilian society.

Spanish culture and conquest accompanied each other. 'Your Majesty', explained the humanist Nebrija to Queen Isabella, 'language is the perfect instrument of empire'. Castilian became in time the predominant lánguage of the peninsula, and a world language in its own right. In the 15th century the first stirrings of Castilian literature found expression in Italian forms, especially in verse. By the late 16th century Spain had begun to export its own native produce. Verse and drama of the period adopted themes from European and American history, while in return America, Italy and the Netherlands—everywhere, in fact, that the Spanish soldier went—became receptive to Spanish influence. It has been pointed out that the early 1580s saw the triumph of Spanish prose and poetry, with the republication in 1580 of Garcilaso de la Vega's verse, and the issue in 1585 of Fray Luis de León's immortal treatise *On the Names of Christ*. By a historical accident the same years witness the peak of Spanish imperial fortunes, with the unification of the Iberian peninsula under Philip II in 1580. Hand in hand, culture progressed with the advance of empire, as though in fulfilment of Nebrija's declaration.

Spain after 1559 was living in the post-Erasmian age, for by then the teachings of the Dutch humanist, once predominant in the peninsula, had been edged out as dangerously Lutheran in content. The last prominent survivors of the Erasmian tradition, like Juan de Valdés—who was eventually forced to flee to Italy—were too liberal to be tolerated in Spain. But the peninsular Counter-Reformation was not exclusively reactionary. It could point back to the reforms of Cardinal Jiménez de Cisneros as laying the basis for a healthier Church, and in the mystical school of the late 16th century it produced a movement without equal in Europe. The poetic and contemplative genius of Luis de León, the mystical verse of St John of the Cross, were excelled only by St Teresa of Ávila, whose contribution as reformer, religious leader and woman of letters, entitles her to world stature.

The Golden Century

By the 17th century only faint flickerings of Erasmianism remain, notably in the writings of Cervantes. Miguel de Cervantes (1547–1616), whose *Don Quixote* was published in 1605, dominates the literary achievement of the period. *Quixote* was a profoundly Spanish novel, but it also surveyed Spain's part in European history and the relevance of the Spanish situation to the universal human condition. Its author's popularity extended beyond the peninsula: in the Low Countries, for instance, nineteen editions of works by Cervantes were published between 1607 and 1670. Of particular value to the historian is Cervantes' perceptive survey of contemporary Spain, and his insight into social and religious manners. He was also, and more obviously, a critic of his times; *Don Quixote* reflects the many weaknesses and shams of Spanish society in the early 17th century. In this it anticipates the criticism and disillusion to be expressed later by Francisco de Quevedo and other writers. Under Philip II, however, the time had not yet come for the pessimism of Quevedo. Writers were still conscious of being spokesmen for the power of their country, the arbiter of the world. Distilling the hopes of a generation, one poet could write in 1584 that under Philip:

Tiempo vendrá en que el mundo dé aposento
a un pastor solo y a una monarquía

(the time will come when the world admits one shepherd only and one monarchy). Others took pride in the achievements of a host of distinguished novelists and dramatists—Lope de Vega and Tirso de Molina among them—who were to make this the golden age of Castilian literature. 'This our Spain', a writer claimed, 'once considered crude and barbarous in the use of language, today exceeds the most flourishing culture of the Greeks and Latins.'

As in literature, Spaniards were at first heavily influenced by Italy in art, sculpture and architecture. Initially relying on Italian forms, they soon evolved a style of their own. In architecture the move to a purer Castilian style was first made by Juan de Herrera (1530–97), creator of the Escorial. Herrera had been educated chiefly in Italy but he initiated a native school which dominated Castilian architecture for half a century after his death. In sculpture the reign of the first two Philips coincides with the shift from an imaginative but severe Mannerism to a more popular and evocative style; both these approaches were Italian in origin, but both also reflected the change of mood in the Spanish religious and cultural temper. Under Philip III sculpture reflects a more fervid and popular religiosity, symptomatic perhaps of a growing preoccupation with internal problems.

In painting, El Greco (1541–1614) bestrides the period as the almost exact contemporary of Cervantes. He came to Spain only in the 1570s, a thorough adept of the Venetian school of painting. Again, despite its Italian origins and its close relation to contemporary Mannerism, Greco's art was intensely personal and Spanish, particularly in the overriding religious theme that dominates all his painting. He can be considered the last of the Spanish Mannerists, before the advent of Baroque in the early 17th century. The Baroque under Philip III and Philip IV continued to emphasize the mysticism which is associated with El Greco. But it included also a secular realism that became basic to all the great Baroque painters. Ribera was one of the first to combine these two apparently conflicting themes: Velázquez was the greatest. Though best known for his court portraits, Velázquez (1599–1660) used his canvases to cover the whole range of social life, with a technical perfection and a respect for humanity that places him at the sum-

mit of the Spanish achievement during the golden century. The irony is that this summit should have been attained in a time of political decline and spiritual decay. The moral collapse of Spain, which begins at the time of the Thirty Years' War, preceded by nearly half a century the evaporation of its immense cultural resources.

True to one of its most beneficial functions, the Spanish aristocracy played the necessary role of Maecenas to national culture. Philip II led the way not only with his foundation of the Escorial, but also through the rich library with which he endowed it. The court was a natural centre for the distribution of reward for artistic merit, and grandees such as the Duke of Alba were prominent among those granting their patronage to men of culture. The favourable results of this are clear, the unfavourable ones not so obvious. Aristocratic dominance of culture dictated the investment of money, which was poured into magnificent palaces and churches, but not into the universities; into family portraits and new altars and books of chivalry, but not into books on science and agriculture. Literacy became essential, but not learning. The small social importance of the bourgeoisie revealed itself in the general lack of bourgeois patronage of art in Castile, although in Valencia and in Barcelona the commercial classes played a more distinctive role in this respect. The successes of Spanish culture were therefore in a sense distorted. They depended almost exclusively on the patronage of a class which was beginning to lose its social and moral capability towards the middle of the 17th century. To this was added the restricting hand of the Inquisition, a constant threat to the development of original speculation in the arts and sciences.

The Prudent King

On the death of Charles V in 1559, the Habsburg possessions were divided between Philip II, who was given Spain, the Netherlands and the Italian territories, and his uncle Ferdinand, who received the Imperial crown and the hereditary Habsburg lands of central Europe. In addition, Philip received all the overseas possessions of Spain, thus securing control of a world empire which would be extended still further during his reign by the annexation of Portugal and the conquest of the Philippines. Spanish ships dominated the world's oceans and Spanish soldiers were garrisoned in every continent of the world. At the centre of this vast structure sat a man whom historians have had singular difficulty in comprehending. The prudent king, *el rey prudente*, was a man of extreme reserve and seriousness. A devoted husband and father, four times married, he was also a profoundly religious man, utterly dedicated to the interests of his faith. Retiring in mid-reign to the magnificent palace-monastery of the Escorial, which he had had built in the hills north-west of Madrid, he led a life of complete austerity among the monks of St Jerome. It was here that he received, on both occasions with remarkable impassivity, the news of the victory of Lepanto in 1571 and of the defeat of the Armada in 1588.

The famous Spanish infantry regiments (pike and musket) known as the 'tercios', remained virtually undefeated for almost a century. Spanish garrisons were to be found in all parts of the empire, Italy as well as Flanders, and Spanish soldiers were renowned for their courage and discipline on the battlefield. In this engraving from Strada's 'De Bello Belgico' (1651 edition) infantry and cavalry are shown relaxing after the fall of Valenciennes in 1567.

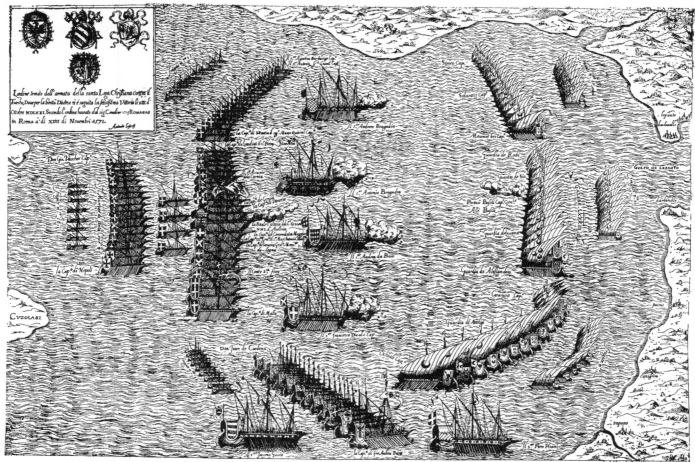

The victory at Lepanto (1571) was the most spectacular Christian success in the long struggle with the Turks for supremacy at sea. In this schematic drawing each fleet is shown led by its flagship—Christians on the left (with Don John's ship in the centre), Turks on the right.

By dividing his empire between the Spanish and imperial thrones, Charles V had sought to preserve an unwieldy inheritance from total disruption. In effect, however, he had withdrawn from the Empire, now split by Lutheranism and princely ambitions, and by retiring to Spain had emphasized where the chief interests of his dynasty lay. It became Philip's task to preserve that inheritance from the contagions that had wrecked the Holy Roman Empire. As a consequence, Protestantism and aristocratic or regional disaffection became the two plagues against which Philip was to exercise his energy in his newly acquired territories. The great attention which both representatives of the Habsburg dynasty were now obliged to devote to internal problems reduced their range of common interests, and for the next half-century Madrid and Vienna were to pursue policies which were often frankly discordant both at home and abroad.

The difference of interests between the two Habsburg crowns sprang from both religious and territorial considerations. Despite Spanish pressure on Vienna, the emperors, and particularly Maximilian II (1564–76), insisted on pursuing policies of political compromise with religious opponents. In their view, this seemed the best way of preserving imperial authority in a bitterly divided Germany. The emperors were also hostile to the general tenor of the Council of Trent, which ended in 1563; to them the Council had served more to exacerbate than to allay religious discord. Philip, on the other hand, saw the decisions of the Council—at least in their doctrinal aspects—as the climax to a great movement which would reclaim Europe for the Church. He had very serious differences with some of the Tridentine decrees, particularly those which might increase papal interference with the Spanish Church, but he took care to see that Spanish theologians and clergy were present in their numbers to promote the interests of Spain. Imperial pretensions also clashed with Spanish authority on two major fronts: in the Netherlands, which were under

Spanish rule but were also part of the Empire; and in Italy, where their respective spheres of influence frequently overlapped.

The only other Catholic powers of consequence in Europe were France and the Papacy. With neither of these was Spain entirely at ease. The Valois-Habsburg struggle of Charles V's earlier years continued to embitter Franco-Spanish relations. Under Philip II undue intervention in the French religious wars had the unfortunate effect of uniting the majority of political factions in France against Spanish hegemony, and when eventually in 1593 a Bourbon, Henry IV, emerged as king of France it was on a national programme of war against Spain. With the Papacy Philip was hardly better placed. Their territorial aims collided in Italy, where both had fundamental interests, and in Europe as a whole Philip was unwilling to support papal policy if it tended to benefit powers that were rivals of Spain.

Spanish imperialism in Europe was consequently exercised in virtual isolation. It was a universal monarchy whose enemies were not limited to any one nation or religion. Catholic France, Protestant England and Muslim Turkey came to be its bitterest opponents. Spain was accordingly obliged to utilize all the resources of the peninsula and of the overseas empire in an unflagging struggle on several fronts to maintain its hegemony in Europe.

The potential of the Spanish monarchy was formidable. Its army was the finest and most powerful in the world; its infantry regiments, known as *tercios*, remained undefeated in any major battle for the best part of a century. With *tercios* garrisoned after the mid-16th century in both Italy and Flanders, Spain was capable of striking directly at any enemy in either northern or southern Europe. One relatively weak point in the monarchy's defences was its lack of adequate naval forces in European waters: this, however, was on occasion remedied handsomely, as in the case of the fleet assembled for the battle of Lepanto; and in any case Spain's sea power in the Atlantic proved itself almost invulnerable to the attacks of the Protestant maritime nations. To finance this great war machine Charles V had been obliged to rely on extensive loans from bankers and on revenue from the Castilian crown, but already before the accession of Philip II a new and apparently inexhaustible source of wealth was obtained in the form of silver imports from the American mines at Potosí in Bolivia. Without such an income an aggressive foreign policy would have been impossible.

Muslim Menace, within and without

The first two decades of Philip's reign were devoted almost exclusively to the problem of the Mediterranean. There the threat came from the vigorous and expanding Ottoman empire. Spain, with its long history of struggle against the Moorish invaders, was the obvious leader of the attempt to stem the tide of Islam. There existed moreover a direct threat to Spanish supremacy in the western Mediterranean, and to its lonely outposts on the north coast of Africa. The princes of Italy also looked to Spain for help. Philip's earliest move in this campaign, however, proved disastrous. This was the expedition which he sent against the island of Djerba in 1560. Half the Spanish fleet and thousands of garrison troops were lost to the Turkish naval forces. This reverse left the Mediterranean open to Turkish and African corsairs, but it also compelled Philip to reassess his tactics and to rebuild his scattered forces.

In 1565 the Turks were again on the offensive, this time against the island of Malta, held by the Knights of the Order of St John. On this occasion the Spanish relief forces lifted the siege and routed the Turks. It was the first significant victory to be achieved against the hitherto irresistible Ottoman power, and it began the turn of the tide in favour of the Christian nations. The initiative could not, however, be seized by Philip, for from this date he was to be overwhelmed by commitments which strained the already scattered resources of Spain. In the Low Countries the beginnings of a revolt led by the Netherlandish aristocracy obliged him to draw off some of his best troops from Italy and send them northwards under the command of the Duke of Alba. A couple of years after this, in 1568, a serious uprising occurred in the mountains of the Alpujarras in Granada. It was the revolt of the *Moriscos*, the converted Moors.

The *Morisco* population of Granada, which had been forcibly converted to Christianity at the end of the reign of Ferdinand and Isabella, had long laboured under the suspicion and persecution of the authorities. Resolute in their hostility to an alien faith and to alien customs which they were compelled by the authorities to adopt, they refused to accept integration into the Christian community. What precipitated even further repression seems to have been awareness in the Spanish government that agents of the *Moriscos* were in secret contact with the Turkish rulers of Constantinople and north Africa. An internal problem was therefore aggravated by the existence of an outside threat. Goaded by decrees ordering abolition of their traditional customs and abandonment of their native language and ceremonies, the *Moriscos* of Granada eventually burst into revolt on Christmas Eve 1568. Taking to the Alpujarra mountains, they organized a vast uprising which kept the best soldiers of the crown at bay for two years. At last, in 1570, Philip's half-brother, the young Don John of Austria, at the head of a regular army, managed to put an end to the rebellion, and the *Moriscos* were expelled from Granada and scattered into the other provinces of Spain. This, as Spanish statesmen very soon realized, was to postpone rather than to achieve a solution.

With its best generals and troops pinned down in the Netherlands and in the Alpujarras, Spain in these years was more vulnerable than it had ever been since the advent of the Habsburg dynasty. The suppression of the *Morisco* rebellion was therefore a great relief. It was also very timely: for it enabled Philip to respond to an urgent call for help from Italy. In 1570 the Turks had landed on Cyprus, a possession of the republic of Venice. The fall of Cyprus threatened to bring economic difficulties to Venice and to be a resounding victory for the Ottoman empire, with serious repercussions for Christian Europe. The Pope, alarmed by

the menace, rallied to the help of Venice and finally persuaded Spain to join in a crusading league against the Turk. Together the three powers raised a huge fleet which, under the command of Don John of Austria, put to sea at last in the autumn of 1571. In October the Christian forces met the Turkish fleet off the Greek coast, in the Gulf of Lepanto, and inflicted a crushing defeat on it. Miguel de Cervantes, wounded in the battle, was to describe it later as 'the greatest occasion that past or present ages have seen, or that future ones can hope to see'. Although the triumph neither drove back the Turks nor destroyed their naval power permanently, it did more than this, for it restored confidence to the heart of Christendom. The initiative had now returned to the nations of the west, and Spain rode forward on the crest of the offensive.

The year of Lepanto also saw the extension of Spanish imperial power to its farthest limits with the occupation of the Philippine Islands—named after the king's son—and the foundation of the city of Manila by the great conquistador of the Pacific, Miguel López de Legazpi. In a sense 1571 may be regarded as the *annus mirabilis* of Spanish naval power, which had now established its authority in the world's three greatest seas—the Mediterranean, the Atlantic and the Pacific. In Spain itself the decade was to end with the annexation of Portugal by the troops of Philip II in 1580, two years after the death of that country's unfortunate King Sebastian in a crusading expedition into Morocco. With the Muslim threat both within and without the country reduced to manageable proportions, and with the union of all the realms of the peninsula under one crown, Philip may be said by 1580 to have reached the peak of his greatness.

The Shadow of Defeat

Success in southern Europe, however, was already being overtaken from the north by the long shadow of defeat. The revolt in the Netherlands, (described in detail in Chapter III), which Alba had believed he could crush by the execution of its aristocratic leaders and the subjection of the population, had soon broadened into a war of national liberation. Alba's policy of pacification by violence failed, as did the more moderate policy of his successors. Even Don John of Austria, victor of so many other battles, was unable to find a proper solution during the two years that he spent as governor in the Low Countries until his death in 1578. His successor Alexander Farnese, Duke of Parma, followed a carefully thought out military and diplomatic policy, but was unable to win the north either by conciliation or by conquest.

The loss of the Protestant Netherlands was not merely territorial. It was the first great dent in the fabric of the monarchy, and illustrated the weakness of the famed *tercios* of Spanish troops before the determination of a small people. In Protestant Europe, and particularly in Elizabethan England, the opponents of Spanish hegemony saw in the success of the Dutch a sign for the future. English intervention on the side of the Dutch in 1585 was only the culminating point of two decades during which English naval forces, both official and unofficial, had harrassed the Spanish lifeline to the Low Countries through the Channel. English diplomatic, religious and colonial interests became the principal threat to the preservation of Spain's empire, and forced Philip to direct his attention to his greatest antagonist—Elizabeth of England.

In Lisbon, where he stayed from 1581 to 1583, he found time to ponder two urgent questions: how to maintain his sea communications with the Netherlands, and how to repress the activities of pirates like Drake and Hawkins who were marauding freely over the Spanish shipping lines in America and even in Europe. To these questions there was one clear answer: to strike a decisive blow at England and thereby to end the source of all his troubles. The plan which was proposed as the most promising was for an armed invasion of England: a great naval armada from Spain was to pick up the necessary troops from Parma's army in the Netherlands. By 1586 preparations were under way for the building of the mightiest fleet ever to negotiate European waters. 'The objective of this armada', wrote the Duke of Medina Sidonia, who was eventually to command it, 'is no less the security of the Indies than the recovery of the Netherlands'. When it sailed at last in

1588, however, it attained neither of these aims. Instead, it failed to collect Parma's troops, was harrassed by the English ships in the Channel and ravaged by the weather. In the end only a few survivors and half the ships managed to stagger back to Spain after a nightmare voyage round the north of the British Isles and the coast of Ireland.

Philip received the news of this disaster with his customary impassivity. He could not fail, however, to realize its significance. In European waters Spain had let the initiative pass to the Protestant maritime powers of the north. The Dutch territories were now irrecoverable (although Philip, throughout his reign, refused to accept this conclusion). And with the rise of independent Dutch power the momentum of empire began to pass to the north. By the next reign Dutch captains had begun to make inroads into the Portuguese colonies in Asia and America, and Amsterdam replaced the cities of the Catholic monarchies, Lisbon, Seville and Antwerp, as the new commercial entrepot of the world.

If the Armada had failed to secure the Indies fully, the English at least gained no advantage in America from its defeat. On the contrary, despite a noticeable increase in buccaneering in the Caribbean, the English and Dutch privateers were unable to profit with impunity from their raids, for the Spanish government had finally woken up to the vulnerability of its position and particularly after 1586 had strengthened its defences in the Atlantic and the Pacific. It was to the Atlantic and the Indies that Philip had to turn more and more as his position in western Europe was undermined by the Protestant powers and ultimately by Catholic France.

Philip had managed to secure peace with France in 1559, but his interest in his northern neighbour deepened with the years, as the religious wars of France threatened repeatedly to bring the Huguenot party to power. A Protestant France would not only be a severe reverse for the Catholic Church; it would also cut off the Netherlands from the south and menace Spanish lines of communication throughout the continent. Philip consequently thought it essential to lend his support at all times to the Catholic party in France. When after the assassination of Henry III in 1589 it became clear that the only serious candidate for the throne was the Huguenot king of Navarre, Henry de Bourbon, Philip sent an army into France from the Low Countries to support the Catholic League. This intervention was the last in a series of ill-calculated enterprises. In 1593 Henri de Navarre declared himself a Catholic and prepared to unite all anti-Spanish forces behind him in an effort to eject foreign troops from national territory. In 1595 Henri declared war on Spain, to be joined the following year in formal alliance with England and the United Provinces. Faced by this coalition, Philip found his energy and money running out in a war from which he now stood to gain nothing. In 1598 he made peace with France by the Treaty of Vervins, though England and the Dutch preferred to continue the fighting. Almost simultaneously he granted the Spanish Netherlands a measure of autonomy under the rule of his daughter Isabel and her husband. It was the beginning of a policy of retreat. As yet, Spain had lost nothing, but it had overreached itself both politically and militarily. In this atmosphere of doubt and crisis, Philip in 1598 came to the end of his momentous reign.

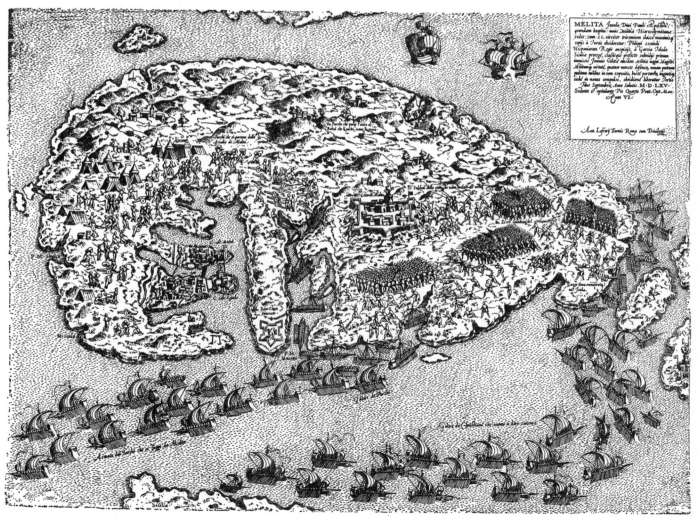

Malta relieved: in 1565 the Knights Hospitaller endured a fierce siege of four months before Spanish troops (seen here landing on the right) came to their aid. Castel Sant' Elmo has fallen to the Turks; San Michele and Sant' Angelo are almost overrun.

The silver mines of the New World were essential to the Spanish economy. A drawing from the Indian Poma de Ayala's 'Nueva Cronica' of 1613 shows a Peruvian mining town, with the main compound centred round the church and heavily-laden llamas being led towards it from the workings.

America's Silver

Before going further.we must pause to examine the economic and religious background to Philip's reign. After the division of the Habsburg territories between the Empire and Spain, the latter came increasingly to depend on its overseas possessions as the guarantee of its power in Europe. No doubt it was awareness of this that made Philip lose interest very soon in the possible acquisition of the imperial dignity: he saw that excessive Spanish commitment to central Europe would divert the nation from its real sources of power. Although central Europe remained a centre of Spanish diplomatic activity, and within a few years was to see the rebirth of vigorous Spanish influence, it took second place to the other concerns of Philip's world empire. Of these concerns the most important was America.

By the 1550s the age of discovery and conquest had been succeeded by that of evangelization and consolidation. The friars began their preaching in the Indies almost from the time of discovery; after them came the administrators, and by 1563 the last of the *audiencias* or provincial councils had been established to assist the viceroys in governing the American continent. The next period witnesses the gradual extension of royal power at the expense of the original colonizers of America. The crown insisted on its right to control town government, administration of the Indians, and exploitation of the mines. Through the Council of the Indies, it sought to bring America under a tutelage as close as it exercised over Spain. This attempt at centralization was boldly asserted, but in an age when slow communications hindered the speedy dispatch of administrative orders it never really succeeded. Gradually an independent-minded colonial class grew up, impatient of the restrictions imposed on it by crown policy and jealous of the profits to be acquired from the labour of Indians and of imported African slaves.

In the 1550s this spectre of a settlers' revolt had hardly begun to materialize. Instead, the crown could look forward to an era of unending wealth, as the mines of America began to pour out their riches. The discovery and utilization of the mercury amalgam process in extracting silver, and the opening of the silver mines of Potosí in 1545, accelerated the flow of precious metals from the New World to Spain that had begun almost with the conquest. From the mid-16th century the influx of silver (and some gold) reached phenomenal, and ultimately disastrous, proportions. By the 1590s a recorded annual average of seven million *pesos* was being sent from America to Spain, and of this the crown was officially getting over two millions a year. Far from preserving the Indies in European waters, Philip was clearly preserving his European empire in the Indies, for the greater part of this American treasure was used to pay off the troops and financiers supporting the Spanish cause in the Mediterranean and in the Low Countries.

The importation of precious metals was only one aspect of an imperialist policy that linked the commerce and economy of two oceans and three continents. Spanish naval supremacy in the Atlantic and the American Pacific, maintained for all the 16th and most of the 17th century, gave its most convincing proof of strength in the system of regular trading fleets. Behind the system lay a doctrine of monopoly, whereby Spain alone decided which commodities could be manufactured and traded between different parts of the monarchy. The monopoly was extended even to ports of departure and call. Ships could sail to America only from Seville; in America only certain ports could receive goods from Europe; and inter-American and Philippine trade was again restricted and often totally prohibited. Only subjects of the crown of Castile could trade to America, a provision that excluded not merely all foreigners but also Catalans and others subject to the crown of Aragon. Spain thus became the sole direct, legal recipient of silver and other goods from America, while in that continent it was assured a closed and guaranteed market for its own products.

The Spanish monopoly of this market was, however, unworkable. Delayed sailings and bad overland communications could easily interfere with supplies. The resulting scarcity of goods created an opportunity for sailors of other nations who, undeterred by penalties which might be as severe as death, were quick to profit from a trade that brought in bullion. Particularly after Philip II had incurred the enmity of the two Protestant maritime powers, religious reasons were added to others as a motive for illicit trade and piracy. So began the privateering war in the West Indies which, while it scored few or no successes in the way of territorial annexation, seriously embarrassed the security of Spanish towns in America and often dislocated trade. The occupation by Drake and Hawkins of Santo Domingo and Cartagena in 1585–6 wakened the government to the size of the threat, and it is safe to say that for the rest of the reign of Philip II, and despite the failure of the Armada, the buccaneers in America were kept at bay.

It had nevertheless become painfully obvious that adequate defence of a world-wide monarchy was impossible in the face of growing Anglo-Dutch naval strength, and that the financial cost involved was prohibitive. After 1580 the problem became even more acute, for the Spanish crown now took over the obligation of defending the extensive Portuguese possessions in South America and Asia. Portugal also fell into the unfortunate position of drawing upon itself the enemies of Spain. With limited resources, Philip inevitably concentrated on the needs of the Spanish territories and neglected the needs of the Portuguese. Sailing into the breach so obligingly left open for them, Dutch traders and privateers were already before the end of the reign making inroads into the colonies of Portugal in eastern Asia, supplanting them everywhere, particularly in Japan, as the chief European traders in the area.

The Cost of Empire

In 1557, a year after his accession to the throne, Philip was forced to declare himself bankrupt. In doing this he admitted that the monarchy was unable to pay back immediately to international financiers the vast sums that Charles V had borrowed from them in order to fight his battles on the distant frontiers of the Holy Roman Empire. To this extent, therefore, the bankruptcy was a pointer to things past. But it also proved to be an omen of things to come, for during his reign Philip was twice more obliged to declare himself bankrupt: in 1575 and 1596. Each occasion illustrated still more clearly the burden of empire on what passed for the greatest monarchy in the world.

Castile, as the *arbitristas*, or writers on economic affairs, were to emphasize tirelessly in the 17th century, was unique in allowing its European dependencies to live off the mother country. Charles V had begun the trend by relying more and more on financial help from the peninsula to further his struggle in Germany. Since only Spain (or, more correctly, Castile) showed itself willing to pay for imperial commitments, Charles and his son looked increasingly to it as the mainstay of their endeavours, and after the 1557 bankruptcy Philip was driven to rely on Spain alone for help. The taxes paid by the people of Castile lubricated the wheels of Habsburg imperialism, although the income from this source could hardly suffice for all purposes and had to be increased regularly by raising the rate of taxation. Happily Philip could draw on the riches of the Indies to an extent undreamt of by his father. In the 1590s, when silver imports were at their peak, the proportion received by the crown came to about one fifth of the annual revenue of the treasury. Marginal as this sum may appear to be, in fact it tended to be the most vital part of royal income, the more so as it took the form of bullion, which could be negotiated internationally in a way that the coinage of Castile, debased with copper under Philip III, could not.

All this money, accumulated with intense effort by officials of the crown, or borrowed after difficult negotiations from such financiers as cared to risk their money despite previous declarations of bankruptcy, poured out from Spain to pay troops in Africa, the Netherlands, Italy and America. Above all the Netherlands. Spanish troops were employed continuously in the Low Countries from 1567 to the end of the reign and beyond, so that for over thirty years Philip was committed to the steady employment of men and money in a vain and desperate attempt to subdue the rebel provinces of the north. All his imperial resources were geared to this one problem of the Dutch, and it continued to be a principal concern of the treasury even during the confrontation with the Turks and with England. The complex financial transactions that were necessary in order to pay accounts in a country that was largely cut off by English and French hostility, led to the use of *asientos*, or financial contracts, by which prominent international merchant bankers advanced money to the crown and agreed to pay it at a specified place in the Netherlands or any other country where it was needed. As Charles V had become indebted to the German bankers, so Philip became indebted to the Italians for his imperial programme, and Genoese financiers came to be a mainstay of his treasury.

The difficulties occasioned by the empire are illustrated in the details of the 1575 bankruptcy. It was calculated then that the crown owed to bankers the total of eight million ducats, and that the general commitments of the monarchy put it into an annual debt of 68 million ducats. By the end of the reign even these sums had been inflated far beyond all possibility of liquidation. In 1566, the year of Protestant image-breaking in Antwerp, the Low Countries figured as a negligible item in royal finances, since revenue from these provinces easily covered the cost of the Spanish garrisons. By 1574 a debt of over four million ducats had already begun to accumulate in the Netherlands. The war against the Dutch became a bottomless well which, for the best part of a century, drained away the resources and manpower of Spain.

The full impact of this situation was not felt until the generation after Philip's death, but already within Spain some of his subjects were beginning to weigh the cost of empire, and finding it too great.

The Inquisition

Philip assumed control of the monarchy at a time of religious crisis in Europe. His father had abdicated the throne after a generation of unsuccessful and costly warfare against the rising tide of the Reformation. Although Philip's foreign policy accepted the realities of the international situation and was not blindly pro-Catholic, the king himself was unswervingly orthodox and totally uncompromising in religion. For him, as for his father, the preservation of the Faith was an overriding obligation, the extirpation of heresy a fundamental duty. It was therefore with shocked horror that Philip learned in 1558 of the existence within Spain of adherents of those very doctrines that had led to the disintegration of his father's German territories.

Protestantism in Spain was virtually still-born. It had no more than a handful of adherents, mostly in Valladolid and in Seville, and even these were to all appearances totally wiped out by a series of *autos-de-fé* which the Inquisition held between 1559 and 1562. Philip was himself present at one of those held in 1559. To a remonstrance from one of the victims on this occasion, Philip is said to have replied: 'If my son were to oppose the Catholic Church, I myself would carry the faggots to burn him'. The story

may be apocryphal, but it mirrors the profound devotion of Philip to a cause now in danger not only in Germany but in England and France as well. The defensive measures he took relied for their execution on the apparatus of the Spanish Inquisition.

Two government decrees in particular aided the vigilance of the inquisitors. The first of these, issued just before Philip's return to Spain, was the establishment in 1558 of a rigid censorship and control of all books, both native and imported. The second was a decree in 1559 ordering all Spaniards at foreign universities to return home: only four colleges, in Italy and Portugal, were excepted from this rule. The censorship decree gave legislative support to the moral authority already being exercised by the Index of forbidden books issued by the Inquisition, while the second measure followed other European countries in sharply restricting academic freedom. Together they laid the basis for a system of intellectual control which could easily be paralleled in other countries but which in Spain was operated with unique efficiency, through the activity of the Spanish Inquisition.

The drive against foreign books and heretical literature was not the beginning of a new trend so much as the culminating point of an operation that had begun under Charles V, in the form of a campaign against the writings of liberal Catholics and especially of Erasmus. Philip's decrees must therefore be set in the context of a long-term movement of retreat from the intellectual freedom of the Renaissance, and towards ideological conservatism. This development can be described as the transition from an 'open' society having creative links with the world outside to a 'closed' society recoiling upon itself. The symbol and architect of this development is Philip himself, a solitary figure consigning himself permanently to the peninsula after 1559, and later almost immured in the monastic splendour of the Escorial.

The role of the Inquisition in the annihilation of Spanish Protestantism has often led to an undue emphasis on this aspect of its activities. In fact the most important part of the tribunal's work was to do not with foreign heresies but with the religious and social position of racial minorities in the peninsula. The Inquisition had been set up under Ferdinand and Isabella as a weapon against Jews who became converted to Christianity through material necessity but continued to practise their former religion in secret. The Moors of Spain were also subject to the tribunal after their forcible conversion in the early 16th century. Against both these minorities the Inquisition waged a persecution which was nominally religious but in social significance racial. The result was that the move towards religious unity in the monarchy, which Philip so warmly welcomed, was carried out only at the expense of racial disunity. It is at this point that the religious problem and that of the *Moriscos* overlap, for the pressure of the Inquisition on the *Moriscos* had the sole effect of emphasizing their racial separateness and compelling them to make common cause with the Muslim powers of the Mediterranean. The defensive posture of Spain became pointless if there continued to exist within the country large minorities hostile to the presuppositions, whether theological or political, governing Spanish society: religious unity within the 'closed' society could therefore be achieved only if the racial problem were first solved. Philip made no contribution to its solution, and bequeathed the issue to his son.

Government by Pen and Ink

The government of Spain in this period has quite properly been taken as the model of a centralized absolute monarchy. In the realm of policy, the king's powers were absolute and unquestioned, tempered only by the dictates of conscience and religion. With Philip, the absolute monarch was also a bureaucrat, for he assumed direct personal responsibility over a great mass of administrative work touching on all aspects of imperial policy. Even very minor aspects of administration commanded his attention, and he corresponded in person with all his subordinates, writing voluminously in his almost illegible scrawl, correcting their faults down to the smallest grammatical error in their reports. Of all the monarchs of his day, it can truly be said of Philip that he ruled in person. Whether this was a desirable achievement is another matter. No one man could adequately arrogate to himself responsibility for all the decisions to be taken in so vast an empire, and inevitably efficiency was impaired and urgent matters were delayed as officials waited for the necessary royal decision to be taken.

The drawbacks of personal rule were to some extent mitigated by the existence of a system of administrative councils whose definitive organization can be traced back to the reforms of Ferdinand and Isabella. The councils, whose powers covered not only administration but also legislation and judicial matters, could be divided into two classes. In the first class fell those with specialized interests usually relating to Spain, such as the Council of the Inquisition and the Council of Finance; also in this category came the Council of State, which took precedence over all other councils and normally specialized in the field of foreign affairs. In the second class came the regional councils, whose business concerned specific areas of the Habsburg monarchy: such were the Councils of Castile, of Aragon, of Italy, of Flanders, of Portugal and of the Indies. Conciliar government organized on so broad a basis nevertheless failed to live up to its promise. Often the councils were submerged under purely judicial business while the real administrative work was being done elsewhere by the king; and when they were allowed executive powers the king sometimes ignored their decisions. The councils were also often filled by indifferent administrators with little devotion to good government. For all this, they remained throughout the centuries of Habsburg rule in Spain the essential organs of government, their efficiency depending largely on that of the man in whose hands matters of State lay, whether king or prime minister.

From the time of Charles V one other individual, besides the king, was of considerable importance in the exercise of authority. This was the king's secretary, who controlled much of his correspondence, and also acted as a liaison officer between him and the councils. There were in addition other secretaries attached to the central government, notably those who helped in the business of the councils. Their key position, together with that of the king's secretary, greatly aided Philip's efforts to smooth the running of the administration. The only danger lay in the pretensions to eminence which the royal secretary might make in view of his undeniable importance. This problem arose in dramatic fashion, in the case of Antonio Pérez.

Although Spain was theoretically an absolutist country, this did not preclude the existence of some sort of constitutional government. In fact, Spaniards had a respectable history of provincial self-government through the *cortes* or parliaments which each of the political units in the Iberian peninsula was entitled to hold at regular intervals. The realms of Navarre, Aragon, Valencia, Catalonia, Portugal and Castile were all entitled to their *cortes*, but there was no parliament for the country as a whole. This fact emphasizes the strange paradox that, for all his 'absolute' rule, Philip had less political power in Aragon than he could exercise at will in America. Absolute in Castile, he was obliged to respect the virtual autonomy of other realms whose *fueros*, or constitutional liberties, guaranteed their independent rights and property. In Aragon, for example, not only were there separate *cortes* and a separate legal and financial system, there were also a separate judiciary, executive and army. Castilians were generally excluded from office in Aragon, and no Castilian troops were allowed to cross the realm. This surprising disunity of the peninsula can in part be traced back to the failure of Ferdinand and Isabella to bring about a complete union between their respective inheritances. The result had been that much of the so-called Spanish empire was strictly speaking a Castilian empire, and that the Indies— *las Indias de Castilla*—were a patrimony only of the crown of Castile. The difference in interests and viewpoint that arose as a result of this situation was to be of great importance in the subsequent history of Spain.

Of the *cortes* of Castile it need only be said that well before the reign of Philip II they had ceased to play any effective part in the government of the country. Originally representing the three estates of nobility, clergy and towns, they were in the early 16th century reduced to the representatives of eighteen specified towns, and their sessions were limited exclusively to deliberation and petition, their powers over taxation and legislation being virtually annihilated. This was consonant with the absolutist policies of

Philip. In the other *cortes* held in the non-Castilian realms, all the traditional estates still assembled, but except in times of crisis they took no initiative which might clash with the will of the crown.

Spain under Philip therefore presented the incongruous picture of an absolute monarchy which was not absolute throughout its own metropolitan territory. There is a further paradox in the fact that substantial liberty of political thought was allowed within this partly absolutist structure. Under Philip the great Jesuit historian Juan de Mariana began to set on paper his belief that unregulated royal power leads to tyranny, that government under God is based on the consent of the people, and that extreme tyranny may at times be cured by regicide. These concepts, enshrined in his *De rege et regis institutione* (1599), were circulated without provoking criticism in Spain. Other thinkers of the century were similarly concerned to set up principles on which just authority could be established. That Philip regularly summoned the *cortes* of Castile, although he had little need for its deliberations, is adequate proof that the king himself was willing to ascertain the wishes of his subjects. Further evidence of this tendency is given in the freedom allowed to *arbitristas* throughout the 16th and 17th centuries, to put forward their radical criticisms and suggestions for reform.

The Black Legend

There were in Philip's reign two personal agonies which had international repercussions and which consequently deserve a brief mention: these were the tragedy of Don Carlos and the affair of Antonio Pérez. Don Carlos was Philip's son by his first wife and was born in 1545, his mother dying in childbirth. From his early years Carlos began to show signs of that abnormality which was to some extent already apparent from his physical appearance. In his late teens the Infante started to exhibit symptoms of mental derangement, accompanied by rages, violence and open hostility to his father. The political implications of this were apparent, for Carlos was heir to the throne, and Philip could not fail to envisage the consequences of his son succeeding him. When in 1566 Philip discovered that Carlos had made contact with the Dutch rebels in a plot against himself, he overruled his own personal feelings and superintended the secret arrest and confinement of Carlos in 1568. Six months after his imprisonment Don Carlos died in mysterious circumstances.

Rumour and legend invented the most lurid explanations for these events, and it was claimed that Philip had ordered the execution of his own son. These theories have now been largely discounted, but at the time they gave to a Europe smarting under Spanish imperialism even further evidence of the sinister character of the king of Spain. Europe was the more ready to believe this, as one of those who claimed that Philip had poisoned Don Carlos was Philip's own secretary, Antonio Pérez.

Pérez, who became secretary of State in 1571, was a brilliant and sinister young man whose influence over the king enabled him to climb (as a contemporary wrote) 'so high that His Majesty would not do anything save what the said Antonio Pérez marked out for him'. Ambition eventually led to his ruin. Political and personal rivalry with Juan de Escobedo, secretary of Don John of Austria, who was then in the Netherlands, led Pérez to convince Philip that Escobedo was plotting against the monarchy, and Philip thereupon agreed to let Pérez get rid of Escobedo. Accordingly, Pérez had Escobedo assassinated in 1578. When he was later arrested on suspicion of the murder, Pérez attempted to implicate the king and fled into Aragon, where the king could not pursue him. This was in 1590. The year after, in defiance of the *fueros* of Aragon, Philip sent in troops to crush a rising, led by aristocratic dissentients, which had broken out in favour of Pérez. This was the first step ever taken by the Castilian crown to suppress regional discontent in the *fuero* provinces of Spain, and provided a precedent for similar action taken in Catalonia by Olivares in the next century. The secretary fled abroad, secure in the possession of State papers implicating Philip in Escobedo's murder, and continued to attack the king from abroad.

In both these cases, Philip was the object of a campaign of vilification, most of it directed from abroad; in both, he had a

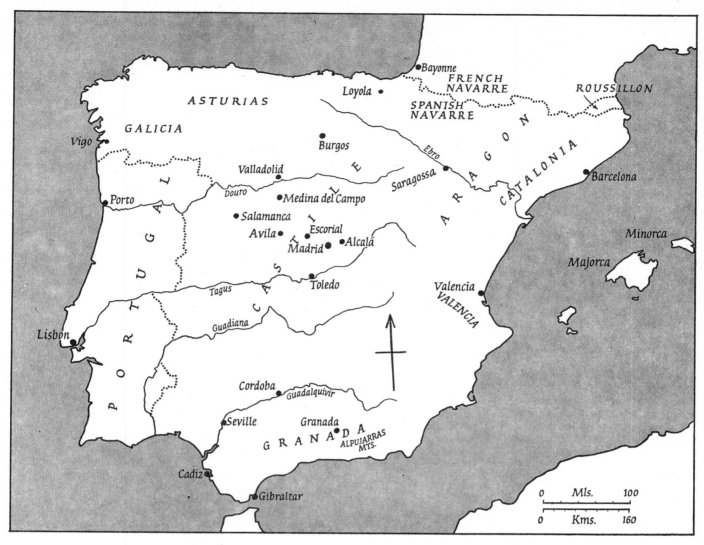

ASTURIAS

GALICIA

Vigo

Burgos

Valladolid

Porto

Douro

Medina del Campo

Salamanca

Avila

Escorial

Madrid

Alcalá

Toledo

Tagus

Lisbon

Guadiana

Cordoba

Guadalquivir

Seville

Granada

GRANADA

ALPUJARRAS
MTS.

Cadiz

Gibraltar

Bayonne

FRENCH
NAVARRE

Loyola

SPANISH
NAVARRE

ROUSSILLON

Ebro

Saragossa

A R A G O N

CATALONIA

Barcelona

Minorca

Majorca

Valencia

VALENCIA

| 0 | Mls. | 100 |
| 0 | Kms. | 160 |

Spain in the 17th century, showing the chief sites mentioned in the text.

heavy burden of guilt to bear, in the first instance for unavoidable harshness to his own son, and in the second for his connivance in the sinister activities of his secretary. The two incidents became an integral part of the *Leyenda Negra*, the Black Legend of a cruel and despotic king in command of a nation which was itself treacherous, superstitious and fanatically cruel.

When the failures and triumphs are weighed together, Philip still emerges as the great king of a nation which reached its apogee of greatness under his rule. He himself would have liked best to be remembered as the servant of the Faith which he maintained all his life and which fortified him in his moments of deepest failure: to this extent El Greco's canvas of *The Dream of Philip the Second* is a description of his life's purpose. For all his greatness, he never succeeded entirely in winning the love of his people. Even in 1580, at the height of his success, Philip was (to quote a Spanish Jesuit) 'not as esteemed and loved as he used to be, nor so much lord of the wills and hearts of his subjects'. It is true that he was reticent and avoided the populace, yet at his passing in 1598, reported the Venetian ambassador, 'although change is universally popular, yet nobles and people, rich and poor, universally show great grief'.

'The Most Barbarous Stroke'

Succeeding to his father at the age of twenty, Philip III was all that his father had not been: he was physically unfit, weak in personality and politically incapable. He relied for all official decisions on an experienced grandee, the Duke of Lerma, and it was truthfully said of him by the Venetian ambassador that 'the king has no other will than that of the duke'. With Lerma began

the long series of ministerial favourites, or *validos*, who were to govern the monarchy in the name of incapable kings until the end of the Habsburg dynasty in Spain.

Whatever the failings of the new government at home were to be, abroad in Europe the servants of the monarchy pursued a realistic policy towards the enemies of Spain. The unprofitable war against the three great nations of western Europe was brought to an end by stages. Peace with France had already been concluded in 1598, just before the death of Philip II, but the new government ratified the treaty. Efforts to continue the struggle against England were failures, and an attempted invasion of Ireland proved abortive. When James I came to the English throne in 1603, he showed himself willing to talk peace, and a treaty was accordingly concluded in 1604 which brought that conflict to an end. Relations were further improved with France in 1615 by a marriage alliance between the two countries whereby Louis XIII married a Spanish princess and the Infante Philip married a French princess. In England the extraordinary influence wielded by the Spanish ambassador Gondomar over James I guaranteed good relations with Spain.

Peace on two fronts left Spain free to deal with the Dutch, and at this late stage a remarkable amount of military initiative was won back for Spain with the help of money and troops offered by the Genoese brothers Spinola. Despite their aid, however, the Spaniards were obliged to reconcile themselves to the loss (in their eyes, temporary) of the northern Low Countries, and a truce (rather than a peace) was agreed upon between both sides, to run for twelve years from 9 April 1609.

Spanish commitments in Italy and the central Mediterranean

The Count of Gondomar, Spanish Ambassador to England 1613–1622, wielded a great influence over James I. He is satirized here as the Black Knight in Middleton's 'A Game at Chess', put on at the Globe theatre to celebrate the failure of the Spanish marriage negotiations in 1623.

brought the government face to face once more with the perennial problem of the Turks. Several successful naval expeditions were made against them both in the eastern Mediterranean and in Africa. What dwarfed the threat from this quarter, important as it remained, was the realization in Spain that the most serious challenge of all came from within the country's own frontiers, from the *Moriscos*.

The misfortunes of the *Moriscos* duplicated in many respects those of the Jews of 15th century Spain. Like the Jews, they suffered from forcible conversion, social discrimination and persecution. After the rebellion of the Alpujarras the *Moriscos* of Granada were scattered throughout the other realms of the peninsula, carrying their resentment with them. *Moriscos* elsewhere in Spain, particularly in Valencia (which contained the vast majority of the *Moriscos* of the peninsula) laboured under conditions of servitude. The acceptance of a Christianity which most of them despised made no difference to their position, for they still suffered disabilities on account of their race. Several repressive edicts issued both by the government and by the Inquisition forbade them to use their own language or follow their own traditional customs. The authorities, in other words, were in general trying to deprive the *Moriscos* of their national identity on the grounds that this was essentially Muslim in character and hindered their integration into the Christian community: genuine conversion in religion alone was not enough.

There was some justification for the official attitude. Most of the *Moriscos* remained Muslims at heart, and continued to practise their religion in secret, stubbornly resisting all attempts to catechize them. The fact that genuine conversion brought no improvement in their civil position confirmed many in their old faith. All this was galling enough to the administrators of Spain, but other factors precipitated the eventual resort to expulsion.

Once the *Moriscos* came to be regarded as inassimilable, the whole question took on a different light. Their high birth-rate threatened to swamp the Christian population. Between the middle and end of the 16th century, for instance, the *Moriscos* of Valencia increased by seventy per cent while the Christians increased by only fifty per cent. This fear of numbers became allied to the old fear that native *Moriscos* might aid an invasion of Spain by Turkish forces. In 1580 at Seville a *Morisco* conspiracy abetting invasion from Morocco was discovered. In 1602 they were plotting with Henry IV of France. In 1608 the Valencian *Moriscos* asked for help from Morocco. In the words of one historian, 'fear entered into the heart of Spain'.

The Duke of Lerma assumed direct responsibility for the action now taken. On 9 April 1609, precisely the day the Twelve Years' Truce was signed with the United Provinces, the king signed an order for the expulsion of all *Moriscos* from Spain. The operation was carried out in stages, beginning with Valencia, since this province contained most of them. The troops and navy of Spain stood by at the embarkation points, to prevent any incident and to hasten the expulsion. About 275,000 *Moriscos* were expelled from Spain out of a resident total of nearly 300,000. Apart from children under the age of seven, who were as a rule kept back forcibly, all *Moriscos* were driven out and no attempt was made to distinguish the Christians from the Muslims among them. In the judgment of Cardinal Richelieu, it was 'the boldest and most barbarous stroke in human annals', and other contemporaries, both foreign and Spanish, agreed in deploring the operation. What the *Moriscos* themselves felt may be gauged from the words of the *Morisco* in *Don Quixote*: 'Wherever we are we weep for Spain, for we were born there and it is our native land, and nowhere do we find the shelter that our misfortune demands; and it is in Barbary, and in all the parts of Africa where we hoped to be received, cared for and feasted, that we are most abused and maltreated'.

Although the economic effect of the expulsion on Spain as a whole has in the past been grossly exaggerated, there can be no doubt of its repercussions on the economy of the eastern half of the peninsula, in the non-Castilian realms where the *Moriscos* formed a considerable proportion of the population. The nobility of Valencia were bitterly opposed to the loss of their principal labour force, and the middle classes in Valencia city suffered bankruptcy. It was the greatest of the many errors in the Duke of Lerma's domestic policy, and the one that would be most remembered by later *arbitristas*.

Madrid Habsburgs and Vienna Habsburgs

While Spain continued to uphold its military prowess abroad, at home it entered on a period of decay which was exhibited most clearly in the conduct of affairs at Madrid. Control of government by *validos* enthroned the rule of faction; favouritism and venality together led to open profligacy in expenditure. The *valido* himself had his own minions, Lerma having as his favourite a certain Rodrigo Calderón, ennobled as the Marquis of Siete Iglesias, and later arrested and executed after the downfall of his master. Court conspiracies against Lerma led eventually in 1618 to his dismissal and the installation as next *valido* of his son the Duke of Uceda. The pattern was in this way set for a perpetual round of party intrigues and replacement of ministers, without any continuous leadership that could rely on more than factional support. The chief casualty of all this was the crown. The nobles lost their veneration for the king's person, and the most elementary needs of the royal household were neglected, with the result that while on the one hand great festivities were held in public by the royal ministers, on the other, as a contemporary observed in 1601, 'His Majesty has nothing with which to pay the wages of his servants, and even the needs of his table have to be obtained on credit, a thing which has never happened before in the royal household'. The absurdity of some government decisions is best illustrated by the extraordinary order, given in 1601, to transfer the whole royal court and all its dependents from Madrid to Valladolid, on the excuse that the cost of living would be lower in Valladolid. This change of capital lasted only five years, and turned out even more wasteful than if the court had remained in Madrid. The general picture is one of increasing opulence, as seen in the swollen dimensions of the court circle, and also of greater financial difficulties, as seen in the debts of the royal treasury.

The end of the reign of Philip III saw the monarchy gravely embarrassed in its leadership, and there seemed little probability that any minister could break out of the charmed circle. When one minister did try to do so in the next reign he was defeated by the same irresponsible factiousness that was in the end to bring down the Habsburg monarchy in Spain. But before this happened, the whole structure of the monarchy had been shaken by the return of that general European war from which the weakness, rather than the policy, of Philip III had obtained a respite.

The return of war was precipitated by events in central Europe.

The converted Moors, or 'Moriscos', lived in greatest numbers in the Alpujarra mountains near Granada until they were dispersed through Spain after the rebellion of 1568–70. Morisco women are shown above in Braun and Hogenberg's view of Granada (published 1572) wearing their *characteristic wide breeches and voluminous veils. Moriscos continued to play an important part in the economy until they were finally expelled altogether from Spain in 1609. The Alhambra, the great Moorish palace of Granada can be seen in the background on the hill.*

Despite the lack of sympathy between the Austrian and Spanish Habsburgs in the reign of Philip II, there had always remained a close degree of diplomatic contact and even of practised co-operation, since in the last analysis the common enemies of the Habsburgs, in both eastern and western Europe, were the same. Containment of France in the west and the Turks in the east was the common aim of both branches of the dynasty. Towards the end of the reign of Philip III, a series of events brought the two branches more closely together and led Spain into its last major offensive as an aggressive power.

At the beginning of the 17th century the Spanish party at the Austrian court was large, and growing. The Emperor Rudolf, who was also king of Bohemia, was weakening both mentally and physically, and part of the support for Spain came from those who looked for a strong successor to both crowns, perhaps even a union between the Spanish and Austrian monarchies, as under Charles V. Spanish diplomacy was also active in Germany on other account, the promotion of the Catholic League among the German princes, to balance the league formed by the Pro-testant princes which was threatening to bring in France against the Habsburgs. A common policy with Vienna was vital on one other issue: the possibility of concerted action in the Netherlands when the Twelve Years' Truce with the United Provinces expired in 1621. As a trump card to further all these interests, Spain had the sympathy and friendship of the Archduke Ferdinand of Styria, who was elected king of Bohemia in 1617 and Holy Roman Emperor in 1619. One additional advantage was the arrival in Imperial territory in 1617 of the new Spanish ambassador, the Count of Oñate, whose efforts were devoted wholeheartedly to furthering the Spanish cause in the Empire.

These intimate links between Madrid and Vienna, completed by the accession of Ferdinand to the imperial throne, brought both powers together in Bohemia, where an anti-Spanish coup in 1618 raised the spectre of an international conflict. After the troubles in Prague, Spanish troops were immediately put at the disposal of the imperial government. Their use in central Europe and on the Rhine brought Spain into a long, costly and ultimately fatal war that was to last for thirty years. In 1621, the year that Philip III died, the truce with the Dutch expired, and Spain entered on an era that led to the sunset of its splendid empire.

The Power of Ancient Privilege

The Spanish Habsburgs spent their lives among the people of Castile, to whom therefore most of the following observations refer. What must be kept in mind is that Spain was not a single unit but a sometimes uneasy alliance between peoples and nations with their own history, language and customs, who understood the word *España* in a different sense from that which it held in the realms of Castile. The attention usually paid by historians to Castile, at the expense of Aragon, Navarre and Portugal, can be excused in part by the fact that Castile played a preponderant part in the affairs of the Spanish monarchy. For all the differences within the peninsula, however, and for all the resentment felt by regional separatism against Castilian domination in the 17th century, the subjects of the crown gloried in the name of *España*. 'España, madre de nobles!' exclaims a character in a play by Tirso de Molina. To be of the race of Spain was the highest of all claims: even today the historical holiday common to both Spain and Spanish America is the *dia de la raza*, the day when the Spanish race discovered America. In the rest of Europe the excessive national pride of Spaniards often gave offence, but to natives of Spain it was their birthright. Charles V, Spanish neither by language nor by race, vindicated the Spanish position before all Europe on a famous occasion in 1536. Speaking in Spanish to an assembly of prelates in the Vatican, he was interrupted by a French bishop who could not understand him. 'Do not expect from me, the emperor informed him, 'to hear any language but Spanish, which is so noble that it deserves to be known and understood by all Christian people'.

First in importance among the institutions of the Spanish people came the Church, governor of the daily lives of all Span-iards from the king downwards, and principal driving force in the establishment of the world-wide monarchy. The number of clergy alone would have differentiated Spain as being primarily an ecclesiastical society. Critics at the time formulated serious objections to the preponderance of the clergy in economic and social life, but such considerations need not detract from the value of the spiritual work of Spanish clergy in the 16th and 17th centuries, which overshadows the achievement of any other European country in this period. At the Council of Trent it was Spanish theologians and bishops who formed the vanguard of

EL FVERO:
PRIVILEGIOS
FRANQVEZAS Y LIBER
TADES·DELOS·CAVALLEROS
hijos dalgo del Señorio de Vizcaya, confirma
dos por el Rey dõ Pelippe II. nueſtro Señor, Y por el
Emperador y Reyes sus predeteſſores.

VIZCAYA

CON LICENCIA REAL.
En Medina del Campo, por Franciſco del Canto,
M. D. LXXV.

The nobility of Spain, insisting on the maintenance of its ancient privileges, formed a political and social élite. Above, the privileges and liberties of the nobility of Biscay ('Vizcaya') confirmed by Philip II in 1575.

the conservative orthodox party which finally prevailed. It was a Basque, Ignatius Loyola, who founded the Society of Jesus, and a fellow Basque, Francis Xavier, who became the apostle of Asia. A Catalan, Peter Claver, saved the Spanish conscience by his work among the negro slaves at the end of the Atlantic crossing. Teresa of Avila renovated the contemplative life in a country which had never known the Reformation, and by her writings established a claim to literary greatness. The names, which can be multiplied, are symbols of a society in which religion and religious values were fundamental to all activity, so that it can be stated that a basis of Spain's greatness was its unswerving adherence to the Catholic religion.

Effective power both in Church and State lay in the hands of an élite which consisted almost exclusively of the higher nobility. The golden age of Spain was also in many respects the golden age of its aristocracy, which flourished under Habsburg absolutism. From the superior nobility, or grandees, were chosen the ministers, generals, ambassadors and viceroys of the crown. These servants of the monarchy were a competent minority among the throng of incompetent nobles who frequented the court, but their numbers tended to decline in time, as the crown found that non-Castilians and even non-Spaniards were more proficient for the tasks in hand. But so long as the aristocratic class, drawing on its ancient privileges, demanded and obtained control over all aspects of central and local government, and political and social life, the values of the nobles took pride of place in Spain. Under Philip II several of the grandees distinguished themselves as patrons of the arts and letters, among them the dukes of Osuna and Alba. Criticism can be levelled less easily at these than at the lesser courtiers and nobles, and all those throughout Spain who, thanks to their nobility or *hidalguía*, claimed the right to live in unproductive leisure. The extraordinary premium set on noble lineage in

Spain far exceeded similar social prejudices in other countries, and had correspondingly more deleterious effects on the national economy.

The aristocracy was particularly sensitive to the charge, made by its enemies both within and without the country, that many noble houses were of mixed racial origin and could not boast *limpieza de sangre*, purity of blood. The cult of *limpieza*, whose importance in the social and political history of Spain is fundamental, demanded that all pretendants to any public office in Church or State should prove they had no Jewish or Moorish blood in their veins. This requirement, based originally on religious grounds, gradually acquired racial overtones, and the aristocracy was particularly susceptible to criticism because in its long history it had intermarried with the other races of the peninsula.

The aristocratic model of a leisure class was accepted by one other numerous and unproductive group: that of university graduates. The two main universities of Castile, Alcalá and Salamanca, aided by others of lesser renown, turned out every year numerous graduates in theology and law who had little hope of making a living out of their meagre education. When they did not augment the band of picaresque vagabonds, they served only to swell the ranks of the clergy or to burden even more heavily a bureaucratic system which laboured under the weight of superfluous personnel. To a very large extent this picture of too many officials and too little efficiency may be blamed on the readiness with which an increasingly impecunious crown created and sold new administrative offices to meet the constant demand from university graduates.

Historians have often spoken loosely of the absence of a bourgeoisie in early modern Spain. In its narrowest sense, such a class is easy to identify in Spain, though it is true that its size and significance varied from one epoch to another. An urban class devoted to commerce, finance and industry could be found in all the major cities of the peninsula in the early Habsburg period. In some regions, as in the north of Castile, the success of this class depended on the maintenance of a trade mechanism, and when the great international fairs of Medina del Campo collapsed, the bourgeoisie of the area declined in function and numbers. To the difficulties produced for the bourgeoisie by economic uncertainty can be added the general lack of municipal independence, above all in the kingdom of Castile, where the towns by the time of Philip III had lost their own autonomy as well as their influence in the *cortes*. The lack of a vigorous bourgeoisie may also be traced back to the unfilled gap created by the expulsion of the Jews in the 15th century, but more significance should be attached to the fact that in a society with a predominant aristocratic ethic the middle classes tended to channel their profits into the acquisition of aristocratic status rather than into competition with growing foreign interests in Spain.

At the bottom of the social ladder, the basis of Spain's economy and the most numerous class in the realm, came the peasantry. The position of the peasant-farmer deteriorated under the early Habsburgs and did not improve in the course of the 17th century. For one thing, the wage level of the peasant remained largely constant between the middle of the 16th century and the beginning of the 17th, at a time when the level of prices was rising steeply in Spain. But more significant was the financial dependence of the rural classes. On the whole they laboured under obligations to an ecclesiastical or secular lord, particularly in the more feudal realm of Aragon, and were as a consequence subject to regular heavy taxation which threatened their livelihood. Secular lords tended to exploit their lands rather than invest in them, and this forced small farmers to borrow capital on their own behalf, with the result that in years of depression the peasant class became heavily indebted to moneylenders. A final blow against the prosperity of the rural areas, and one which was never remedied despite the sober advice of economic advisers, was the weight of government taxation, which affected consumers no less than producers, the most notorious levy being the sales tax on all consumer goods, the *alcabala*. For all this, the peasant population remained politically stable, and it is a surprising fact that Spain was the one country in western Europe in this period not to experience any large peasant revolts.

The Peso in Trouble

Spain in 1621 was still at the peak of its power, and its aggressive policy in Europe on the eve of the Thirty Years' War presented to its enemies the spectacle of a monarchy not to be provoked with impunity. But already for almost a generation a succession of *arbitristas* had been bewailing the miserable and ruinous state of the country. Prominent among the early writers was Luis Ortiz, who as early as 1557 analyzed the monetary difficulties of Spain. It was not until after the death of Philip II, however, that the complaints of universal decay came flooding into print. Martín González de Cellórigo and Sancho de Moncada, two of the most intelligent of the early critics, produced their work at the opening of the century. Shortly after the death of Philip III, Pedro Fernández Navarrete published in 1626 his *Conservation of Monarchies*. The date of his work makes it a fitting commentary on the previous two reigns.

As the basic text for his discourses Navarrete relied on a memorandum presented in 1619 by the Council of Castile to the king. In this document the council had complained that the depopulation of the realm had been largely caused by excessively heavy taxation; that the crown had been too lavish in its granting of favours; that the cities, and particularly Madrid, were overcrowded with nobles, clergy and other unproductive classes; that money was being lavished by the upper classes on luxuries; that the peasant farmers, 'whose position is the most important in the state', were being neglected by the government; and that there were too many ecclesiastics in the kingdom. Basic to all these complaints was a realization that the economic and financial state of the monarchy had taken a turn for the worse, though the council was unable to diagnose any overriding cause for all these ills beyond the awareness that Spain was living beyond its means.

Some earlier writers, however, such as Martín de Azpilcueta in 1556, had already begun to grasp the fact that the economic crisis was to some extent connected with the import of American bullion.

Thanks largely to the researches of the American historian Earl J. Hamilton, it has in recent years been possible to define more closely the relation between bullion imports and the price inflation which struck Spain in the 16th century. A comparison of the volume of precious metals imported into certain parts of Spain in this period, and the movement of commodity prices, seems to indicate some influence of silver on the level of prices. The rise in the cost of living hit those who existed on small fixed incomes and also hurt wage-earners whose pay did not keep pace with the inflation; in other words, the greater mass of the population suffered. Those who profited included producers and manufacturers, who did not, however, reap the full benefit of the price rise since productivity seems not to have expanded greatly after the first half of the 16th century, and profits tended to be used in buying land and status rather than in further investment. The great landowners also benefited from the rise in agricultural prices, but any profits from this were not passed on to the class of producers, the peasants, who fell into debt and bankruptcy as their costs exceeded their income. The sum of all this was that the rich grew richer and the poor grew poorer, presenting contemporary *arbitristas* no less than modern historians with the incredible picture of a wealthy and often profligate noble élite in a country where the mass of the people lived not far from beggary. To add to the difficulties of inflation, Castile suffered from repeated monetary debasement, a sign and a result of government inability to control the economy of the country. Philip II had been firmly opposed to debasement of the Castilian coinage, but under his son the silver content of the coins in circulation was steadily eliminated, to the profit of the royal exchequer, and a largely copper coinage took its place. Although this was supposed to have the same face value as coins which used to have a bullion content, it was immediately quoted at an unfavourable rate, and monetary inflation became a standard feature of the troubles of subsequent years.

Spanish peasant women sit cooking at open-air fires while fishermen haul in a shoal of tunny fish near Cádiz. Cádiz, like Seville, received the Spanish treasure fleets from the New World, and its prosperity attracted attacks such as Essex's sack of the town in 1596.

Crisis in Castile

Against this background of economic crisis the problems outlined by Navarrete may well be taken as representative of the most glaring ills of the monarchy. Depopulation of the countryside, particularly in Castile, was gathering force by the end of the 16th century. Deserted villages throughout the realm bore witness to the pressure, usually from taxation, that made the peasantry flock to the towns. These in turn expanded phenomenally under Philip II. The terrible plague years 1599–1600 began a fall in population. In the first half of the 17th century the inhabitants of Spain (excluding Portugal) decreased from eight to perhaps six millions. Navarrete cites as further causes of depopulation 'the host of colonists who leave for the New World', and the lamentable expulsion of the Jews and *Moriscos*. The *Morisco* problem leads Navarrete to criticize the policy of the monarchy towards its minorities, and the refusal to admit *Moriscos* to social equality: 'it is a most malign policy of State for princes to withdraw their trust from their subjects'. The comment reveals the growing disillusion of thinking Spaniards with some of the policies of their government.

The overcrowding of Madrid, which had grown from about 5,000 people in 1530 to over 60,000 in 1597, mirrored both the drift from the countryside and the growth of a large parasitic population living off the court. 'All the streets of Madrid are full of vagabonds', reports Navarrete. To him this vagabondage was not principally the result of unemployment. It was caused by the large number of persons who lived off the money from investments, office, and ecclesiastical charity. In addition there was a plethora of those who, glorying in the noble title of *Don*, considered themselves above the need to degrade themselves by work. The ethos of the noble class, which in Spain as in other European countries considered manual labour an undignified activity, attained in Spain the most ludicrous heights of expression and ultimately undermined confidence in the aristocracy. It was even considered no contradiction to combine nobility and vagabondage: indeed the new ideal of the 17th century became the man of aptitude who lived by his wits rather than by labour—the *pícaro*. The degenerate and perversely romantic figure of the *pícaro*, which dominates the literature of the early 17th century, personifies the decline of the Spanish ideal from its great era of chivalry and the Reconquest.

In discussing the financial commitments of the monarchy, Navarrete touches on one point which is fundamental. 'All monarchies', he notes, 'have usually enriched the head of the empire with the spoils and tribute of their provinces . . . Castile alone has followed a different way of ruling'. The needs of the monarchy, the upkeep of royal government, the defence of the peninsula, the garrisoning of Italy, Africa and the Netherlands, and aid to other provinces and states, all were supplied out of the coffers of Castile. On one province alone, aided of course by American silver, fell the entire cost of empire, and the Castilians, far from benefiting freely from their position at the head of the monarchy, were committed regularly to paying for the defence of other nations. Even within the peninsula Castile had an obligation to maintain garrisons in other provinces, but these realms had no corresponding obligation to pay taxes to the Castilian exchequer. With this burden on its back, it is not surprising that Castile betrays very early the symptoms of that economic decline which came to affect most of the peninsula.

Contemporary preoccupation with the role of the nobility was a sign of social self-criticism, but little was done to remedy the situation. Navarrete criticizes aristocratic extravagance and the love for sumptuous building, gilt coaches and luxurious food, but there is no evidence that the tastes of the nobility were ever effectively restricted. Nor was anything done about the large number of young men who every year swelled the ranks of the clergy and depleted those of the industrious classes. The very high proportion of clergy to the rest of the population, above all in Catalonia, was of great concern to economists and certainly to the government, which could not tax the clergy directly. The brake exercised by the Church on economic growth in Spain is a factor almost impossible to exaggerate.

Navarrete's most important plea echoes that of the Council of Castile in asking for a fair deal for the Castilian peasant. To some extent this demand may have implied criticism of the privileges accorded to the gild of sheepowners, the *Mesta*, whose flocks were guaranteed grazing rights over large tracts of territory that might have been developed for tillage. More specifically, however, Navarrete asks for the government to guarantee peasant farmers an adequate price and market for their agricultural produce, and to enable them to escape the grasp of the tax-collector and the moneylender. Faced with its own financial difficulties in an age of mounting inflation, the government could hardly attempt to stem the tide (and perhaps defy vested interests) in order to help the lower classes. Its own dismal efforts to legislate on trade matters in order to right an unfavourable balance of trade and to protect native manufacturers, were completely unsuccessful, as were all other ventures in the field of economic regulation.

What brought the crisis home to contemporaries was the glaring contrast between the might of Spain abroad and the poverty of Castile within. The upkeep of the monarchy abroad was paid for with silver, as European bankers would accept nothing else, but at home the kings of Spain were forced to live off a copper coinage. A phrase of Hamilton sums up this picture: 'the golden age in literature and the silver age in money were succeeded by a bronze age in the seventeenth century'.

The Sun Sets

If the crisis of Spain is to be defined as the turning point from an era of greatness to one of decline, the critical period is centred on the reign of Philip III. It was then, in 1600, that Martín González de Cellórigo issued his *Memorial* criticizing the paradoxical plight of Castile, flooded by silver from America yet totally bereft of it since it had drained away to foreign countries, so that in Spain 'what causes its poverty is its wealth'. The rapid interchanges between price inflation and monetary inflation, in a country where money was gained only to be lost by depreciation, bred an atmosphere of economic insecurity where wealth soon ceased to be wealth. This was a climate ill-suited to long-term investment in industry and enterprise, and lent an air of unreality to the entire image of a powerful Spain flourishing on its Indies. 'It seems', wrote Cellórigo, 'as though one had wished to make of this realm a republic of enchanted beings, living outside the natural order of things'.

Many of the *arbitristas* only aggravated this unreality by their choice of remedies. Utopian solutions continued to be proposed up to the very end of the Habsburg dynasty. The few who made realistic suggestions, such as the Jesuit Juan de Mariana, who in 1609 attacked the debasement of the currency, were either ignored or disciplined. It was left to the genius of Cervantes to sum up finally in 1605, in *Don Quixote*, the personification of the national dream which gloried in chivalry and empire but lived in reality in a wretched world of picaresque pretensions.

Beyond 1621, then, stretched a landscape of unfulfilled aspirations. In the Thirty Years' War Spain entered a conflict that sealed the loss of the Netherlands and began the shrinkage of the monarchy. The decade 1610–20 witnessed the first serious check to an expansion of the trade with America, and shipping for the rest of the 17th century decreased in volume. The decline of Spain appeared still more obviously to be the decline of Castile rather than of the kingdoms on the periphery of the peninsula, and this imbalance in fortune was felt most strongly by Portugal, weary of its long subjection, and by Catalonia. The increasing burden of empire would lead Olivares in the next reign to attempt to extract some financial support from these other realms, an attempt which aggravated the internal crisis of Spain and led to the permanent loss of Portugal. After Olivares there was virtually no minister with the imagination or courage necessary to arrest the decay of the empire. The greatest monarchy in Europe stood on the threshold of military, economic and moral collapse.

III THE DIVIDED NETHERLANDS

Rebellion, liberty and nationhood

CHARLES WILSON

'What are you afraid of? A handful of men, a worm turning against the King of Spain? You are fifteen provinces, and we are two. What have you to fear?'

WILLIAM THE SILENT in answer to Don John of Austria's delegates at the Conference of Geertruidenberg in 1577.

'Think of God's wrath

and of the contempt of foreign peoples and princes. Think of the hateful yoke which you let rest upon you and your children.' The appeal came from William of Orange in 1572, during the worst days of the struggle against Spain. Less than fifteen years before, William had been a Councillor of State under Philip II, a knight of the Golden Fleece, Stadholder of Holland, Zeeland and Utrecht. What had turned a loyal minister into a rebel and a peaceful country into a desert of hatred and death?

That Spain ruled the Netherlands at all was due simply to the fact that Charles V had inherited both Flanders (from his father, Philip le Bel) and Spain (from his mother, Joan the Mad). There was nothing in this necessarily to cause friction. Charles was as much a Fleming as a Spaniard; the Netherlands were anyway not a political unit and his constitutional position varied from province to province (he was not a 'king' in the Netherlands at all) and he was at pains not to offend local pride. Nor had the religious division assumed hopeless proportions, though the persecution of Protestants had already begun. All this changed after 1555, when Philip II succeeded his father.

In the Netherlands Philip was a foreigner. He spoke no Flemish and little French. His religious faith was of a more fanatical brand and he was no respecter of the constitutional rights of heretics. Spanish bureaucracy and bigoted religious persecution went hand in hand. Philip strove to impose Catholic conformity on his subjects, and as his ministers used harsher and ever more autocratic methods, even Catholics were roused to revolt. It became a national issue.

The Spaniards could find no solution but rule by terror, and their brutalities shocked even 16th century Europe. After 1567 the Netherlands were ruled by a series of military governors, of whom the Duke of Alba was the first and most ruthless. Public executions became daily events; whole towns were pillaged and their populations massacred. It was this policy of repression rather than any common principles which kept the northern provinces together.

The fact that resistance hardened in the north and eventually led to the formation of the Dutch Republic was partly a geographical accident. The dividing line was neither linguistic nor religious (there were thousands of Catholics in the north throughout the revolt). The north could be defended; it was much more difficult to defend the south. As conditions became intolerable, Protestants naturally fled north. Many of the personalities whom we think of as typically Dutch were immigrants from Flanders.

The apalling agony which the Netherlands had to suffer before this could be achieved left an indelible mark on the national memory. The language of protest comes through even in paintings with subjects remote from contemporary history. Beggars in a street will be seen to have been punished by horrible mutilations. The Crucifixion procession will be driven forward by a military escort, while a stricken populace looks on helplessly. The 'Numbering' at Bethlehem will show the forced registration of Flemish townsmen for a new tax. In Breughel's *Massacre of the Innocents* (opposite) the peasants pleading for mercy are the country people of Flanders, Herod's troops are the armoured lancers of Spain and the grim commander who leads them is Alba himself.

Granvelle, Bishop of Arras (*left*), had read Philip's speech for him at the abdication. As his chief minister under the regency of Margaret of Parma, he advised moderation, but had to bear the odium of Philip's increasingly intolerant policies. For Philip, there could be no political unity without religious unity. This was the source of his persecution of Jews, Muslims and Protestants, and the root of the revolt of the Netherlands.

The progress of the revolt is depicted in a series of engravings by Frans Hogenberg. *Right:* William of Orange (then still a Catholic and officially a loyalist) pacifies a Calvinist mob at Antwerp in 1567, an action which earned him names like 'servant of Antichrist' from the crowd and small thanks from the king.

The 'Sea Beggars' capture the Brill. In April 1572 a force of privateers owing nominal allegiance to William seized the port of the Brill. It was the first step in the establishment of a free Netherlands. Alba's troops failed to recover the town and from here the revolt spread to Flushing and other ports along the west coast.

The Duke of Alba (*right*), single-minded and pitiless, tried for six years to stamp out opposition by terror. Initially this was a total success. The execution of the popular leaders Egmont and Horne left the rebellion in despair and chaos.

William of Orange (*below*) by tenacity, diplomatic skill and courage held together the revolt against Spain.

The **'Spanish Fury'** – perhaps the worst horror of the whole war. In October 1576 the Spanish garrison at Antwerp mutinied, broke out into the town and sacked it with unrestrained savagery. Houses and churches were pillaged, property carried off or destroyed and thousands of people perished in a few hours.

William was murdered in 1584, but he had accomplished much. The Union of Utrecht (1579) had laid the foundations for the United Provinces. As Count of Holland and Zeeland he lived quietly at Delft. Here the assassin, Balthazar Gérard, surprised him as he came from the dining room with his family.

The austere Calvinist church
eventually triumphed in the north.
This view of the Grote Kerk at
Haarlem was painted in 1673. The
building has been whitewashed
and denuded of images. A table
replaces the altar and the real centre
of the service is the pulpit.

Rich and poor confront each
other at a village Kermesse (*right*).
This is a Flemish work by David
Teniers the Younger; the class
differences are displayed perhaps
more blatantly than they might
have been in the north. The
peasants are given a touch of the
grotesque and it may well be that
the gentry who pay them a visit are
Teniers himself and his wife. The
château in the background has
been identified as Dry Torens,
which he rented.

A comfortable bourgeois world developed im the first decades of the 17th century. Northern painters loved to recreate this world based on wealth gained in commerce, and to dwell on the simple but often rich surroundings of the typical Dutch family. In this interior by De Witte (*above*) the lady of the house at the virginals is unostentatiously dressed, but the marble floor and the carpet, which is probably Persian, betray evidence of wealth.

Sea power was the key to Dutch freedom and soon became the key to wealth. The United Provinces rapidly turned themselves into the leading maritime nation in the world. An alliance of the Dutch against the hated Portuguese was sought and obtained by the king of Kandy in Ceylon when he welcomed Joris van Spilberghen, the Dutch captain, in 1602 (*above*). By 1658 the Dutch had replaced the Portuguese, although Kandy remained independent.

New Amsterdam (*below*) was founded in 1626 when Manhattan Island was bought from the Indians for a few pieces of cloth and some beads. By 1664 it had 'an earthen fort, within which stands a windmill. The church rises with a lofty double roof. On one side is the prison, on the other the governor's house. At the waterside stands the gallows.'

The Dutch East India Company, established in 1602, had trading posts all over the East – in China and Japan, India, Ceylon, Malaya and Indonesia. Hugly was founded in 1640 and became the company's headquarters in Bengal. This view (*above*), with the Dutch flag flying and Dutch ships on the Ganges, dates from 1665. In India the Dutch had eventually to relinquish power to the British, but they maintained a vast and profitable empire in Indonesia.

Trade with the Far East was established in the early 17th century. *Right:* 'the herbe Cha' i.e. tea, which by the mid-century was imported in large quantities from China, was considered of particular benefit after over-eating and drinking, 'for it is a very great dryer of gross humours, and dispels vapours'.

Brazil, as a Portuguese (i.e. for a time Spanish) possession, was a natural lure to Dutch ambitions. Pernambuco was captured in 1630 and attempts were made to colonize and open up the country to trade (*left:* Dutch colonists outside their house). But the venture did not succeed and the Portuguese regained control in 1660.

For their country – its flat fields, canals, towns and villages – the people of the northern Netherlands felt a warm affection which was freely expressed in the arts of landscape, genre and still-life. Vermeer's famous *View of Delft* (*left*) shows his native town with almost photographic realism: nothing is emphasized, nothing is 'composed', yet it remains a painting of endless fascination.

The small town of Delft enjoyed a celebrity out of proportion to its size. It was here that the State of Holland had resolved in 1575 to throw off allegiance to the king; here Holland and Zeeland concluded an act of union the following year; and here in 1584 William the Silent had met his death. During Vermeer's time it was noted all over Europe for its fine glazed and painted china.

73

Commerce flowed into the ports of the north, and Amsterdam rapidly became a vital commercial centre. In the Exchange (*above*) merchants from all over Europe could meet freely. It was founded in 1611 to deal in commodities and Dutch East India Company stock. Amsterdam's civic pride was grandly expressed in her new Town Hall by Van Campen, started in 1648 as a sort of architectural manifesto of independence. The view on the right shows the side elevation from one of the canals.

The States-General meeting in the Binnenhof in 1651 (*left*). This assembly was the sovereign voice of the seven provinces, yet each of the states kept its own sovereign status and organs of government – militia, fleet, council, stadholder, provincial estate, taxes. To gain the unanimity of all the provinces needed a system of perpetual referendum from the States-General itself back to the local dignitaries.

More charitable institutions existed in the United Provinces than anywhere else in Europe. *Right:* two of the woman governors of the Old Men's Home, Haarlem, painted by Frans Hals when he was old and poor, and himself receiving alms from the city authorities.

Leo Belgicus: when in 1583 Michael Eytzinger first used the image of the lion to portray the Netherlands (most of the 17 provinces used a lion in their armorial bearings), they were still officially considered as one political group, although the revolt was in full swing. In 1648 the Peace of Westphalia was signed, bringing to an end the Thirty Years' War and also bringing official recognition of the independence of the seven United Provinces. The lion was then used to represent the new nation.

Rebellion, liberty and nationhood

CHARLES WILSON

THE LIFEBLOOD OF SPAIN was drained away by the Eighty Years' War with the rebellious provinces of the Netherlands. The same long struggle led to the birth of a new state in Europe: a state which was to become the pattern of modernity while Spain was to become the pattern of archaism. In some ways this is paradoxical, because in constitution and social structure the Netherlands were themselves a medieval anachronism in the time of the 'new monarchies' like that of Philip II.

The Netherlands territories which had passed from the House of Burgundy to the House of Habsburg were a curious mixture of feudal and urban institutions, of great contrasts of wealth and poverty, a tangle of counties, duchies, signories, each with its special relationship to the nominal suzerain. Some of its noble families, like the Lannoy and Croy families, were ancient. Others were of more recent origin—the Bergens and Nassaus—and the new families tended to come from Brabant rather than from old Flanders. In spite of the power and wealth of the cities, it was the nobility, greater and lesser, and especially those of Walloon origin, who still dominated the politics of the Netherlands in the first half of the 16th century. They were, by and large, a *rentier* class, living, or trying to live, on the income from their landed estates. And as their domains passed under the suzerainty of the Habsburg Empire of Charles V, new strains and stresses added to their problems and helped to multiply the political commotions of the age.

For the first time, a group of the nobility, not yet large but growing in numbers, showed a growing consciousness that a gulf separated the interests of this whole region from those of its dynastic overlord. Englebert of Nassau, brother of the grandfather of William the Silent, was among those who first became aware of new tensions between overlord and people. Nor was it accidental that this embryonic consciousness of Netherlands unity coincided with serious economic problems for the whole of the governing class in the Netherlands as elsewhere.

From the late 15th century onwards, and at a swifter pace in the 16th century, men everywhere began to feel the impact of inflation. Its causes were, and still are, much debated. Were they primarily the increased demand for goods from a growing population? Or did they lie in the expanded supply of money now available from the growing stream of silver which flowed from Central America via Spain to the source of goods and services represented by Antwerp? The answer is still obscure, the result is not: a decline in the value of money. It was felt most acutely by those members of the landowning *rentier* class whose incomes were more or less fixed, either by law or custom or merely by inertia. An astute tradesman might well benefit by it. This is not to say that the springs of opposition to the Habsburgs in the Netherlands in this early phase were simply economic; only that the economic troubles which plagued the nobility and gentry made them more sensitive to the demands of an overlord which increasingly appeared to them inequitable and unreasonable.

A Land of Cities

Yet this was only one aspect of an economy and a society in a state of flux. The social predominance of the nobility at this stage of Netherlands history is evident from the part they played in the early opposition to the Habsburgs. Yet the whole of this area (which included the present-day Benelux countries, together with the north-west of France) already bore an aspect very different from the comparative rural emptiness of contemporary Europe. More than anywhere else in the contemporary world, except northern Italy, this was already a land of towns. The total popu-

The Low Countries in the 16th century were already among the most densely populated areas of Europe, and a high proportion of this population lived in towns. Utrecht (top of page), with its many tall church-steeples crowded within medieval walls, numbered 20,000 people. Groningen (left) was only a little smaller with nearly 15,000. In this engraving one can see part of the Renaissance fortifications, the triangular bastion in the foreground being designed for artillery warfare.

lation was not far off a couple of millions. A high density of population was closely connected with a uniquely advanced system of farming. While abundant labour was available to produce the commercial crops needed by the town populations—cheese, butter, meat, hops, madder, oil-seeds, flax, mustard, and later on tobacco—the basic food of the people, corn, was increasingly imported from the Baltic. Throughout the Netherlands, an intensive agriculture developed, employing many techniques which were to penetrate other European countries only centuries later—crop rotation, fodder crops, row-cultivation, systematic manuring and the like. Yet, as Slicher van Bath, the historian of the subject has remarked, the total picture of rural life in the Netherlands was 'not a picture of wealth but of scarcely controlled poverty'. Agriculture was not an independent way of life for the peasantry; it was the means of 'making a living for an increased and dense population . . .' By nature, the terrain was poor, not rich. Technically advanced as Netherlands farming was, it was far from meaning high living standards for the farming community, far from bringing high rents to the landowners. As so often, society was achieving technological progress at the cost of complicating its socio-political problems.

Everywhere, at intervals of a few miles, rose busy centres of trade and industry, richly planted with the steeples of splendid cathedrals, abbeys, and churches, and ringed by walls and fortresses. Until it was overtaken by Antwerp in the 15th century, Ghent, the great Flemish textile city, was among the half-dozen largest cities of contemporary Christendom. The population of Antwerp had risen from a few thousand inhabitants in the 14th century to a hundred thousand by the mid-16th century. Here was a great market for the cloths of England and Flanders, the eastern spices brought in by Portugal, the bullion from Spanish America. Here the kings of Europe sent their agents, as Elizabeth sent Gresham, to arrange loans from the German bankers, like the Fuggers of Augsburg, who operated on the Antwerp exchange. But there were other sizeable cities of trade and industry too. Liège and Utrecht each numbered twenty thousand people by the beginning of the 16th century. A much larger group comprising Leiden, Delft, Haarlem, Amsterdam, Gouda, Dordrecht, Middelburg, Louvain, Maastricht, Groningen and many others numbered between ten and fifteen thousand people. Scores of smaller market towns and large villages made up the rest.

These ancient towns were the centres of long-established industries—textiles, metals, leather, silk, and many other crafts. Closely organized under guild or municipal control, they were now feeling the chill winds of competition. As the great markets like Antwerp grew, the conservative patterns of the traditional industries came under pressure. The changing demands of new markets and new customers brought into being new industries and new products. Across the North Sea, a similar change had already begun in England. Industries were moving out of the old corporate towns into the free and unregulated countryside. So also in the Low Countries. The largest towns were growing as centres of trade. But the older urban industries were yielding to new technologies that were taking root in the comparative freedom of the countryside or smaller towns. The traditional textile industries of cities like Ypres, Ghent and Brussels were in decay by the mid-16th century. They could no longer compete with the imported cloths of the English nor with the rapidly growing cloth manufactures of the country districts and newer towns. Free from antiquated municipal regulations, these new industries could take on or shed labour freely. Round Ypres, Lille, and at smaller, newer towns like Hondschoote, Armentières, there came into being new industries supplying cheap, brighter, lighter cloths to the great markets of Antwerp. Around Liège and Namur iron works and coal mines sprang into being. Around Valenciennes enterprising capitalists manufactured serges. Throughout Flanders, carpet-making and linen manufacture spread through scores of small workshops and cottages.

Trade and shipping were likewise expanding as the exchange of goods between the Baltic and Biscay developed. Fishing and fish curing, salt and grain, created bulk cargoes for ships plying between north and south. Broadly, the northern provinces concentrated their economic efforts on shipping, fishing and agriculture. The southern provinces contained the largest centres of trade, industry and finance. Before it was disrupted by the war, the economy of the south was more advanced and diversified than that of those northern provinces which were later to form the Dutch Republic.

Turmoil and Transition

On the eve of the rebellion against Spain, the whole economy of the Low Countries was in a state of turmoil and transition: growth on the one hand, decay on the other; great contrasts of wealth and poverty. In the rapid inflation that preceded the outbreak of violence in the 1560s, some social groups gained and others lost. Among the losers were unquestionably many of the noble landowners. Their costs were rising more rapidly than their incomes. William the Silent himself was to live his life in a permanent state of semi-bankruptcy, plagued by debtors. His problems were not unique. The entire Nassau clan and their allies in revolt were similarly harassed. William's brother, John, Stadholder of Gelderland, ultimately found himself unable to meet his baker's and butcher's bills and departed ignominiously to Germany. Many noble families suffered a similar fate.

At the other end of society there began to appear a floating mass of unemployed or under-employed labour. This army of casual workers by dockside, mine, forge or loom formed the closest approximation to a classic proletariat in contemporary Europe. They were vulnerable to the fluctuations of the market economy, vulnerable to famine: to heresy too. Such, briefly, was the social background against which the politics of the Low Countries moved swiftly into violence in 1566 and 1567.

It is always tempting—as Clarendon observed of the English Civil War—to see a great crisis of human history casting its shadow before it. The revolt in the Low Countries was preceded by earlier troubles which in retrospect look like harbingers of the Eighty Years' War. The last decades of the 15th century saw the nobility and cities of Flanders opposing their new overlord, Maximilian. The Inquisition did not have to wait for Philip of Spain. It was introduced by Charles V in 1523, and in that year the first heretic was burnt at the stake. Sixteen years later open revolt flared up in Ghent, traditionally a restless city. It was ruthlessly suppressed. Radical Protestantism appeared in the 1530s in the shape of fanatic Anabaptists at Haarlem, Mennonites in Friesland. Calvinism was a later arrival, but by the 1550s it too was spreading, especially in the south.

The three future strands of revolt can therefore be discerned in the pattern of events—discontent among the nobles, suspicion and unrest among the town rulers, heresy especially among the lower orders in town and countryside. All this against a background of economic change that was widening the amplitude of the swings between cycles of prosperity and depression. Trade and industry were coming to be increasingly controlled by new and fluid forms of capital. The organizing merchant capitalist would invest or disinvest in the light of his judgment about the future. Increasingly the employment and welfare of thousands of workers in the new rural textile industries hung precariously on his economic predictions and decisions. Here was fertile soil for the seeds of heresy and social discontent.

A king determined to rule

Yet it is easy to exaggerate the potential of revolt before 1559. The countervailing forces of reasonableness and stability were also powerful. Radical fanaticism was still offset by a generally equable Erasmian humanism, an easygoing temper in Church affairs. When Charles V decided to abdicate in October 1555, onlookers could discern few omens of future disaster. Indeed the abdication was a moving occasion for all beholders. The emperor, in black, was supported on the shoulder of his former favourite ward, William, prince not only of the small principality of Nassau-Dillenburg, but of a quarter of Brabant, and the distant sovereign principality of Orange, as well as of large stretches of Luxembourg, Flanders, Franche-Comté and Charolais. Overcome by emotion, the emperor wept. Everyone in the distinguished assembly followed suit. Only a few perceptive onlookers noted uneasily that Philip, the heir, had to ask the Bishop of Arras to read his speech for him. As a native of Ghent, Charles had been forgiven much. The new ruler spoke no French, much less Flemish.

Philip himself could see no reason why his new Netherlands subjects should find unreasonable the policies he at once introduced. The seventeen provinces which composed his dominions had, after all, come together not so much by reason of any compelling sense of unity, but of dynastic accident and force. These were simply the territories his father had managed to accumulate. Their constitution, if anything so vague could be dignified with the title, was a collection of private treaties that guaranteed mutual rights and privileges between lords, towns and sovereign. Their inhabitants spoke with at least four tongues, and between Walloon and Fleming there were old enmities. In this patchwork of provinces, Philip's own authority was characteristically varied. Of Brabant, Gelderland, Limburg and Luxembourg he was duke. Of Flanders, Holland, Zeeland and four other areas he was count. In the other six provinces his titles were even less exalted. Nowhere was his authority that of king as it was in Spain. In principle, the fact that he was a foreigner caused no insuperable problem. Even those who were to rebel against his policies would piously maintain the fiction of loyalty to his person. Outwardly,

there was little to suggest that this rich but politically untidy, socially divided jumble of provinces would be likely to offer effective opposition to the will of a determined sovereign.

The fundamental trouble was not that Philip was an alien but that he proposed to govern by alien methods and enforce his will by alien troops. The loose and ramshackle political arrangements he surveyed from Brussels failed utterly to satisfy his pedantic, spasmodically tidy mind. Philip was determined to rule.

At once tension began to sharpen between ruler and nobility. The nobles resented the presence of three thousand Spanish soldiers, widely suspected as evidence of the tyrannical intentions of the new regime. On top of this came the proposals (1559–61) to increase the number of episcopal sees and transfer the right of nominating bishops to the crown. The objects of the plan were plain: to enforce the Inquisition, extinguish the Erasmian spirit and thoroughly subject the Netherlands Church to State. For once, resistance was universal and total. Nobility, clergy and towns were swift to see their ancient rights and freedoms threatened. A medieval society, loose and vague as it was, closed ranks against the close central bureaucracy which Philip immediately established under Cardinal Granvelle, in his efforts to bring his new dominions into line with developments in Spain, France and England. 'Turk like' (as Walter Ralegh said) Philip tried 'to tread under his feet all their national and fundamental laws, privileges and ancient rights'.

Thus was inaugurated the phase of resistance that has been dubbed 'the revolt of medievalism'. The title contains a positive element of truth. The leaders in these early days were all great nobles, all Knights of the Golden Fleece, who had the right to advise the ruler with a freedom that Philip neither understood nor appreciated. All had their great estates and correspondingly elevated local status. Among the great nobility, the Count of Egmont was Stadholder of Flanders, the Count of Horne was Admiral-General, William of Nassau was Stadholder of Holland, Zeeland and Utrecht. As the forces of Spanish persecution pressed hard on Erasmian latitudinarianism, the appeal of positive Protestantism to the nobility increased. Louis of Nassau, William's brother, was a Lutheran. The Marnix brothers, Brabanters, were Calvinists. Here, as in France, Calvinism made especially rapid

Fanatical outbreaks of image-breaking mark the course of the Reformation in the Low Countries. It was common for the mob to break into Catholic churches, throw down every statue they could reach and smash the stained glass.

The execution of Counts Egmont and Horne in 1568 deprived the opposition of two of its leaders but served only to inflame hatred against Spain. The third leader, William of Orange, fled to Germany and prepared for a long struggle.

progress among the lesser nobility and gentry. By the spring of 1566 there were already four of five hundred minor nobles ready to make common cause against Philip—in theory anyway.

In theory only, because the threads holding together this motley collection of combative, highspirited but lamentably unconstructive magnates and squires, Catholic, Lutheran and Calvinist, were slender. Orange alone consistently stood by his considered philosophy of tolerance. 'However strongly I am attached to the Catholic religion, I cannot approve of princes attempting to rule the consciences of their subjects and wanting to rob them of liberty of faith.' Others, Catholic and Protestant, were much less liberal. The apparent unity of 1566 therefore soon disintegrated. William of Orange, consummate diplomatist though he was, was totally incapable of preventing Philip's regent, Margaret of Parma, from exploiting the obvious political, personal and religious differences between the magnates.

Neither the resolution nor the judgment of Egmont or Horne was to be relied on. As feudal magnates they naturally felt the pull of old loyalties to authority. As Catholics, they were shocked by stories that reached them from the textile manufacturing districts of Flanders; here itinerant Calvinist preachers, the so-called 'hedge-preachers', were rousing their *alfresco* congregations to an hysterical enthusiasm that was the prelude to wild outbreaks of violence and orgies of image-breaking. What were these old loyalists to make of maniacs like Hendrik van Brederode, descended from an ancient feudal family of Holland, who egged on his fellow Calvinists to outright rebellion against their lawful monarch? Even Orange suffered an agonizing moral predicament in these years. He could not approve the rebels' plans to seize Antwerp: to them, already rejoicing in their title of 'Beggars', Orange could only look like a temporizer and traitor. The 'medieval' revolt was thus hopelessly split. By the time the Duke of Alba arrived, with another four regiments of foot and a thousand cavalry that crossed the Alps from Milan to Brussels, the rebels were in disarray, their prospects zero.

The first stages of the Spanish terror, imposed by Alba, were unquestionably effective. The arrest and execution of Egmont and Horne, followed soon by the dismal failure of Orange's attempted invasion from Trier, left the resistance in chaos. Orange's own morale was unbroken, but he was now a bankrupt refugee. And as he fled, so did thousands of others. This was the first of those successive waves of emigration which were to drain away the Protestant spirit and economic enterprise of the southern provinces over the following decades. These successive blood-transfusions were to prove one of the formative, and still only partially understood, phenomena of the war. For the energies lost to the south went largely—though not wholly—to the north. England (East Anglia especially), France and Germany also benefited.

Characteristically, Alba now overplayed a strong hand. By filling his new 'Council of Blood' with Spanish thugs like Vargas, by deliberately terrorizing the people—five hundred were arrested on a single March day in 1568—and above all by threatening to impose on all commerce the potentially paralysing excise (called the Tenth Penny), Alba succeeded in unifying again an opposition that was already crumbling for want of any common objectives. Now the forces of feudal privilege, mercantile interest and Calvinist obstinacy were revived, even temporarily reconciled, against the Spanish terror.

The *rentier* nobility, its income falling as prices rose, was the more resentful that its ancient powers and privileges were over-ridden by the new, alien bureaucracy demanding higher tribute. Merchants saw in the Tenth Penny a sample of that dynastic disregard for the welfare of trade that was to make anti-dynasticism a continuous theme of Dutch politics for more than a century. Declared Protestants formed only a small minority of the population. At this stage they were almost certainly more numerous in the southern than in the northern provinces. But their discontents and aspirations likewise fed on unemployment, poverty and economic uncertainty, and in these the years 1565–6 abounded. Relatively small though their numbers were, they showed everywhere a reckless courage bred of fanaticism and despair.

Under Alba's reign of terror no one was safe from secret denunciation. Informers flourished. This print shows accusations being pinned up on doors and walls.

The Sea Beggars

Yet when these imponderables have been taken into account, the most decisive event of these six years of Alba's rule was a military one. On 1 April 1572, a contingent of 'Beggars' who had taken to the sea, marauding and raiding under letters of marque from William of Orange, seized the small port of the Brill, west of Rotterdam. Their leader was William de la Marck, a picturesque figure as depicted by Motley. 'A wild, sanguinary, licentious noble, wearing his hair and beard unshaven according to ancient Batavian custom, until the death of his relative Egmont should have been expiated, a worthy descendant of the Wild Boar of the Ardennes, this hirsute and savage corsair seemed an embodiment of vengeance. He had sworn to wreak upon Alba and upon Popery the deep revenge owed to them by the Netherland nobility, and in the cruelties afterwards practised by him upon the monks and priests, the Blood Council learned that their example had made at least one ripe scholar among the rebels.' His comrades in arms were likewise untroubled by those humane scruples which consistently guided Orange's own conduct of affairs.

The Siege of Haarlem was among the most horrifying incidents of the war. The city lay on an isthmus about five miles wide. Surrounded by Spanish troops in December 1572, it withstood fierce assaults for seven months. Even Alba wrote that 'never was a place defended with such skill and bravery as Haarlem'. After the surrender all the garrison and about two thousand citizens were butchered.

The Sea Beggars captured the Brill by storm. Its fall was the signal for a general northern rising. Other ports along the great estuaries that split up these provinces into an alternating pattern of sea and islands fell in rapid succession to the rebels—Veere, Zierikzee, Flushing; then Enkhuizen further north. Dordrecht, Haarlem, Gouda, Hoorn and others followed. Social factors may in some cases have strengthened the forces of resistance. The fishermen and skippers of Flushing were frustrated and angered by Spanish interference with trade and shipping that left them unemployed and starving. Perhaps they were that much less shocked when the Sea Beggars desecrated the church and vestments at Flushing and tortured and killed the local monks.

The capture of the Brill was fortuitous: but the subsequent strategic exploitation of the whole area north of the great rivers made concrete reality of a shrewd appreciation written for William in 1571 by Geldrop, one of his friends. To concentrate on the south (Geldrop had written) was a mistake:

'Country and circumstances were nowhere so favourable for the enemy as there, while on the contrary, once you have got a foothold in the maritime provinces, it will be easy to resist all attempts at expulsion. Next time, therefore, Holland should be the objective. There is to be found the converging point of trade routes which he who obtains a firm footing there will be able to command. It will be unnecessary to occupy more than a few towns, by preference in the neighbourhood of the Zuider Zee. That will at once give to our privateers a safe retreat and a market. The enemy, hampered by the rivers and lakes, will not easily surprise us there. Town after town will choose our side and a free trading commonwealth will arise, which will be an example to Brabant and Flanders, tempting them similarly to throw off the yoke, or which, if they prove incapable of doing that, will be able to keep them cut off from all trade and traffic.' Here was the core of future strategy.

The accession of the Brill and neighbouring ports meant that the entire western and a large part of the southern flank of the rebels was secured by sea power against Spanish attack. Control of the western approaches to Holland and Zeeland meant that supplies could be brought in by sea; so could relieving forces; and hard-pressed victims of siege from north or east could be extricated or relieved. That the full implications of the *coup* were not immediately appreciated by the rebels (including William of Orange himself) does not lessen their importance. Yet these successes did not by any means immediately or automatically create an impregnable fortress against Spain: they only created the physical conditions in which a fortress could be built. Enemy forces could still find their way in by routes landwards from south-east and east. Towns *north* of the famous river-line had earlier been sacked with all the accompaniment of slaughter, rape and arson that were the normal fate of the defeated. Alba's son, Federigo de Toledo, had ravaged Naarden with frightful atrocities. Zutfen had fared as badly as the towns of Flanders and Brabant. Even after the seizure of the Brill, a new Spanish attack was launched from the east via Amsterdam (still officially anti-Protestant and anti-rebel). Haarlem fell to hideous brutalities after a siege of seven months. Alkmaar just survived, thanks to ruthless flooding by the Sea Beggars. And at Alkmaar (as a later saying had it) 'began the victory'. But in 1573 the future was not so plain as all that. Antwerp had yet to be sacked by mutinous Spaniards, Leiden to endure the worst of all the sieges. Even in 1576, Zierikzee, south of the Brill across a few miles of water and islands, was still under siege by the Spanish forces. But certainly the focus of resistance had now shifted from the south to the north.

Rebellion split and confused

By this time a profound change had transformed the character of the rebellion. The cloak of medievalism had not been entirely cast off, but a distinct modernity was beginning to show through its rents. Proscription, emigration and death had severely reduced the numbers of the northern nobility. The disorders had reduced the wealth and influence of those who remained. They were now largely replaced in the administration by merchant oligarchs from the towns. From July 1572, when the first independent meeting of the States of Holland took place at Dordrecht, the effective government of the province lay with States and Stadholder. Out of the nineteen members of the States of Holland, only one was now noble; but twelve smaller towns joined the former six large ones as members.

The irony of all this was to become plain only later. For as the rebellion had spread from the seizure of the Brill onwards, the Beggars, led mainly by the minor nobility, had joined hands with something like a Calvinist proletariat to oust the apathetic 'establishment' of magistracy and office holders. But now a new element came forward to take a firm hold on the reality of power. Men like Jan van Hout and Jan van der Does who came to the fore in the siege of Leiden were by now Protestants. So (nominally) were most of the new magistrates who now assumed office in the north. But spiritually these men were still descended as much from Erasmus as from Calvin. Humanists, *politiques*, they had no intention of surrendering the liberty they had won from the Spaniards either to a Calvinist theocracy or to mob rule. Increasingly, Roman Catholics were purged from the town governments. Agreements to allow them liberty of worship were torn up and dishonoured. But politically Calvinism was also kept at arms length. So was democracy.

The genius of William the Silent was never more necessary than at this time. Since 1573 he had finally thrown in his lot with the rebels and joined the Reformed Church. In 1575, while long arguments were still in progress between the two sides, the States made him their 'High Authority'; yet the fiction was still maintained that the war was not against Philip but against his evil servants and counsellors. Even Roman Catholics still looked to William as their best hope. So did the *politiques* and the uncommitted everywhere. For a time, and especially after Antwerp had been ravaged by Spanish troops in 1576, there still seemed to be a chance that William might succeed in unifying the entire Netherlands. Under the Pacification of Ghent, a treaty between the rebels and the Estates General, all the provinces agreed to join together to repel foreign armies; the rule of Calvinism was to be recognized in Holland and Zeeland, while Holland and Zeeland agreed not to crusade against the Catholic religion elsewhere.

This was a moment when it seemed as if the whole of the Netherlands might still make common cause against Spain. Yet the 'Pacification' contained fatal contradictions. History and culture might point towards a united Netherlands. Strategy and geography made it unlikely. To these were added socio-political differences between north and south. In the south, especially in the Walloon provinces, the influence of ancient noble families—Lannoy, Ligne, Montmorency, Croy, Lalaing—was virtually undiminished. As in the English Civil War, the alliances and animosities of the great families were a powerful determinant of political change. In the face of Spanish atrocities, the old feuds might give way temporarily to union. But no sooner did the threat weaken than they reappeared. Without outside help, even the infinite patience and diplomatic skill of William could not avail against the inherent anarchy of the magnates.

For the moment, exhilarated by the demonstration of unity, the nobility in the States General might accept a new sovereign. The necessity for an overlord was still strongly felt. The successive choices which were made demonstrate the profound conservatism that still coloured the revolt. The first selection was Archduke Matthias of Austria, an amiable and reasonably honest cipher. His successor, the Duke of Anjou, was neither amiable nor honest. Only the desperate need of influential friends could have reconciled Orange to an ally so palpably unreliable. The last choice, the English Earl of Leicester, was a more plausible but hardly less disastrous one.

Meanwhile, on the Spanish side, the military governorship went to Don John, half-brother of the king: he was the emperor's son by the notorious, extravagant and ungovernable Barbara of Blomberg, laconically described by Motley as 'the washerwoman of Ratisbon'. So weak was Don John's position that he was compelled to accept the condition that all Spanish troops should forthwith leave the Netherlands. No sooner had he made his festive entry into Brussels than William of Orange followed with his own, amid universal rejoicings.

Yet once again the hopes of union were swiftly despatched. The underlying religious and class conflicts between the signatories of the Pacification were too obvious not to be exploited. The old social order was still intact in the south; it had not been revolutionized by surprise attack as it had in the north since 1572. The terms of the Pacification itself were imprecise and evasive. The Catholics could hardly be expected to look on passively while the Calvinists proselytized throughout Flanders, ousting Roman Catholics everywhere. Even Amsterdam had at last yielded to Calvinism. Haarlem too. The aggressive violence of the Calvinist movement destroyed the unity of 1576, and revealed for the first time the visible dualism that was to be the Netherlands' future. The Protestant Union of Utrecht of 1579 and the Catholic Union of Arras revealed how split and confused the rebellion now was. And though the Utrecht Union was not exclusively northern, it was to be the basis of the later Republic.

Groping towards government

In 1580 the revolt was at a low ebb. The government and military operations had now been taken over by Alexander Farnese, later Duke of Parma, son of Margaret, Duchess of Parma, the former regent. Farnese was the ablest of all the Spanish commanders. He was not only a brilliant military commander: he was also an astute diplomatist who exploited every aristocratic feud between Orange and the still powerful, quarrelsome nobility of the south. Thus he added diplomacy to geography to secure his military base in the south. Swiftly he seized Maastricht, bullied the Duke of Aerschot into alliance, and frightened the Count of Rennenberg, Stadholder of Friesland, Groningen and Overijssel (where Catholics were in a large majority) into surrender. By 1582 city after city was giving in. Zutfen and Bruges fell first, followed by Ghent, Brussels and finally in 1585 Antwerp. The whole of Flanders and Brabant, as well as the north-east, was now in danger. All the earlier military gains were lost, political hopes blighted.

But it was not only territory that was threatened. On 10 July 1584, William of Orange was assassinated at Delft. Without him, without his powers of persuasion, his profound belief in tolerance, the hopes of a united front seemed doomed. Of course the revolt represented many deeper forces than the personal devotion and patriotism represented by William. But if older historians sometimes overlooked these deeper social forces that underlay the revolt, modern analysts are sometimes in danger of underestimating the contribution of individuals to historic development. William had undoubtedly made his mistakes, but he had achieved the virtually impossible in holding together a team of rebels that had few genuinely common aims except a determination to oppose Spanish rule. As Sir George Clark has said '. . . no one who has any faculty for responding to human greatness can doubt that this man was great. He never shrank from responsibility but never magnified his office; he had no equal in constancy or resource.' He had won the confidence of the new class of city rulers and had astutely managed to conceal since 1579 the fact that the spearhead of the revolt was now essentially the Calvinist minority. Yet his own *Apology* (1580) revealed how much medievalism there still was even in his make-up. His *leitmotif* was the wrongs he, as a loyal vassal of his lord Philip II, had suffered—the seizure of his lands, the abduction of his son. To recover and secure his rights he had acted under the authority of the Estates, the only true repository of power. But just as the feudal action of the nobility had turned into a revolution of the whole nation to defend *their* lives and privileges, so now the feudal oath of the Stadholder symbolically turned into a pledge to the nation: *Je maintiendrai Nassau* became *Je maintiendrai*.

The loss of William seemed irreparable. A quarter of a century after it had begun, the revolt was in total disarray. As Farnese piled blow upon blow, the rebels could do little more than exchange bitter recriminations among themselves. By 1585 little territory was left to them except Holland, Zeeland, Utrecht and some fragments of the eastern provinces. The old class structure, old institutions and the old concept of authority had disappeared in confusion. Yet at this crucial moment two events of vital significance took place. First came the ludicrously unsuccessful exploits of the Earl of Leicester, who arrived with a contingent of

English troops in 1585–6 to assume the post of Governor-General. The details of this woebegone farce are not relevant here. Enough that Leicester upset the Holland oligarchs by trying to prohibit trade with the enemy (a main source of state revenue) and by trying to hand over the Holland administration of finance and the navy to a central Council of State; by hobnobbing conspicuously with the Calvinist zealots at Utrecht, his residence; but above all by failing signally to achieve any military success. On 18 May, at Arnhem, he pronounced his own political epitaph, 'I am weary, I am weary, Mr. Secretary', and departed.

Leicester's contribution to history was to reveal his own ineptitude and the failure of his allies, the body of extreme Calvinists who hoped to add to their victory in religious affairs a theocracy in the state. Totally misjudging the balance of political and social forces in the emergent state, Leicester threw his lot in with the wrong party. He failed utterly to appreciate the strength of the relatively conservative town magistracies. Purged of popery they certainly were by now, but they still regarded themselves as the secular guardians of what they saw as their liberties and privileges. These were the 'libertines', professedly Protestant, Calvinist mostly, sometimes indifferent or empirical, but generally the repository of the old Erasmian tradition.

Nothing clarified the emerging character of the new state more sharply than Leicester's attempt to create a strong central government of a Calvinist colour. All the underlying forces of merchant oligarchy, Erastianism and local autonomy that were to characterize the future Republic of the Seven Provinces were immediately aroused and fused in opposition. His failure also marked the end of political paternalism. As Professor Wernham has said, the Dutch 'had tried Spanish princely rule; they had tried French princely rule; now they had tried English princely rule; all with disastrous results.' Henceforth, experiment in government was to be strictly domestic. That, alas, did not mean it was to escape disaster or disillusion.

A match for Spain

The second revolution of the 1580s was in the international scene. Queen Elizabeth's policy towards the Netherlands revolt had often seemed timid, hesitant and vacillating. But it was in part calculated. She had no love of rebels anyway, but a Franco-Dutch alliance which would bring the French up the Channel to the Brill and Flushing seemed as alarming a strategic menace as the presence there of Spain itself. Her ideal was probably a return to the old jumbled arrangements of Charles V. Now in 1588, Elizabeth's mind was made up for her. The pope deposed her as a heretic. Philip prepared the Armada against England.

For the Duke of Parma, as Farnese had now become, this proved the beginning of the end. The Spanish grand strategic design was defeated by the joint efforts of English and Dutch naval power. Parma was compelled to waste a whole campaigning season, his troops locked in Dunkirk and Nieuwpoort, while a Dutch squadron blockaded the Flemish ports. Then from 1590 onwards, he too had to turn southwards to France again (as Alba had had to in 1572), this time to protect Paris against Henri IV. These international involvements could not have come at a worse moment for Parma. The defence line provided for the rebels by the great rivers was not absolutely impregnable; it was nevertheless the most formidable obstacle he faced. And now his resources were weakened and squandered against England and France, and his lines of communication with his bases in the southern Netherlands were longer and more vulnerable than ever. Once more, the outcome of the conflict was powerfully influenced by international contingencies that could be foreseen by neither side.

By 1592 when Parma died, in disgrace, the tide had turned decisively against Spain. From 1590 the rebels, now commanded by a strategist of genius, Maurice of Nassau, William's son, began to recover territory taken by the Spaniards. Throughout the 1590s, to the south, east and north, Maurice fought his way back towards the German and French boundaries. His army was punctually paid, well armed, and thoroughly disciplined. Its commissariat was excellent, its morale high. Maurice himself, who had studied mathematics at Leiden University with Simon Stevin, was one of the best military engineers in Europe. He had also grasped firmly the importance of sea-power, as did his political masters. 'In the command of the sea, and in the conduct of war on the water resides the entire prosperity of the country', said the States of Holland in 1596. It was no exaggeration. Then, even more than today, the entire territory of Holland and Zeeland was a patchwork of polders, lakes, meres, dykes, rivers and canals. All warfare here, as the Spaniards were repeatedly made to realize, was amphibious. And amphibious warfare was a technique the Spaniards never mastered.

The transformation of the 1590s was not only one of diplomacy but of social structure, economy and morale. Not all Parma's brilliant successes of the 1580s were reversed, but most of the eastern territories lost earlier by the rebels were recaptured and

Cruelty and bloodshed during Alba's regime reached a pitch hardly to be equalled even in modern times. This print shows a husband searching hopelessly among the ashes of the pyre where his wife had just been burnt. Charred bones still stick to the stake, but the little child looks on uncomprehending.

of occupation. Militarily defenceless and socially stagnant, the south was beginning to suffer an inevitable failure of morale as the hopelessness of its situation became ever more apparent.

Maurice was a strategist of infinite care rather than of *panache*. Later, the Orangist party were to be accused by the merchant oligarchs of subordinating the national interests of the Republic to the exigencies of a Calvinist crusade. In 1600 the boot was still on the other foot. It was the States General who had to egg on Maurice to invade Flanders in an attempt to rouse the south to new rebellion against Spain. The results were a bitter disappointment. On the other hand the south was by now apathetic, physically drained of its powers of resistance; much of its enterprise and spirit had migrated and been absorbed in the growing cities of the north. It was therefore unable to profit by success. The smoking ruins of Ostend were surrendered by Maurice to Spain's brilliant new Genoese commander, Spinola, but the northerners held on to two strongpoints south of the Scheldt, Aardenburg and Sluis, which gave them virtual control of the approaches to Antwerp. The campaign had ended in stalemate. Three years later, in 1609, the stalemate was confirmed by the Twelve Years' Truce.

Entrepot of the Western World

By now the economy of the north Netherlands was launched into an era of astonishing expansion. So far from its energies being drained by war, or consumed by domestic quarrels, the Republic of these years, like England in the 18th century, throve on the problems by which it was beset. Already, by 1600, the Dutch trading system was shaping towards its later goal, as the entrepot of the Western world.

The growth of the merchant shipping fleet of Holland is as good an index as any of this astonishing expansion. In 1532 Holland commanded the services of some 400 seagoing ships: a century later the number had risen to at least 2,500 and the average size of the ships had doubled. Many were of the so-called '*fluit*' or 'flyboat' type, really a seagoing barge, cheaply built and operated and specially designed to carry bulk goods like grain and coal at the lowest freight rates.

The dykes, which had been vital to the country's agriculture, became even more vital to her defence. This woodcut shows the criminal activity of damaging the dykes, which was heavily punished.

Maurice plunged far beyond the river line into the south, beyond Breda and the Scheldt.

While the energies of the north were beginning to spill out from the redoubt behind the great rivers, the southern Netherlands were contracting politically and economically. The new governorship of Archduke Albert (married to Philip's daughter Isabella in 1598) was itself less odious than earlier regimes, but the people were still contemptuously terrorized by the Spanish army

Leiden University was founded in 1575, during some of the bitterest years of the war, and quickly gained a reputation among the universities of Europe.

In the early 17th century it attracted teachers and students as eminent as Scaliger and Grotius. This engraving shows one of the original buildings.

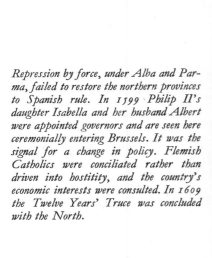

Repression by force, under Alba and Parma, failed to restore the northern provinces to Spanish rule. In 1599 Philip II's daughter Isabella and her husband Albert were appointed governors and are seen here ceremonially entering Brussels. It was the signal for a change in policy. Flemish Catholics were conciliated rather than driven into hostility, and the country's economic interests were consulted. In 1609 the Twelve Years' Truce was concluded with the North.

This merchant fleet operated in the 16th century in an area bounded by Britain to the west, Bergen to the north, the Gulf of Finland to the east, Gibraltar to the south. Its function was to exchange, through the warehouses of the ports on the Zuiderzee and (to a lesser extent) of Zeeland, the products of the Baltic—corn, timber, iron—against the salt and wine of Biscay; to bring the wool, herrings, coal, and minerals of England into the stream of European trade, and send her in return a large variety of European and colonial exports. Until the Revolt, none of the northern towns could compare with the riches of Antwerp. Amsterdam still had less than 3,000 houses in the mid-16th century. Its most affluent citizens were still only of modest wealth compared with those of the great cities of the south. In the correspondence of Thomas Gresham, England's leading economic diplomat of the Tudor age, Amsterdam featured only as a town 'where you could buy wainscoting'.

In the 1590s this 'classical' system of Dutch trade, heavily concentrated on the Baltic, began to expand. In the north the Dutch developed the North Atlantic fisheries and pushed their trade round the North Cape and into the White Sea as far as Archangel. The growing surplus of grain in the Baltic was carried south far beyond Gibraltar to supply the increasing hunger of the overpopulated Mediterranean. The first voyage to Guinea took place in 1593. By 1600 there was a general trade to the Gold and Slave Coasts of Africa. Houtman reached Java via the Cape in 1595 and 1602 saw the founding of the East India Company. The Brazil trade was opened up in 1600. All this expansion provided abundant and vivid evidence of enterprise and capital accumulation: yet the much larger if less spectacular trade between Baltic and western and southern Europe remained the foundation of the economy. This was (as contemporaries wrote) the 'mother trade', 'the vital nerve', 'the spine', of Dutch trade. The centre of all this activity was Amsterdam, now a city of 100,000 people, firmly con-trolled since a *coup d'état* in 1578 by a small oligarchy of Protestant trading families. In rapid succession, its citizens established a produce and stock exchange, a commercial bank and a loan bank, and watched the yield of customs double between 1590 and 1611.

In the nature of things, this expanding economy was commercial and maritime, rather than industrial. Yet some industries, of a rather special kind, grew rapidly and contributed notably to the growing prosperity of the Republic. They could be described as 'riparian', flowering as they did beside the stream of raw materials which passed through the Dutch ports—grain, metals, timber, silk, sugar, wool—or semi-finished products like imported German unbleached linens or English cloth 'in the white' (i. e. undyed and unfinished). Zaandam, amply supplied with Baltic timber, was the centre of the most advanced shipbuilding technology of the age. Leiden, industrially moribund at the time of the siege, enjoyed a revival from 1575 to 1620 that raised its population from 12,000 to 45,000 and made it the most concentrated centre of woollen manufacture in Europe. Its raw materials came from a variety of foreign countries from Spain to Turkey and Saxony. At Amsterdam, breweries, distilleries, sugar refineries, textile dyeing vats, tobacco-cutting factories and a dozen other finishing or refining industries flourished. Bookbinding, diamond-cutting, printing and small workshop industries ministered to the needs of a growing urban population. Haarlem, with nearly 40,000 citizens, bleached and finished millions of yards of coarse linen imported from Germany. The Republic could boast no city as large as London, but more medium-large ones than England.

'Antwerp changed into Amsterdam'

A striking feature of this changing society was the high proportion of newly-settled citizens. From the Union of Utrecht onwards, the Sephardic Jews were to play a unique role (in the history of

Amsterdam especially). More numerous, richer and more powerful were the former southern Netherlanders, ranging from great
capitalists to skilled workmen, who were soon to be found everywhere, and especially in the trading and manufacturing towns of
the Republic. Of the three hundred largest clients of the newly-
founded Amsterdam Bank of 1611, more than a half were former
southerners. Among them were the two largest stockholders of
the Dutch East India Company, Dirk van Os and Isaac le Maire.
The two families of the Trips (patrons of Rembrandt, Maes and
other artists), and of the de Geers, who jointly dominated the trade
with Sweden, were both from Liège. William Usselinckx, formerly
of Antwerp, was the moving spirit behind proposals for a West
India Company. When the company finally materialized in 1621,
at least half (and perhaps more) of its directors were southerners.
About a third of Amsterdam's population in 1600 was of southern
origin. 'Here is Antwerp itself changed into Amsterdam', as one
of the newcomers wrote in 1594.

Industrially, the influence of the refugees from the south was
even more striking. Driven away from Walloon and Flemish
industrial towns and rural areas, thousands of skilled workers
found their way north to Amsterdam, Haarlem, Middelburg,
Leiden, and other northern towns between 1567 and 1620 and
even through the 17th century the drain continued. Amsterdam
had the services of four hundred silk workers who took refuge
there from Antwerp. Others transferred the former linen bleach
industry of Flanders to Haarlem. But the reconstruction of the
Leiden cloth industry is their most striking and fully documented
achievement. It was from small southern industrial towns like
Armentières, Poperinghe and Hondschoote that the architects of
the new northern enterprise came. Flanders had early discovered
how to make a cheap, light, attractive worsted that sold well in the
Mediterranean markets and indeed to urban customers everywhere. The capitalist organizers of the new Leiden industries like
the Le Pla brothers, Hennebo and de la Court were southerners.
So was a vital element in their skilled labour force. Many of the
refugees (to be found abundantly in Sandwich, Norwich, Col-
chester, Canterbury also) were dedicated Calvinists.

To look (as we can) at the dossiers of the new arrivals in the
cities of the north from the 1560s until the 1620s is to realize the
tremendous drain of religious enthusiasm and economic skill
suffered by the south. At a conservative estimate perhaps one
tenth of the total population of the south fled to the north. But it
was the expertise and quality of the refugees rather than their
mere numbers that told. Nor were most of them merely seeking a
comfortable bolthole. The river line was not an automatic defence,
only a potential one. One reason why it became increasingly
effective was the rising morale and increasing wealth of the
population it sheltered as the determination and skill of the
newcomers stiffened the forces of northern resistance.

As the Revolt progressed, government both local and (so far
as it existed) national or federal came to mirror more faithfully
the growing importance of the towns, their trade and manufactures. In the province of Holland, which provided between
fifty and sixty per cent of the revenue of the Republic, the towns
sent their delegates to the provincial States which they dominated.
The States in turn sent their delegates to the States General where
again, by virtue of their growing economic preponderance, they
usually had the last word.

The new Republic was far from being a unified state. In reality,
it was little more than an alliance of seven sovereign provinces.
The States General, an assembly of delegates of the provinces and
bound by their instructions, was responsible for foreign policy.
The Stadholder's position was eminent but ambiguous. He headed
the armed forces but was theoretically only the minister of the
provincial States. But vestigial relics of his earlier office as chief
lieutenant of the monarchy remained. He still had a say in the
election of certain regents. There was often to be some natural
confusion therefore as to who was the borrower and who was the
lender of power.

As a class, the 'regents' who governed the towns and through
them the Republic, represented a unique social and political
phenomenon of the new Republic from its creation to its end.
There was nothing like them elsewhere in Europe. Who were
they? 'Out of the uppermost stratum of the merchant class' wrote
Huizinga, 'little by little a class of magistrates was formed, which
never completely detached itself from the soil of business.' Their
influence was not uniform. In a large city like Amsterdam they
were immensely powerful. Ten powerful family groups led the
city from the *coup d'état* of 1578 onwards, suppressing after a year
or two any pretensions of other local institutions to have a say in
affairs. In the rural, inland provinces like Friesland and Groningen,
even in a smaller town like Leiden, their status and influence was
less. Generally their rule can be described (in Gustav Renier's
words) as 'a social dictatorship of the upper middle class', ben-
evolent, enlightened and in harmony with the structure of power
and wealth in the new society. But it was now a self-perpetuating
oligarchy untainted by any of those suspicions of democracy which
had once characterized the cities of the Netherlands (especially in
the south) and had threatened to revive again in the 1570s.

Power: theory and practice

While the war against Spain was in progress, such awkward
problems as the relationship of the States and their regent
members with the Stadholder had been conveniently suspended.
By relieving the external pressures that had preserved a precarious
domestic unity, the Truce brought these crucial political (and
religious) issues into the open once more. William the Silent was
by appointment in 1558 Philip II's Stadholder or royal lieutenant

The internal peace of the Netherlands
during the years of the Truce was violently
disturbed by the controversy between
Remonstrants and Counter-Remonstrants.
Its origin turns on an abstruse theological
point, but its consequences rapidly became
political. This satirical print showing the
coach of state brought to a halt by quarrels
among those pulling it urges the contestants
to 'Be courageous and prevent worse; the
Spanish treason lies in wait'.

The Netherlands at the time of the revolt. Geography has been held by recent scholars to be the decisive factor in the final political division.

Map labels:

The original Seven Provinces, and Drenthe
Border of the Spanish Netherlands
Frontier of United Netherlands in 1648

NORTH SEA

GRONINGEN · Groningen · FRIESLAND · DRENTHE · OVERIJSSEL · Vecht · Enkhuizen · Hoorn · Alkmaar · ZUIDER ZEE · Zaandam · Amsterdam · Haarlem · Naarden · GELDERLAND · Zutfen · COUNTY OF HOLLAND · The Hague · Leiden · Rhine · Utrecht · Arnhem · Delft · Gouda · Rotterdam · Leck · Nimegen · The Brill · Waal · Maas · Cleve · Dordrecht · DUCHY OF CLEVE · Zierikzee · ZEELAND · Bois-le-Duc · Essen · Veere · Middelburg · Breda · Flushing · DUCHY OF BRABANT · Ostend · Bruges · Antwerp · Rhine · Cologne · ARCHBISHOPRIC OF COLOGNE · Niewpoort · Ghent · Scheldt · DUCHY OF JULICH · Dunkirk · COUNTY OF FLANDERS · Brussels · Louvain · DUCHY OF LIÈGE · Maastricht · DUCHY OF LIMBURG · Aix-la-Chapelle · Calais · Hondschoote · Ypres · Lys · Limburg · Poperinghe · Armentières · Lille · COUNTY OF ARTOIS · COUNTY OF · Liège · Maas · Scheldt · Valenciennes · Cambrai · Arras · HAINAUT · Sambre · BISHOPRIC OF LIÈGE · COUNTY OF NAMUR · Namur · Ourthe · DUCHY OF LUXEMBOURG · Enclaves of the C. of Artois · B. of Cambrai · To B. of Liège · Oise · Somme · Luxembourg · Moselle · ARCHBISHOPRIC OF TRIER

Mls. 0 — 50
Kms. 0 — 80

in Holland, Zeeland and Utrecht. Even after he had joined the rebels, the argument ran that he was still fully in possession of his office. The regents still continued to look for a father figure, a sovereign of some sort. Accordingly William was military and diplomatic chief of the embryonic federation. Yet increasingly, after William's death, Oldenbarneveldt, as advocate or pensionary of the States of Holland, had come forward as its principal civil and political officer. He was, in particular, author of the Truce of 1609. What was to be his relationship with Maurice, who inherited his father's military and diplomatic offices?

Although the two leaders had originally got on well, it was improbable that Oldenbarneveldt could indefinitely maintain friendly relations with the Calvinist, anti-Catholic, anti-Counter-Reformation, anti-Spanish, anti-peace elements. Maurice himself remained remote and discreet, the perfect chessplayer. But he was surrounded by a war party. Some of its members were moved solely by material interest—professional soldiers, privateers, contractors. Others were fanatical Calvinists who genuinely feared a renewal of Spanish-Catholic aggression from the south. Others, like Usselinckx, architect of the West India Company project, ingeniously combined faith in Calvinism with a faith that Calvin-

ism could be made to pay. Slowly these missionary forces, now vocal among the lower orders everywhere and especially powerful among the former southerners in high places at Amsterdam and elsewhere, polarized around the person of the prince. Religion, dynastic ambition and the belief that Spain's colonial trade was wide open to an attack by Dutch enterprise, all combined to precipitate the clash between Oldenbarneveldt and Maurice.

Two related and explosive elements entered into the politico-religious situation. One was the theological controversy between two Leiden professors, Arminius and Gomarus. The details of the quarrel are by now almost incomprehensible—according to Gustav Renier, 'they were the frantic endeavours of honest men to encompass divine mysteries within the narrow limits of human reason.' Arminius was not satisfied with the orthodox presentation of the doctrine of predestination. 'Gomarus,' he said, 'attributes to God the causes of sin . . .' Gomarus replied: 'The doctrines of Arminius make men more arrogant than those of the papists.'

The political consequences of the quarrel went wide and deep. Gomarus had the support of most of the Protestant ministers. Arminius enjoyed little overt general support from the regents.

Maurice himself was (understandably) said to have misunderstood the entire problem and confused both the persons and theologies of the contestants. But on one point Arminius attracted regent support: by proclaiming the right of all public authorities to arbitrate in church affairs, he underscored the political advantages of his viewpoint to the civil rulers as against the Gomarist insistence that the church was sole judge of doctrine. Moreover, many who were not declared Arminians nevertheless sympathized with their refusal to follow the Gomarists in their call for a holy war against Spain. Rapidly accused by the Gomarists of crypto-popery and treacherous intent to betray the Republic to Spain, the Arminians in 1610 addressed a 'remonstrance' to the States of Holland, denying the charges of their opponents. The Gomarists promptly issued a 'counter-remonstrance'. Henceforth the Arminians were known as Remonstrants, the Gomarists as Counter-Remonstrants.

These controversies, obscure and tedious as they now seem, were immediately related to the struggle for power. Against the view of the common people, who continued to regard the Prince of Orange as their natural *Hooge Overheid* or Supreme Authority, another view had crystallized among the regents. It had been formulated most clearly by Hugo Grotius, pensionary of Rotterdam, close friend and colleague of Oldenbarneveldt, and already a lawyer, philosopher and historian of international reputation. The ancient Batavians, Grotius argued, were ruled traditionally by their patricians, while the powers accorded to their leader were limited, purely a matter of convenience. Extended history and elaborate paradox steadily led to the ineluctable conclusion: the States, not the monarchy or its heirs or assigns, were, legally and historically, the repository of true sovereignty.

There were other elements in the contest. Amsterdam, with its powerful contingent of rich and influential southerners, many strongly Counter-Remonstrant, had never forgiven Oldenbarneveldt for suppressing the plan for a Dutch West India Company as a move in his diplomacy that had produced the Truce with Spain. In the person of Reinier Pauw, burgomaster of Amsterdam, Oldenbarneveldt faced one of his most intransigent opponents (and later, his most unrelenting judge). Disturbances now broke out everywhere as town governments tried to control the quarrels of Remonstrants and Counter-Remonstrants. At Rotterdam there was a characteristic *fracas* when a local pastor who had denounced all Remonstrants as 'seducers and enemies of the Church' was expelled from the town by the police guard. In scores of towns, the would-be liberal regents found themselves having to deprive the Counter-Remonstrant majority of the right to worship as they thought fit. By 1614, the Counter-Remonstrants were claiming that Prince Maurice was for them. In 1617 he declared himself publicly in their favour. The final breach came, ironically, at the Brill, keystone of northern victory in 1572.

The States of Holland had taken powers to recruit special professional levies (*waardgelders*) to preserve order and check mob violence. Maurice, as commander-in-chief, suddenly transferred some of his own soldiers to the Brill and coolly refused to agree to the local magistrates' suggestion that they should raise their own *waardgelders*. His action was the decisive start of an attack on regent authority throughout the Republic. In the following year Oldenbarneveldt and Grotius were both arrested. Grotius made a dramatic escape but on 13 May 1619, Oldenbarneveldt was condemned and executed. His alleged offences included charges that he had promoted provincial ambitions in church matters, heresies, edicts against true Christians and accepted bribes from foreign powers, etc. Meanwhile, the Synod of Dordrecht, summoned in the previous year, pronounced in favour of strict Calvinist orthodoxy and demanded that the Church should be free from civil interference.

To all outward appearances, the States party, representing local regent autonomy, the Erasmian tradition in religion and business as usual, had irretrievably lost the day. The fact that the war with Spain was renewed in 1621 and that conflicting trade interests in the Indies were a major stumbling block to further peace seems to confirm that view. Yet the purge of Remonstrant and Catholic regents that followed Oldenbarneveldt's execution had less effect than might have been expected. In reality, the differences between

the two parties were far from clear-cut. Few even of the incoming Counter-Remonstrant regents had any intention of accepting a theocracy in practice. The essential medievalism of orthodox Calvinists (like Voëtius, the *doyen* of the divines at Utrecht, who excommunicated a pious woman from his congregation because her husband was usuriously employed in a pawnshop) was as distasteful as it was inconvenient to the merchant class generally. There was a widespread consciousness that the new Republic was strategically weak, its long lines of communication at sea highly vulnerable, its hardwon liberties fragile. In spite of a noisy minority of war-mongers, prudence usually prevailed. The newly constituted regent oligarchies resumed their daily tasks of trade and government. The Republic, though once again plunged into war, resumed its economic progress towards a peak of prosperity that was to be reached in 1648.

All this turmoil in a dynamic, economically expansive, though far from democratic society, presented a stark contrast to events in the north, Calvinism was antipathetic to the forces making for a specifically northern culture—to poets like Hooft, Breero and Vondel, composers like Sweelinck. Its churches were clinical, spacious, swept but not garnished. Divorced increasingly from humanism, Calvinism lost its contact with education. As science and the enlightenment succeeded Renaissance, the Calvinist Church was to live largely beyond the mainstream of culture. In the south, under the Archduke Albert, institutions developed very differently. Here, government during the Truce immediately set itself to enforce the Counter-Reformation in all its rigour. The political influence of the (largely Catholic) Walloon nobility had always been a problem. Old feuds between the families of Nassau and Croy lay behind the long drawn out quarrel of Aerschot and William. The years of the Truce emphasized and widened the division between north and south. In 1612 the papal legate himself observed that the Archduke aped all the usages of Spain and its court. A horde of Spanish bureaucrats and Jesuits even insisted that the English Merchant Adventurers' request to move their staple from Middelburg to Antwerp in 1615 should be viewed strictly as a threat to the Roman Catholic faith and be refused accordingly.

The dominant theme of the south steadily became aristocratic-bureaucratic. This was *par excellence* a 'Court culture', in a country that had once been the setting of great towns of trade and industry. Now their economic importance suffered a sharp decline. The Flemish countryside might continue to surprise foreigners by its still advanced agriculture. Antwerp did not, as is sometimes suggested, become totally bankrupt or deserted. But its population and prosperity declined. By 1600 its population had dwindled to 50,000—half its numbers of the 1560s. Its importance as a market became local, not world wide. The cloth and linen manufactures declined in face of competition from the Dutch and English. The industries which survived best were those, like lace and tapestry, which catered for an aristocratic market. But the native aristocracy ennobled by the Spanish regime had made its money more from office and land than from business.

Art, the Mirror

The aesthetic symbol of the new order was the Baroque church. Its shattered images were now replaced by great circular arches and curving scrolls, majestic tombs, marble monuments and figures that described magnificently sweeping gestures of glory, hope, and despair. Towering above all rival artists in the south was one of the greatest geniuses of the age, Peter Paul Rubens. Much of Rubens' art—his realism and colour, his portrait technique—was as Netherlandish as that of Rembrandt or Hals. All reflected the essential unity of the art of the Low Countries. But his feeling for design and sensuous beauty he owed to that southern orientation which characterized Counter-Reformation Baroque. While his fellow artists in the north—Jan van Goyen, Jan Steen, the van der Veldes—were struggling to eke out a living by combining painting with inn-keeping or peddling bulbs or linen, Rubens commanded a princely income and lived in style in an Italianate palace sumptuously furnished and decorated.

Like Netherlands culture as a whole, Netherlands painting now stood divided. Contrasted with Rubens and his school were the painters of the Northern School which was at its most brilliant through the second and third quarters of the 17th century. Its dominant theme, as Arnold Hauser has said, was a 'middle class naturalism . . . which attempts not only to make spiritual things visible, but all visible things a spiritual experience.' A storm as violent as any as the 16th century had witnessed was to end in the peace of de Hooch's interiors, Vermeer's domestic scenes, Cuyp's grazing cows, flower paintings and skating scenes. The cultural breach between north and south was never complete. Northern artists like Jan Both and Nicolas Berchem continued to look to Italy and its sun-drenched landscapes for inspiration. The greatest genius of all, Rembrandt, was to achieve a penetration of the human personality that owed little to the naturalistic *genre* of his contemporaries. Here was an impressionistic freedom, an audacity of line and subtleties of colour that raised portraits, biblical scenes and domestic sketches above period and locality. So too in the south, the sensuous beauties, the soaring Baroque goddesses and angels of Rubens, had no immediate parentage or succession. For a great northern humanist (and Calvinist) Constantyn Huyghens, 'the chief and Apelles of them all is P. P. Rubens, whom I rank as one of the wonders of the world . . . there is no-one . . . who in wealth of invention, in daring beauty of form or in perfect variety of all kinds of painting, shall rival him.' It was characteristic of the greatest of the visual artists of north and south (as it was of Erasmus and Grotius) that only technically were they 'typical' or local. In their broad humanism they were for all time and all men. None of them ever wholly lost an intuition that the divisions of the old Burgundian territories, even of Europe itself, might one day be repaired.

Revolt or Civil War?

The most influential conception of the Netherlands Revolt created by 19th century historians, liberal and Calvinist alike, idealized it as the spontaneous popular uprising of Holland and Zeeland in 1572; a popular sovereignty which created a new, modern, liberal, Protestant state—the seven United Provinces—totally dissociated spiritually and historically from the ten southern provinces of the old Burgundian state. Such interpretations, in their simplest form at any rate, have been largely discredited. The idea of a manifest Protestant destiny has given way to a different concept: this emphasizes the sense of cultural if not political unity that already existed among the Burgundian provinces as a whole before the revolt and minimizes the differences between the rebellion of north and south. It recalls the earlier economic and cultural predominance of the southern provinces, but stresses the advantages that geography was to bestow during the revolt on those areas of Holland and Zeeland which enjoyed the natural strategic protection of the great rivers—Rhine, Maas and Waal—and the great island-studded estuaries. Lacking any such natural protection, and still subject to the ancient social order, the southern provinces fell away, declined and reverted finally to Spanish rule. The north, first 'conquered' then 'protestantized' and socially transformed by rebel forces drawn from all areas, classes and religions, went on to weather the storm. The Netherlands were to emerge in 1648, after eighty years of war, irretrievably split, not by any predestined or inherent differences of character, religion, culture or aptitude but by geography and the arbitrament of war.

This thesis, expounded brilliantly by Professor Geyl and his followers, remains basically intact, though it is now seen to raise its own problems of interpretation. It is still not wholly clear how much of a 'conquest' the revolutions of 1572 were, how far they began with an unpremeditated descent by the Sea Beggars on the Brill, or how far they were the work of a small but determined minority from within. Yet even if that question can ever be resolved, there remains another. Time after time, the rebels were saved by contingencies that arose far beyond the boundaries of the Netherlands. For the revolt was itself part of an international ferment. Alba and Parma both had to divert major forces southwards to France at a crucial moment. At other times, Spanish troops mutinied and dispersed because a bankrupt regime that had undertaken military adventures far beyond its means or competence had no money to pay them. The final rift between Spain and England in 1588 was crucial for the success of the rebels.

Under Albert and Isabella the Southern Netherlands regained part of its earlier prosperity, though valuable commerce had migrated north. Catholic, aristocratic and proud, southern culture gives an impression of ease that belies its economic plight.

Again, former generations of historians may have over-emphasized factors of religion or personal leadership. Yet there can be no doubt that the Netherlands struggle was in some measure a civil war; underlying it were differences of social structure between north and south. The religious split that characterized all classes sometimes reflected genuine personal convictions; sometimes religion was merely a façade for a struggle for power between individuals or classes. The persuasive statesmanship of William the Silent played a crucial role in holding together a strangely assorted team of rebels through the defensive phase. Yet even he could not break through the obstinate barriers of feudalism which time and again thwarted his crusade for union and independence in the south. The Walloon nobility proved fatally vulnerable to Spanish influence. That Maurice's military genius was equally vital to the phase of advance is certain. The persistence of the 'Orangist' interpretation of Dutch history is an instinctive tribute to the indispensable genius of the dynasty. So long as these factors of social structure, contingency and personal genius are allowed for, there is no risk that the determinism which used to see the Dutch Republic as the ineluctable outcome of Protestant nationalism will be replaced by another that sees it as the simple outcome of geographical circumstances.

William the Silent and—until 1614-18 at least—Maurice too were engaged in performing a feat which historians busily simplifying the issues have not always recognized clearly. The Netherlands Revolt was not a single revolt stemming from a single grievance or a single group of rebels; it was a congeries of revolts. At any moment—even in those early stages sometimes called 'the revolt of medievalism'—we can discern strains within the entire Netherlands society quite distinct from the discontents of the nobles and gentry. Radical Protestantism, anti-clericalism, inflation, unemployment, starvation, the decay of ancient cities and corporations, the rise of new industries and social groups, the fears and suspicions of middle-class merchants and magistrates—all contributed to make this a dynamic, turbulent, potentially explosive society. These revolts, as Professor Smit has said, 'sometimes run parallel, sometimes conflict with one another, and at other times coalesce into a single movement.' If all this churning discontent was not to end in an orgy of self-destruction, inspired leadership was vital. There was only one source from which it was forthcoming: the House of Orange.

The creed of a minority

The resistance of the nobility and town oligarchies was crucial: they represented powerful forces in society. Yet noble opposition was often patchy, hesitant and devious. Their armour was vulnerable to monarchical force and political persuasion. They were difficult to unite, easy to divide by astute diplomacy and the appeal to orthodoxy, the rules of social order and plain bribery.

Calvinism, on the other hand, represented everywhere a small minority, smaller even in the north than in the south. Yet what it lacked in numbers it made up for by intrepid fanaticism. The Reformation had come relatively late in the Low Countries. Yet here as elsewhere, the Calvinists were able to take advantage of the laxity of church organization and clerical morality to launch an irresistible drive for supremacy. The results varied widely from one region to another. Considerable areas of Roman Catholic predominance survived in north Holland, Utrecht, and the Eastern Provinces. But further south in large areas of Holland and Zeeland and northwards in Drenthe, Protestantism was in the ascendancy by 1600. By 1650, half the population throughout the whole Republic had ceased to be Roman Catholic.

In short, Calvinist fanaticism was the most powerful single propellant behind revolt. As in many revolutions since, it was the creed of a minority. The later spread of the Reformation on a more general scale was a *result* of the Revolt, but by this time the area of Protestant penetration was limited to the northern provinces. The comforts of Protestant doctrine had most appeal for the humbler orders of society; the uprooted, dispossessed and those vulnerable to the idea that work was a religious duty. But there was no neat equation between faith and class. Like mid-Victorian socialism, Calvinism appealed to a combination of idealism and discontent at every level of society. The rank and file of Calvinism came from the artisans. But the twelve thousand victims of Alba's Council of Blood were plucked out of all strata of society. The general anticlerical, Protestant appeal comprehended many who, like William of Orange himself, Oldenbarneveldt and many others of the noble and regent class, found their resolution fortified by the doctrine of predestination in times of stress. The divisions *within* Protestantism were perpetuated less by theological differences—Gomarism versus Arminianism—than by differing opinions on the relation of church and state. Calvinist Oldenbarneveldt certainly was: he was no less determined not to yield to theocratic pressure in politics nor to agree to the persecution of other creeds for political reasons.

Slowly a new politico-religious situation crystallized in the north. As one town after another seceded, the churches were purged of popish and superstitious ornaments, priests, monks and nuns pensioned or expelled. Those Roman Catholic regents who still remained were turned out. The time-servers kept quiet. Then the Calvinists moved in. Their weapons were educational and charitable. Through school, orphanage and almshouse, the lower orders were converted with relative ease. Further up the social scale the difficulties of Calvinizing increased. Well-to-do burghers and patricians resented the dictatorship over morals, ethics and politics implied by the theocratic logic of a fanatic minority. They clung to older traditions of humanism, good manners and tolerance. Their strong stake in material wealth, at risk not only in Holland but throughout the Christian world and beyond, helped to foster ideas of empirical tolerance and diplomatic expediency. Externally the policy of the new federation was increasingly to be aimed (if not always with success) at non-alignment. Internally, the regent class was concerned at the growing tension between their own aims and those of the combined forces of Calvinism and dynasticism—Orange now replacing Habsburg as the symbol of suicidal idealism. *A furore monarchorum, libera nos, Domine.*

The roles of the nobility and the Calvinists in these complex shiftings, quarrels, alliances in the Republic were in a sense complementary. The political decline of the former, the consolidation of their power by the latter, can be clearly traced. Likewise, it has become plain that the Dutch Republic emerged in part from the southern Netherlands: that some of its most vigorous entrepreneurs and most intransigent Calvinists—even great, though perhaps atypical, organizations like the Dutch West India Company—were largely the creation of southerners. The social situation was not static but dynamic. Migration, movement, flexibility were its essence.

A republic of merchants

There remains one social group, and that perhaps the most central, whose role is still cryptic and obscure. Leicester's failure as Governor-General was his failure to understand it. The Republic that emerged from the revolt was a Republic of merchants. Although the oligarchs who ruled city after city were not always themselves actively in trade, they were intimately connected by blood and interest with merchants who were. Here and there we can glimpse the dogged, obstinate resistance this class could oppose to men or measures that threatened their conviction that they and their welfare were coterminous with the welfare of the whole society. Now and again, as at the siege of Leiden, they come on stage to play a role of distinction and heroism. More often, their contribution was silent, ambiguous, anonymous; yet none the less indispensable.

In the early stages of revolt, their role was often cautious, timid, passive. At Amsterdam, until the *coup d'état* of 1578, the ruling regents were Catholic, anti-rebel. Slowly, as the revolt advanced, and especially as its forces became concentrated in the north, their role everywhere underwent a change. Negative conservatism gave way to positive conservatism. One political organizer of genius was thrown up from this class to share power with the Stadholder: Oldenbarneveldt. His ultimate reward for ignoring the instinctive avoidance of the personality cult that typified his class was execution. As a group the regents remained politically tentative, ideologically empirical. Though out of sympathy with Calvinist theocratic ambitions, few of them were actively Arminian or avowedly anti-Calvinist. Most were deeply suspicious of dynasticism of any kind, opposed to diplomatic entanglements that threatened their trade and capital by sea or land, searchers after rules of law and neutrality that would not only keep them out of other people's wars but enable them to profit by them. Such were the policies later outlined in *The Interest of Holland* (the work of Pieter de la Court, a rich Leiden merchant). Although it appeared only half a century later, it crystallized republican, oligarchic opinions that were already a hundred years old among the merchant community. Essentially collective, almost anonymous, their characteristic monuments are those vast canvases of Frans Hals or Jan de Bray from which the directors of cloth guilds, orphanages and old folks' homes, gaze down on posterity; sober, prudent, prosperous, but essentially uncommitted. These were the *politiques* and they were numerous and powerful.

It was the formation of this rich, self-perpetuating oligarchy, which in reality governed the loose-knit federal Republic even in times of so-called Orangist supremacy, that made the new state unique even in the Europe of 1609. Till then, Venice had represented the nearest approach to the model of a mercantile economy. But never before had an entire territorial state so deliberately chained and confined dynastic ambition and subordinated state policy to the interests of trade. In this the Republic was sharply distinguished from the obedient provinces of the south where new bureaucracy and old aristocracy ruled in double harness. The next half century was to see a display of economic virtuosity that made the Republic a prodigy of technology, productivity and wealth. But it also left it uniquely vulnerable to attack by sea and land in a world of almost continuous and ubiquitous war. The consequences of this weakness were not lost on contemporaries. 'The United Provinces', observed Thomas More tartly, 'are like a fair bird suited with goodly borrowed plumes, but if every fowl should take his feather, this bird would rest near naked.' This was the theory on which the enemies of the Republic, Spanish, English and French, were to act successively during the rest of the 17th century.

IV PEACE IN GERMANY

The Empire before 1618

CLAUS-PETER CLASEN

'Would God we might establish genuine peace in Germany!

We fear that a great storm is gathering in the Heavens:

may God almighty graciously deign to disperse it!'

FRANKFURT DELEGATES AT AUGSBURG DIET 1566

Between the two conflicts

of the Reformation and the Thirty Years' War Germany enjoyed a period of relative peace—the Peace established at Augsburg in 1555—which allowed her to become one of the most prosperous regions of Europe. Her political problems were unsolved. She was ruled by the Emperor, the seven Electors, thirty archbishops and bishops, fifty princes, fifty abbots, one hundred counts and fifteen hundred imperial knights; there were in addition sixty-six self-governing imperial cities. The religious split likewise remained wide open, the north being mainly Protestant, the south mainly Catholic. But the quarrel, if it had not abated, was at least waged by the pen rather than by the sword. By compromise, by fear, by the sheer complexity of the problem, a precarious balance was maintained.

Many rulers made great efforts to develop the economic resources of their states. Land under cultivation increased. Population and revenue rose steadily, though prices did too, and development was often at the expense of the poorest classes. But urban life continued to prosper and the small courts of German princes were able to evolve distinct personalities and to encourage independent cultural enterprise in a way that often recalls the story of the Renaissance in Italy.

An important centre of Catholic culture was Munich, the capital of Bavaria. It had a permanent papal nuncio and the Dukes, beginning with Albrecht V, exercised an energetic influence over its religious life. Albrecht's son and successor, Wilhelm, called 'the Pious', abdicated and retreated to a monastery in 1597; his son, Maximilian I, made a regulation that at the sound of the Angelus everyone should kneel down, even in the street, dismounting from their horses and getting out of their coaches.

In the 17th century Maximilian was to become the leader of the Catholic League and play a prominent part in the Thirty Years' War. But at the end of the 16th, under Albrecht and Wilhelm, Munich was among the most delightful capitals of Europe, beginning the transformation of its architecture that was to give it such distinction, and attracting to its court some of the most eminent artists and musicians of the time. One of the latter was Orlando di Lasso, born at Mons in 1532 and coming to Munich in his late twenties. Here he attained an international reputation. The Emperor Maximilian ennobled him and Pope Gregory XIII gave him the Order of the Golden Spur. He died in 1594.

The illustration opposite shows him directing a musical gathering at the Bavarian court. He stands on the extreme left, while an orchestra of assorted string, wind and keyboard instruments performs music of his own composition. The names of the players are recorded in the cartouche below. Above them the motto from Ecclesiasticus reads: 'A concert of music in a banquet of wine is as a signet of carbuncle set in gold.'

Mineral wealth was efficiently exploited. Saxony, the Harz mountains, Tirol and Styria were among the important mining areas, producing iron, copper and coal. This illustration of a mine (*above*) shows smelting in the background, quarrying on the left and on the right a watermill supplying the power needed for refining processes. In the centre at the back, a man with a barrow emerges from the bowels of the earth.

The free cities, business centres in an increasingly financial world, produced a vigorous middle class who imitated the great courts in culture and manners. *Below:* Jobst Friedrich Tetzel of Nuremberg sits down to a meal with his friends; Spanish fashions are *de rigueur*, and the gold plate is clearly being displayed with some pride.

The imperial palace at Vienna, the Amalienburg (*above*), was begun in 1575 by Rudolf II. An extra storey was later added.

Bremen (*below:* the façade of the Town Hall, 1609) and **Hamburg** (*right*) typify the wealth of north German towns. Both belonged to the powerful Hanseatic League, a commercial union of free cities with trade links all over the world.

Nuremberg, in the heart of Germany, was among the most powerful of the free cities. Part of it is shown diagrammatically in a drawing of 1625 by Hans Bien. On the island is the Elisabethkirche; beside it, with the rooms at first-floor level exposed, is the complex of houses belonging to the knights of the German Order. A large hall occupies the building at the top.

Polite society before 1618 took its ease in the parks and gardens that were being laid out on a grand scale. In the picnic shown here with the palace and old town in the background, almost every aristocratic entertainment is included, from

jousting to making daisy-chains. The garden itself is formal (there is even a maze on the island in the river) but the picnic party have wandered into the open countryside, foreshadowing a later taste for the picturesque. The artist was Lucas van

Valkenborch, a Fleming who left Antwerp at the time of Alba's persecutions and settled in Germany. He executed a series of these paintings in about 1585 when he was living near Vienna under the patronage of the Archduke Matthias.

A 'Kunstkammer', or private museum, became the ambition of every prince and rich burgher. The ceremony on the right, to all appearances a matter of civic solemnity, in fact marks the delivery in 1617 of a new *Kunstschrank* (literally 'art cupboard') to Philip II Duke of Pomerania. It had been ordered five years earlier from Philip Hainhofer of Augsburg, with the intention that it should contain a complete survey of art and science and that all the notable artists of Augsburg should contribute to it.

The 'Antiquarium' of Munich, begun in 1570 to house the collection of Albrecht V of Bavaria, rivalled even the Vatican. The long hall, decorated with Italianate and neo-Roman frescoes, was lined with antique figures and busts in niches – some genuinely old, some patched from authentic fragments, some complete forgeries.

The curious, the ancient and the costly were what attracted collectors. Frans Francken the Younger painted a *Kunstkammer* (*above*) which includes a typical assortment of objects – a Madonna and Child, a river-god copied from the antique, seashells (large ones in the foreground, smaller ones in a drawer at the back) and much heavy plate and jewellery.

'I will make you fishers of men.' In this crowded canvas painted in 1614 by Adriaen van de Venne, Christ's words are taken as an ironic text for the whole contemporary religious situation. Protestants and Catholics face each other across the river. Protestants are on the left. In the foreground stand well-known theologians. Further back, by the open space on the bank, are Prince Maurice of Orange (hat in hand), and his young son Frederick Henry (bareheaded), James I of England, Christian IV of Denmark and Louis XIII of France (then still in his minority, siding with the Protestants for political reasons).

On the right bank are Catholic theologians, including

Cornelus Musius, and in the middle distance again the heads of state: Philip III of Spain (richly dressed, his hand on a stick), his sister Isabella, regent of the Netherlands, and her husband Albert. Members of their court surround them. Further back is the Pope amid a vermilion crowd of cardinals. In the water, parties from both banks try to drag naked men and women into their own boats. One is manned by Protestant ministers, another by bishops and priests. Over them all, uniting one side with the other but disregarded by everyone, shines the rainbow of God.

The Lord's vineyard – according to this allegory by Cranach the Younger – will prosper now only under the Lutheran Church. On the left Catholic bishops, priests and monks destroy the vines, burn the tools and fill the well with stones; in the foreground they are being dismissed and paid off with a piece of gold by Christ. On the right all goes well under the devoted care of Luther, Melanchthon and other Reformers.

Hopes of reconciliation had risen when the Council of Trent (*right*) was first convened in 1545. But the Protestant point of view was given no hearing and when it ended in 1563 the two sides were further apart than ever.

A wave of witch-trials swept Germany in the 16th and 17th centuries. Satan's hand was seen on all sides, and those suspected of witchcraft were ruthlessly persecuted. This propaganda picture by Frans Francken the Younger (1607) shows several occult practices in progress. In the centre a group of witches weave spells with magic books and instruments, while to their left another signs a pact with a devil. Behind her a naked witch is having her back rubbed with ointment to help her fly. On the post in the centre another prepares to take off on her broomstick.

In the solid comfort of a rich German household, life could be civilized, elegant and reasonably secure, even after the Thirty Years' War had devastated some parts of the country and threatened others. The wedding scene in Bremen depicted by Wolfgang Heimbach (*above*) gives a wealth of detail in costume, furniture and manners.

Jewelled pendants, sometimes of incredible intricacy, enjoyed a vogue all over Europe. Often, as in the example *left*, they include allegorical figures in miniature architectural settings, enamelled and hung with precious stones and pearls.

The Empire before 1618

CLAUS-PETER CLASEN

Hunting was the chief pastime of princes, an aristocratic privilege that bore heavily on the peasant farmers whose lands suffered. There was no lack of game. Deer, wolves and wild boar abounded in the forests, and the common people were forbidden to kill them under severe penalties.

THE TRUCE of 1609 between Spain and the Netherlands was temporary only. Each side saw it as a suspension, not an end of hostilities, and each used it—Spain diplomatically, the Netherlands economically—as a means of preparing for the last round: the round which would reunite all 17 provinces under either the Habsburg Crown or the States General. That last round would duly begin on the legal expiry of the Truce, in 1621. But, like the first round, it was not isolated. As in the previous century, the struggle was soon generalized; only this time, it was involved not in the ambitions of the Atlantic powers but in the internal tensions of Germany—a Germany which for the last half-century had been largely exempt from ideological war.

By 1552 it had been clear that Charles V's attempts to destroy German Protestantism had failed. So his successor, King Ferdinand, and the imperial estates agreed to legalize it. They did so by the Peace of Augsburg of 1555. By this treaty it was agreed that the imperial estates, i. e. the princes and cities who were represented at the imperial diet, were not to be molested on account of their Lutheran or Catholic religion. The imperial estates and the imperial knights were to have free choice between the two religions. The subjects, however, had to accept the belief of their princes or be expelled. The Catholics succeeded in inserting three special clauses of great political consequence in the treaty: first, the secularization of ecclesiastical property such as monasteries was declared legal only up to 1552. In other words, secularizations after 1552 were illegal. Second, in imperial cities with both Protestant and Catholic population, both parties were to be left in their rights. Third, prince bishops and abbots who converted to Protestantism were obliged to resign from their position. The last-mentioned clause, the *Reservatum Ecclesiasticum*, closed the territories of all bishops and abbots to the further expansion of Protestantism. In return Ferdinand granted that the nobility and towns in ecclesiastical territories should be allowed to practise the Lutheran belief if they had done so for a long time. This so-called *Declaratio Ferdinandea* was, however, not included in the treaty.

To be sure, the Peace of Augsburg did not prevent the growth of violent tensions between the two religious parties which finally exploded in the Thirty Years' War. But thanks to this compromise, the structure of the Empire remained basically intact during the long period from 1555 to 1618 while France and the Netherlands were engulfed in religious and civil wars. This was the more remarkable because that structure had been threatened with disintegration in the 15th century, and although several attempts had been made to preserve it by reform, most of those attempts had failed. In spite of this the Empire, as guaranteed by the Peace of Augsburg, did remain a political reality.

As had been laid down in the Golden Bull of 1356, the emperor was still elected by the seven prince electors, i. e. the three archbishops of Cologne, Mainz and Trier, and four lay princes—the king of Bohemia, and the princes of the Palatinate, Saxony and Brandenburg. These seven electors also formed the first curia of the imperial diet. The second curia consisted of thirty archbishops and bishops, and fifty secular princes, who each had a vote at the imperial diet. Fifty abbots and other prelates were represented as a group by one vote only, a hundred counts and lords by two votes. The fifteen hundred imperial knights who ordinarily ruled a few villages only, had no representation. In the mid-16th century, sixty-six imperial cities were represented in the third curia. From an economic point of view, the Habsburgs were considered the wealthiest rulers in the Empire, followed by the Prince Electors, the Dukes of Bavaria and Württemberg, and the Landgrave of Hesse. The Empire had two highest law courts, whose competence had never been clearly divided. They only differed in that one, the Imperial High Court (*Reichskammergericht*, established 1495) was under the influence of the estates, while the other, the Aulic Court (*Reichshofrat*, established 1559) was under the exclusive influence of the emperor.

The Riven Empire

However, in the second half of the 16th century it was no longer the rivalry between emperor and estates which caused the great political crises, but solely the mounting antagonism between the religious parties. Religion entirely dominated politics.

By 1555 all the duchies in central and north Germany were Lutheran. The prince-bishoprics of north-east Germany were also on the point of falling to Protestantism. In south Germany the Palatinate, Baden, Württemberg and Ansbach were Protestant. The Habsburg territories, Bavaria and the south German prince-bishoprics nominally remained Catholic but large numbers of their inhabitants had turned to Lutheranism. Apart from Cologne and Aachen, all important imperial cities were either predominantly or entirely Protestant. In the mid-16th century Calvinism also appeared in the Empire, being introduced as the official religion by Frederick III in the Palatinate in 1562 and in the following years by several smaller counts.

Neither the Protestants nor the Catholics seem to have accepted this distribution of the confessions as permanent. At first the Protestants were on the offensive, the driving force and leader being the Palatinate, whose princes rule in Heidelberg. The reasons for this are various. Calvinism itself was a radical creed, regarding Catholicism as a satanic form of religion. There was also a deep-rooted feeling of insecurity at Heidelberg because at the imperial diet of 1566 an attempt had been made to exclude the Calvinists formally from the Peace of Augsburg. This radicalism was fostered by emigré theologians from France, the Netherlands and Italy, convinced, from their own experience, that the Catholic powers were bent on exterminating Protestantism in the whole of Europe. Heidelberg thus became the refuge and citadel of Calvinism in Germany, and as such was to play a fateful part in the next century. The radicals of the Palatinate showed their hand early. At the imperial diets of 1556, 1559, 1576 they and their German friends demanded that the *Reservatum Ecclesiasticum* be formally abolished. These attempts failed; but in fact the *Reservatum* was often defied, and in the latter half of the 16th century all the bishoprics east of the river Weser were reformed.

A major crisis came in 1582 when Gebhard Truchsess, Archbishop-Elector of Cologne, was converted to Protestantism. Encouraged by John Casimir of the Palatinate, he then started to reform his prince-bishopric. Realizing that if Gebhard succeeded, Catholicism in north-west Germany would disappear, that the electoral college would receive a Protestant majority and that the rebellious provinces in the Netherlands would get new support, the Habsburgs and Bavaria interfered by force. Receiving no help from the Protestant princes, Gebhard was defeated and fled. The Protestants were not more successful at Strasbourg where in 1592 Johann Georg von Brandenburg was elected bishop by a Protestant group while the bishop of Metz, Charles of Lorraine, was elected by the Catholics. Johann Georg finally resigned in 1604.

From the 1570s and 1580s on, the renascent Catholic church took up an extremely aggressive course, pushing the Protestants to the defensive. By 1571 Protestantism had been wiped out in Bavaria. The Counter-Reformation was particularly ruthless in the Habsburg territories where a large section of the nobility, the towns and villages had accepted Lutheranism. By 1590 Lutheranism had been suppressed in Lower Austria, by 1596 in Upper Austria, by 1603 in Styria and Carinthia. Only the nobility preserved their freedom of worship. Dismissing the *Declaratio Ferdinandea* as invalid, the Archbishop of Mainz and the Abbot of Fulda commenced to exterminate Lutheranism in the 1570s. In the 1580s Protestantism was wiped out in the prince-bishopric of Würzburg, around 1600 in those of Bamberg, Hildesheim, Osnabrück, Münster, Paderborn, Cologne and Trier. A new crisis arose in 1581 when the city of Aachen, swollen by refugees from the Netherlands, turned Protestant. But in 1593 the Aulic Court rejected the claim that Aachen had the right to admit the Augsburg Confession, and in 1598 the Catholic rule at Aachen was restored by force.

These violations or alleged violations of the Peace of Augsburg by both Protestants and Catholics created growing bitterness on both sides. Aggressive and distrustful, both parties were prepared to use any means to force through their demands. At the diets of 1556, 1559, 1576 and 1594, the Palatinate and its friends proposed that taxes for the war against the Turks should be refused unless the Protestant demands were met. The Catholics on the other hand warned the Emperor that they would leave the diet if he yielded to the Protestants. In 1562 and 1575 the Palatinate endeavoured to use the imperial elections, first of Maximilian II and then of Rudolf II, to push its demands. Invariably the Palatinate failed because Saxony and most other Lutheran territories were opposed to these radical aims and methods. This was partly due to their engrained hatred of the Calvinists. Above all, Augustus of Saxony refused to support a policy which endangered the compromise achieved in 1555.

This growing religious hostility finally disrupted the imperial institutions. It wrecked the fiscal system, and thereby the defence of the empire. The Emperor badly needed financial support for the war against the Turks, who in spite of the armistice of 1568 had never stopped their raids against Styria and in 1593 launched a large-scale attack to conquer all Hungary. The Palatinate declared in 1576 and 1594 that these wars against the Turks served not the defence of the Empire but the expansion of the house of Habsburg. Therefore taxes to finance the war could not be voted by a majority at the imperial diet, but were to be regarded as voluntary contributions only. Similarly, in 1582 the whole curia of the imperial cities refused to pay taxes unless the city of Aachen was guaranteed the right to decide its own religion. In 1590 the Catholic estates refused to support military action when the Spaniards invaded north-west Germany and exterminated Protestantism wherever they found it. The same religious hostility also wrecked the legal system. From 1588 on, a commission charged with the final revisions of sentences by the Imperial High Court was no longer summoned by the Archbishop of Mainz because the Protestant Administrator of the bishopric of Magdeburg (which had been reformed after 1555) would have sat on it. As a result the whole jurisdictional process collapsed; in order to escape a sentence, one only had to put in an appeal. In 1598 a special commission was empowered to revise these sentences; but the problem was not solved. Among the sentences were four

which, following the stipulation of the Peace of Augsburg, condemned the secularization of four monasteries after 1552 as illegal. Realizing the dangerous legal consequences, the Palatinate and its friends suddenly declared that the Imperial High Court had no jurisdiction in disputes concerning the Peace of Augsburg and simply left the commission. At the diet of 1603 they announced that confessional questions could not even be decided by a majority of the diet but had to be left to the voluntary agreement among the imperial estates. The imperial diet began to turn into a congress of almost sovereign states.

Tension Heightens

By disrupting the constitutional organs of the Empire whenever their own demands could not legally be upheld, the Palatinate slowly brought the internal tensions of the Empire to breaking point. On the other side, Duke Maximilian of Bavaria emerged as leader of a militant Catholic group. In December 1607 he simply overpowed Donauwörth, an overwhelmingly Protestant imperial city, on dubious legal grounds. Deeply disturbed, the Protestants demanded at the imperial diet of 1608 that the Peace of Augsburg be expressly confirmed. When the Catholics refused to guarantee the legality of the reformation of prince-bishoprics and monasteries after 1552, the Palatinate and its allies left the diet. Shortly afterwards they formed a military alliance, the Union. The Catholic estates responded by forming a counter-alliance, the League.

War almost erupted in 1610 over the question of Jülich. When Duke Wilhelm of Jülich died childless, Brandenburg and Neuburg who claimed to be the heirs, occupied his four duchies and by the treaty of Dortmund arranged for a joint administration. As both Brandenburg and Neuburg were Protestant, the fate of Catholicism in north-west Germany was again at stake. The Emperor Rudolf II thereupon voided the treaty of Dortmund and declared the duchies under his own administration. This in turn brought in Henri IV of France who could not tolerate a new Habsburg bastion at his north-western frontiers. He was already conspiring with the Union to drive the Habsburgs out of Jülich and even the Netherlands, when he was assasinated on 14 May 1610. In the end the Prince Elector of Brandenburg, who had accepted the Calvinist belief, retained Cleve-Mark and Ravensberg, while the Duke of Neuburg who had been diplomatically converted to Catholicism, kept Jülich and Berg.

During the same years a much more explosive crisis was emerging in the territories of the Habsburgs. For years there had been dissatisfaction within the Habsburg family with the inefficient rule of Rudolf II. In 1608 he was forced to hand over to archduke Matthias the government of Hungary, Austria and Moravia, retaining only Bohemia, Silesia and Lusatia. As the price of their support the estates, under the leadership of the Calvinists Georg Erasmus von Tschernembl and the brothers von Starhemberg, demanded freedom of religion for the towns. In Bohemia Rudolf II did indeed, by the 'Letter of Majesty' of 1609, grant free practice of religion to both the nobility and the royal towns. A permanent committee, the *defensores*, was to represent the Protestant interests. But the Catholics were determined not to be defeated. After the childless Matthias they designated the archduke Ferdinand as Emperor and proceeded to ensure his succession. The support of the Spanish Habsburgs (who had claims on the Hungarian and Bohemian crowns) was won by the secret treaty of Graz, by which Ferdinand promised to cede to Spain Alsace, the Landvogtei of Hagenau and the Grafschaft of Ortenau as soon as he had inherited them. This treaty was to have far-reaching consequences in the following years. Meanwhile the 'acceptance' of Ferdinand as king of Bohemia was pushed through at Prague. Once 'elected', Ferdinand, who had already exterminated Protestantism in his Austrian lands, set out to destroy it in Bohemia. When the *defensores* called a meeting of the Protestant leaders he rejected their complaints and forbade further assemblies of the kind.

The Bohemians now rose in revolt. On 13 May 1618 they threw the royal governors out of the window and, following the political theories of the west European Calvinists, declared the estates the organ of popular sovereignty. The Union announced that the violation of the Letter of Majesty was a matter of concern to all

The crude religious satires of the Reformation continued throughout the century. This titlepage to a 1584 edition of one of Calvin's minor works is aimed at the familiar target of Catholic reverence for relics.

Protestants. After Matthias' death, on 20 March 1619, events quickened. Ferdinand succeeded in being elected Emperor on 28 August 1619. However on 22 August his acceptance as King of Bohemia had been declared unconstitutional by the Bohemian estates. On 26/27 August 1619 they elected in his place the representative of the most violent anti-Habsburg policy in the empire: Frederick V, Prince Elector of the Palatinate. This was the spark that fired the powder-keg. The rebellion of the estates in Bohemia and the tension between the confessional blocs in Germany erupted in one great conflagration. The disastrous religious division in the Empire produced a war which was to bring untold misery over the German people.

Structure of Government

Preoccupied with political history, German historians have centred their attention on the tragic course of events which led to this catastrophe. They saw a Germany descending from the heights of the Reformation to the ruin of the Thirty Years' War and concluded that the whole period was one of stagnation and decay. However, once we realize that the political history of the Empire does not exhaust German history of the period, new questions present themselves: what for example were the inner conditions in the territories?

In the first half of the 16th century, the centre of government in any state had been not a formally organized council but the chamber of the prince. With the help of a few powerful councillors and secretaries, the prince himself had taken all important decisions. Now, following the example of Austria, most territories, such as Saxony in 1574 or Bavaria in 1582 organized this amorphous group of advisers as a definite council, the *Geheime Rat* or privy council. But even this council had advisory functions only: the government still retained a strongly personal character.

Another council, the *Kammergericht, Regierung* or *Ratstube* as it was variously called, had both jurisdictional and administrative functions. It served as court of equity and of appeals, and was also in charge of feudal matters, new legislation, or negotiations with the estates. A third body, the *Rentei* directed the technical side of financial administration.

Commoners, especially lawyers, increasingly occupied the highest positions in the government. In Hessen, for instance, the percentage of commoners in government rose from 20% before 1509 to 70% after 1536. In Württemberg the percentage of high officials with legal training rose from 69% between 1520 and 1550 to 85% between 1551 and 1568. Often these high officials were related to each other. In Hessen 70% of the councillors in the three governing bodies belonged to 25 families only.

Over against the prince and his court stood the estates or parliament of each principality. The period from 1555 to 1618 was the time of their greatest influence. Originally the estates had consisted of three houses, but in many territories the clergy disap-

peared as a separate house after the Reformation. In general the nobility and the towns formed the estates. In some south German territories such as Baden, Trier or Bamberg, where the nobility had gained the status of free imperial knights, towns only were represented in the estates. In very few territories such as Friesland or Tirol, the peasants had their own representatives. Ordinarily the estates were summoned by the prince though in a few territories they had the right to assemble on their own. In Württemberg 15 diets were held at irregular intervals between 1550 and 1618, mostly lasting five to ten days only, sometimes however not less than five weeks. First all houses met in a common session, to hear the proposition of the prince; then they divided to discuss it separately. In general the decision of the majority prevailed in each house. Whenever the houses took divergent views, the government would try to negotiate a common agreement. The need for money was the original and most frequent reason why the estates were called. Almost always they eventually took over the debts of the government. But they established their own financial administration which in some territories, such as Württemberg or Brandenburg, was completely independent of the government. Often the government consulted the estates on new legislation, law codification, price and trade policy, the canalization of rivers etc. In some territories such as Württemberg the estates were represented by permanent committees. In spite of sharp wrangling over taxes, many princes took a patriarchal attitude towards the estates. With his own hand Duke Ludwig of Württemberg wrote under a letter to be forwarded to a committee: 'Your faithful father and protector until my death, may the Holy Trinity help me, Amen'. Though the estates controlled the purse and often demanded that they be consulted in matters of alliances, war and peace, the prince and the governments always remained the stronger part, administering justice, initiating new laws and directing foreign policy. Frequently the estates referred to their rights and privileges, but only the Prussian estates in 1663 offered a theoretical defence, basing it on the contract theory of government.

In all territories comprehensive laws, *Landesordnungen*, were issued in the late 15th and all through the 16th century, often remaining in force well into the 18th century. The aim of these laws was to establish order in territories divided by manifold customs and privileges. But they also reveal to what extent the 16th century prince felt responsible for the material and spiritual well-being of his subjects. For example, the ordinance issued in Ernestine Saxony in 1556 dealt at length, and in minute detail, with the different economic groups of society. The peasants were forbidden to engage in brewing or to sell their crops before the harvest. They were ordered to heap up balks between the fields, to plant a few trees every year and to keep bees. Detailed regulations were made for servants, wage labourers, messengers and wood-cutters. The towns were told that fewer houses should be built of wood and that better use should be made of quarries and clay pits. A long part of the ordinance was devoted to 'police', which in the 16th century greatly affected personal life. It was laid down how swearing, adultery and fornication were to be punished, how much credit an innkeeper was to grant to a peasant with horses and to one without. Lastly, legal problems, such as the competence of lower and higher courts and fees for judges and clerks, were dealt with.

Under the impact of increased expenditure and rising debts, some princes sought to raise the productivity of their estates and to stimulate the productive forces in their territories. Exact knowledge of the nature and amount of income, of the size of the population and wealth of the country was a prerequisite for an economic policy. Most noteworthy were the efforts of Landgrave Wilhelm of Hesse. Between 1569 and 1589 he caused to be drawn up a series of surveys which reported the results not descriptively but in statistical tables. In 1569 government officials were sent out to investigate on the spot the jurisdictional rights in every village, the exact number of inhabitants, the amount of services, military obligations, the forest and hunting rights. In 1571 a census of the whole population was taken, including children and servants, followed in 1574 by a precise assessment of all forests etc. On the basis of these and other reports the central government established large statistical surveys, covering the whole of the lower duchy.

A *Book of Estimates*, written between 1569 and 1575, lists the expected revenue and expenditures in every district, another volume the actual revenue and expenditures. A third volume contains altogether thirty pieces most of which are statistical surveys, written in black, red, green or blue ink. There are lists of all forests and their owners, of the population in every village, of land owned by the landgrave, of sheep, calves and cows raised, and butter and cheese to be expected, of the gold and silver value of the different currencies etc. Marvellous new maps by outstanding cartographers such as Arnold and Johann Mercator and Wilhelm Dillich supplemented the surveys.

Part of a page from the 'Book of Estimates' drawn up for the Landgrave of Hesse. The left-hand column lists the names of towns, the others give the amounts to be paid under various land-taxes.

Some governments interfered directly in the economy. Württemberg issued not less than 31 ordinances for practically all branches of the economy: for glass-makers, weavers, bakers, millers and other crafts. Regular trade wars were waged against nearby imperial cities to protect the nascent industrial production of the duchy. Great care was taken to foster the most important branch of the economy, wine-growing. New plants such as cauliflower, cucumber and melons were introduced. Cherry trees became frequent and mulberry trees were planted for the raising of silk worms and the production of raw silk.

Figures and Facts

As in other countries, in the Empire too questions of economic and financial policy became the subject of investigation by high government officials, the cameralists, and also by scholars and lawyers. Georg Obrecht (1547–1612) discussed measures to raise the revenue, methods to conduct statistical surveys and to establish government-run saving banks. Jakob Bornitz (c. 1560–1625) wrote on the nature of money and the varieties of revenues, Christof Besold (1577–1638) on the necessity of public treasuries and Kaspar Klock (1583–1655) on the various forms of taxation.

The accurate work of these 16th century officials enables us to study the movement of population. Sebastian Franck and his contemporaries were surprised and worried by the steady growth of population. Indeed at Augsburg the number of tax payers increased by 14% between 1558 and 1604. In 20 villages of the district of Weimar the number of peasant holdings rose from 720 in 1541 to 1,023 in 1588. A recent investigation has shown that in an area of 100,000 square kilometres with 676 towns and 14,193 villages, the population increased yearly by 0.55% from 1520 to 1610. The whole population of Germany is supposed to have risen from 14 millions in 1560 to 16 or 17 millions by 1618. Of course the overwhelming majority of people lived in villages. In the lower duchy of Hesse 73% of the people lived in villages, 27% only in towns. In the hereditary lands of Saxony, where the flourishing mining industry caused a high density of towns, 68% of the population were villagers, 32% townspeople. However the 137 communities of this area which officially were called towns

and markets, were rather small: 55 (40%) had less than 500 inhabitants, 94 (68%) less than 1,000, 123 (90%) less than 2,000. Many of these burghers had their own fields, meadows and gardens. Only 14 towns had more than 2,000 people, the largest being Leipzig with 7,500 people. Dresden, the capital, had 6,450 inhabitants.

The capitals of other territories were not much larger. By 1600 Heidelberg had 6,300 people, Stuttgart 9,000, Munich 10,000. The largest cities were the commercial centres, Stettin having 12,200 people by 1600, Frankfurt 18,000, Hamburg 22,500, Breslau and Magdeburg 30,000, Cologne about 40,000, and Augsburg, the largest city of the Empire, about 50,000.

The largest social class were the poor, not the middle class. In 1558, 47.7%, i.e. almost half the tax payers of Augsburg, had no property at all. Another 24.7% had not more than 300 florins. In other words, 72.4% of the Augsburg population were either propertyless or had modest possessions only. Whenever a bad harvest sent grain prices up, the poor came close to starvation. During the great famine of 1570, every week the Augsburg town council sold to the poor at a reduced price 23,000 loaves of bread and 37 centners of lard. Social conditions were not better in small towns. In 9 out of 15 small towns in electoral Saxony in the mid-16th century, more than half the tax payers with real property had not more than 100 florins. The large mass of journeymen, servants and those who had no real property, is not even included here. The peasants were not better off. In the villages of ten representative districts of the duchy of Württemberg in 1544, 42% to 57% of the tax payers had not more than 50 florins' worth of property. Altogether 65% to 83% had not more than 150 florins.

Of course the lower classes, particulary in the cities, were hardest hit by the rise of prices. At Augsburg for example, the prices of rye, barley and oats rose from 1550 to 1618 by 69%. The wages of bricklayers'men, of journeymen bricklayers, journeymen carpenters and unskilled building workers rose by 47% only. In other words the real income of the great mass of urban wage labourers decreased.

	Could be bought by 1 Florin (1 Florin = 60 Kreuzers)
42.8 lbs of beef	
14.2 lbs of lard	
12 lbs of carp	
17.6 lbs of linseed oil	
10 lbs of flax	
67 herrings (about)	
13 dry cod (about)	
150 cabbages	
300 bricks	

	Prices:	
1	lb of beef	cost 1.4 Kreuzer
1	lb of lard	cost 4.2 Kreuzers
1	quart of milk	cost 0.7 Kreuzer
1	lb of carp	cost 5 Kreuzers
1	lb of linseed oil	cost 3.4 Kreuzers
1	lb of flax	cost 6 Kreuzers
100	herrings	cost 1.5 Florins
180	dry cod	cost 14 Florins
100	cabbages	cost 40 Kreuzers
100	bricks	cost 20 Kreuzers

Table giving the approximate purchasing power of the florin at Augsburg in 1558.

A Fruitful Land

The great increase of population led to an extension of cultivated land all over Germany. Villages which had been abandoned after the Black Death were again settled. New land was won in forests, on mountains, in swamps and from the sea. In east Friesland 40,000 hectares of land were won by dykes in the 16th and early 17th centuries. Naturally the size of the farms and the position of the tenant varied greatly in the different parts of the Empire. In south-west Germany small farms dominated, leased on a hereditary basis or (less often) for a specific period of time. Ordinarily the land was divided among all the children. The lords there did not cultivate large estates, but lived on rents and payments of the

Beggars waiting for alms outside a church, from a German edition of Petrarch's 'De remediis utriusque fortunae'. Even when the harvest was good, a large proportion of the population lived on the brink of extreme poverty, and when it failed masses of both town and country folk were reduced to beggary.

peasants. The services and dues of the peasants were fixed. Serfdom still existed, but did not constitute a burden. In Bavaria the farms were passed on to the children undivided and retained an impressive size. However, there was a large mass of landless labourers. Upper and Lower Austria were shaken by a violent peasant uprising from 1594 to 1597, caused by the heavy burdens and services imposed in consequence of the Turkish wars. Northwest Germany was predominately a land of free, small peasantry who in the 16th and 17th centuries acquired full rights of inheritance. The government carefully guarded the independence and stability of the peasants against encroachments by the lords.

While in the territories west of the Elbe river, the position of the peasants did not decline in the 16th century, a catastrophic deterioration occured in the eastern lands: Brandenburg, Mecklenburg, Pomerania, Silesia and Prussia. Originally the position of the peasants in these colonial parts of Germany had been better than in the west. However, from the late 15th century, their position changed. Prompted by the profitable export of grain, the east German nobility, the Junkers, who themselves cultivated their estates, deliberately set out to annex the peasant holdings. Through their control over taxation, the nobility forced the territorial princes to rule that they had the right to buy the land of the peasants even against their will. Since they already possessed rights of jurisdiction and police over their peasants, the rest was easy. Thus in the Mittelmark 35% of all large estates which existed in the 19th century had been formed in the 16th century. As the Junkers needed more labour, they increased the services of the peasants—in Mecklenburg from 3½ days a year in 1500 to three days a week in 1600. The peasant was forbidden to leave his farm and his children had to offer their services first to the lord. Only indirectly was the peasant still the subject of the prince. It was this new servile relationship which distinguished the east from the rest of Germany.

While the peasant in central and west Germany ordinarily sold his products in the nearby town, the Junker in the east grew for export. Prussia and Pomerania together with Poland became the large supply store of grain for western Europe: 75% of the grain was exported via Danzig, the rest via Königsberg, Riga and Stettin, and shipped to the great markets at Amsterdam, Hamburg and London. Russia, Poland and Hungary also supplied the German cities with cattle and oxen. In Germany the breeding of cattle and pigs declined because meat prices rose very much less than those of grain. The great markets for cattle from southeastern Europe were Vienna, Breslau and Brieg, for those from Poland and Russia Posen, Frankfurt-on-Oder and Buttstädt, a small town north of Weimar where sometimes 16,000 to 20,000

animals were traded on a single day. However, towards 1600 the large cattle from north-west Germany and the Netherlands were pushing the smaller eastern cattle off the markets in central and west Germany.

Though the wine-growing area in Germany had already reached its greatest extension by 1500, wine-growing occupied a very important position all through the 16th century. However, the competition of beer, which was much cheaper, was already felt by the winegrowers. At Nuremberg three times as much beer as wine was consumed between 1551 and 1570.

The second half of the 16th century saw the beginning of a literature on farming in Germany. In 1570 Conrad Heresbach published his *Rei rusticae libri quattuor* which discussed the location of the farm, the tasks of the farmer, manager and servants, the climate, soil, crops, sowing, harvesting, barns, meadows, gardens, fruit trees, fences, hedgerows, forests, animals, chicken, ponds, bees etc. Similar books were written by two pastors, Martin Grosser in Silesia (1590) and Johann Coler in Brandenburg (1591). The book of Abraham von Thumschirn, which originated

Titlepage from 'Weinbuch' by Johann Rasch, 1582, showing wine-casks, the merchant or landowner and the labourer tending the vine.

as instructions for the estates of Augustus of Saxony, was of a more professional nature. These books give excellent insight into German agriculture in the 16th century. For example we learn that carrots, parsnips, lamb's lettuce, radish, turnips and cabbage were grown in fields; that hemp-seed, rape and cole seed and poppy were grown for oil; woad, madder, dyer's safflower and saffron for producing dyes. The authors of these books were well aware of the importance of good manure. Heresbach recommended stable manure, compost, vegetable manure, marl, unslaked lime and ashes, and praised lucerne and lupin both as manure and fodder.

In the period from 1555 to 1618 handicraft and industrial production flourished in Germany as much as ever. Silesia, Westphalia, the lower Rhine and Swabia were known for their weaving and knitting, north-west Germany for its copper and brassware and tins, central Germany for pottery and glass, south Germany for products of wood and precious metals. Important centres of mining were Saxony, the Harz mountains, the Siegerland, the Lahn-Dill area, Tyrol and Styria. Iron-mining, smelting works and the production of tin-plate played an important role in the upper Palatinate.

Some resourceful princes themselves engaged in industrial enterprises. Acquiring 2800 *Kuxe* (shares in a mining company which entitled the owner to a part of the profit against payments for maintenance), Augustus, Prince Elector of Saxony, was in a

German trade and finance is proudly displayed in this allegory by Jost Amman. In the centre are represented the qualities needed in a merchant—Integrity, Discretion, Knowledge of languages—while the sides form a panorama of the businessman's world, from money-changing and calculating risks to tying up bales and nailing barrels.

In 1556 George Agricola the elder published the 'De re metallica', a digest of processes connected with mining and similar industries. Various stages are shown here in glass making and blowing, with the finished articles packed in a crate on the right.

position to influence the price movements of iron and copper ore, of vitriol, alum, cobalt and coal. He encouraged new mining techniques and improved the stamping mills and iron mills. Duke Julius of Brunswick re-established the decaying iron pits and iron forges at the northern and eastern slopes of the Harz Mountains, which produced an excellent thin steel, and exported culverin and arquebuses. The sullage was used for the production of cannon balls.

Saxony and Westphalia are good examples of how the German economy adapted itself to changing conditions. When the large labour force of Indian and Negro slaves in the Spanish colonies offered a good market for coarse cloths, enterprising merchants, especially in Nuremberg, extended and encouraged the production of cheap linen in Saxon and Bohemian towns which were affected by the decline in mining. Production was organized in the form of the *zunftkauf*: representatives of the great merchant houses negotiated with the guild the amount and variety, the quality and price of linen they would buy. The agreements had to be approved by the town council. As the individual weaver was free to join the agreement or not, his economic independence was safeguarded. These arrangements often covered large areas and were kept for decades. The prosperity of many Saxon and Silesian towns in this period was due to the flourishing production of linen.

In Westphalia the merchants organized production among the poorer people in the country, in opposition to the urban guilds. In southern Westphalia they developed the large-scale manufacture of scythes, sickles, or ploughshares; in northern Westphalia, with Osnabrück as the centre, a flourishing linen industry. Most of the linen was exported via Hamburg. Thus Germany was characterized by a diversified economy, orientated towards export. It was only the Thirty Years' War which destroyed this promising development.

Commercial Interests

Some of the great commercial centres such as Augsburg, Strasbourg or Ulm had lost their position by the second half of the 16th century. At Augsburg not less than 70 internationally known houses collapsed between 1556 and 1584 in consequence of the bankruptcies of the Spanish and French crowns. However other cities maintained their position or even rose to prominence. The Nuremberg merchants realized the great opportunities in eastern Europe. Some moved to Leipzig for good, others opened branches at Breslau, Posen, Danzig, Warsaw and Cracow. Leipzig with its three yearly fairs gained increasing signifiance as a commercial and financial centre for eastern Europe.

The Hanseatic cities of the north similarly sought to adjust themselves to new circumstances. In 1557 they adopted a new statute levying a tax on the 63 towns which were members of the League and appointing a permanent syndic. However the solidarity among the towns continued to decay. Also the eastern Baltic was lost after the conquest of Livonia by the Russians and

Swedes in 1558, and in England the privileges of the League were severely curtailed. In spite of these reverses, however, the commerce of the Hansa flourished. With 1,000 ships of altogether 45,000 *last* (unit of ship capacity equivalent, in Germany, to two tons) by 1600, its fleet was larger than that of England, France or Spain and second only to that of the Dutch. As a result of the wars in the Netherlands, Hamburg, Lübeck and Danzig enjoyed a very profitable trade with Spain and Portugal, and Hanseatic ships even traded in Italy and Crete. But the basis of the commerce of the Hansa remained the trade between east and west. The number of its ships passing through the Sound rose from 202 in 1497 to 1,568 in 1597: from 20% to 23.5% of the whole traffic. Of the 4,500 passages made through the Sound yearly between 1601 and 1610, 80% were from or to Hanseatic towns.

Unlike Cologne, which failed to profit from the arrival of foreign merchants after the fall of Antwerp, Hamburg welcomed immigrants. Ignoring the principles of the Hansa, it granted full equality of status to the Portuguese, the Italians, the Lutherans and Calvinists from the southern Netherlands, the south German merchants and the English Merchant Adventurers. Thanks to this policy Hamburg soon experienced an unprecedented prosperity. Lübeck still entertained a very lively trade with Norway, Sweden and Danzig but its dominant position was lost. At Stettin the great firm of Loitz, grown rich on the herring trade, strove for a monopoly of the salt trade in the north-east, and was also engaged in the trade of copper and grain until it collapsed in 1572. The Pomeranian and Prussian nobility had greatly invested in this house. Thanks to merchants from the Netherlands, Emden (which was not a member of the Hansa) in 1572 harboured not less than 572 ships with a tonnage of 21,000 *last*, equalling the whole English fleet. However by 1600 Emden's position had already declined.

Frankfurt-on-Main too owed its rise largely to the arrival of refugees. Between 1554 and 1590, 1,212 Walloons and Flemings were accepted as burghers. Among them were many textile workers and, above all, Lutheran and Calvinist merchants from Antwerp with immense riches and trading connections all over Europe. Between 1585 and 1589 not less than 70 rich merchants and bankers and 30 wealthy jewellers from the Netherlands settled at Frankfurt. Of the 125 richest burgers in 1618, 65 were Belgians and only 45 Germans and 15 Jews. The two Frankfurt fairs which had formerly played a significant role within Germany, between 1560 and 1630 rose to be leading centres of international trade, famous in particular for books, silks and jewels.

Frankfurt also became the financial centre of Germany, although in international finance it never achieved the significance of Amsterdam or London. The Frankfurt exchange was founded in 1585 when 82 great merchants established an official rate of exchange. Held in front of the *Römer* during the second week of the fair, the exchange played a prominent role in the financial relations between Italy and upper Germany on the one hand and the Netherlands and England on the other. As purchases at the fair were ordinarily made on credit, the granting of loans from fair to fair developed into a special form of money-lending, the loan *a deposito*, which was considered a very profitable form of investment. Using differences in the rate of exchange and interest, merchants took loans of hundreds of thousands of florins in other markets, in order to lend them *a deposito* at Frankfurt at a higher rate. Johann von Bodecke of Antwerp, the richest merchant at Frankfurt, together with his brother lent *a deposito* not less than 148,000 *thaler* between 1606 and 1609, making a profit of 6,455 florins in 1607 alone. After the catastrophe of Antwerp, the exchange business increased immensely at Frankfurt. Bodecke's investments in bills of exchange were of about the same size as his investments in loans *a deposito*. 'Dry exchange' was also used by the great Frankfurt merchants. To the anger of the German merchants, more French, Flemish and Italian than German was heard among the 150 great merchants who regularly attended the fair. Indeed trade and finance in Germany largely lay in the hands of Belgians and Italians, many of whom had, however, permanently settled at Frankfurt, Nuremberg and in other German cities. The old German houses of the Fugger, Welser or Imhof had lost their dominance.

Because of the confusion of currency, exchanges were also established in other German cities: at Hamburg in 1558, Cologne in 1566, Danzig in 1593, Lübeck in 1605, Königsberg in 1613, Bremen in 1614, Leipzig in 1635. None of these, however, could compete with that of Frankfurt.

All through the 16th century, this confusion of currencies in the empire was ridiculed in sermons, broadsheets, satires and caricatures. Repeatedly, in 1524, 1551, 1559, 1566, 1570 and 1571, the imperial authorities tried to bring order into the chaos. In 1559 the florin of 60 *kreuzer*, in 1566 the Saxon *thaler* of 68 *kreuzer* were decreed as imperial currency; but the variety of currencies persisted. In the second half of the 16th century, when the price of silver greatly exceeded the silver value laid down for the coins, the various states, contrary to the currency laws of the Empire, began to mint inferior small coins. This immediately resulted in wild speculation. The value of the larger coins rose continuously, while the small coins lost 20%, 50% or even more of their nominal value. Contrary to the laws of 1570 and 1571, the princes also established a great number of coining presses, leasing them at a profit to unscrupulous mint-masters. These shady practices led finally to the fantastic inflation of the years 1618 to 1623.

Inside the Protestant States

The growing role of the government, which we noticed in the inner administration and in economic affairs, can also be observed in the life of the Protestant and Catholic churches in our period. Though Lutheranism had spread widely as a popular movement, it was the secular authorities who organized the movement as a Church. Decisions had to be taken on its immense property. In Saxony, after deduction of payments for pastors, schools and the poor, the income from church property was used for the expenses of government. In Hesse 59% of church property was reserved for church, university, schools, hospitals etc., 38% for the needs of the court and the administration, and 3% for remuneration of loyal services. Numerous other questions had to be decided such as the organization of the church, appointments or changes in ceremonies. As the jurisdictional powers of the bishops were no longer recognized, the theologians emphasized the duty of the secular authorities to act in the emergency. Consequently, as many independent churches were established as there were territories, principalities and imperial cities.

Though decrees on religious matters had been issued since the 1520s, it was in the period from 1555 to 1600 that the Protestant churches were definitely organized. Hundreds of church ordinances prescribed the details of doctrine, ceremonies and organization. In Württemberg for example the Great Ordinance of 1559 decreed the *Confessio Wirttembergica* as the doctrinal standard, and gave detailed directives as to baptism, confession, absolution, catechism, Lord's Prayer, singing, dress of pastors, topics of sermons etc.

Though the prince, as *summus episcopus*, was at the head of the church, there had to be a machinery for its administration. Three types of Protestant church government can be observed in the Empire. In Saxony the prince and his councillors made all important decisions on appointments, salaries or visitations. There was no central governing body of the church, though a consistory was established for matrimonial jurisdiction. In every district a superintendent was appointed to supervise the clergy through visitations and synods. The congregations were only the object of pastoral care: they had no part in the administration of the church. This type of church government was also adopted by Mecklenburg (1552), Pomerania (1563) and other north German territories. The Hessian church on the other hand provided for the office of elders and for a certain self-government of the church through synods of the clergy. The church of Württemberg developed a bureaucratic form of government. The Church Council, consisting of theologians and lawyers, was divided into a theological and political section. Together with the four general superintendents, the Church Council formed the Synod, the highest organ of the church. The duchy was divided into 28 superintendencies which were inspected twice (later once), a year by the superintendents. Extracts from their reports were submitted to the Synod. Important decisions were subject to the approval of the government and the duke. This type of church governement was adopted also by Baden-Durlach, the Palatinate and in 1580 also by Electoral Saxony.

A remarkable instrument of church government was the regular visitation. In the Saxon Ordinance of Visitation of 1580, 126 questions were formulated of which 52 had to be addressed to the pastor and the deacons. Some dealt with church attendance: do people take walks during the service; do they work on Sundays? Others concerned family life: are there tyrannical husbands, disobedient wives and unruly children? The pastor was also interrogated on the ceremonies he used at baptism, weddings and burials, and on the payments and services of his parishioners. Then in the absence of the pastor, the parishioners were asked 74 questions on the form of the church services and the life of the pastor. Does the pastor gamble? What are his relations with his wife? Do they keep buildings and fences in good shape? Do they waste the rectory timber?

Two areas of different forms of church service can be discerned in Lutheran Germany. The north and central German territories and the imperial cities in Franconia followed Luther who had retained as much as possible of the old forms, eliminating only what contradicted his doctrine of justification. Besides the mass, there were still matins and vespers. There were the chants of the priests, the choirs of boys, the same liturgy, and even the Latin language. Before communion, the believer went to confession. Communion was considered part of every Sunday service, though eventually the sermon became the centre of the service. Though marriage, ordination and extreme unction were no longer con-

Germany during the early 17th century. The Swiss Confederation was in theory part of the Empire until 1648.

sidered sacraments, the ceremonies were largely the same. Exorcism at baptism was kept, the old liturgical vestments were worn, the five liturgical colours, church vessels, crosses, pictures and altars were retained. In a few territories Sunday services were still held in form of the high-mass and the consecration of bread and wine with elevation, bells, incense and altar boys were customary. People continued to cross themselves. In general, more ceremonies and practices of the old church were retained in the north and east than in the west and south of the Empire.

South-west Germany was influenced by the example of Zwingli's church service. The extremely sober service was meant only to promulgate the Christian message. The Lord's Supper was celebrated a few times a year only. The liturgy retained hardly anything of the mass. There were no crosses, candles, liturgical chants or colourful vestments.

Besides the sermon, Luther's catechism became a favourite means of instruction in many Lutheran churches. Prints of the catechism were hung up in the church. The different sections were explained in lessons and sermons and had to be memorized. In addition, the common people were expected to know the Lord's Prayer, the Confession of the Faith and the Ten Commandments. Confirmation was introduced in Hesse in 1539 and soon adopted by most other territories. The glory of the Lutheran Church service was the chorale, which was particularly cultivated in Saxony, Thuringia and Silesia.

The calibre of the Protestant pastors in the second half of the 16th century was not high. Many had formerly been teachers, sacristans or artisans and had never attended a university. Sometimes a pastor had to be reminded to buy a bible or a book of homilies. Occasionally he was told to reserve a quiet room in his house as a study. Many a pastor had to till his own fields. Sometimes pastors were forced by noblemen to hand over part of the church property, to serve as clerks or even assist during the hunt. Repeatedly the pastors accused the peasants of not rendering their stipulated dues or services, bringing poor sheaves as tithes or refusing to repair the rectory though rain leaked through the roof. Only towards 1600 did the intellectual level and the prestige of the pastors begin to rise.

In the second half of the 16th century, the Lutheran churches were shaken by several violent theological quarrels which for the most part resulted from Melanchthon's deviations from Luther in questions concerning free will, good works and communion. In 1548 Melanchthon was branded a traitor by Flacius Illyricus for accepting the Leipzig *Interim*. In 1552 fierce feuds broke out over the problems of good works, the validity of the law, the ubiquity of Christ's body, and in 1558 over free will. As these venomous polemics threatened to increase the divisions among the Lutherans, the princes interfered, pressing for a common agreement. Finally in 1580, after 20 years of negotiations, 51 territories and principalities and 35 imperial cities, (i. e. two thirds of the German Lutherans) accepted the *Formula Concordiae* as a standard for the understanding of the Scriptures. For various reasons several Lutheran princes did not accept the *Formula Concordiae*.

Furthermore there were still the Calvinists, deeply divided from the Lutherans by their view of the Lord's Supper. While the Calvinist refugees in the duchies of Jülich, Cleve and Berg and in east Friesland established genuine Calvinist churches, Calvinism in the Palatinate appeared in a very modified form, without the doctrine of predestination and without an independent church organization.

Catholic Renewal

In the Catholic church, the situation had become desperate by the middle of the 16th century. In Bavaria a visitation revealed in 1558 that most priests were ignorant of the doctrines of the church, sometimes even of the number of the sacraments. Instead of books, the officials found women and children in the houses of the priests. The officials reported that most priests were drunkards, wore the dress of soldiers, and spent days and nights in inns. No wonder that their parishioners turned to Protestantism. In 1553 it was reported that the people in many towns and villages of Bavaria disregarded oral confession, extreme unction, fasting and pilgrimages, and took the sacrament under two kinds. The Catholic church in Germany lacked the strength for an inner renewal: reform had to come from abroad.

As is well known, the Council of Trent laid the basis for the long process of regeneration. Pope Gregory XIII in particular considered the fate of Catholicism in the Empire of prime importance for the whole church. A special congregation for Germany, which had been established by Pius V, was reorganized in 1573. A system of permanent nuncios was established at Vienna, Graz, Munich and Cologne. The Collegium Germanicum, founded by Pope Julius III in 1552, was enlarged by Gregory XIII in 1573. Towards the end of the 16th century, former students of the Germanicum began to play decisive roles in the empire as diocesan and suffragan bishops, as canons, vicars-general and professors of theology.

The history of the renewal of Catholicism in Germany is closely connected with the Jesuits. From their first settlements at Cologne (1544), Vienna (1551) and Ingolstadt (1556), they quickly spread all over Catholic Germany. In 1600 there were altogether 1,111 Jesuit fathers in Germany, in 25 colleges, 9 residences and 3 noviciates. Through their aggressive devotion to the church, they soon aroused the bitter and lasting hatred of the Protestants. The fact that many of the first Jesuits were foreigners, particularly Italians and Spaniards, heightened the distrust and tensions.

The Counter-Reformation in Germany had two aspects which were effective simultaneously: the extermination of Protestantism and the revival of Catholic piety. Protestant officials and guildmasters were deposed, preachers and teachers expelled. The clergy, teachers, and graduates of the universities had to render an oath on the Tridentinum. Commissions visited towns and villages. Thousands of Protestants were ordered to leave within a few weeks and had to sell their property for less than its value. In the bishopric of Würzburg they also had to pay a property tax of 2% for leaving the territory. Many small towns suffered irreparable economic losses: the town of Karlstadt in Franconia, for example, lost the immense sum of 72,233 florins when 80 burghers were

driven out in 1586. Soldiers were stationed in obstinate towns. In one town the Bishop of Würzburg himself interrogated all suspects. The few who recanted were at once taken by soldiers from the town hall to the confessional chair in the church. Protestant books were burned in great bonfires. Precise lists of communicants were drawn up, and those who did not go to communion were punished by stiff fines.

The suppression of Protestantism would not have had a lasting effect if at the same time the church had not undergone an inner regeneration. The fate of reform largely depended on the personality of the bishop or prince. For years many bishops took little action. But even if a bishop was willing to initiate reforms, his cathedral chapter might impede all efforts. In many dioceses lasting reforms were taken only by the end of the 16th or even in the 17th century. Often as a first step a synod of the clergy was called. New ordinances concerning marriage, holidays, or fasting were issued, reformed statutes for the religious orders decreed. Commissions were sent to all archdeaconries to examine every priest. Concubines were chased away, priests forbidden to go hunting etc. Whenever the Jesuits were called in, a great step towards reform had been taken. They soon founded or took over seminaries, schools and universities, educating the young generation in the new spirit. As in the Protestant Church, catechisms were widely used, particularly those of Peter Canisius, the greatest of German Jesuits. The doctrines which distinguished the church from the heretics, such as those of the supremacy of the pope or the veneration of the Virgin Mary, were particularly stressed. The Jesuits developed new methods of pastoral care, encouraging frequent confession and communion, and paid diligent attention to the sermon. They conducted missions among the people, founded lay fraternities for students, burghers and noblemen and organized spiritual exercises for the clergy. As if bent on chafing the Protestants, they revived old forms of popular piety, such as the cult of relics, pilgrimages, and gorgeous processions. Sculpture and painting were put in the service of the church, and found expression in the great blossoming of the Catholic Baroque.

Impatient with the laxity of the bishops, some princes, such as the Dukes of Bavaria, took the task of reforming the church into their own hands. In 1570 Duke Albrecht of Bavaria established a government council, the *Geistliche Rat*, which practically assumed episcopal functions. Its reform measures were backed by the full power of the government. Under Duke Maximilian, even the highest councillors had to attend mass daily. At the 'Turks' Prayer' and the Angelus bell, everybody had to kneel down, people had to get down from their horses and travellers out of their coaches. A system of spies and informers was organized which watched the religious life of all.

But in spite of all efforts, the rebirth of Catholicism in Germany took decades. In many dioceses one third of the priests still lived in concubinage in the second half of the 16th century. It was only in the early 17th century, after a new generation of priests had gone through the seminaries that the Catholic church in Germany began to recover its full life.

Minorities and Madness

The sectarian movements which had burst forth in the Reformation, did not completely disappear after 1550. The spiritual Protestant Caspar Schwenckfeld had many devotees and 'Schwenckfeldian' circles, mainly of wealthy people, existed in several cities such as Augsburg and Ulm. In the villages of the lords von Freyberg, regular Schwenckfeldian congregations were established. Though Anabaptism had been exterminated in Saxony, Franconia, Bavaria and Austria, small Anabaptist groups survived in Westphalia, east Friesland, in the area of the lower Rhine, Hesse, Alsace and Tirol. In both Swabia and the area of the Upper Rhine the Anabaptists penetrated into 230 towns and villages. But even here Anabaptism was far from being a mass movement. In Swabia only about 1,200 believers are known to us after 1550, in the area of the upper Rhine about 700. Still Anabaptism here lived on until the Thirty Years' War. Unlike the early urban congregations, most of these Anabaptists were peasants and village artisans of modest conditions. The Anabaptists were not only dogmatically divided into several groups such

The Anabaptists were one of the most persecuted sects of Europe, equally reviled by the Protestant and Catholic Churches. The 'Hutterite Anabaptist Dovecote' appears on the titlepage of a work of 1607 ridiculing their communistic beliefs.

as Swiss Brethren and Mennonites, but each congregation was almost independent. Only rarely were meetings of numerous Anabaptist leaders held to establish common doctrines and practices, as in 1557 at Strasbourg or in 1591 at Cologne. As stubborn Anabaptists were ordinarily executed in Catholic and expelled in Protestant territories, many believers emigrated to Moravia where powerful lords allowed them to settle on their lands. The Hutterites, who emerged as the strongest Anabaptist group in Moravia, established communities which practised complete communism of production and consumption. By 1589 57 Hutterite communities with approximately 17,100 believers were counted in Moravia. An elected bishop and the assembly of the leaders of the individual communities were the highest authority. Admired by numerous visitors, the Hutterites experienced their happiest development from 1565 to 1590. In 1622 they were driven out of Moravia by the victorious Habsburgs.

In spite of the intolerance of the Protestant churches, original thinking did continue. Valentin Weigel, pastor at Tschopau in Saxony (1533–1588), and Jakob Böhme, the great shoemaker-philosopher at Görlitz (1575–1624) developed profound mystical systems which were to influence the religious and philosophical thinking far into the 18th century. Influenced by medieval mysticism, Johann Arndt, Lutheran superintendent at Celle (1555–1621), wrote his famous book on the 'Four Ways of True Christianity' (1605/09) which paved the way for Pietism.

The preoccupation with spiritual matters generated one of the most gruesome madnesses in modern history: witch hunting. In Germany witch trials on a larger scale dated only from the bull *Summis desiderantes* of Innocent VIII in 1484 and the publication of

the infamous *Malleus Maleficarum*, or 'Hammer of Witches' in 1487. Luther's constant obsession with Satan may also have kindled the fears of the people. Both in Catholic and Protestant territories the persecution of witches lay in the hands of secular courts which employed the inquisitorial process. Denunciation was encouraged. The relatively mild regulations for trials of sorcerers which had been laid down in the Penal Statutes of Charles V in 1532 were disregarded. Because of its diabolic powers, witchcraft was considered an 'exceptional crime' which did not restrict the judge to ordinary procedures. Unlimited torture was used to procure statements which were considered valid confessions. All those denounced under torture as witches, were immediately arrested. Following the example of Saxony the death penalty was pronounced whether a witch had inflicted harm or not.

From the second half of the 16th century onwards, witch-trials assumed unheard-of proportions in both Catholic and Protestant areas. The persecution raged most wildly in the ecclesiastical territories of Trier, Mainz, Würzburg, Bamberg, Fulda, Ellwangen, Salzburg, in the duchy of Brunswick-Wolffenbüttel and in the Austrian possessions on the upper Rhine. In the prince-bishopric of Trier 306 witches were executed between 1587 and 1593, in the prince-bishopric of Würzburg 180 between 1627 and 1629. Among the victims we find children, peasants, burghers, burgomasters, lawyers, physicians, priests and ministers, but by far the largest number were women. Several enlightened men sought to resist the craze, of whom the earliest and most radical was the Calvinist physician Johann Weyer (1573) and the most eloquent the Jesuit Friedrich Spee (1631); but they wrote in vain: the persecutors always prevailed, at least until well after the Thirty Years' War.

Teaching, Learning and Reading

In the 16th century church and school were closely connected. Indeed, it was the Reformation which gave the great impetus to primary education. In the duchy of Württemberg 19 schools existed in towns before the Reformation in 1534. In 1559 the duchy had already 194 schools of which 156 were primary schools. In 1600, 434 schoolmasters were counted of whom 371 taught in German exclusively. In neighbouring Catholic territories of similar size, schools existed in 16 towns and 12 villages only by 1600. Though the parents were not obliged to send their children to school, the number of pupils increased steadily. Some girls also went to public schools; more however had private lessons. With the help of Luther's catechism, the children learned to read and write. Ordinarily arithmetic was not taught in schools. Most children went to school in winter only though some schools stayed open in summer too. As a rule the teacher was also sacristan and in this capacity in charge of humiliating tasks such as ringing bells, setting the clock or cleaning the church.

'Latin schools' were established by many Protestant towns. From the 'Latin school' the pupil would pass on to the *paedagogium* which offered the final linguistic preparation for the university. In many Protestant territories, the governments also established residential schools in former monasteries where gifted boys received free board and instruction on condition that later they would enter the service of church or state. The most famous schools of this type were the three 'Princes' Schools' in Saxony and the four 'Monastery Schools' in Württemberg. In 1570 altogether 219 boys were in these schools in Württemberg. While in Saxony the boys could later enter the legal or medical professions, in Württemberg the 'Monastery Schools' were reserved for future ministers. The academic gymnasia such as those at Strasbourg or Altdorf or the excellent Calvinist schools at Herborn and Burgsteinfurt added to their curricula courses in philosophy or even law and medicine.

The foremost aim of instruction was to instill *sapiens et eloquens pietas* as Johann Sturm, the great educator of Strasbourg, called it. The ability to write and speak Latin fluently was considered the absolute prerequisite for further studies. Subjects such as history or geography were not taught but picked up by reading the ancients. However all educators agreed that the learning of Latin constituted a terrible burden, postponing the study of the arts for many years. Melanchthon himself was aware of the heathen

By some strange paradox, the persecution of witches reached its height in Europe just at the time when modern science was beginning. In Germany it assumed nightmare proportions. This woodcut shows a wholesale burning of witches in 1555.

A German burgher and his wife at home, with their numerous offspring. Middle-class prosperity had increased to such a degree that critics were complaining of luxury and extravagance. This family has a maidservant to look after the children.

character of ancient literature. But the humanistic tradition was still strong enough to demand that the theologian express himself in classical Latin.

The excellent Jesuit schools and colleges offered the same type of grammatical-rhetorical education. According to the *Ratio Studiorum* of 1599, six years of training in languages were followed by a three years' course in philosophy, and in case of future priests, by a three years' study of theology. The Jesuits carefully appealed to the student's honour, organizing frequent competitions, disputations and declamations. Above all, the Jesuit schools distinguished themselves through their dramatic performances.

The number of German universities rose from 14 in 1517 to 25 in 1618. Four more were founded in the following five years. Of these 29 universities, 17 were situated in Protestant and 12 in Catholic territories. The leading Lutheran universities were Wittenberg and Rostock. In almost all Catholic universities the Jesuits eventually gained control of the faculties of philosophy and theology. Many of these universities did not have more than 400 to 500 students. However Wittenberg claimed between 1,800 and 2,000 students. The proliferation of universities was due to the religious divisions and to the ambition of the princes who wished to train their future officials in their own universities. All that was required to found a university were several thousand florins for salaries and scholarships and the buildings of a large monastery. A few universities such as Heidelberg retained an international flavour, one third of its students being non-German speaking foreigners: in the 1570s they were predominantly Walloons, Dutchmen and Frenchmen, after 1600 east Europeans. Owing to the demand for pastors and officials, the faculties of theology and law greatly increased, while that of medicine attracted few students only.

The government which had founded the university also issued its statutes and supervised the administration and the teaching. As in the preceding centuries, the student had to pass through the faculty of philosophy before entering the faculty of theology, law or medicine. The methods of teaching were also traditional: the lecture and the weekly disputation. There was little room for independent thinking either in Protestant or Catholic universities. The highest truths in religion, philosophy and science had been established. All the professor had to do was to explain them. If a professor taught divergent views, he was punished and dismissed. In spite of his epochal discoveries, the great astronomer Johannes Kepler was refused a chair at the Lutheran university of Tübingen in 1611 because he leaned towards the Calvinist doctrine of the communion. In the end, however, the dogmatic divisions among the Protestant territories offered more possibilities for independent

thinking than the Catholic universities, controlled by the Jesuits.

Germany retained the leading position in the world of book printing and publishing during our period. While up to 1589 rarely more than 500 books were annually printed in Germany, the number rose to 1,059 in 1600 and 1,780 in 1613: a figure which was not reached again until 150 years later. It was during this time that Frankfurt and Leipzig rose to eminence. In 1613 Frankfurt had altogether 21 publishing and 8 printing houses, publishing and printing having become separate enterprises since the second half of the 16th century. Between 1565 and 1630 legal, medical and scientific literature formed the outstanding branches of publishing at Frankfurt. Frankfurt publishers, such as Hieronymus Feyerabend distinguished themselves by bringing out a great number of books of popular interest, such as chronicles, biographies, works of geography, arithmetic books, sample books for sewing and embroidery, cook-books, herbals and popular literature such as Reineke Fuchs. Great artists such as Hans Sebald Beham, Jost Amman or Hans Burgkmaier were regularly employed by the publishers, ornamenting about 200 books with thousands of marvellous wood cuts on practically all aspects of German society.

Through its fairs, Frankfurt became the centre of the international book trade between 1560 and 1630. 170 to 200 visitors from 72 to 85 cities of the whole of Europe visited the two annual book fairs. After an Augsburg book dealer had published a catalogue of books offered at the fair in 1564, other publishers followed his example. In 1598 the city of Frankfurt published the first official catalogue which was to appear regularly for 150 years, forming the basis of the international book trade. The number of books announced rose from 550 in 1565 to 1,757 in 1618. Of 21,941 books announced between 1564 and 1600, 65% were in Latin, 30% in German, the rest in French, Italian and Spanish. The subjects covered most were theology, jurisprudence and medicine.

Up to 1590 three times as many books were published in the south and west as in the north of Germany. From 1590 on, however, book publishing in the north increased rapidly, reaching 44% of all books published in the decade before the Thirty Years' War. Between 1611 and 1620 Leipzig brought out annually 225 items on the average, followed by Frankfurt with 178, Cologne 140, Wittenberg 78, Augsburg 42, Strasbourg 38, Magdeburg 33, Rostock 30 and Nuremberg 27. The preponderance of Protestant Germany is evident. Of course the great mass of slanderous lampoons, libellous pamphlets, satirical poems and squibs which flooded Germany were never listed in the catalogues. They were printed clandestinely and sold by hawkers in market places, in taverns and at the gates of colleges.

Germany was also leading in a completely new field, modern journalism. From the early 16th century on, numerous reports on political events, *Zeitungen* as they were called, had appeared. Up to 1599, 877 are known. In 1575 Augustus of Saxony together with other princes established a regular exchange of reports from agents abroad. More successful was the commercial venture of Michael Eytzinger who from 1580 to 1583 reported on the conflict between the Protestants and the Spaniards at Aachen and in the prince-bishopric of Cologne. In 1597 one Samuel Dilbaum organized a monthly newspaper at Augsburg. Shortly before 1609 Johann Carolus at Strasbourg started publishing weekly reports in quarto format which contained news from not less than 17 European cities. Vienna had such a newspaper in 1610, Frankfurt in 1615, Berlin in 1617. Other Protestant cities quickly followed. Soon the newspaper affected daily life. The poet Fischart already ridiculed the 'newspaper believing public' and its craving for news. The schoolmasters also began to fulminate against parents who neglected the education of their children and ran to book-shops and drinking places in order to read newspapers: 'this they think is *summum necessarium*, the most needful thing'.

The Makers of Manners

What actually was the daily life of the Germans in this period? Let us first look at the upper classes. Hundreds of castles and palaces were built by princes and noblemen in the fashionable Italian style all over Germany: at Dresden, Wismar, Heidelberg and other towns. The furniture in these palaces, the cabinets, tiled stoves, wood panelling, chandeliers, the mirrors of Venetian glass and the tapestry were of exquisite craftsmanship. The gardens were often divided into geometrical patterns, and ornamented with arcades, mazes, statues of marble, variegated flower-beds, fountains, grottos, ponds and aviaries. In 1559 the first lemon, orange and citron trees were planted at Stuttgart. In 1562 the imperial ambassador at Constantinople brought lilac and gilly-flower to Vienna.

Aspiring to assert their dignity, many princes kept stately courts with hundreds of carabineers and bodyguards, with trumpeters, lute and guitar players, pipers, conjurers and fools whom they dressed now in green, now in red, grey or blue. Some young princes attended a university or travelled to France or Italy. However, sophisticated princes like Moritz of Saxony or Heinrich Julius of Brunswick, who wrote plays for the stage, were exceptions: the chief pastime of most princes was the hunt. Albrecht of Bavaria proudly recorded that on 1,852 hunting expeditions between 1555 and 1579 he had slain with his own hands 2,779 stags, 1,784 does, 220 fawns, 150 foxes, 50 hares, 525 wild boars, 2 bears and 23 squirrels. For many princes drinking was the favourite entertainment. Regular drinking orders were founded. An unbelievable extravagance was displayed at princely weddings which often lasted eight to ten days. At a wedding at Liegnitz in 1587 the following amount of meat was consumed: 54 Polish oxen, 6 cows, 97 goats, 267 sheep, 55 calves, 16 pigs, 46 sucking pigs etc. The quantities of beer and wine consumed were equally astounding. Great ingenuity was employed in preparing the dishes. At a great banquet at Stuttgart in 1603, 90 different dishes were served: 'pasties of most ingenious designs and all colours of the rainbow; some represented birds, swans, cranes, standing upright and stretching their necks forward, and many-coloured peacocks contemplating themselves in their own glasses'. On festive occasions there were prize fights between wild animals, tournaments, prize shootings, ring-runnings, sleigh rides, masquerades, ballets, dances, plays and pantomines. Often the festivities ended with dazzling displays of fireworks at which likenesses of the pope, the sultan or the Tsar of Russia were burned.

Towards the end of the 16th century, Spanish influence receded and French language, dress and manners became fashionable. The princes at Heidelberg were the first to write their letters and diaries in French. French dictionaries, grammars, and translations of French novels appeared in growing numbers. Several courts were graced by great composers, such as Munich by Orlando di Lasso and Dresden by Heinrich Schütz. Frequently Italian and Dutch artists worked for princes and art collections were established. In the hope of meeting their immense expenses, many princes employed alchemists who offered to transmute base metal into gold.

Three details from a print published in 1587 showing peasant life. It is a feast day. Outside an inn the local people eat, drink, fight and vomit.

The German nobility showed great differences in culture and living standards. Accompanied by a 'hofmeister', the young nobleman in Austria would attend a Latin school, and then a Protestant or Catholic university. Many Austrian nobles studied law at Padua, Bologna or Siena. Often the stay in Italy was part of the tour through southern Europe, France, the Netherlands and England, the *nobilis et erudita peregrinatio*. The nobleman who entered the service of the Habsburgs was expected to know Spanish, Italian and French. The libraries of the Austrian rural nobility covered an amazing range of interests: theology, humanistic, historical and legal studies, occult and natural sciences, mathematics, agriculture, ancient literature and modern poetry and novels. Hans Ludwig von Küfstein became known through his fine translations of Spanish and Italian prose and poetry. We owe to these cultivated gentlemen some of the most fascinating descriptions of Russia and the Ottoman empire in the 16th century.

Several noblemen in south and west Germany also showed a high level of culture. All of them endeavoured to keep up their social distinction—in dress, residence, gait, speech, pew in church and burial. But living on rents and interest, the nobility was affected by the rising inflation. Their impregnable castles on mountains and in woods were often very narrow within, crowded with stalls for the cattle. Hutten already complained of the nobleman's rural delights, the continuous bleating of the sheep, the lowing of the cattle, the dung and barking of hordes of dogs, the shouts of the workers in the fields, the quarrels between the retainers, the squeaks of barrows and wagons and the howling of wolves at night. Having lost their military and political position, some families showed signs of degeneracy. The young nobles, Richard von Solms wrote, have no other occupation than to sleep until high noon, loaf around the rest of the day, flirt with the women, play with dogs, and then drink half through the night. Next to this, they think of nothing but their dress. Indeed, extravagancy was considered the chief cause of the insolvency of the nobility. Many young noblemen entered the service of princes, but occasionally their behaviour left much to be desired. One court ordinance forbade them to relieve themselves in front of ladies, to defile rooms and corridors with 'urine and other dirt' to throw bones and pour beer on each other. But it is only fair to add that far into the 18th century, many able administrators came from the ranks of the nobility.

Burghers at Home

Even the burghers were affected by the luxury of the time. In 1565 one preacher complained of the many changes of fashion during the last fifty years, the varieties of chains, cloaks, mantles, furs, ruffles, gowns, caps, collars, hats, boots and jackets. Trunkhose, formerly the dress of soldiers, were very fashionable for a while. The pastors were greatly disturbed by the luxury in women's dresses. They also thundered against bleached hair, wigs, naked arms and throats, the use of cosmetics, painted brows, eyes, cheeks and lips. In vain the authorities endeavoured to limit by law what sort of dress each social order, the burgomasters, the rich merchants, the artisans and the wage earners were allowed to wear. Stern critics complained that one could no longer distinguish the maidservant from the burgher's daughter.

Of course women in the 16th century had more to mind than their looks. The wives of burghers and the ladies of the nobility alike were in charge of the minute details of the household, collecting recipes and supervising the kitchen. While bread was bought, fine pastry was baked at home. The housewife had to take care of the preserving of fruit, the pickling of meat, the smoking of ham and sides of bacon. Pigs had to be butchered. Tallow candles were dipped or moulded. While all perfumed soaps were bought, the ordinary white soap was made at home. All burgher women did fine needle work such as embroidery, knitting and bobbinet work. Often there were many children. Care

was taken to educate the children in music from their early childhood on.

Many burghers kept a garden with a *Lusthaus* outside the city. The popularity of the bath houses seems to have declined owing to the danger of contagious diseases, particularly syphilis. As physical exercise for burghers the Tyrolese physician Guarinonius recommended fencing, jumping, wrestling, carrying of loads, cutting wood, threshing, throwing stones, and climbing mountains. There was a variety of ball games both for men and women. Sleigh rides were an old pastime. Theatrical performances, especially by English companies, became very popular. In spite of the pastors, dancing was one of the main enjoyments of the time. Stern preachers were also alarmed by the rising interest in novels. Girls who had hardly learned to read, devoured seductive novels such as *Tristán* from Spain or *Lancelot* from France. Among the burghers chess, checkers, backgammon, card playing and gambling at dice remained favourites.

The ordinary food of the burgher was simple: cabbage, turnips, beans, beef, veal and pork, chicken, geese, fish, roast venison, barley, groats and oatmeal porridge, and as desert cheese and fruit. But at weddings, childbirth, or christenings, great extravagance was displayed. The authorities finally interfered by limiting the number of guests and quantities of food for each social class. The 16th century German knew many opportunities for convivial gatherings: the host of feastdays, carnivals, fairs, shooting matches, the harvest goose, the new wine, the welcome, the good-bye etc. Heavy drinking was greatly encouraged by the custom of standing drinks. While wine and beer still dominated, brandy slowly became popular. The preachers warned that 'bestial eating and drinking' ruined the health and impaired potency. Guarinonius lamented in 1610 that the majority of people did not live beyond thirty or forty. However that may be, famous spas such as Gastein, Wildbad, Wiesbaden or Ems were greatly frequented. At that time already, games of chance were fashionable and morality light at the spas.

Oddly enough, we know little yet of the daily life of the most numerous class, the peasants. In spite of all sympathy, Sebastian Franck called them savage, cunning and untamed. Sebastian Münster wrote in 1588 that together with their servants and animals they lived lonely in miserable huts of mud and wood, with no floors but the damp earth, covered only with straw. Their food, he said, was black rye bread, oatmeal porridge or boiled peas and lentils, water and whey their daily beverages. A coarse smock, a pair of shoes and a felt hat made their attire. But there were many regional differences.

A scourge of the peasants was the hunting passion of the princes. Villagers near the hunting reserves were forbidden to fence in their fields or drive away bears, wolves and wild boars even with small dogs. During the hunt, the peasants suffered great damage from the troops of horses galloping across their fields. The peasant himself had to attend the hunt with carts and horses, carrying all the hunting paraphernalia forwards and backwards, leading along the hounds, hewing roads and the like. Though there was great abundance of wild animals in the forests, the peasants were forbidden to hunt themselves. In many territories banishment or even capital punishment was pronounced on those caught hunting in the game reserves.

Numerous wood engravings tell us that at the weddings or carnivals the peasants made good for the hardships they suffered. There we see those uncouth figures as they stuff themselves, drink from huge mugs, vomit under the table, fondle their women, hop around to peasant tunes and beat each other up in big brawls.

In general all too little is known yet of Germany between 1555 and 1618. However all evidence suggests that the pale picture of a stagnating society is one-sided. Germany around 1600 had a rich and varied, if earthy culture. But it is true that this civilization sank into ashes once the soldiers took over in 1618.

V THIRTY YEARS' WAR

The European Civil War

H. G. KOENIGSBERGER

'They came marching, this day then that, one from sunrise the other from sunset, he from south and they from north, and have wanted to contain and assuage the fire, but only increased its fury.'

PASTOR JOHANN GEORG DORSCH, of Bad Peterstal, Black Forest,
preaching on the occasion of the Peace of Westphalia.

'I was born in war',

said one of the women who had followed the armies in 1648; 'I have no home, no country and no friends—war is all my wealth and now where shall I go?' Her regret at the ending of the war was her own, but in another sense she spoke for a whole generation. No one born in Germany after about 1610 knew what peace was like. Few could remember how the war had started or why it was being fought; they knew only that year after year the great straggling armies marched and countermarched across their land, burning, pillaging and destroying, and that hunger and disease killed thousands more than the guns.

The war began with the revolt of the Protestant Bohemians against their king, the Catholic Holy Roman Emperor, Ferdinand II. Ferdinand called on his Habsburg and Wittelsbach cousins, the King of Spain and the Duke of Bavaria, to aid him. The revolt was crushed. But the other Protestant powers, however tardy in their aid to Bohemia, could not allow Austria to be totally dominant. Half-heartedly and inefficiently, they continued the war. When the Twelve Years' Truce between Spain and the United Provinces ended in 1621 they found natural friends in the Dutch. England sympathized. So did Denmark, whose King, Christian IV, invaded the imperial lands in Saxony in 1625, but was routed by Tilly and driven back.

Again the Protestant powers rallied in defeat and a new champion emerged—the warrior king Gustavus Adolphus of Sweden. At first brilliantly successful, hailed as a saviour by some, hampered and betrayed by others, Gustavus finally met disaster at Lützen. Once again the Emperor seemed invincibly in the ascendent. Once again, another power could not allow the victory. This time it was France who intervened. Richelieu, anti-Protestant at home, was even more anti-Habsburg abroad. In May 1635 he declared war on Spain. Fighting spread to the soil of France and then to Italy. Almost every state in Europe was now ranged on one side or the other; almost every frontier was a potential battlefield. The quarrel was no longer Germany's. Exhausted and bleeding, it could do nothing but wait for the great powers to settle its destiny. It waited another thirteen years.

The sufferings of this long war for the civilian population were aggravated by the way the armies operated. Most soldiers were mercenaries, serving a particular commander for pay. If he, or his employer, had no funds, they had to live off the country. Troop movements were often dictated not by strategy but simply by the necessity of finding fresh lands to plunder. The best generals were those who could hold the biggest army together at the least expense. Wallenstein was a genius at such logistics, but it tended to create a situation that no one could control. The armies were paid to make war; they went on making war in order to be paid.

The detail shown opposite is from a painting by Philips Wouwerman (himself a true child of the war—he was born in 1618) showing a mêlée of cavalry and infantry. Wouwerman spares us the horrors which Callot records with such terrible realism, but he does convey some sense of the frenzy of a conflict that had degenerated into a weary and hopeless slaughter—a conflict whose lasting monument is that sardonic masterpiece of the mock-heroic, *Simplicius Simplicissimus.* . Here is how Grimmelshausen, in his measured and reasonable words, describes the career of the mercenaries. 'Nothing but hurting and harming and being in their turn hurt and harmed, this was their whole purpose and existence. From this nothing could divert them—not winter or summer, snow or ice, heat or cold, wind or rain, mountain or valley, swamp or desert, ditches, ramparts, water, fire . . . . or the very fear of eternal damnation itself. At this task they laboured until at last, in battles, sieges, assaults, campaigns, or even in their winter quarters, which is the soldiers' paradise, one by one they died, perished and rotted.'

On May 22nd 1618 a group of Protestant Bohemian noblemen, wishing to bring to a climax their quarrel with the Emperor over their religious and constitutional rights, seized two of the imperial governors, Martinitz and Slavata, and threw them out of the high window of the Hradčany Palace at Prague. For good measure, their secretary was flung after them. The famous 'defenestration' was a fiasco since none of the three was even seriously hurt, but the flame of revolt was alight.

The Siege of Magdeburg in May 1631 (*above*) and its frightful sack by the imperial troops of Tilly's army, is one of the most barbarous incidents of the war. Practically the whole town was destroyed by fire and 24,000 men, women and children are said to have died.

Wallenstein was murdered in 1634 when Ferdinand became convinced that he was plotting against him. Wallenstein, roused from sleep, was killed by an English captain, Walter Devereux. His body was dragged from his bedroom 'by the heels, his head knocking upon every stair'.

The effects of the war on the ordinary people of Germany can be glimpsed in the writings and illustrations of the time. One of Callot's etchings (*above*) shows a group of discharged mercenaries dying at the roadside or begging their way through the streets. Grimmelshausen has a vivid description of one such old comrade: 'A man came limping into the room on a stick. He had a bandage round his head, his arm was in a sling and he was dressed in such wretched rags that I would not have given a penny for them. As soon as the innkeeper saw him he showed him the door, for he stank abominably and was so overrun with fleas that you could have peopled a fair-sized village with them.' *Below left:* soldiers loot and burn a village while the inhabitants flee, a scene that must have been repeated many times. *Below right:* unemployed mercenaries set upon a band of travellers. Behind a tree, the figure of death mockingly points to an hour-glass.

The princes of Germany were faced with a series of difficult decisions. Those who tried to take advantage of the situation were often those who miscalculated most disastrously. Many of the smaller powers, following the lead of John George of Saxony, were ready enough to change sides when this would save their own states from the worst effects of the war. On the Catholic side the leading personalities were the Habsburg Emperor Ferdinand II and Maximilian of Bavaria. **Ferdinand** (*above left*), elected as the Bohemian revolt broke out, devoted his whole reign to the war but victory eluded him. Tilly, the only effective general he could trust, died in 1632, after suffering crushing defeats by Gustavus Adolphus. Wallenstein seemed to be as dangerous a friend as any foe. Even Ferdinand's greatest success, the Peace of Prague in 1635, only brought upon him the lasting opposition of France. He died in 1637, his difficulties no nearer to solution. **Maximilian** of Bavaria (*above right*), leader of the Catholic League, was a prince whose support was vital to Ferdinand. It was gained by lavish payment in money and the promise of Frederick's lands and electoral title when the revolt was over. His jealousy of Wallenstein harmed the imperial cause, and led to his own country being overrun by the Swedes, but at the end of the war Maximilian was one of the few who emerged with profit. He died three years afterwards in 1651, at the age of seventy-eight.

The **Protestant leaders** were motivated by a variety of considerations. **Christian IV** of Denmark (*above*), for reasons of personal and national aggrandizement rather than religious fervour, led a Protestant attack on the Empire in 1625. But the failure of promised English subsidies and the death of his two strongest supporters, Mansfeld and Christian of Brunswick, left him dependent on his own limited powers of generalship. He was routed at Lutter in 1626 and by the peace of Lübeck, three years later, had to renounce all further claims to intervene in German affairs. In 1643 he challenged Swedish supremacy in the Baltic and was again completely defeated. **Gustavus Adolphus** of Sweden (*above right*) came near to succeeding where Christian had failed. He took his army – the most efficient in Europe since its nucleus was conscript instead of mercenary – into Germany in 1630 and in spite of the mistrust of many northern princes succeeded, by his brilliant victory at Breitenfeld, in becoming acknowledged leader of the Protestant cause. Sweden's dominance, however, lasted less than three years. In November 1632 Gustavus was killed at Lützen and although his forces were victorious he was irreplaceable. Gustavus is a figure of great fascination, quite apart from his military prowess. In his own kingdom he initiated a host of reforms, constitutional and legal, promoted education and developed the country's economic resources. He took a lively interest in a whole range of intellectual topics, from navigation to the decipherment of runes. **Frederick V**, Elector Palatine (*right*), was twenty-seven when the rebels at Prague offered him the crown. For a year 'the Winter King' enjoyed the empty honours of royalty. In November 1620 his forces were defeated at the Battle of the White Mountain and he lost both his new kingdom and his ancestral estates of the Palatinate.

Queen Christina was only six years old when her father, Gustavus Adolphus, was killed. She depended heavily upon her Chancellor, Count Oxenstierna, until his death in 1654, when she abdicated.

Axel Oxenstierna, described by Richelieu as 'an inexhaustible fountain of sagacious counsel', acted as regent during Christina's minority, though temperamentally they were widely different.

The fortunes of Sweden became closely tied to the war in Germany through the expansionist policy of Gustavus Adolphus, who was killed on the field of Lützen (*right*) leading a cavalry charge. Two years later the Swedish army was crushed at Nordlingen. Oxenstierna, however, made the best of the situation by improving his alliance with Richelieu and the Swedish armies continued to win tactical victories in Germany. In 1654 Oxenstierna died; Christina abdicated, became a Catholic and retired to Rome where she lived until 1689.

The Royal Palace at Stockholm (*left*), which in the time of Gustavus Adolphus and Christina was a rambling edifice of various dates. It was destroyed by fire in 1697, and rebuilt in the 18th century.

The armaments industry was developed, under Gustavus, by Netherlanders, until it was the most efficient in Europe. This view (*below left*) shows the Julitabroeck foundry.

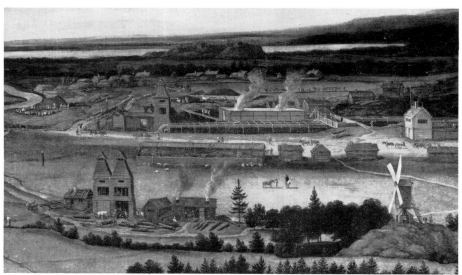

Christina's successor was her cousin Charles Gustavus, who renewed traditional Swedish policy by invading Poland and Denmark. In 1657, campaigning in Poland, he was surprised by a Danish attack in his rear, marched his army across the frozen water of the Little Belt to Zealand and beat them at the battle of Ifverös (*right*).

The camp became the setting for thousands of lives – not only of soldiers but also of the hordes of civilians who lived off them. In the scene on the *right*, by Sebastian Vrancx, bodies of pikemen and cavalry in armour prepare to move off in formation. All around reigns the bustle and business of the non-combatant population: wagons, packhorses, women with their children, vendors of meat, vegetables and every commodity – the world of Simplicius and of Mother Courage.

A Dutch officer, his bed pitched inside an occupied mansion, dictates a letter while the messenger waits, booted and spurred. *Right:* ill-clad and hungry Spanish troops gather for the winter siege of Aire-sur-la-Lys, on the borders of France and Flanders – an incident in the long struggle between Richelieu and the Habsburgs. The town fell on December 7th 1641.

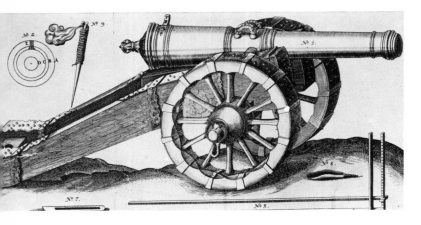

'**The Harquebusier**' (*left*), according to Cruso, a contemporary author, 'was first invented in France, in the time of the wars in Piedmont'. The amount of armour varied. The 'harquebus' or carbine could only be fired at lengthy intervals.

Artillery made enormous progress during the Thirty Years' War, developing from a doubtful auxiliary to an indispensable part of warfare. Gustavus Adolphus made himself an expert on it. The cannon shown here (*left*) is of a kind used at the beginning of the war. Military organization largely depended on the practice of individual commanders, but increasingly such matters as equipment, exercises and tactics tended to become standardized.

'**The Cuirassiers**' says Melzo, another military writer, 'although inferior to the lancers, should also be led by men of rank and valour' (*lower left*). They wore armour similar to that of the lancers but carried two pistols in holsters on either side of the saddle instead of a lance.

'**The Lancer**' wrote Cruso, 'should be a man of quality, able to pay for his own troops.' The lancer shown here (*bottom left*) is wearing half-armour (without greaves) although it was often thought necessary to his dignity that he should have full armour.

Troops rally from their billets as an approaching enemy is sighted (*below*). Advance guards place themselves outside the town. Trumpeters blow the call to arms. Lancers assemble in the square, collecting their lances from where they are stacked against one of the buildings.

The Pikeman usually kept close in battle to the Musketeer in order to defend him while he reloaded. Here the Pikeman braces his pike against his foot and draws his sword. Pikemen still formed a large part of every army.

The Musketeer supports the heavy barrel of his gun on a stand; at his side he carries a powder flask for priming and bandolier holding separate charges of powder. He is instructed to take the bullets from 'his mouth, or wherever he normally keeps them'.

The Caliverman was employed in skirmishes rather than pitched battles. A Dutch manual tells how 'he shall blow of the match speedily and well, and with the two forefingers cover the pan lid for the sparks'.

The end came at last when both sides had reached the point of exhaustion. This commemorative painting shows the scene in the Rathaus of Münster on May 15th 1648 when the delegates swore the oath of ratification to the Treaty of Münster. The men with their hands raised are Netherlands representatives. On the other side of the table, holding a copy of the oath, their hands on a Bible, are the plenipotentiaries of Spain with (on the right of the picture) their chaplain, in a black cloak, and secretary, in red. The room had been decorated with foliage and flowers for the occasion. The treaty was read aloud, first in French, then in Dutch. Then both groups of delegates swore the oath in turn (Ter Borch represents them as swearing simultaneously) and the Spaniards kissed the crucifix.

The European Civil War

H. G. KOENIGSBERGER

Under the flag of war the sun is immersed in clouds, angels devastate crops and vines, and death strides among men; a broadside of 1627.

IN THE SPRING of 1618 Europe was at peace. There was nothing usual about this. War was endemic in European society. Men deplored it and would blame those responsible for breaking the peace, although they rarely agreed on the identity of the culprit. A particular war, men agreed, might have been avoided; but war as such seemed to be part of the natural order. Princes and their juristically schooled advisers, happily confirmed in their own feelings by the dazzling logic of Bodin's theory of sovereignty, argued that all sovereign states had the right to wage war by virtue of this very sovereignty. It seemed, moreover, that warfare had many moral and practical virtues. The duc de Rohan voiced a common opinion when he wrote that external wars occupied ambitious and unquiet spirits, banished luxury, made a people warlike, increased its reputation among its neighbours and was the best means of preventing civil wars.

Rohan, the leader of the Huguenots in a succession of civil wars, knew what he was talking about. But civil wars had their own justifications: the right of resistance to tyranny. This classical concept, which had never completely died in European thought, had received a new and sharp edge in the religious wars of the 16th century. The rulers of that century had done their best to maintain the religious unity of their countries; but, outside Spain and Italy, they had been singularly unsuccessful. In England and France, in the United Provinces and the Swiss Confederation, in the Empire, in Poland and in Hungary, heterodoxy had obstinately persisted and was constantly threatening to turn political and constitutional disputes into civil wars, fought for the very best of Christian reasons.

Not all those who took up arms felt that they needed a Bodinian or a Christian justification. Oppression by the local nobility or royal officials, or just sheer misery, were sufficient reasons for repeated armed uprisings by French, Austrian and Swedish peasants, even though, on occasion, they too were not averse from quoting the Bible to justify themselves. Armed robbery on land and piracy at sea were ubiquitous and often organized under the most august auspices. Dutch and English pirates, encouraged by their governments, systematically preyed on Spanish and Portuguese shipping. The king of Spain retaliated by licensing the Dunkirk privateers. Both this ruler and the emperor set the Uskoks, a piratical frontier community on the coast of Dalmatia, to attack Venetian shipping. The Barbary pirates of North Africa hunted Christian ships from the eastern Mediterranean to the shores of Iceland and forced the European maritime powers to conclude ignominious, and far from effective, treaties to safeguard their shipping. Out on the oceans and in the overseas colonies the peace treaties of the European powers were all but completely disregarded; and practically every one thought it perfectly proper to hunt for Negro slaves in West Africa or to pay local chieftains for doing so. The ethos of the European upper classes was essentially military. The majority of young noblemen received a military education, either privately or in one of the military academies which were just beginning to be popular. The more enterprising would learn the art of war in the service of a well-known general. A large proportion of the high officers of the first half of the Thirty Years' War had been trained in the 'schools' of Spinola or Maurice of Nassau.

Nevertheless, for two decades the forces of peace had been in the ascendant. One after another the great wars had been settled: between Spain and France in 1598; between Spain and England in 1604; the emperor and the sultan concluded a truce in 1606, and Spain and the United Provinces another, for twelve years, in 1609; Denmark and Sweden made peace in 1613; Sweden and Russia in 1617. By the spring of 1618 the Swedes and the Poles were on the point of arranging a truce and so were the Poles and the Russians. Men were aware that these treaties did not settle all the disputes which had previously led their signatories into war; but they were to look back with regret to the good years before 1618. All the evils which followed seemed to arise directly from the Bohemian revolt. Contemporaries did not think that this event was a sufficient explanation for the great war; but most of them were agreed that this was when it started.

The Bohemian Revolt

The Defenestration of Prague, when two royal governors of Bohemia and their secretary were thrown out of a seventy-foot high window of the Hradčany Palace on 23 May 1618, was the result of a genuine conspiracy and confirmed those who viewed all history and politics in terms of conspiracies. Count Thurn and his friends who were responsible for the act wanted to prevent any possible reconciliation between the king and the Bohemian estates. It was, however, an ominous sign that the affair was half bungled from the start. The three victims unaccountably escaped with their lives. Tradition has it that they fell on a refuse or dung heap. The secretary was compensated for his harrowing experience with the title of Freiherr von Hohenfall—Lord of the High Jump. An element of the grotesque was to remain a characteristic of the Bohemian rebellion until it finally turned to tragedy.

But from the beginning it was more than a conspiracy. Kepler had predicted in his prognostic calendar for 1618—hackwork with which he tried to earn money for his serious astronomical and astrological studies—that in May there would be much trouble in places where there was great political liberty. The likelihood of trouble, though not of course the date, was not difficult to prognosticate. Ferdinand, the nephew of the old Habsburg emperor Matthias, who had recently been 'elected' king of Bohemia, had shown his intentions twenty years earlier, as duke of Styria. A former student at the Jesuit university of Ingolstadt, this amiable, music-loving, spendthrift and indigent mediocrity was as determined to fulfil his duty to God, as a prince and a true Catholic, as ever his elder cousin, Philip II of Spain, had been. He had taken his coronation oath to observe the liberties of his subjects; but these liberties, he said, had nothing to do with religion. He had simply banished the Protestant leaders of the Styrian estates and had replaced them with his own officials. Counter-Reformation and political absolutism could clearly be made to work hand in hand. When they encountered the alliance of Protestantism and anti-absolutist estates no compromise was likely to last for long. Nor was it possible to isolate the Bohemian conflict, as Ferdinand had successfully done in Styria. Some of the Calvinist Bohemian magnates had for years been in touch with other Calvinist leaders: with Erasmus von Tschernembl, the leader of the Upper Austrian estates; with Charles Žerotin, the governor of Moravia; with Bethlen Gabor, the Calvinist prince of Transylvania who, with encouragement from his overlord, the sultan, was manoeuvering for the crown of Hungary; above all with Christian of Anhalt, the ambitious minister of the elector Frederick V of the Palatinate. It seemed a formidable combination. Frederick was the nephew of Maurice of Nassau and the son-in-law of James I. No one knew how far family and religious sentiment might not commit the two great Protestant powers. If Frederick could be substituted for Ferdinand as king of Bohemia, there would be a Protestant majority in the electoral college, perhaps a Protestant emperor. The Austrian Habsburgs would be left powerless, petty princes of three or four Alpine duchies whose estates would prescribe their policies. Spain might then well find it impossible to hold northern Italy and the Netherlands.

Such seemed to be the potential escalation of disasters as it presented itself to Ferdinand and to Oñate, the Spanish ambassador in Vienna. In July 1618 they carried through a *coup d'état* by arresting Cardinal Khlesl, the leader of the old emperor Matthias's peace party. All compromise was now ruled out.

The pamphleteers were first in the field. Scioppius (Kaspar Schoppe) admonished the emperor to exercise vengeance against heretic and rebellious princes and to exterminate the inhabitants of cities that had changed their religion, 'even the very children and infants', so that they should not lose their eternal life. The Protestants, with as yet comfortable shudders, quoted Scioppius' Latin in German translation and then replied in kind, urging the Christian duty to resist tyranny. In the autumn of 1618, fighting started in Bohemia. But as yet there were few soldiers; the government in Vienna had not prepared for war. The Bohemians had their chance. But this was no repetition of the Hussite wars of two hundred years before, when the fight for religious and political freedom had found an echo in all classes. Now, the German-Czech nobility had no use for the peasants as allies and very little for the towns, except to get money from them. Even Tschernembl, the friend of the Huguenot intellectuals, Hotman and Duplessis-Mornay, and the one leader of the rebellion with a grasp of the political realities of the situation, was a prisoner of his aristocratic preconceptions and his rigid Calvinist thinking about the role of the lower magistrates in resistance to tyranny. Thus the social basis of the rebellion remained disastrously narrow, and its leaders never managed to shake off the deadly flavour of mere conspiracy. Anhalt dangled election to the Bohemian throne before the romantic eyes of Charles Emmanuel of Savoy and persuaded that inveterate old hunter of elusive crowns to pay for an army for the Bohemians to be led by the Catholic mercenary leader, Count Ernest of Mansfeld. Anhalt then double-crossed Savoy and persuaded the Bohemians to elect his master, Frederick V. This happened on 27 August 1619. A day later the electors at Frankfurt, ignorant of events at Prague, made their choice of a new emperor (Matthias having died earlier in the year). The Protestants, including Frederick, unable to reach agreement among themselves, voted for Ferdinand. Ferdinand, still acting as king of Bohemia, voted for himself. Only later did Frederick learn of the Bohemian offer and, after a period of hesitation, accept it.

The Catholic Counter-Stroke

During the following year, Anhalt's light-hearted cleverness and the Bohemian nobility's political and military incompetence frittered away their remaining opportunities. Only in the summer of 1620 was the Catholic party ready for its counter-stroke. Maximilian of Bavaria had reorganized the League of the Catholic Princes of Germany. Ferdinand had to pledge him Upper Austria for his campaign expenses and, secretly, promise to transfer to him the Upper Palatinate and Frederick's electoral dignity. Spain mobilized its army in the Netherlands to attack the Rhine Palatinate. Sigismund III of Poland, worried by the prospect of a Hungarian-Bohemian Protestant alliance, sent a corps of Cos-

sacks. Even Pope Paul V, though rarely inclined to look beyond Italy, sent money to Munich and Vienna. John George of Saxony was promised Lusatia for preferring loyalty to the emperor to loyalty to his Bohemian neighbours and co-religionists. The government of Louis XIII, hoping to preserve peace in Germany and prevent Spanish intervention, arranged a truce between the armies of the League and of the Protestant Union and thus, inadvertently, freed Maximilian from fear of a Protestant counter-move against Bavaria. On 8 November 1620, Maximilian's Belgian general, Tilly, annihilated Frederick and Anhalt's army in the battle of the White Mountain, outside Prague.

Twenty-seven noblemen and burghers were executed in Prague; the Protestant preachers were banished; the estates lost all effective powers. A new Bohemian nobility, of German, Italian, Spanish, Flemish, even Scottish origins, joined the few remaining German-Czechs who had chosen the imperial side and, like these latter, did well out of wholesale confiscations of the estates of the rebels. Their loyalty was not to the Bohemian tradition but only to the house of Austria in whose service they had made their fortunes.

It should now have been possible to make peace. If the fate of Bohemia terrified Protestant Europe, it was still only the fate of rebels within the emperor's own dominions. But the Palatinate was a different matter. Here was a major principality of the Empire, in a strategically sensitive area, straddling the middle Rhine, in which none of the great western European powers could afford to disinterest themselves. That it should now have become the connecting link between the power struggles of western Europe and the complex religious and political struggles of the Empire and of northern and eastern Europe was due not so much to the frivolous scheming of Anhalt and Frederick V as to the ambitions of the Wittelsbachs of Bavaria. Maximilian was now officially also Elector Palatine. His brother was Archbishop-Elector of Cologne. Several of his cousins held smaller principalities, both secular and ecclesiastical. It seemed natural that Maximilian should be the leader of the Catholic German estates, pursuing the double objective of preventing any further losses to the Protestants and of preventing the house of Austria from infringing the German liberties, i.e. the power of the princes. The foolishness of his distant cousin, Frederick V, opened up the further prospect of acquiring his lands and titles for the Bavarian line of the Wittelsbachs. In Bavaria, Maximilian had a centrally situated state of some one million inhabitants in which both Protestantism and the opposition of the estates had been eliminated two generations earlier. Almost absolute powers of taxation and a regime of careful economy gave him a substantial income. As head of the Catholic League he had a fine army, commanded by Tilly, one of the best generals of the age.

To Maximilian his ambitions appeared both just and realistic in their limitations. But almost immediately the inherent contradictions of his aims became apparent. By obtaining from Ferdinand the transfer of the Upper Palatinate and the electoral dignity he set a most dangerous precedent for the extension of imperial power in Germany. The Protestant princes of the Empire, and especially the electors of Saxony and Brandenburg, did not accept the transfer. From the beginning the self-proclaimed champion of the estates had raised half of them against himself. The marauding campaigns of Frederick V's generals, Mansfeld, Baden-Durlach and Christian of Brunswick, gave Tilly the excuse to move into the Rhine Palatinate; but so did a Spanish army from the Netherlands. From this moment the course of events escaped from Maximilian's control, and all of Tilly's victories could never restore it to him.

Spain's Role

In the spring of 1621 the twelve years' truce between Spain and the United Provinces of the Netherlands ran out and was not renewed. In Spain the quest for a *monarquía universal*, a world empire, had died with Charles V; the universal championship of an aggressive Counter-Reformation had died with Philip II. But the idea of a Spanish empire (now sometimes actually referred to by this name) which should play some not very clearly defined, but certainly Catholic-Christian and politically pre-eminent, role

In the cynical view of the satirists, the Thirty Years' War was nothing but a lucky-dip for the princes of Europe. In this print, the Emperor (2) sits on his throne on the right, his feet on the lion of the Palatinate, while Wallenstein (6) presents him with the city of Prague. The two men in the foreground trying their luck are probably Spinola and George of Branden- burg. Other rulers wait hopefully to see what will fall to their share. On the ground are rich spoils in the form of money and plate; in the distance the towns of Germany whose fate is being decided; and along the top, hanging from a long spear, are other prizes—crowns, ducal robes and the armour of the successful general.

in Europe and the world—this was an idea which still filled the minds of many of the Castilian grandees. As viceroys of Naples and governors of Milan, as ambassadors in Rome, Venice, Prague and Brussels, they had chafed under the inactivity imposed on Spanish policy by Philip III's favourite, the duke of Lerma. In 1618 they won control of the Council of State in Madrid. When the young Philip IV succeeded his father in 1621, their victory was complete. The most intelligent, ambitious and determined of their number, the Count-Duke of Olivares, now enjoyed the unshakeable favour of the king.

There was much discussion, in Brussels and Madrid, over the wisdom of renewing the war with the Dutch 'rebels'. They had made use of the truce to capture the carrying trade from western Europe and the Baltic to Spain. Worse still, they had never ceased their piracy on the oceans and their attacks on the Spanish and Portuguese overseas colonies. In these twelve years, said Don Carlos Coloma, they had gained as much reputation in the Indies as the Spaniards had in a hundred and twenty. If they were allowed to continue, said Don Balthazar de Zúñiga, first the Indies would be lost, then the rest of Flanders, the Spanish dominions in Italy, and finally Spain itself would be in danger, for it would have lost that which had made it great. Once again, the argument from the potential escalation of disasters confirmed those who were tem- peramentally inclined towards an aggressive policy. The contrary arguments from the Council of Finance were overruled. The young king understood only this, that he was not responsible for the debts left by his predecessors. Neither he nor anyone else could know that the recent reduction in the silver shipments from America was not due to temporary difficulties but heralded a permanent decline. It seemed enough to Philip IV to declare his pious intention not to burden his subjects any further. Velázquez's portraits of the king show, with incomparable insight, the pathos of a man who is half aware of his personal inadequacy for the role he is called upon to play. But Philip never wavered. With the enthusiastic support of the nobility and clergy of Castile, but of few others, he led his country for 44 years from disaster to disaster.

Once war had been decided, Spanish policy remained perfectly consistent. All hope of success must depend on keeping open the road between Spain and the Spanish Netherlands. There were three alternative routes: (1) by sea; (2) the old 'Spanish Road', via Genoa, Savoy, Franche-Comté and Lorraine; and (3) via Genoa, Milan, the Valtelline, the upper Rhine and Alsace. To safeguard the first, the Catholic King was willing to contem- plate marrying his sister to the heretic Prince of Wales (later Charles I), perhaps even, to please the English, to agree to the restoration of Frederick V to the Palatinate. There was some feeling of relief in Madrid when neither possibility materialized; but, clearly, Spain was not engaged in a Catholic crusade. The two overland routes both presupposed Spanish domination of northern Italy and the co-operation of the emperor. When, in 1624, the abortive negotiations for the English marriage were followed by a desultory naval war, Madrid proposed to Vienna a Habsburg league which the pope and other Catholic powers would be invited to join, specifically to safeguard the road to the Netherlands and to co-operate against common enemies. These included France, as well as the Protestant powers; for in October 1624, Richelieu had sent French troops into the Valtelline.

This league was never formally concluded, but co-operation between Madrid and Vienna became very close. The Valtelline became one of the focal points of the war. Its Catholic inhabitants were under the political authority of the Protestant Grisons League, allied to, but not part of, the Swiss Confederation. Spanish, French and Venetian attempts to control the Valtelline passes became entangled in the religious and family feuds of the Grisons. Francophile Salis and Hispanophile Plantas murdered each other and invited, or helped to expel, the troops of one or other of the great powers. A former Protestant pastor, George Jenatsch, made himself virtual dictator of the Grisons, manoeuver- ing with ferocious virtuosity and at least one change of religion, until he himself was finally assassinated (1639). In the end the Grisons kept the Valtelline but granted Spain the right of free passage.

'A Calvinist International'

If Spain had made a deliberate choice to restart the Netherlands war, so had the United Provinces. Their decision had become virtually certain when Maurice of Nassau had won his long duel with Oldenbarnevelt and the regents' party. The opportunities seemed splendid and the risks not too great. At sea the Dutch were supreme. A chain of modern fortresses and the most professional and best-paid army in Europe guarded the provinces on their land frontiers. Behind these, life could continue peacefully and placidly, with perhaps more personal freedom than anywhere else in Europe. For some years there were hopes of inducing the southern Netherlands to overthrow their Spanish government. But the Belgians, though anxious for peace, were loyal to the king of Spain. Until the later stages of the French war, they, too, suffered relatively little from the frontier war.

Both friend and foe recognized that the United Provinces were the centre of all resistance to the house of Austria. In Maurice's words, they were fighting for their own and for universal liberty. Dutch ambassadors and agents worked in London and in Constantinople, in Stockholm and Moscow. With Venice there was a regular alliance; later, there was to be another with France and— a great dynastic *coup* for the house of Nassau—a marriage alliance with the Stuarts. The greater part of Europe's trade with the Baltic was carried in Dutch ships. Netherlanders, many of them religious or political refugees from the south, formed important settlements in the German North Sea and Baltic ports. From there they spread their activities to Scandinavia and Russia. The Marcelis mined Norwegian copper, exported Russian grain and helped to organize the Russian armaments industry at Tula. Later, they became the king of Denmark's economic advisers and organizers of his war effort. The De Geer and the Trip combined interests in Swedish copper, brass and iron with the armaments industry of the lower Rhine and Belgium. In Paris, the Hoeufft supplied Baltic naval stores to the growing French navy and arms for the French troops. These firms had capital resources, commercial and industrial expertise and, above all, family connections. They intermarried and formed partnerships. Their brothers or cousins sat in Amsterdam and had access to the world's richest money market and the best commercial information. Belgian and Portuguese-Jewish connections gave them entry to the Ibero-Indies trade, and the Spanish government's elaborate system of licensing ships and cargoes could not prevent this commercial penetration.

Here was a 'Calvinist international' that was much better organized, and potentially much more powerful, than Christian of Anhalt's correspondence club of incompetent aristocrats. But it was not a conspiracy against Spain nor against the Catholic religion. While others fought for religion and politics, these Calvinist capitalists were out to make money. One of them, the Antwerpner Jan de Witte, financed Wallenstein's armies. In 1645 the Amsterdam money market was perfectly happy to equip naval squadrons for both the Swedes and Danes to fight each other. Most of these firms probably preferred to finance the war efforts of the Protestant powers; all of them were willing to trade with Spain, even in war materials. Maurice of Nassau cheerfully maintained that the Dutch would bring provisions to the devil if they were not afraid that hell-fire might burn up their ships. Spain could not carry on the war without the provisions which the Netherlanders or their agents alone could provide. The United Provinces could not pay for its soldiers and warships without the wealth which this trade with the enemy helped to bring into the country.

Both sides were fully aware of the baleful implications of this sordid symbiosis. But, even after the long stalemate that followed the Spanish capture of Breda (1625)—Velázquez deliberately painted the scene as the beginning of a reconciliation—both sides always found good reasons for continuing the war. Olivares still believed in victory. His creatures in the Council of State—the praetorian buccaneers of the 1610s had been pushed out or had died—took their cue and added unwarranted innuendos against Spinola's loyalty when that most brilliant and faithful of the king's generals pleaded for peace. In that year, 1628, the Dutch admiral, Piet Hein, captured the Spanish silver fleet in the West Indies. The balance of the war was beginning to tilt against Spain. From the

Caribbean to the South Atlantic and the Indian Ocean, the Dutch pressed their attacks. For the first time, a European war was becoming a world war. The Gold Coast, Cape Verde, parts of Angola and half of Brazil, all of them Portuguese possessions, fell into Dutch hands during the 1630s and early 40s.

The war, however, imposed heavy strains on the United Provinces. Taxes were high; the Dunkirk privateers continued to take a heavy toll of Dutch shipping; and as long as powerful imperial armies fought in Germany, the military position remained precarious. The war with Spain seemed to be fought more and more for the benefit of the house of Nassau and its hangers-on, for the shareholders of the West India Company which was conquering Brazil, for a handful of millionaire firms with interests in the war economies of the different European states, and for the spiritual satisfaction of the orthodox Calvinist preachers. The regents' party, gradually edging back into key positions, and the East India Company, jealous of the southerners who directed the West India Company and more worried about English than about Spanish trade rivalry, all these would have liked to end the war on any reasonable terms. But many were also afraid of renewed civil and religious strife, once the country was at peace again. For a long time Prince Frederick Henry's military successes, his virtual toleration of the Remonstrants and his moderation towards the regents' party seemed preferable to anything that might happen if he were seriously opposed.

The Rise of Wallenstein

The Dutch had always been sensitive to the military situation in north-western Germany. When Tilly smashed Frederick's supporters on the middle Rhine, during the early 1620s, their situation became critical. They needed a new ally and they found him in Christian IV of Denmark. Christian, in his capacity of Duke of Holstein, had for a long time indulged in that favourite Protestant pastime, the secularization of ecclesiastical lands. His brother was bishop of Schwerin, his son of Verden, and he himself now had his eyes on Bremen, Osnabrück and Halberstadt. Any further advance by Tilly into north-western Germany would put an end to all these ambitions. In 1625 the United Provinces and England offered him an alliance and money to intervene in Germany. To Christian it seemed a splendid opportunity to act as the leader and saviour of the Protestant princes of the Empire and to balance the recent victories of his great rival, Gustavus Adolphus, over Poland.

It was a sad miscalculation. The Danish Council of State washed its hands of the affair. The Dutch were themselves hard pressed and had little money to spare. English help in money and troops, though not negligible, was quite inadequate for the ends pursued. Nevertheless, Maximilian was sufficiently alarmed by Christian's plans to urge the emperor to raise an army of his own in support of that of the Catholic League.

Ferdinand entrusted the organization of this new army to a Bohemian country nobleman, Albrecht von Wallenstein. Wallenstein had remained loyal during the Bohemian rebellion and had received princely rewards out of confiscated estates. Together with Prince Liechtenstein, the imperial governor of Bohemia, several of Ferdinand's ministers in Vienna, and the financier De Witte, Wallenstein had formed a consortium which farmed the Bohemian mint and issued a depreciated currency (1622). Many of the north-German princes had been systematically depreciating their coinages since 1620; but the Bohemian inflation topped them all. Liechtenstein may have made up to 10 million guilders profit; De Witte certainly over 30 million. Wallenstein used his profits to buy himself the duchy of Friedland in northern Bohemia and, altogether, more than fifty noble estates.

From the beginning, Wallenstein treated his army command as a big business operation. Through De Witte he raised loans in all important financial centres, from Venice to Lyons, and from Antwerp to Nuremberg and Hamburg. He made contracts with rich noblemen and businessmen to raise regiments. Systematically and deliberately he outbid Maximilian, so that Tilly found whole regiments disappearing from Bavarian into imperial service. Wallenstein's Bohemian estates supplied much of the grain and fodder this army needed. Iron founders, gunsmiths, powder

Germany in 1648; the inset shows the main territorial changes made by the Treaty of Westphalia.

grinders, brought from Germany and Italy to Friedland, started a minor industrial revolution in the duchy and made it into one of the principal centres of the European armaments industry. The army itself, however, flooded into north Germany and forced the German princes, provinces and cities to pay for its upkeep. This was the famous system of contributions, huge taxes in money and provisions, imposed on friend, neutral or foe at the point of the gun and the halberd, for the upkeep of the army and the profit of its colonels and generals. The system was not new, except in detail; but never before had it been used so ruthlessly and on such an immense scale. Wallenstein demonstrated that it was possible to raise mercenary armies of over 100,000 men and build up a most formidable military machine on a quite narrow territorial and industrial basis, provided one's financial and administrative organization was really good, and provided also that one was willing to spread both recruitment and the maintenance of the army over large areas of a relatively rich country. The lesson was not lost on the kings of Sweden and, later, Prussia, who found that independent princes, with the help of conscription and the backing of a regular civil service, could do even better than an upstart adventurer with a genius for organization. This pattern was not really broken until the appearance of the national mass armies of the French revolutionary wars and the advance of military technology in the 19th century, which completely changed the scale of the demographic and industrial basis that a country would need if it wanted to be a great military power.

The war in Germany was very different from that waged by Spinola and the princes of Nassau in the Netherlands, where the siege and capture of a relatively small city, like Breda or Bois-le-Duc, was glory enough for several years' campaigning. In Germany there were no chains of fortresses. Few cities had modern defences; for fortification was an expensive business, neglected during the half century of peace before 1618 and difficult to make good, once the war had started. Most cities, therefore, could not hold up a determined assailant for more than a few days or weeks. From 1620 onwards, when Mansfeld had marched his unpaid army from Bohemia to the Palatinate, Alsace and East Friesland, the character of campaigning remained similar: relatively small armies, with all their impedimenta of baggage and munitions trains, soldiers' wives, prostitutes and children, and a host of hangers-on turning their dishonest pennies at the expense of soldiers and civilians alike—such armies would crawl slowly in pursuit of each other over vast distances, engulfing villages and small towns on their way, picking up every local disease and spreading it in their tracks. The wastage rates were enormous. In 1626 Wallenstein chased Mansfeld from Dessau, on the Elbe, through Silesia to Hungary where Bethlen had promised support against the emperor. Mansfeld's army practically disappeared during this march. Wallenstein's survived only just sufficiently to frighten Bethlen into making peace.

During the winter Wallenstein again recruited a huge army. Tilly had won one of his brilliant victories, the battle of Lutter,

Lapländer. Liff — Länder. Schotländer.

A German caricaturist's idea of the army of Gustavus Adolphus, composed of barbarian Laplanders, Livonians and Scots. The animal is meant to be a reindeer. The caption ends with a plea to God to protect the poor fatherland.

against Christian IV (27 August 1626). But in the campaigns of 1627 and 1628, it was Wallenstein's much larger army which carried the imperial standards on a broad front through Brandenburg, Pomerania, Mecklenburg and Holstein, right into Jutland. On 7 July 1629, the emperor and Christian IV concluded the peace of Lübeck, by which Christian was allowed to keep Denmark and Holstein but had to leave his unfortunate German allies to face Ferdinand's revenge.

Vistas of Possibility
No emperor since Frederick Barbarossa, in the 12th century, had been as powerful in Germany as Ferdinand II was in 1629. With half of Germany occupied and the other half open to blackmail by Wallenstein's armies, there might well have been a chance to set up a strong central monarchy in Germany, or even to set course for the universal monarchy of the house of Austria which its enemies always accused it of pursuing. Wallenstein may have toyed with such ideas. He spoke of plans to drive the Turks from Constantinople, to set up a huge new empire in eastern Europe. But no one in Vienna had any such plans. The objectives of the house of Austria remained limited and tactical; yet they were such that they could not help but confirm all current suspicions of the over-mighty power of the house of Habsburg.

It was Madrid, rather than Vienna, which grasped the potentialities of Wallenstein's control of the German Baltic ports. If a Spanish-imperial fleet were built in the Baltic, perhaps with Danish and Hanseatic help, the United Provinces could be struck in their Achilles heel, their vital Baltic trade. Olivares wanted no more than that. But could any outside power believe, or afford to believe, that Spanish-imperial sea power in the Baltic would not be permanent and overwhelming? Even though the plan did not prove immediately feasible—neither Habsburg resources nor the available ports were adequate for such an ambitious scheme—the mere project was bound to bring in a new and powerful enemy: Sweden.

The plans of the court of Vienna were rather different. Ferdinand and his clerical advisers saw their chance to restore the Empire to the state it had been in at the time of the Peace of Augsburg, in 1555. This meant that the Protestants would have to restore all the ecclesiastical property which they had acquired since then. It might even mean that imperial cities, such as Augsburg, would have to accept a Catholic government. John George of Saxony and the other Lutheran princes of the Empire who had hitherto faithfully and not unprofitably supported the emperor, would never willingly accept such a reversal. But Ferdinand published the Edict of Restitution on 6 March 1629. Very soon it became clear that it was not an altruistic act, designed simply to right the wrongs which the Catholic church had undoubtedly suffered since 1555. Germany was treated to the unedifying spectacle of a race between Habsburg and Wittelsbach to capture the reconstituted prince-bishoprics. The Habsburgs won, with the splendid prizes of Magdeburg, Bremen and Halberstadt for Archduke Leopold William (already bishop of Passau and Strasbourg), against the less important Osnabrück, Minden and Verden for the Wittelsbachs. No other house had a chance; but the lesser pickings of this feast, the monasteries, prebends and schools, were disputed loudly and embarrassingly by the different monastic orders.

There is no evidence that Ferdinand wanted to destroy German Protestantism or to transform the Empire into an absolute monarchy. But it looked like that to the German princes. His general, Wallenstein, openly showed his contempt for them. The electors should depend on the emperor, he said, not the emperor on the electors, as hitherto. Or, less ominous but even more wounding: 'Herr Tilly is a slave to the Bavarian commissars . . . The good old chap will gain a martyr's crown for the patience he has to show to these varmints.' And this upstart had been created a prince of the Holy Roman Empire, enfeoffed with the ancient duchy of Mecklenburg whose dukes the emperor had deposed for rebellion (1628). It was becoming only too clear what a dangerous weapon Maximilian had pressed into the emperor's reluctant hands when he had insisted on the destitution of his cousin Frederick.

France Intervenes
In the meantime the war had flared up in Italy. This was inevitable once France began to play an active role in European politics again. Throughout the 1620s, France had been preoccupied with her internal problems and with her unsatisfactory relations with England. In 1627 a number of relatively minor irritations brought the two countries into open war. The Duke of Buckingham, then all-powerful in England, thought that he could carry off a brilliant *coup*: the occupation of the island of Ré. This would help La Rochelle and the Huguenots if they rebelled again, bring commercial and piratical profits to England, inhibit French naval building before it became really dangerous and, above all, present Buckingham as a champion of Protestantism to Parliament. Richelieu took the threat very seriously. But the English just failed to capture the island and, by 1629, Richelieu had, once and for all, broken the military power of the Huguenots.

'Princes command peoples and interest commands princes,' wrote Richelieu's great antagonist, the duc de Rohan. The decision which Richelieu now took to intervene in Italy was, in his own view, dictated by interest and was duly admired by Rohan himself. Yet was this the real interest of France? Richelieu's rival, Michel de Marillac, and his circle did not agree. France was not menaced, they argued, and it was wrong to fight other Catholic powers when these were engaged in a life-and-death struggle with Protestant powers. The French people were poverty-stricken, overburdened by taxes and rebellious. The power of the crown was still shaky and must first be strengthened. Richelieu did not altogether deny these arguments. The deliberate choice which he made was partly based on a different appreciation of the danger to France arising from the startling victories of the house of Austria. But the cardinal stressed equally the glory and reputation which the king would gain from the war. In the course of the 1630s, Richelieu was to develop realistic and moderate war aims, based on the idea of interlocking guarantees for future peace as a system of collective security against aggression. This certainly was reason of state actively applied to the true interests of France, perhaps of Europe. But the decisions of 1629/30 were mixed with a good deal of that traditional military pride of the European aristocracy which made warfare almost an end in itself. As to the cost, 'War is one of the scourges with which it has pleased God to afflict men,' Richelieu wrote to Marillac; and with this solace the French peasants had to be content.

The occasion for French intervention was provided by a Spanish-imperial act of aggression in Italy. The last Gonzaga Duke of Mantua died in 1627. His heir was a French subject, Charles, Duke of Nevers. Fearing that the French might obtain a foothold on the Lombard plain, Madrid and Vienna decided on preventive military action against Mantua. Many contemporaries were, later, to regard this war, with its unsatisfactory outcome, as the turning point in the history of Spanish power and of the emperor's position in Germany which, it was argued, was fatally weakened by the diversion of troops to Italy. Yet the evidence is all the other way. The Spanish-imperialist armies were highly successful against the French. If Richelieu was able to conclude the favourable Peace of Cherasco (19 June 1631) which gave France Pinerolo, and Nevers the imperial investiture with Mantua, this was only because the imperial position had meanwhile suffered a disastrous setback in Germany.

This setback had very little to do with the Mantuan war and almost everything with the inability of Ferdinand's corrupt and incapable council to develop a rational imperial policy on the basis of Wallenstein's victories. In the summer of 1630 the emperor travelled to Regensburg to persuade the Catholic electors—Protestant Saxony and Brandenburg refused to participate in the meeting—to elect his son, Ferdinand, as King of the Romans, and to participate in the Spanish war against the Dutch. The family interests of the house of Habsburg could not have been more blatantly preferred to those of the Empire. The electors countered with the demand for Wallenstein's dismissal and for a large reduction of the imperial armies. Wallenstein had many enemies at court. They persuaded Ferdinand that the Catholic and Protestant princes of the Empire might make common cause against him, or even join the King of Sweden who had just landed in Pomerania (26 June 1630). Ferdinand should prove that he did not wish to change the Empire into an absolutist monarchy. On 13 August the emperor gave in and dismissed his general. Wallenstein's financial organization, shaky during the previous year, now collapsed altogether. De Witte jumped into a well in his own garden.

Having thrown away his ace, the emperor quickly lost the other tricks. The electors refused to join the war against the United Provinces, they pressed for peace with France, and they did not elect young Ferdinand King of the Romans. Maximilian forced the emperor to accept Tilly as the new commander-in-chief of the greatly reduced imperial, as well as the League, armies. At the same time Maximilian negotiated an alliance with France which was formally concluded, in the Treaty of Fontainebleau, on 30 May 1631. Richelieu's armies had been defeated and his diplomats bungled their part of the negotiations at Regensburg; but thanks to Bavaria he had won a major victory over the house of Austria. He followed it up by an alliance with Sweden (Treaty of Bärwalde, 23 January 1631).

Sweden: a Leader of Genius

In the twenty years before this treaty the young Gustavus Adolphus of Sweden had modernized and centralized the administration of his country. He had done this in alliance with the high nobility, more especially the Oxenstierna family. He had encouraged Louis de Geer and other Netherlanders to build him the most modern armaments industry in Europe and to develop the old copper mines of Falun until Swedish copper came to enjoy a virtual monopoly of the European copper market. When the Swedes conquered Riga and other Livonian ports from Poland-Lithuania, another Netherlander, Pieter Spierinck, organized for the king the systematic exploitation of the export tolls on grain. The social cost of Gustavus' policies was high, and there were some economic setbacks. The peasants, burdened by high taxation, plagued by recruiting for the army, and often handed over, willy-nilly, to suffer further exploitation by the aristocratic recipients or

usurpers of crown land, were almost annually goaded into local riots and rebellions. In 1626 the Spanish government alternated its habitual *vellón* inflation with one of its periodic attempts at deflation, and the bottom fell out of the copper market. Nevertheless, Sweden maintained its predominant position in copper. By foisting copper coins on conquered territories, and by De Geer's astute manipulations of the markets in Hamburg and Amsterdam, the Swedish crown still extracted large sums from this export.

Gustavus Adolphus had already had to fight for his crown, and for Swedish independence, first against Christian IV who would have liked to revive the Union of Kalmar (the late-medieval union of the three Scandinavian kingdoms under the Danish crown), then against Sigismund III of Poland, his cousin, whom Gustavus' father had deprived of the Swedish crown. The claims of the Polish Vasas were the more serious as they involved a threat to Swedish Protestantism, for Sigismund was an enthusiastic champion of the Counter-Reformation. The motivation of these wars seems to have contained strong economic elements. Both Denmark and Sweden claimed the *dominium maris Baltici* which meant, in practice, that they would levy tolls on each other's and everyone else's shipping wherever they could: the Danes in the Sound, and the Swedes at the entrance to the Neva and in any Baltic port they managed to control. Both countries, no doubt, wished in this way to protect and encourage their own shipping and commerce; but this was only a small fraction of the total Baltic trade. Ultimately, Denmark and Sweden, unlike the United Provinces, fought for economic and financial advantages because these were the tools of power.

The Swedish-Danish war had ended, with some Danish advantage, in 1613. The Swedish-Polish war, however continued intermittently, partly because Sigismund would not give up his claims to the Swedish crown and partly because Gustavus was doing well out of it. By 1622, Livonia was in Swedish hands. In 1626, Gustavus invaded Prussia and began to speak airily of attacking the emperor, once he had finished with Poland. The confrontation began when Wallenstein, nervous for his right flank, sent troops to help Sigismund. The collapse of Denmark precipitated the crisis. Once again, the argument of the potential escalation of disasters justified a war of aggression. As early as the beginning of 1628, the Swedish *Riksdag* accepted Gustavus' analysis of the dangers threatening Sweden, 'the open conspiracy (by the emperor and the king of Poland) to deprive us of all trade and navigation, and . . . of the sovereignty of the Baltic.' In September 1629 France mediated the truce of Altmark between Sweden and Poland. The Polish problem was now isolated from Germany and Sweden was free to intervene in the general war. Sweden retained the right to collect the export tolls of the Prussian ports. As much as the copper exports, and more than the French subsidies promised in the Treaty of Bärwalde, these tolls were to be the financial basis of Gustavus Adolphus' campaigns in Germany.

No one in 1630 thought that Swedish intervention should be taken lightly; few realised just how formidable it was to be. The Swedish army, hardened in the long years of war on the Livonian and Prussian marches against the redoubtable Polish horsemen, knew all about the most modern Spanish and Dutch tactics and it added some new ideas of its own, notably the close co-operation of musketeers with cavalry and the greatly increased use of field artillery. This army was backed by a country more thoroughly organized for war than any other in Europe, and it was commanded by a leader of genius. By all contemporary accounts Gustavus Adolphus was the most charismatic personality to appear on the European scene since the death of Henry IV. This big blonde 'Goth' from the barbarian north who spoke most European languages fluently and with *éclat*, who liked good literature, music, food and drink, whose Protestant convictions were sincere but not intolerant, who was immensely sure of the justice of his cause and of his ability to lead it, who used his personal charm to balance his quick and terrifying temper and his bouts of repulsive self-righteousness—this man could inspire enthusiasm where the other two outstanding leaders of the age, Richelieu and Wallenstein, could inspire only cold admiration and awed hatred. He was served by men of exceptional ability: Axel Oxenstierna, his chancellor; the Netherlanders who ran the Swedish economy; and his generals, Horn, Banér and Torstensson. It was more than luck: it was intelligent and unprejudiced selection, as well as loyal support of those once chosen (a point whose importance Richelieu never tired of stressing to Louis XIII). It was Gustavus Adolphus who made the reluctant Swedish nobility open their ranks to foreigners, Netherlanders and Germans, Balts and Scots, and even more unwillingly, to men of lower birth, administrators and diplomats, financiers and professional men.

'The Lion of the North'

Gustavus unfolded his German campaign carefully and ruthlessly, advancing from one strategic conquest to the next, and meanwhile first persuading, then blackmailing the unenthusiastic Protestant princes of northern Germany into increasingly dependent alliances with him. At the same time he expanded his armies by much the same methods that Wallenstein had used. By March 1632, he had some 140,000 men under his command, of whom only 13,000 were Swedes.

The king's shattering victory over Tilly, at Breitenfeld near Leipzig (7 September 1631) stilled for the moment all Protestant misgivings over Swedish reason of state and over the king's role in the catastrophe of Magdeburg—the city whose smoking ruins showed the result of trusting Gustavus' promises of relief from Tilly's besieging army. After Breitenfeld, even John George of Saxony spoke for a moment of electing Gustavus emperor. The king wanted nothing so quixotic; but he was certainly not averse from re-arranging the map of the Empire to suit his own interests. Once again, ecclesiastical lands became the most convenient prize with which to reward German allies and Swedish generals. The famous liberty of the German princes soon appeared to be in greater danger from the 'Macedonian domination' of Sweden than from the autocratic but legalistically-minded emperor.

Richelieu had hoped that Gustavus Adolphus would strike directly south, through Bohemia to Vienna. It was on this presupposition that he had signed his alliance with Bavaria; and this alliance was necessary to him, not only because it gave him a counterbalance to the house of Austria in Germany, but also because it was meant to prove to the pope, and even perhaps to himself, that the war in Europe had nothing to do with religion. But for Gustavus a direct attack on Vienna appeared both tactically difficult and strategically unrewarding, for it would not necessarily break the main sources of imperial power. A move south-westwards, on the other hand, to the Rhine and the Alps, would bring him control of the still undevastated, rich states of southern Germany, would isolate the emperor from Spanish help from Italy and the Netherlands, and would finally allow a decisive campaign eastward down the Danube. At Christmas 1631 the king held court at Mainz. There he informed the French ambassadors that he would 'devastate Bavaria by pillage, fire and blood,' unless Maximilian laid down his arms. Richelieu, placed before the choice of a victorious Sweden and a crumbling Bavaria, threw Maximilian to the wolves. For France it was a diplomatic defeat. For Bavaria it was disaster. Maximilian, the triumphant leader of the Catholic estates of Germany had, after all, only played sorcerer's apprentice, unleashing forces he could not control. On 5 May 1632 Gustavus Adolphus and Frederick V entered Munich.

This was the high water mark of Swedish power. In January 1632 Wallenstein had once more taken command of the imperial armies, with more extensive powers even than during his first command. With Spanish money and with the credit which his name still carried he managed to finance a new army. From Bohemia he invaded Saxony. Gustavus, to save his most important and most unreliable German ally, John George, had to turn north. Throughout the summer the two armies faced each other and fought without decision. The king continued to make grandiose plans: a firm league of Protestant German princes under Swedish leadership; then one more great campaign, and his 'knee on their neck and a dagger at their throat' would force his enemies to accept the peace he would dictate. After that he would turn to Poland and partition that kingdom with Russia.

On 6 November 1632, at Lützen, once again on the plains of Leipzig, Gustavus attacked Wallenstein. A decisive victory seemed within his grasp, for Wallenstein had already dispersed half his army into winter quarters and many of his units only arrived on the field of battle in the course of the day. But Gustavus himself fell while leading the charge of one of the Swedish regiments. His army fought on until, at dusk, Wallenstein was forced to retreat. But the victory meant little, for Gustavus Adolphus was irreplaceable.

Axel Oxenstierna who now took over the direction of Swedish affairs for Gustavus' six-year old daughter, Christina, shed the more fantastical of the king's plans, notably those concerning Poland, and brought the rest down to earth. In January 1633 he defined Swedish war aims as security for Sweden and some 'satisfaction', i. e. compensation for her efforts on behalf of the German Protestants. These remained Sweden's basic terms until the final peace treaty, though views changed as to what exactly was meant by them. For these terms the Swedish nobility was willing to continue to fight: there were still many splendid personal prizes to be won by successful generals, and the cost to Sweden itself was relatively slight. *Bellum se ipse aleat*, let war feed itself, Mansfeld's and Wallenstein's old maxim, was being practised with ever more brutal efficiency by the Swedish commanders.

Wallenstein Falls

Wallenstein is reported to have remarked that Gustavus Adolphus' death was well and good, 'for two cocks on one dung heap could not get on.' But what did he now crow about? Was he a Bohemian or Czech patriot, wishing to make himself king of an independent Bohemia? or a German patriot, struggling to free Germany from Swedes, Spaniards and other foreigners? Was he a traitor to the emperor, aiming only at self-aggrandizement, or did he intend to impose peace on a war-weary Europe? These and other interpretations have all been learnedly, and often passionately, canvassed in the historiographical treatment of the *Wallenstein problem*. Seen in such terms of motive, with or without elaborate psychological underpinning, the solution to the problem is likely to remain speculative even if, as now seems possible, much hitherto unused material may become available. There is little doubt that Wallenstein's rapidly deteriorating health, throughout the year 1633, impaired his powers of making clear decisions. But much more important was his complete failure to understand the role which the commander of even the largest, most successful and most personal army could play in a 17th century state. He could sell his army to another war lord, the Swedes or the French, as Bernard of Weimar was to do a few years later. That would have simply meant exchanging one master for another. Yet, by themselves, Wallenstein and his army could never impose any political settlement. Unlike the New Model Army, fifteen years later, Wallenstein's army stood for nothing; it could command no political or religious loyalty. The very aims of its commander were bound to be secret. Only if Wallenstein had first used his power to impose his will on the imperial government could he then have hoped to carry through whatever plans he may have had. Julius Caesar is said to have remarked that Sulla did not know the ABC of political power when he retired from the dictatorship of Rome. In Caesarian terms, Wallenstein was a child-in-arms. He did not even see that there was a Rubicon to be crossed.

Without decisive leadership, Wallenstein's party at court disintegrated during the summer and autumn of 1633. After that, his enemies had little difficulty in winning over his senior officers. Having made their choice, these officers improved their case by freely inventing such evidence of treason as might still be lacking against their commander. At last, Ferdinand was convinced; but his conscience had still to be put at rest by a formal trial accorded to his general. His confessor assured him that it did not matter that the accused knew nothing of this event. The death sentence was executed against Wallenstein and three of his loyal followers at Eger, on the night of 25 February 1634, in a manner highly reminiscent of Machiavelli's admiring account of the more lurid deeds of Cesare Borgia. The double-crossing generals, the treacherous colonels and the murderous soldiers who committed the deed, were all richly rewarded by a grateful emperor.

The war exposed Spanish economic weakness. Catalonia rebelled, and Portugal seized the opportunity to shake off the rule of Spain. In 1640 John Duke of Braganza was proclaimed King John IV of Portugal.

The year 1634 was a good one for Ferdinand II. In September his son, Ferdinand of Hungary, together with Philip IV's brother, the Cardinal-Infante Ferdinand of Spain, annihilated the Swedish-Protestant army at Nördlingen. The Swedes had to evacuate southern Germany altogether. In the north, most of their German allies, led by Saxony, made peace with the emperor. In the Peace of Prague (May 1635) the emperor only gave way on the Edict of Restitution—not indeed revoking it, but shelving it for 40 years. But all alliances between the German princes were forbidden and their troops were to form an imperial army which was to take an oath to the emperor. It was a brilliant victory for the emperor and, secondarily, for Saxony which kept Lusatia and obtained Magdeburg in addition. The peace-loving, beer-drinking Lutheran prevaricator, John George, had done rather better than the austere Catholic power politician, Maximilian of Bavaria.

But the war was not over. The very extent of the Spanish-imperial victory forced Richelieu's hand; for the spectre of a Habsburg domination of Europe seemed now more threatening than ever. On 5 May 1635 France formally declared war on Spain.

The first All-European War

The ring of alliances was now complete. The Bohemian rebellion had become the first all-European war in which, of the greater powers, only England, Poland, Russia and the Ottoman Empire remained relatively uninvolved. No bilateral treaty, nor even a treaty between two groups of states, could now end the war. Most of the treaties of alliance contained specific clauses prohibiting separate peace treaties. In any case, how could any government be certain that the enemy with whom it treated would not lead it into a trap, isolating it from its friends and joining forces with its betrayed allies? Only a general peace could now give security, and this could be achieved only through a general peace conference. It took time before the combatants fully understood this, and then it took more time to organize such a conference, to decide its form and to agree on who had a right to be represented and in what capacity; for the question with whom one was prepared to treat raised some of the fundamental issues of the war. What rights, if any, were to be allowed to the Bohemian exiles, to the heirs of Frederick V, to the Catalans and Portuguese, both in rebellion against their lawful king since 1640, or to the Swiss cantons who had not fought at all but were an interested party in the future constitution of the Empire?

In the meantime the war continued. Central Europe could no longer maintain the huge numbers of soldiers that Wallenstein and Gustavus Adolphus had had at their command. Small armies, rarely more than 15,000 of whom often half were cavalry, would now march rapidly over long distances, moving from one un-devastated area to the next until this too was burnt out or until supply lines became too long and the enemy could temporarily concentrate superior forces. Grand strategy in the manner of Gustavus Adolphus, aiming at the annihilation of the enemies' forces and total conquest, was no longer possible. Three times the Swedes swept through Bohemia. Vienna, even Paris, had moments of panic when enemy armies approached. But storming or besieging such great cities was not to be thought of. In the long run, the resources of the anti-Habsburg forces and their fighting ability proved to be superior. In 1638 Bernard of Weimar's German army, in French pay, captured Breisach and with it the control of the Upper Rhine valley and Alsace. The Spanish Road was now all but blocked. In the following year the Dutch admiral, Tromp, sank a great Spanish armada in the Battle of the Downs, in neutral English waters. In 1640 the Dutch followed this up by a brilliant victory over a Spanish-Portuguese fleet off Bahía, which confirmed the Dutch hold on Brazil.

Spain's Weakness

The Spanish monarchy could make no riposte. Its fundamental weakness was now revealed: the narrowness of its base. Castile and the silver from its American colonies financed and defended the empire; the other dominions were, to a greater or lesser degree, onlookers. In 1624 Olivares had suggested that these dominions could be induced to play a full part in the burdens of empire if they could be allowed to share in its fruits: the honours, commands and control over policy that had been all but monopolized by the Castilian ruling classes. It might just have worked. In the 1560s Cardinal Granvelle had made very similar proposals to Philip II. It is not clear whether Olivares knew of these or not; but both sets of proposals suffered a similar fate. Castilian vested interests would not even allow their serious discussion. The results were disastrous in both cases. Philip II fell back on the Duke of Alba's policy of repression and lost the northern Netherlands. Olivares had to fall back on a policy that drove him, slowly but inexorably, into a similar policy of repression which lost him Catalonia and Portugal. This alternative policy was the 'Union of Arms', a scheme for the creation of a common imperial reserve of 140,000 men to whose maintenance all the states of the empire were to contribute in fixed proportions. But without the *quid pro quo* of the original proposal, the 'Union of Arms' was inevitably disliked and distrusted by the non-Castilian dominions. Catalonia was the state with the greatest surviving autonomy and with an archaic and inefficient government that could do little to pacify its feud-riven and bandit-infested countryside. It made practically no contribution to the Spanish war effort. Having for fifteen years failed to get voluntary help, Olivares determined to pitchfork the province into war by attacking France from the Catalan border (1639). The need to defend their country should force the Catalans to support the army, regardless of their liberties. But the Catalans, led by their clergy, did not see it this way. High-handed actions by the Castilian troops were met by riots and these turned into rebellion. By July 1640 the viceroy had been murdered and the authority of the Madrid government in Catalonia had collapsed.

The last available troops in Spain were now sent against the Catalans. This gave the Portuguese their chance. Increasing financial demands for a war effort which had signally failed to protect the Portuguese colonies in Africa and Brazil turned the commercial classes and the nobility against Madrid. The lower classes, vociferously supported by the clergy, had always hated the Castilians. On 1 December 1640, Portuguese conspirators, probably with French backing, seized power in Lisbon and proclaimed the greatest nobleman of the country, the Duke of Braganza, as King John IV of Portugal.

In January 1641 the Catalans transferred their allegiance to the king of France, 'as in the time of Charlemagne.' Peace with France was now impossible, for Philip IV would never consent to the loss of Catalonia and the king of France's honour was engaged to his new subjects. But it was the end of Olivares. In 1643 the Castilian grandees forced his dismissal and exile. Two years later he died, broken and insane—a classically tragic figure whose grandiose vision of a Catholic Spanish-international empire was flawed by the aggressive militarism that was central to the Castilian aristocratic tradition and whose personal character was flawed by the *hybris* that was the indelible mark of this tradition.

The disasters continued. In 1643 the Prince de Condé broke the Spanish infantry's century-old reputation for invincibility in the battle of Rocroi. In 1647, revolts broke out in Naples and Palermo. After Castile, Naples was probably the most heavily taxed dominion of the Spanish crown. But the millions which the Spanish viceroys had to press out of that kingdom forced them into two contradictory policies: they had to increase viceregal authority at the expense of the liberties of the country but, at the same time, they had to grant or sell new liberties and privileges to the Neapolitan nobility without whose support the taxes could not be collected. It amounted to a virtual abdication by the monarchy of authority over the countryside. The nobles, exercising ever-widening powers of jurisdiction, buying up or usurping whole towns and terrorizing anyone still outside their direct power through gangs of bandits whom they protected from royal justice, were progressively reducing the kingdom to anarchy. On 7 July 1647 a popular revolt broke out in the city of Naples and spread immediately to the provinces. It was led by a gifted but unstable fisherman, Masaniello, but was stage-managed by an octogenarian lawyer, Antonio Genoino. Within five weeks very much the same pattern, though without the Neapolitan bloodshed, was repeated in Palermo and western Sicily. These revolts were directed both against the Spanish viceregal governments and against the nobility. Both in Naples and Palermo the original leaders disappeared within a week, after setting up their popular dictatorships. But effective control over the two capital cities remained with the revolutionaries for many months. Only step by step and, finally, with the help of a Spanish fleet, did the two viceregal governments and their noble allies re-establish their authority (spring 1648).

Peacemakers

The position of the Austrian branch of the house of Habsburg, if not quite as critical, had also deteriorated decisively. The loss of Alsace allowed French armies to invade southern Germany at will. In 1641 the young elector Frederick William of Brandenburg broke the Peace of Prague and declared his neutrality. Bavaria did the same in 1647. The German princes had recaptured the right to an independent foreign policy, and the emperor implicitly recognized this when he agreed that they were to be represented at the peace conference. Imperial hopes revived in 1643, when Christian IV of Denmark, old now but still incurably optimistic, broke with Sweden. But the Swedish riposte was devastating. Torstensson overran Jutland and then turned south to crush an imperial army sent to help the Danes. When Christian was also defeated at sea he had to accept the Peace of Brömsebro (1645); by which he had to give up to Sweden the islands of Gotland and Ösel and the province of Halland for 30 years. Denmark thus lost her strategic strong points in the eastern Baltic and only just managed to keep her most important strategic and financial asset, the control of the Sound.

This was also the end of Danish attempts to mediate at the two peace conferences, of Münster and Osnabrück, which had begun meeting in 1643. The role of peacemaker was now taken up by Venice and the papacy. Neither power had been completely neutral. Venice, the ally of France and the United Provinces, had disputed the Valtelline with Spain and, for short periods, had actually been at war with the house of Austria; but from 1630 onwards she had withdrawn from the European struggle, and from 1645 she had to fight a bitter war against the Turks for the defence of Crete. The Venetian senate was therefore most anxious that the Christian powers should stop fighting each other and become aware of the renewed danger to Christendom from the Turks.

The position of the papacy was more complex. Paul V (1605–21), Gregory XV (1621–23) and Urban VIII (1623–44) had all supported the Catholic cause. But, right from the beginning of the war, Rome had found it difficult to decide which of the powers most truly fought for this cause, and this problem was complicated by the pope's purely political interests as a territorial prince in Italy. Not unnaturally, successive popes had tended to prefer Bavaria to Austria and, with more serious consequences, France to Spain. Most of this support was diplomatic; welcome, no doubt, but as Maximilian remarked about one of the papal diplomats at his court: 'Father Giacinto demands great faith and patience, but we and the soldiers a great sum of money.' And money Rome gave only very sparingly. To the scandal of contemporary Catholics, but to the undoubted enrichment of the Church and of the world, far larger sums went to the papal nephews. Instead of adding to the slaughter in Germany, the popes and their families paid for the Baroque age of Rome, the squares, palazzi and churches of Bernini and Borromini, the paintings of Pietro da Cortona and Poussin. Paris, Madrid, Amsterdam and London all had their patrons and artists, some of them—Rembrandt and Velázquez—the greatest of the age. But it was Rome which became, for the last time in its long and splendid history, the greatest single centre of art and architecture in Europe.

All this did not interfere with papal mediation at the peace congress. But when Rome would not sanction any Catholic concessions to the Protestants, or even to accord them diplomatic recognition, the powers found that they could do without papal services. The Curia was aware of this dilemma, but was bound by its most venerable traditions. The final, and unheeded, protest by Innocent X against the peace treaties was, however, a diplomatic blunder, for it showed starkly the gulf between the political-religious claims of the papacy and the realities of European political life.

While the delegates negotiated, the Catholics at Münster and the Protestants at Osnabrück, there was no truce and the parties still tried to improve their bargaining position in successive campaigns. The wonder is therefore not that it took five years to make peace, but that it was made at all. The almost universal corruption of the delegates of the smaller states and of Sweden helped to smooth away many minor difficulties. They invented a special word for it, *Realdankbarkeit* (practical gratitude). The decisive move was made by Ferdinand III and his principal adviser, Trauttmansdorf. Pressed by Maximilian, who threatened to make a separate peace, and against the violent protests of Spain, they accepted French claims to Lorraine, Alsace and the bridge-heads of Breisach and Philippsburg. This meant the irrevocable end of the Spanish Road and, effectively, the end of the close alliance between the two branches of the house of Austria. Philip IV drew the logical conclusion from this situation and came to terms with the United Provinces. Spanish recognition of the complete independence of the United Provinces and the closing of the Scheldt were hard to swallow but did not call for any change in the position as it had existed for many years. The Orange party and the French did their best to wreck the negotiations; but Frederick Henry had died in 1647, his son William II was still very young, and the province of Holland was determined to have peace. It was signed in January 1648.

After this, it was relatively easy to persuade Brandenburg and Sweden to divide Pomerania between them. Sweden also obtained the bishoprics of Bremen and Verden and was thus firmly established on the estuaries of three great German rivers, the Oder, the Elbe and the Weser. Brandenburg was given Magdeburg and Halberstadt, in compensation for western Pomerania—this time at the expense of Saxon claims. Maximilian had to be content with the Upper Palatinate and the electoral dignity. Charles Louis, son of the unfortunate Frederick V, was allowed to return to the Rhine Palatinate, with an eighth electorate especially created for him.

Post-War Settlements

More important than these details was the final settlement of the relations between the emperor and the princes. Although still fighting on the imperial side, they were effectively supported by France and Sweden. Step by step, Trauttmansdorf had to retreat before their combined pressure. In the end, the sell-out of Spain

The glad tidings of peace are trumpeted throughout Europe, when the Treaty of Westphalia is signed. In the foreground lie the shattered implements of war. Beyond, the ship of peace carries the news to Stockholm, Paris and Vienna.

proved to have achieved practically nothing. The princes and imperial cities were confirmed in their absolute right to determine the religion of their subjects, although, for the first time, a few concessions were made to the heterodox, notably the right to emigrate. The Calvinists were now included with the Lutherans in the peace. The 'normal' year for the ownership of ecclesiastical property was to be 1624—a more favourable date for the Protestants than 1627, the date set in the Peace of Prague. Finally, the imperial estates retained, as of right, the ancient and disastrous practice of making alliances and waging war.

What was left of the medieval universalist ideals, as represented by the pope and the emperor, had now completely disappeared. The pope was ignored. Ferdinand III had virtually to write off the Empire. From now on his house concentrated its efforts on a very different political structure, a multi-racial but Catholic Danubian empire in which the emperor was a virtually absolute ruler. At the same time, the statesmen of the age had become acutely aware of the danger of a protracted general war. Something had to be found to replace the old universalist ideal, and this turned out to be the idea of a universal guarantee of peace. It was the merit of Richelieu and his circle that they worked out this idea systematically and made it the basis of French war aims. Originally, Richelieu claimed only such territorial acquisitions for France as would enable her to fulfil her obligations in such a system of collective security; but even during his lifetime, the very successes of French arms led to an expansion of French territorial claims. Mazarin compromised the original plans still further until, to the rest of Europe, French war aims did not appear to differ in essentials from those of all the other powers.

Nevertheless, in a modified form, Richelieu's system was written into the peace treaties. The signatories guaranteed the treaties, if need be by force of arms, against any disturber. The new constitution of the Empire was thus made part of the public law of Europe and guaranteed by non-German powers. To later generations of Germans it seemed that these powers were deliberately trying to keep Germany weak. There is some truth in this. Yet the division, and the consequent political impotence, of Germany was primarily the fault of the German estates; for it was the inevitable result of their 'liberties' for which, in a sense, they had fought the Thirty Years' War—even when, like Maximilian, they had fought as the emperor's allies. But in any case, the politicians of 1648 really did want a secure and reasonably permanent peace, and no other way of obtaining it was remotely feasible.

It was not really the fault of the peace makers that the treaties, signed on 24 October 1648, did not after all turn out to be either secure or permanent; nor did this prove that their basic ideas were wrong. It was rather that they had not gone far enough in settling all specific disputes and that they were not able to eradicate the tradition of the quest for military honour and the spirit of aggression. France and Spain did not make peace in 1648. Mazarin was

riding on the crest of the wave of military success and hoped for even better things; Philip IV and his new adviser, Don Luis de Haro, imagined that, with the Dutch war off their hands, they could hold France and reconquer Catalonia and Portugal. Despite the desperate exhaustion of Castile they were almost right. The Fronde neutralized France for five years—time enough for Madrid to settle the revolts of southern Italy (1648) and to reconquer Catalonia (1652). The Catalans received back all their old liberties. The Spanish monarchy thus reverted to its old policy of alliance with the the local ruling classes of its various dominions—the policy that had kept the Spanish empire in Europe alive for two hundred years and was to do so for another fifty.

Spain should now have concluded peace with France, but Philip IV, ageing and obstinate, still found his honour engaged over Portugal and over the person of the Prince de Condé who had fled from France and become the commander of Philip's armies in the Netherlands. It was, however, not really Philip's fault that he became involved in another war, with England.

In 1652 the old and exasperating rivalry between the English and the Dutch had escalated, through the Navigation Act of 1651 (an attempt to cut out the Dutch carrying trade from foreign countries to England) and royalist privateering from Dutch ports, into open naval war (1652–54). The English, with considerable strategic and technical-naval advantages, came well out of this war, and this success perhaps helps to explain English enthusiasm for the almost purely aggressive war against Spain, in 1656. Mazarin offered Cromwell Dunkirk for an offensive alliance. It would be useful against the Dutch. Perhaps it may have seemed useful also against the French if, as now seemed likely, they captured the whole of the Spanish Netherlands. The rest was pure imperialism: conquest in the West Indies for the sake of both religion and trade.

The English naval war was not a complete success. The capture of part of a Spanish silver fleet and the still undeveloped island of Jamaica were balanced by heavy shipping losses. But Dunkirk was captured by an Anglo-French army, after its victory over Condé in the battle of the Dunes. In 1659 France and Spain finally concluded the Peace of the Pyrenees: France received Artois, Roussillon and Cerdagne, and Philip IV's daughter, Maria Theresa, married Louis XIV. In 1662 Charles II sold Dunkirk to France—a striking demonstration of the basic futility of Cromwell's war with Spain.

Once again Philip IV had concluded a peace treaty to have his hands free against another enemy: the last and the most unforgivable of all, the Portuguese. But it was now too late. The Portuguese had reconquered Brazil from the Dutch. It did not matter that this was possible largely because of the hostility of the old Amsterdam patriciate to the West India Company whom they starved of financial and naval support to resist the Portuguese attack. For the Portuguese it was a notable victory, bringing with it new financial resources and much-needed self-confidence. In 1665 they routed the last Spanish army at Villaviciosa. A few weeks later Philip IV died and in 1668 Spain officially recognized Portuguese independence, just as Louis XIV was marching into the Spanish Netherlands. But that war belonged to a different age when the Spanish monarchy had become an object of the ambitions of other powers.

Sweden at War again

Over half of Europe groups of disbanded soldiers were roaming, useless, unwanted and destructive. Discharged officers sat bored and discontented on impoverished estates, nostalgic for the gay life of the camps. In Sweden they controlled the government and the king was one of them. Christina's minority and reign had witnessed an unprecedented rise in the numbers and wealth of a now partly international and very militarist Swedish nobility. They had come to own some two thirds of all the farms in the country, mainly at the expense of the crown. At a *Riksdag* in 1650, the estates of the clergy, towns and peasants combined against the nobles, and the country was on the verge of civil war. Christina took advantage of this crisis to secure the right of succession for her cousin, Charles Gustavus. In 1654 she abdicated, partly because she had become a Catholic in a Lutheran country, partly because she preferred a quiet life among artists and philosophers in Rome to the political struggles which were looming so menacingly on the Swedish political horizon. Charles X Gustavus did indeed make a start with the partial resumption of crown lands (*reduktionen*). But he had been Swedish commander-in-chief before 1648, and, with the enthusiastic support of the nobility, he side-stepped the internal problem and threw Sweden into a new war against Poland (1655).

Poland seemed on the point of dissolution. A Cossack revolt, in 1648, had brought the Russians on the scene as allies of the Cossacks. City after city in Lithuania and eastern Poland fell to their massive attacks. The Swedish action therefore seemed to promise the double advantage of forestalling a likely Russian penetration to the Baltic and of securing for Sweden Poland's Baltic coastline, perhaps even the Polish crown.

Three times Charles X reached Cracow. He won brilliant battles and, at times, the Polish nobility was willing to accept him as their king. But the Swedes could not control the vast areas of the Polish plains. The Poles turned back to their old king, John Casimir, the emperor sent support. In 1657 Denmark declared war on Sweden. It seemed a unique opportunity to reverse the Treaty of Brömsebro, and the United Provinces, fearful of a Swedish monopoly of the Baltic grain ports, urged the Danes on. The result was unexpected. Charles X turned north and, like his master Torstensson in 1643, overran Jutland. Then, in January and February of 1658, he marched his army over the ice of the Little Belt and then, from island to island, to Zealand. Denmark had no choice but to accept the treaty of Roskilde, ceding Bornholm and her remaining provinces in southern Sweden. A few months later Charles re-started the war by attacking Copenhagen. There had been some Danish provocation, but essentially it was an act of aggression. Charles now wanted to recreate the Union of Kalmar, but under Swedish leadership. But in October 1658 a Dutch fleet sailed into the Sound and forced the Swedes to lift the siege of Copenhagen. It was a most impressive demonstration of the uses of sea power. The Dutch effectively dictated the peace they wanted, which was to keep the two sides of the Sound under different political control. The old Danish blackmail of the Sound tolls was finished for good and the Swedish attempt to keep all foreign warships out of the Baltic was frustrated.

It was probably lucky for Sweden that her brilliant but irresponsible king died in 1660. The regency government for his young son, Charles XI, concluded the Peace of Copenhagen with Denmark (1660) which confirmed the Treaty of Roskilde, except that Sweden gave Bornholm and Trondheim back to Denmark. By the Peace of Oliva with Poland, also concluded in 1660, Sweden kept Livonia but not Polish (West) Prussia and Danzig, and the Polish Vasas finally gave up their claims to Sweden. Frederick William of Brandenburg who had manoeuvred unscrupulously between the parties had the possession of East Prussia confirmed in full sovereignty. In 1667 Poland made peace with Russia, at the cost of most of her territories east of the Dniepr.

The Cost Counted

The treaties of the Pyrenees, of Copenhagen and Oliva formed the necessary supplements to the Peace of Westphalia. The period that followed was concerned with new and different problems, its leaders filled with different ambitions. Yet there is much to be said for the old interpretation of the Thirty Years' War, as a single process from 1618 to 1648. People spoke of it in this way and by this name as early as the 1650s. They saw this unity in the central importance of the imperial and of the religious problems, even though the war ranged far beyond the frontiers of the Empire, and even though religion was only one, rarely the most important and certainly a diminishing motive force for the combatants. But the religious motivation was there, however Richelieu might deny it, and it was deliberately taken into account in the terms of the Peace of Westphalia. After 1648 there was a real change. Religion might still produce sympathy or antipathy between states, but it no longer determined alliances nor did it lead countries into war. From 1648 until the French Revolution the European states were engaged in pure power struggles only diaphanously veiled by the laws of inheritance and quotations from Grotius' *De jure pacis et belli*.

All this is clear enough and has been generally accepted; but the immediate effects of the Thirty Years' War on the economic, social and political structure of European society, and on its cultural life, are more difficult to interpret and have remained highly controversial. Only quite recently has it been recognized that the beginning of the war coincided with an economic crisis that affected most of Europe and some parts of the rest of the world, and that this crisis was followed by an economic depression that lasted, in varying degrees of severity, until at least the middle of the 17th century. The causes of the crisis and the depression are not yet fully understood. Almost certainly they were complex, compounded of such phenomena as the German currency inflation which made Dutch and English cloth temporarily unsaleable in central Europe, the vagaries of Spanish monetary policy, the dislocation and unemployment produced by the victory of the 'new draperies' over the traditional cloth industries of England, Holland and northern Italy, a decline of population with a consequent slump in agricultural prices (but why did population decline even in countries unaffected by war?) and the quite dramatic collapse of the Spanish-American trade after 1620—a collapse due, in its turn, primarily to the catastrophic decline of the native population in the Spanish American colonies during the previous hundred years. It seems inconceivable that the Thirty Years' War, with its destruction of life and property, its dislocation of trade routes and its distortion of investment and production for military purposes should not have added to the economic malaise. But exactly how this happened is far from clear; and the reverse effect —that of the depression on the course of the war—has hardly begun to be studied. The United Provinces, with their near-monopoly of the European carrying trade, with their profitable commerce with all the combatants and with their successful break into the Portuguese colonial trade, suffered least of all. The Swiss made neutrality pay very well. The English economy was sufficiently flexible to adjust itself, in the long run very successfully, to the changing economic circumstances. The French did not do nearly so well, and both the Spanish and the Italian economies continued to decline until the end of the century. The anti-economic ethos of a clerical and courtly society, which showed itself in the massive shift of capital investment from trade and manufacture to land purchase and building, caused the relative economic decline of southern Europe compared with the economically dynamic northwest.

The direct effects of the war on central Europe are better known, but their extent is still a matter for debate. The peasant revolt in Upper Austria (1626), with its strongly Lutheran tinge, still followed traditions that went back to the previous century. But another peasant revolt, in Bavaria in 1634, was quite free from religious motivation. The peasants rebelled against the elector who, they said, had delivered the country over to the detested soldiery. The scenes of soldiers' cruelties and the peasants' brutal retaliations, described in Grimmelshausen's *Simplicissimus* and etched in Callot's *Les Misères de la guerre*, are not exaggerated even if, for literary and artistic effect, different incidents may well have been brought together. It is not for nothing that in Germany the horrors of the Thirty Years' War have lived on in popular memory as those of no other war. Of the bigger cities only Magdeburg suffered complete destruction; but scores of smaller towns, and thousands of villages and hamlets, were plundered or burnt or left deserted by their inhabitants. The high mortality rates, however, were due mainly to local famines and to the contagious diseases spread by the soldiers and the refugees in the towns. North-western Germany, Prussia and most of Austria got off lightly. But in Brandenburg, Mecklenburg, Pomerania, in the Palatinate, in Württemberg and in parts of Bavaria population losses were up to fifty per cent or even more. The price paid by the common people for the ambitions of the princes and the arrogance of the churches was high indeed.

It does not seem, however, as if the war changed the secular trends of social development in central Europe. The imposition of a new serfdom on the peasantry of the Baltic littoral, from Denmark to Prussia and Poland and inland in Bohemia and Hungary had started in the 16th century, or even earlier, and was only accelerated by the population losses of the Thirty Years' War. By contrast, in many areas of western and southern Germany, the dissolution of the old manorial system, well advanced in 1618, was all but completed, and depopulation provided better opportunities for the surviving peasant families. Nor is it possible to see the war as a great cultural turning point in the history of Germany. While it lasted there was, naturally, very little money or opportunity for great building programmes or for the patronage of painting and sculpture. But the greatest period of German art had ended as early as the middle of the 16th century and a revival, the South German baroque, began not so long after the end of the war. The Bavarian monasteries, which had bought up cheaply the estates of the impoverished Bavarian nobility, proved to be among the most imaginative patrons of this art. If German literature produced no great dramatist or poet like Corneille or Calderon, Milton or Vondel, neither had it done so in the previous century. But it was precisely the emotional impact of the war which has left us the moving poetry of Gryphius and the devastating satires of Grimmelshausen and Moscherosch: a corpus of anti-war literature as powerful as any before Voltaire. In the middle of the war the Jesuit Spee had the courage to defy the traditions of the church and of his order and publish the first systematic attack on witch hunts and witch trials, the *Cautio criminalis* (1631/32). But it was in music that German creative gifts survived the war most triumphantly. Throughout its course, and often under tremendous difficulties and strain, Heinrich Schütz composed his motets and passions at Dresden, and so did many lesser musicians in courts, cities and village churches throughout the country. It seems as if people fled to music, perhaps even more than to religion, as a refuge and consolation from the almost unbearable ills of the times.

Power Struggles within the Empire

The Thirty Years' War started with a revolution in central Europe; it ended amid revolutions and *coups* all over western, southern and northern Europe. This was not fortuitous. The aim of all European monarchies was the imposition of effective central control over their countries. This brought them into conflict with forces that still retained, from the middle ages, autonomous powers within the country: estates and parliaments, provinces and cities, cathedral chapters, monasteries and universities, and above all the great nobles. Their powers and their respective importance varied from country to country. Often, some of them found their best interest in alliance with the monarchy. The lines were never sharply drawn, not least because the monarchies' own agents, law courts and royal officials, tended to imitate the autonomous corporations, claiming special privileges and immunities and often acting in opposition to royal commands and interests. Nevertheless, the conflict over ultimate power was perfectly clear. It might be temporarily compromised or postponed; it could not be permanently ignored. It was likely to flare up over questions of money and taxation, for here the wishes of the prince and of his subjects were diametrically opposed: the princes needed money

and their subjects did not want to pay. It was, moreover, always possible for these political and constitutional conflicts to become entangled with social movements that had, in themselves, very little to do with political power. From the latter part of the 16th century, religious differences became involved and these tended both to intensify and to internationalize the social and political conflicts in any particular country. Religious motivation and religious organization could become the basis of revolutionary movements spanning, at least temporarily, all classes, from the artisans of the cities to the highest nobility. Such was the case with the Huguenots, the Holy League and the Sea Beggars during the French and Netherlands civil wars in the 16th century. In Austria and Bohemia, however, where the cities were small, only the peasants could form a popular wing of a revolutionary movement; but the peasants here had their own, terrifying, revolutionary traditions, and the nobles, fearful of extending the revolution to their own estates, refused to accept the peasants as allies. In every case, however, in which religion was involved, the contestants tended to take up rigid attitudes, compounded of the self-righteous conviction of the justice of their own cause and intense distrust of the sincerity of their opponents. As a result, old and almost traditional struggles for a different balance of power within a state tended to turn into civil wars, fought à outrance for complete victory. Such civil wars inevitably forced both sides to look for allies outside their own country and to merge their private quarrels with the current international power struggles.

To many Germans this seemed to be precisely what was happening in the Holy Roman Empire during the Thirty Years' War, and this on two different levels. The first, the Bohemian revolt, was the classic case of an aristocratic-religious rebellion against a centralizing monarchy which turned into a deadly struggle for ultimate power during which both sides called on outsiders for help. The second—precipitated by the first—that of the struggle between the emperor and the estates of the Empire, was much more complex since the estates were, in fact, semi-independent princes and since the religious issue cut across the constitutional question. On the other hand, popular movements could not possibly become involved in this struggle, since no prince could put himself at the head of a movement which (as Maximilian of Bavaria found in 1634) must threaten him as much as the emperor. The outcome of the power struggle in the Empire was not a foregone conclusion. Indeed, it was only the intervention of Sweden and France which led to the decisive defeat of imperial power in Germany. Within the majority of the German states the power struggle between the monarchies (princes) and the autonomous forces (estates, parliaments, nobility) had yet to be decided. But the middle of the 17th century was not the time for this. Until 1650, when the great armies were finally disbanded, there could be no question of resistance to authority, and for another generation, at least, the Germans seem to have had enough of political struggles and wars. Characteristically, the stiffest resistance opposed to any German prince during this period came from the city of Königsberg in East Prussia, a province all but untouched by the great war (1662).

The Limits of Absolute Monarchy

In the states of western and southern Europe, however, it was precisely their involvement in the war which precipitated open conflicts for ultimate power. The war, coinciding as it did with the long years of economic depression, made demands on the financial resources and administrative machinery of these states which forced their governments both to extend their administrative competence and to increase taxation. But while these two policies were logically complementary, they proved to be politically incompatible. The bureaucratic machinery for the extension of royal power either did not exist at all or, where it did, was inefficient and ill-controlled. The greater the financial pressure, the more central governments were thrown back on the voluntary co-operation of the privileged classes and corporations. As early as the reign of Philip II, the Spanish government had been forced, by financial pressure and the incompetence and corruption of its own officials, to hand over recruiting and much of the administration and supply of the army to the provinces and cities. Olivares could not give up the monarchy's alliance with the Castilian nobility and was forced to adopt the plan of the Union of Arms which shifted the conflict from Castile, where the monarchy was strong, to Portugal and Catalonia, where it was weak. Since Olivares could not offer the Portuguese and Catalan ruling classes anything that they did not already possess, his political and financial demands inevitably raised against him the alliance of forces that rose in revolt in 1640.

In Naples, and perhaps also in Sicily, the Spanish monarchy was in a somewhat better position because it could offer more to the local nobility: rights of jurisdiction and administrative control over the provinces; even the collection of the rapidly increasing taxation. This alliance of monarchy and privileged classes did not work very harmoniously, and it placed such unbearable strains on the rest of the population that the consequent revolts were directed against both the governments and the nobility. This doomed these revolutions from the beginning.

The basic causes of the Fronde in France were essentially similar. In theory the French monarchy was absolute. Its legislative and executive authority and its almost unfettered powers of taxation were generally accepted throughout the country. In practice, however, the monarchy was limited by the virtually untouchable immunities of classes, corporations and individuals and by the lack of effective central control over the large and heterogeneous bodies of royal officials. As everywhere else, the prosecution of the war demanded both greater centralization and made it more difficult to carry this out. Thus Richelieu had to give up Sully's and Marillac's plans to convert the *pays d'états* into *pays d'élections*. The *intendants*, the most recent and effective agents of royal centralization, were bitterly resented by the other royal officials for interfering with their prerogatives and privileges. At the same time, war finance had greatly increased an already existing ground-swell of social discontent, doubly dangerous because it was often encouraged by the local nobility. The royal minority, after 1643, raised the question, not so much of royal authority as such, as of who had the right to exercise it and how far. It was over this very practical question that the civil wars of the Fronde were fought. Characteristically, the revolts were triggered off by quarrels over taxation and the universal hatred of the tax farmers and government bankers. But, at bottom, the question of finance and taxation mattered relatively little to the privileged classes. Different parties were willing to use popular movements for their own ends but took great care not to commit themselves, or allow themselves to be committed, to social revolution, as had happened sixty years earlier with the Holy League in Paris. The different opposition groups—the parlements, Cardinal de Retz and his followers, Condé, Orléans and the high nobility—always protested their loyalty to the principle of absolute monarchy (although in the case of Condé there was probably implicit a much more medieval view of the monarchy, in which the great nobles, especially the princes of the blood royal, formed the monarchy or state together with the person of the king). Nevertheless, their victory would undoubtedly have seriously weakened the monarchy as against the autonomous forces in the provinces and in the royal bureaucracy. Mazarin's eventual victory was necessary for the complete triumph of royal absolutism under Louis XIV.

The Netherlands had abolished their centralizing monarchy in their successful revolution of the 1570s. But in order to fight their long war against Spain they had found it necessary to set up a surrogate monarchy, the house of Orange-Nassau. The problems of the United Provinces were therefore still essentially similar to those of the great monarchies and they were even more closely linked to the pressures of war. It was when the war had ceased that they exploded into open conflict. Since, at least in the province of Holland, there was no significant noble estate, and since the religious issue, still so prominent in 1619, was all but dead thirty years later, the conflict came to be fought quite openly and starkly for political power. For financial reasons the estates of Holland demanded a substantial reduction of the army. William II saw this as a deliberate challenge to the power of the house of Orange. He had the backing of the other provinces and of the States General, and he tried to cajole and bully the cities of Holland to

support him. An attempted military *coup* against Amsterdam failed, but the regent party was clearly losing the struggle. At that moment William II died (November 1650) and the Orangist party collapsed for want of leadership. For the time being the Orangist attempt to establish a centralized monarchy in the United Provinces had failed.

But the most successful revolution against a centralizing monarchy occurred in England, the one western country which had dropped out of the Thirty Years' War after its first decade. Yet even in England the years of unsuccessful intervention in Germany and against Spain and France had left bitter memories of national failure and had burdened the monarchy with debts which, during the long years of economic depression, forced it to resort to one unpopular financial expedient after another. Characteristically, it was the attempted assertion of the royal authority over an outlying kingdom which caused the first break in Charles I's system (1638)—although in Scotland the immediate issue was not financial, nor directly related to the war, but (as in Bohemia in 1618) religion. But it was the Scottish war which finally ruined Charles I's shaky finances and thus precipitated the conflict between king and parliament.

Revolution and Compromise

The crisis of the European states at the end of the Thirty Years' War was a genuine crisis of societies and of their political constitutions. Even the Swiss cantons experienced it, when war-time prosperity had given way to post-war economic collapse. Then the remains of medieval democracy struck back against their patrician invaders in a peasants' war (1652–53) and an inter-cantonal war, fought belatedly under religious colours (1656). At stake everywhere were not only the patrician forms of government but the existing structure of society. Sometimes that structure was openly challenged from below, as in Naples and Palermo and in the *Ormée* of Bordeaux. Elsewhere, as in England, only some parts of established society were challenged, and the challenge came primarily from the propertied classes. A very similar challenge had been successful in the Netherlands in the 1570s; but the history of both the United Provinces of the Netherlands and the English Commonwealth was to show that the resultant changes produced their own political and social problems and that, to the surprise of contemporaries, they did not solve the fundamental political question of the age, that of the relation of a centralizing monarchy to the rest of the body politic. In France, in Portugal and in Catalonia this was from the beginning the central question, just as it had been in Bohemia and in the Empire. But since 17th century states were complex structures, with widely varying histories and traditions, the political problems were never posed in their pure form (except for the special case of the United Provinces in 1650) but were always entangled with a host of different social forces and personal ambitions.

The results of the revolutions were therefore very varied. The basic class structure of European society remained intact, was indeed confirmed. The genuinely popular and democratic movements were everywhere defeated. The privileged classes remained privileged. But within this very broad framework there appeared enormous differences. France, Spain and the newly-independent Portugal confirmed the absolutism of their monarchies, the special position of the Catholic church in their social and intellectual life and, to a rather more varying degree, the preponderance of their nobilities. In both Denmark and Sweden the monarchies were soon to establish their royal absolutism by *coups d'état* at the expense of the nobility. In Poland, on the other hand, the monarchy had finally lost its long struggle with the magnates, and the king had become a kind of Venetian doge in an aristocratic republic whose nobility was more rapacious and autocratic than the absolute monarchies of western Europe. The greatest transformations occurred in the United Provinces and in England. There, compromise solutions were found: mixed constitutions, the emancipation of intellectual life from clerical control, and the development of open and flexible, even though highly differentiated, social structures. These were the differences which were to determine the course of European history for the next hundred and fifty years.

VI FRANCE: MONARCHY
AND PEOPLE

From Henri III to Louis XIV

MENNA PRESTWICH

'Noble birth is nothing without virtue.'

MOLIÈRE

The roots of France

lay in the agricultural countryside. Foreign conquests, the material splendour of the aristocracy, the growing prosperity of the new *noblesse de robe*—all depended ultimately on the peasants and small farmers who paid their taxes and their rents. Passive, exploited, anonymous—they are the foundations of history.

Between 1630 and 1640 taxation practically quadrupled and prices rose steadily. Travellers from abroad saw peasants who looked 'like so many ghosts, not men'. They lived on rye bread and bean soup and after a bad harvest faced starvation. 'Destruction everywhere...' wrote a Venetian ambassador; 'most of the cattle have gone, so that they can no longer plough ... war and the sight of blood have made the people sly, coarse and barbarous.' Plague flourished in the wake of famine.

Desperation led to revolt. From 1620 there was not a single year which did not see peasant and urban uprisings. Lacking leadership and organization, they were savagely repressed.

As individuals the poor have no ·history, but occasionally in literature, and more often in art, where there was a strong tendency towards social realism, their voices can still be heard. Louis le Nain, the greatest and most compassionate of this school, painted the woman shown opposite in about 1645. It is a detail from a scene of family life. Le Nain does not sentimentalize or exaggerate; the faces of his subjects show a vigorous will to survive. Only the old woman who sits alone with her precious glass of wine has the withdrawn expression of one in whom suffering has destroyed hope.

The last of the Valois, Henri III, never wholly escaped from the domination of his mother, Catherine de Médicis. His reign was a disastrous attempt at compromise between political and religious factions, succeeding only in arousing the hostility of all. In 1589 he was stabbed by a fanatic monk. Henri was a weak neurotic, but he had a strong sense of kingship and upheld the legitimacy of Henri de Navarre's claim to the throne, even though the latter was a Huguenot. *Below:* Henri attends as a guest (at the end of the left-hand row) the wedding of the Duc de Joyeuse, one of his favourites.

Wars of religion split and impoverished France. The Huguenots, or French Protestants, had among their leaders Admiral Coligny, murdered at the Massacre of St Bartholomew (1572), and later Henri de Navarre. The Catholic extremists formed themselves into the Holy League, under the leadership of the Guise family, two of whom were murdered by Henri III at Blois in 1588. *Right:* Admiral Coligny (on the right) with his brothers Odet and François. *Above:* the forces of the League in procession through Paris in 1590. After the death of Henri III the city refused to recognize a Protestant king. The League held out for three years, only submitting when Henri IV changed his religion – 'Paris is worth a mass'. In this picture many wear the Cross of Lorraine in their hats, emblem of the Duc de Guise.

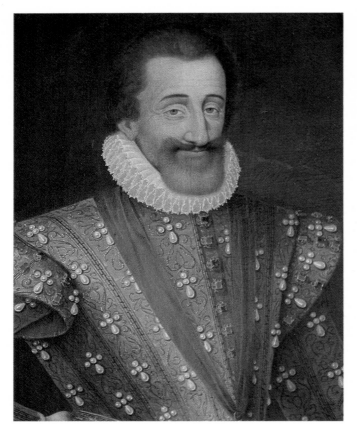

The new king, Henri IV, answered the country's need as no other man could. For him politics was the art of the possible. Relying on tolerance, compromise and reason he eventually won the trust of both Protestant and Catholic. He possessed, besides an acute judgment of men and affairs, a sense of the importance of sound finance.

Richelieu owed his bishopric to his family and his cardinal's hat to his skill as negotiator: his motives were indeed consistently political. He brought stability and greatness to France, achieving triumphs in foreign policy at a high social cost. This portrait by Champaigne shows his intellectual power and controlled determination.

The administration of France was subjected to reform first by Sully under Henri IV and then by Richelieu. Some efforts were made to render taxation equitable, but the system of hereditary public office (facilitated by the *paulette*) hampered improvements. Richelieu tried to promote a new class of disinterested civil servants, the intendants, drawn from the

professional classes, the *noblesse de robe*. Among the most outstanding of his ministers was Pierre Séguier (*below*) the descendant of a distinguished 16th-century legal family, for long in the service of the crown. He became Chancellor of France in 1635; this portrait, showing him with all the trappings of office, was painted by Charles Lebrun in 1661.

A regency – dangerous for any nation – followed Henri's assassination in 1610. Ten years earlier, after the death of his mistress, Gabrielle d'Estrées, he had divorced his first wife and married, for sound business reasons, Marie de Médicis – 'the fat banker', as the Parisians nicknamed her. The future Louis XIII was born in 1601. This allegorical painting by Rubens shows Henri confiding the government to the Queen on behalf of his nine-year-old son. It was under the wing of the Queen Regent that the new 'strong man' of France, Cardinal Richelieu, was to come to power.

A new sense of order entered French architecture during this period. After the fantasies and hybrid forms that had marked the early Renaissance came a fuller understanding, a tighter discipline and a more rational adaptation of classical example to the needs of contemporary urban life. Under the active patronage of the court the result was to transform first Paris and then France. The Place Dauphine (*left*) forms a triangle pointing towards the centre of the Pont Neuf. The Place Royale (*lower left*) is now called the Place des Vosges. Both squares combine Italian regularity with such traditional French features as steep roofs and dormer windows.

Parisian architects looked to Rome but created something that was characteristically French. Lemercier's church of the Sorbonne (*right*), begun in 1635, clearly reflects Italian models. At the Louvre Lemercier blended the earlier work of Lescot with his own in the Pavillon de l'Horloge (*far right*) where the top storey with its caryatids and square dome is entirely his and entirely French.

Spacious squares began to take the place of the narrow medieval streets. The Place Dauphine and the Place Royale were the first examples of modest, fairly plain town houses all grouped behind a unified façade and the façades themselves integrated into a master town-plan. The grandest project of all, the Place de France (*right*) was designed in 1610 but never completed. From a large semi-circular space eight avenues were to open out like a fan, each bearing the name of a French province. The buildings round it were to be markets and civic offices.

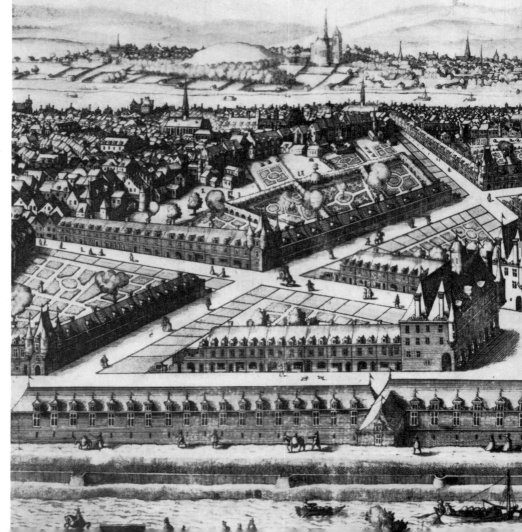

The problem of poverty was not peculiar to France, but French painters – or perhaps the patrons who commissioned them – seem to have been particularly alive to it. The Le Nain brothers from Laon have left a poignant record of rural conditions, including this painting, *Peasants' Meal*, of 1642. For some years, beginning in 1630, France had suffered a series of bad harvests, and there had been sporadic outbreaks of plague. In many areas the independent peasant farmers were forced to give up their holdings and become paid labourers. Sometimes whole villages were abandoned. Le Nain's peasants, in the centre and on the left, seem reasonably well off, and can still afford wine. But the man on the right, with bare feet and tattered clothes, is clearly in the last stages of poverty.

'Monsieur Vincent' – St Vincent de Paul – showed a sensitive response to the sufferings of the poor (which he shared), and founded charitable institutions. The most lasting were the Lazarites and the Filles de Charité who still flourish. This picture (*right*) painted after he was canonized in 1737, celebrates the two foundling hospitals which he set up. The rich women of Paris (Louise de Marillac was his most active helper) are bringing him their jewels, while members of the sisterhood tend the babies.

Jansenism was essentially a theological movement, drawing inspiration from St Augustine and emphasizing the corruption of man, society and the state. Christian perfection dictated a withdrawal from the world, and the Jansenist centre was Port-Royal near Paris. Philippe de Champaigne's daughter Catherine was one of the nuns. In 1661 she was cured of paralysis through the prayers of the prioress, Mère Agnes Arnauld. The artist's *ex voto* painting expresses the atmosphere of deep devotion, the miracle being suggested only by the ray of light from above.

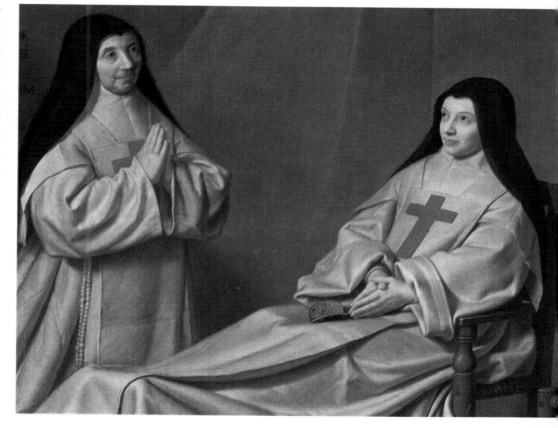

The quiet convent of Port-Royal (*right*) became the stormiest centre of religious controversy in 17th-century France. Jansen attacked empty forms of 'devotion' and authority that lacked spiritual understanding. Jansenism came into conflict with the Church, and in particular with the Jesuits, but made a profound appeal to many thoughtful Frenchmen, including Pascal and Racine. Regarded with suspicion by an authoritarian state, Port-Royal was finally suppressed in 1704, but the movement continued to agitate the Church in the 18th century.

The gap between rich and poor remained vast, despite the efforts of church and state. *Left:* another impassive social comment from the school of Le Nain showing a nobleman distributing alms to beggars.

Social conscience was awake. Charitable institutions multiplied and, though always within the orbit of the Church, the role of lay patrons increased. In 1602 Marie de Médicis founded the Congregation of St Jean de la Charité, at first with five friars from Florence. A new hospital was built in the Faubourg St Germain (*right*) – a well-lit airy room richly equipped even with four-poster beds. In the foreground some of the brethren prepare the food, which is taken to the patients by volunteer helpers.

The full horror of war is mercilessly portrayed in a series of etchings by the Lorraine artist Jacques Callot. He had seen the Thirty Years' War (Lorraine bordered on the Empire), the sieges of Breda and La Rochelle and the French invasion of his own province in 1633. *Below:* soldiers pillage a farmhouse, raping and murdering the inhabitants.

Having paid the debt of conscience, the upper classes – the court aristocracy, the rich bureaucracy and the Parisian financiers – were free to indulge a taste for luxury which was to increase for the next century. *Above*: two glimpses into the life of a rich household – (*left*) baking pies for Mardi Gras and (*right*) shopping in the Galérie du Palais Royal. The couple in this scene are dressed in the height of fashion; the shop behind them specializes in lace collars, ruffs, sleeves and fichus. These two details, as well as the hospital (*left*), are the work of Abraham Bosse, a prolific illustrator of social life.

Richelieu's successor, Cardinal Mazarin, brought with him from his native Italy a taste for the arts. He amassed a huge fortune by government financial deals and spent it on pictures (many from Charles I's collection), sculpture, manuscripts and *objets d'art*.

The young king: in this detail Louis XIV receives his brother into the Order of the Holy Spirit in 1654. The open book contains a picture of the occasion of the founding of the Order.

The fallen minister: Fouquet's trial for embezzlement lasted three years. He was convicted and imprisoned, dying in 1680.

Inauspiciously the next reign began with another regency. Louis XIII died in 1643 when his son was only five. Richelieu had died a few months earlier and the situation seemed threatening. But in the hands of the Queen Regent, Anne of Austria, and her dexterous minister Cardinal Mazarin the regime survived. Louis XIV assumed absolute power in 1661. That year saw the death of Mazarin and the fall of the Surintendant of Finance, Fouquet. Thenceforth Louis shared some of his responsibility with advisers like Colbert, but his ultimate authority with no one.

It was Fouquet who assembled the talents of the architect Le Vau, the painter Lebrun and the landscape gardener Le Nôtre to create the splendid château and grounds of Vaux-le-Vicomte (*above*). The wealth lavished upon this showpiece was one cause of the financier's downfall, but it set the scene for the age to come. The same three artists were taken over by Louis XIV and employed at Versailles.

From Henri III to Louis XIV

MENNA PRESTWICH

The *Guide des Chemins de France*, an early *Guide Michelin*, was published in 1553; it recommended hotels and wines, and described the attractiveness of both countryside and towns, while another account written on the eve of the Wars of Religion, offered the traveller the prospect of 'a great, indeed an infinite number of beautiful cities, towns, and villages, together with innumerable châteaux and attractive houses set in a smiling landscape, cultivated according to the best rules of husbandry'. French poets also painted a captivating vision. Joachim du Bellay compared the swaying wheat of Champagne and the Beauce to the sea, and sighed in Rome for the gentle countryside of Anjou. Ronsard, the poet laureate of Valois France, coming like Du Bellay from the Loire, expressed his sensuous delight in this idyllic and fertile valley when he wrote:

> *Versons ces roses près ce vin,*
> *Près de ce vin versons ces roses*
> *Et boyvons l'un à l'autre.*

The publication of a guide book indicates how much new there was to see in France. The Loire was freshly decorated with the royal châteaux of Blois, Amboise, Chambord and Chenonceaux. The Louvre in Paris, inspired by the Palazzo Farnese in Rome, advertised the new preference for classical models over flamboyant Gothic. Fontainebleau, the greatest of the palaces of Francis I, with its great gallery, stucco work and cartouches, displayed its ornate splendour just outside the capital. In it the king hung the masterpieces of Leonardo da Vinci—the *Mona Lisa*, the *Virgin of the Rocks* and the *Virgin with St Anne*—together with paintings by Titian and Raphael, so that Vasari called Fontainebleau a new Rome. The greatest of French 16th century architects was Philibert Delorme, who was commissioned by Cardinal Du Bellay, the uncle of the poet and the French diplomatic representative in Rome, to build a palace fitting for a great prelate. Delorme also built for Diane de Poitiers, the mistress of Henri II, the enchanting château of Anet, now largely destroyed, which combined individuality with classical feeling and evoked tributes both from Joachim du Bellay and Pierre de Ronsard. In her turn Catherine de Médicis, the neglected wife of Henri II, when a widow and Regent of France, asked Delorme to build the Tuileries. Her marriage united Valois and Medicean taste for splendour. The luxury industries, the pride of 17th century France, such as the silks of Lyons and Tours, the tapestries and enamels of Fontainebleau and the glass blowing of St Germain, derived their stimulus from the Valois court, to which Francis I had attracted such Italian artists as Benvenuto Cellini and Girolamo della Robbia.

Du Bellay wrote that Anet imitated 'tout l'art de l'antiquité', but he was unfair to Delorme's originality. Both the architecture and the poetry of the age displayed a subtle combination of classical forms with national traditions. Renaissance Italy and classical learning provided the catalyst, but national pride, especially strong by the mid-century, played its part. In 1549 Du Bellay inaugurated a new school of poetry, the *Pléiade*, with his *Défense et Illustration de la Langue Française*, declaring:

> *J'écris en langue maternelle,*
> *Et tâche à la mettre en valeur,*
> *Afin de la rendre éternelle*
> *Comme les vieux ont fait la leur:*

A scene from the description by Jean Dorat and Ronsard of the 'ballet de cour' given in 1573 to celebrate the election of Henri, Duc d'Anjou as the King of Poland. A special pavilion was erected in the Tuileries gardens for this spectacle, devised with Italian magnificence by Catherine de Médicis.

> *Si les Grecs sont si fort fameux,*
> *Si les Latins sont aussi tels,*
> *Pourquoi ne faisons-nous comme eux,*
> *Pour être comme eux immortels?*

> *(I write in my mother tongue in an endeavour to enhance it that I may give it eternal fame as the ancients did theirs.*

> *If the Greeks are so renowned, and the Romans too, why do we not do as they did, to be like them immortal?)*

He and Ronsard paraded their loyalties to Vergil and Horace, but they fused these with French traditions, just as the architects combined high-pitched roofs with classical pilasters. It is symbolic of their success that Du Bellay was criticized for using the classicism *patrie* when *pays* would have served.

'The Monstrous History of our Times'

National pride reflects the achievements of the early Valois. The peace of Cateau-Cambrésis in 1559 closed more than a half-century of war, registering the victory of the new nation-state which had destroyed Charles V's dream of a Christendom united under the direction of the Holy Roman Empire. In 1555 Charles V recognized defeat when he divided his lands between his son, Philip II, and his brother, Ferdinand, so that in future France faced not a single Empire but a dual monarchy with separate capitals in Madrid and Vienna. Italy remained a Habsburg sphere, but the cession of

The massacre of a Huguenot congregation in a barn at Vassy in 1562 sparked off the wars of religion. The Duc de Guise (B) and his men force the people in desperation to flee through the rafters.

Metz, Toul and Verdun shifted French power eastwards to the Meuse. The cult of France rings in the poetry of Du Bellay, who assured Henri II that he was about to become Henry IX of England, while in 1559 Ronsard acclaimed him as a new Caesar who had restored the Gallic frontiers:

> *Bornant plus loin ta France et fait boire aux François*
> *Aux creus de leurs armets en lieu de l'eau de Seine*
> *La Meuse Bourguignonne.*
>
> *(Setting more distant boundaries to your France, and giving the French to drink in the hollow of their helmets the Burgundian Meuse instead of the water of the Seine.)*

Du Bellay died in 1560. Ronsard lived to see and to deplore the civil wars, which, endemic for the next half-century, changed the face of France. In 1562 he asked:

> *O toy historien, qui d'ancre non menteuse*
> *Escris de nostre temps l'histoire monstrueuse,*
> *Raconte à nos enfans tout ce malheur fatal,*
> *Afin qu'en te lisant ils pleurent notre mal,*
> *Et qu'ils prennent exemple aux péchés de leurs pères,*
> *De peur de ne tomber en pareilles misères.*
>
> *(O historian who with truthful ink writes the monstrous history of our times, tell our children of all this disastrous ill-fortune, that in reading your words they may weep for our wrongs and learn from the example of their fathers, for fear of falling prey to like afflictions.)*

What answer can a historian give to Ronsard? Why did the strong government of Francis I disintegrate under the later Valois? A major problem, and to Ronsard the insuperable one, lay in the growth of a vociferous and fanatical Huguenot minority. The age of Erasmus had passed; intransigent Calvinism faced reinvigorated Catholicism. Cardinal du Bellay, who had thought Gallicanism a greater danger to the Papacy than Protestantism, and Bishop Caracciolo of Troyes, whose hopes of presiding over the two confessions led only to his deposition, were genial relics. Ronsard invoked a dying humanism when he wrote:

> *Car Christ n'est pas un Dieu de noise ny discorde:*
> *Christ n'est que charité, qu'amour et que concorde.*
>
> *(For Christ is not a God of quarrelling nor of discord, Christ is pure charity, love and concord.)*

Irenical formulas tried at the Colloquy of Poissy by Michel de l'Hôpital, the Erasmian Chancellor of Catherine de Médicis, failed when faced by an uncompromising Calvinist delegation led by Theodore Beza. Beza had once been a close friend of Ronsard, modelling his verses on Catullus and writing odes to a Candida whose existence he disclaimed after his conversion. In 1562 co-existence based on an edict of toleration foundered when the massacre of a Huguenot congregation at Vassy inaugurated the civil wars. The Huguenots rightly blamed the Duke of Guise for this, but they had themselves been organizing mass demonstrations and going armed to meetings. Ronsard declared both his faith in Christ and his love for Ceres and Bacchus, but his exhortation to Beza:

> *Ne presche plus en France une Evangile armée,*
> *Un Christ empistollé tout noircy de fumée,*
> *Portant un morion en teste, et dans la main*
> *Un large coustelas rouge du sang humain.*
>
> *(Preach no more in France a Gospel of violence, an armed Christ blackened with smoke, helmeted, and in his hand a great cutlass red with human blood.)*

fell on deaf ears. By now Huguenot communities were to be found in almost all regions of France, and in 1561 Coligny counted 2,150 of their churches.

But why did a minority movement, originally contained, burst the barricades after 1559? Was this the result of a change in the composition, structure and outlook of the Huguenot movement? Does religion account for the wars which were deplored as much by the Catholic Ronsard as by the Huguenot poet, Agrippa d'Aubigné? Attempts to give the Calvinism of the earlier century a class basis are unconvincing. Its appeal to merchants and artisans has been emphasized, but the lists of convicted heretics show the response of a variety of social groups, including lawyers, civil servants, priests, court circles and peasants. It was the court poet, Clément Marot, a humanist drawn to Calvinism, who translated the psalms into French verse, sung by the artisans and peasants of Saintonge, intoned by martyrs at the stake and chanted by Huguenot troops in battle. Huguenot churches answer to no particular geographical pattern, although proximity to Geneva played its part. The universities helped to spread the new ideas among the professional classes, while social discontent provided fertile soil, especially in areas where tithes were heavy, as in Normandy. But the turning-point came in the reign of Henri II with both the tight organization of the churches, staffed by pastors trained in Geneva, and important conversions at Court. The three Châtillon brothers, Gaspard de Coligny, François d'Andelot and the Bishop of Beauvais, members of the great house of Montmorency, and the two Bourbon princes, Antony, King of Navarre, and Louis, Prince of Condé, all became Calvinists. The importance of such conversions can be illustrated by the case of d'Andelot. As captain-general of the Infantry he had patronage in the army, while in 1558 he conducted a successful proselytizing tour around Nantes, where his wife owned great estates. The defeat of St Quentin in 1557 was seen by the king as a divine judgement on the spread of heresy; by way of expiation he arrested d'Andelot and issued a new edict against Calvinism.

The Politics of Religion

It is an open question whether civil war would have occurred had Henri II lived: it was made inevitable by the political problems inherent in feeble minority government, by the financial and administrative legacies of the wars against the Habsburgs, and by the social tensions which these exacerbated. Ronsard attributed the wars to religious fanaticism, but towards their close the royalist pamphlet, the *Satire Ménippée*, which urged the succession of Henri IV, contemptuously held that simpletons and idiots had been taught this easy answer; the real problem stemmed from the struggles of the three great families, the Guises, the Bourbons and the Montmorencys, for place, power and profit. Henri II had preserved a delicate balance between the Guises and Montmorencys, though the Prince of Condé already considered his pension inadequate for a Prince of the Blood. The accession of

The 'Satire Ménippée' attacking Spanish Catholic intervention in the wars of religion, cast Philip II in the role of the organ-playing Spanish charlatan, advertizing on the parchment behind him his miraculous drug 'Catholicon composé', literally a purgative panacea.

A League satire on Henri III shows him as the Devil, gloating over the murder of the Duc and Cardinal de Guise at Blois 1588; behind him is the characteristic procession of penitents. The next year the king was in his turn to be murdered by the League.

Francis II, a minor, gave power to the Guises, since their niece was married to the king. The *Satire Ménippée* correctly put court conflicts at the centre of the stage, but much depended on the capacity of the principal actors to dominate the crowd scenes.

The great nobles already derived power from tenurial clientage, but the collapse of crown credit gave them new leverage. Debt forced Henri II to make peace at Cateau-Cambrésis, on less triumphant terms than those proclaimed by Ronsard, and hampered crown initiative in the next decades. War finance had led to the sale of offices, with an acceleration of sales from 1542 and a heightened tendency towards hereditary transmission. Government administrative control was enfeebled, especially since courtiers were often rewarded by being given offices to sell. This new source of clientage gave them a grip upon the civil service and the army, so that in 1561 L'Hôpital considered that the Crown had neither hands nor feet. Court factions could also utilize class tensions. Conspicuous spending, a feature of Renaissance society, was enhanced in France by the example of the court and of the splendours of Italy. But in 1559 the gentlemen of France faced both demobilization and the European price rise. In the reign of Charles IX a Huguenot nobleman held that eight out of ten gentlemen were in debt or had sold land, while the rest managed with difficulty. The new purchasers of land were either merchants or office-holders. L'Hôpital connected social resentments, civil disorder and religious disaffection when he said that many assumed the mantle of religion, although they were sceptics and even atheists, and that they included those who had dissipated their fortunes and looked to recoup by making trouble in the kingdom. Ten years later Coligny advised war against Spain, partly on the grounds that Huguenot gentlemen had become so addicted to anarchy and plunder that it was desirable that they should indulge in these tastes outside the kingdom.

But the court factions needed a cause and found it in religious antagonisms. The Netherlands nobles, infuriated by their exclusion from government, successfully manipulated Calvinist discontent. Conversely, the revolt of the Earl of Essex in England in 1601 failed because, although he sought to use the antipathy of country against court, he made no appeal to principle and the yeast of religious discontent was missing. But the Prince of Condé, in debt like Essex, could call on Huguenot organization in his role as Protector-General of the Churches of France, while as a prince of the blood he could appeal to the distrust of the country gentlemen for an Italianate court. The massacre of St Bartholomew registered the failure of the Huguenots to capture the court, but

they had already failed to carry the country. Lacking coherent leadership, the wars had seen them driven south of the Loire. Calvin had quickly sensed the damage which Condé's cynicism inflicted on a religious movement, and he, like Coligny, deplored the aristocratic stamp which Condé gave to Huguenotism. Popular support evaporated, since tithes were not abolished but appropriated by nobles and Huguenot churches, while pastors castigated the social menace of the *canaille*. The Huguenot political theory of a contract between king and people was explosive, but its effect was dampened by a restrictive definition of the latter. Yet the part played by religion as a reason for protracted war shines out in the resistance of towns like La Rochelle and in the conviction of gentlemen such as the Huguenot poet, Agrippa d'Aubigné, who deplored civil war, but yet urged the need to fight for the City of God.

The containment of the Huguenots did not lead to a recovery of power by the Crown. Henri III, the last of the Valois, a flagellant and a transvestite, presided over a corrupt and extravagant court. The beneficiary of his misgovernment was the Duke of Guise, who organized the Catholic League and received subsidies from Philip II. In 1588 and 1589 the monarchy faced its most dangerous crisis before the French Revolution. The Estates General at Blois pressed demands designed in the eyes of the Venetian envoy to make France a republic and the king a doge. Political and social strains lay behind the League, but its fanaticism was provided by the friars and Jesuits. Henri III despoiled the Church and equivocated with the Huguenots: his insistence on the hereditary succession, which meant the prospective accession of Henri of Bourbon, forced the crisis. The Huguenot theory of contractual monarchy was adopted by the League and given a lethal edge when the Church sanctioned assassination. In 1588 the Sorbonne declared Henri III deposed on religious, moral and political grounds; he was murdered in the next year.

Henri IV: 'all things to all men'

Puritanism would give momentum to the revolution of 1641 in England; Catholicism gave it to the revolution of 1589 in France. In the 17th century the Catholic Church was to be the bulwark of the monarchy and the social order; under Henri III it was the religion of radicalism and discontent. The League, like the Huguenot movement, was backed by ambitious nobles and depressed squires, but it had a popular basis in the urban revolutions which, stimulated by the example of Paris, spread rapidly in a period of unemployment and high prices. Communes, drawing on

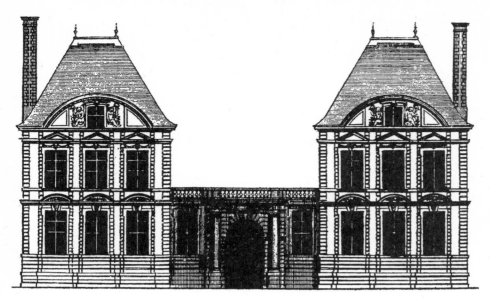

The Hôtel de Sully built 1624–9 was designed for a rich financier by Jean Ducerceau; in 1634 Henri IV's great finance minister, Sully, bought it. This elevation of the entrance as it looked originally shows its richly carved decoration and allegorical figures, reminiscent of another great private house, the Hôtel Carnavalet.

the underworld, organized through guilds and fraternities, were directed by lawyers and petty officials, who found the higher bureaucracy barred by the emergent caste of hereditary office-holders. The murder of Henri III unleashed a movement which menaced degree and property. But just as Calvinist democracy in the Netherlands stimulated a counter-revolution and the return of the southern Netherlands to Spain, so Catholic demagogy alienated many and drove them to support Henri of Bourbon. He was at once the patriot king and the saviour of society.

Sanity and scepticism came to the aid of Henri IV. The *Satire Ménippée* exposed the selfish interests behind the League, enlarged on the social dangers and, anticipating Marx, declared religion to be the opium of the people. Ronsard died in 1585. He deplored both the corruption of the court and also the fanaticism of the League. When he described the Jesuits as 'les mignons de Jésus-Christ', he was maliciously adopting the word currently used of the favourites of Henri III. He already looked to the accession of Henri IV, saying:

> *Rien n'est meilleur, rien plus doux que ce Roy,*
> *Rien plus humain, rien n'est de plus affable.*
>
> *(None better, none gentler than this King*
> *None more human, none more affable.)*

His humanism was shared by Montaigne, whose essays, published in an enlarged edition in 1588, the year of revolution, tried to solve the conflict between faith and reason by separating the two and to give a comfortable basis to scepticism by advocating outward conformity. Montaigne's disciple was Henri IV, who had stayed with him in Guyenne, and who held that Paris was worth a mass.

Ronsard's salute to Henri IV was the first of many; indeed few kings have enjoyed so consistently high a reputation. When Henri was assassinated in 1610 the Jesuits, sensitive to their association with the doctrine of tyrannicide, compared the king who had allowed them to return to France, to St Louis and Constantine. Malherbe, the *doyen* of the Paris literary world, although full of grief at the murder of Henri IV was yet sardonically amused to hear that the Jesuits were pressing for his canonization. This did not materialize, but the coincidence of the murder occurring on a Friday occasioned comment, as in the case of President Lincoln. In a pamphlet published during the minority of Louis XIII the ghost of Henri IV unctuously urged on his son the virtues of moral purity and sound religion such as he himself had upheld. Henri was adaptable during his life, and after his death. He was acclaimed both as the protector of the oppressed and as the guardian of the social order; he was applauded both as the *bon vivant* who wanted the peasants to enjoy chicken on Sundays and as the authoritarian who had stifled ugly democracy in the towns. During the Fronde his constitutional rule was contrasted with the perversion of monarchy by Richelieu; yet he was held up to the

young Louis XIV as a model king. He was blessed by Bossuet, a pillar of orthodoxy, and saluted by Voltaire, a crusader for rationalism, while the physiocrats looked to Sully, Henri's finance minister, as their patron. When kings were denounced during the French Revolution, Henri IV was honourably excepted, while in this century Vichy France praised a king who had based his rule on an industrious, pious peasantry. How far did Henri IV deserve and why did he attract these diverse tributes?

Henri IV had natural charm, while his years in the wilderness confirmed his dislike for dogma and taught him to tolerate what he could not avoid. He was all things to all men, but went his own way. He gave the Huguenots toleration by the Edict of Nantes, while under the influence of Cardinal Bérulle, the leader of the French Catholic Counter-Reformation, his court became a centre of piety, harmlessly directed towards charitable works, and untainted by League radicalism. Two of Henri's ministers, Jeannin and Villeroi, had been Guise clients, but Sully presided over a Treasury staffed by his Huguenot co-religionists. Henri had a Jesuit confessor but a Huguenot doctor, and chose as the tutor for his sons a Rabelaisian sceptic, Vauquelin des Yveteaux, who was attacked as a corrupting influence, since he held that it was conduct, not dogma, which counted.

Henri preserved a delicate balance. His concern was recovery of power for the monarchy and the reassertion of the absolutist traditions of the early Valois. But he knew when to stoop to conquer, when to apply the principle of divide and rule, and when to use both intimidation and conciliation. Thus he struck at the regional influence of the great nobles, but placated them with court pensions. Sir George Carew, the English ambassador, considered that the nobles 'did wholly so frame themselves to obey all the King's commandments and becks, as there is no schoolmaster that hath his subjects in more awe than this king hath these gentlemen'. The Louvre was prefiguring Versailles.

But the office-holders, the 'fourth estate' of the realm, presented Henri IV with a subtle problem. The League had demonstrated the political strains which could result from the demand for offices exceeding the supply. Henri found the *Parlements*, the judicial bodies which enforced royal edicts, intent on preserving oligarchical power. Their moral arguments against the extension of office-holding thinly concealed self-interest. But in 1604 Henri and Sully, needing money, opened the doors of office by the device of the *paulette*, which made hereditary tenure secure on the payment of a small annual tax, whereas previously patents had to be sealed forty days before the death of the holder, an inconvenient rule in an age of plague and sudden death. Office-holders now acquired a stake in the Bourbon dynasty, much as purchasers of monastic land in England supported the Reformation or holders of Bank of England stock invested in the Protestant Succession. The crown gained a revenue, which could be inflated at will by imposing stiffer terms, for although reversion was legalized, the exact terms on which offices were held were confined to nine years. Secondly, the crown could place new offices on the market. The *Parlements*, intimidated by Henri's speeches but sweetened by the easy terms of the *paulette*, offered only soft centres of resistance. Moreover, official sales broke the connections between the nobility and the provincial bureaucracy, so dangerous in the time of the Guises. After the *paulette* Henri could remark complacently that no one in future could point to an office-holder and say that he was the client of this or that nobleman.

Calm on the Surface

Conciliation was nevertheless expensive: pensions eroded the revenues and office-holders looked to a return on their investments. Yet both Henri and Sully appreciated the link between the power and the wealth of the crown, and the dependence of both on a healthy economy. Their concern is understandable. In 1596 Henri IV found military operations against Spain crippled by lack of funds, while the Assembly of Notables at Rouen gloomily discussed the economic depression resulting from the wars. The challenge was met. Under Sully the gross revenue increased by only 11%, but the net revenue doubled. This was achieved partly by a shift to indirect taxes, possible when economic recovery followed peace, but largely by a reduction of administrative costs, for office-holders were made to account. Secondly, Sully was backed by a king who was prepared to curb his pleasure in spending. Court expenditure was curtailed and pensions were shrewdly calculated. Deficit finance weakened other states, but an accumulated surplus enabled Henri IV to build a war reserve in the Bastille. Sir George Carew graphically described Henri walking in the garden between the Arsenal and the Bastille, boasting that 'none other hath such an alley to walk in, having at the one end thereof armour for 40,000 men ready prepared; and at the other end money to pay them, even to the end of a long war'.

Henri looked to prosperity as well as power. Carew admired the king's 'economical faculty, or looking into matters of profit', noting that Henri omitted 'no means of enriching his realm generally'. Agricultural treatises received the *imprimatur* of the court, while Sully allocated funds for improving communications. The luxury industries of the Valois were revived to capture foreign markets and to stop leakage of currency on Italian imports. Carew, observing how 'neat and nimble' French craftsmen were,

Jean Toutin, goldsmith, engraver and enamel painter, incorporated a design for jewellery in this illustration of a goldsmith at work. The revival of the French luxury industries was a deliberate policy of Henri IV, who enticed foreign craftsmen with grants of privilege.

emphasized the success of the royal industries, such as the Gobelins tapestries and the silk carpets, made 'after the fashion of those of Persia', the satins and the velvets, and reported that he had been reliably told that in Paris 'there were about five hundred families which were served all in silver vessels'. At the end of the reign of Louis XIV a French businessman observed that the luxury exports were the Indies of France, and their success had owed much to the impulse of Henri IV.

Henri once said of himself, 'People say that I am mean, but I do three things which have no connection with avarice, for I make war, I make love and I build.' Henri had a galaxy of mistresses. One charming item in the royal accounts runs: '15,000 écus à la Néri, cette belle fille'. Paris was a battered capital when he entered it, but the *Mercure Français* boasted that no sooner was Henri master of the city but masons were at work, while Malherbe in 1608 told a friend in Provence that he would soon be unable to recognize the town. The Valois had loved the Loire. Henri concentrated on the Seine, extending along its banks the Louvre and the Tuileries, set among gardens, planted with mulberries, pomegranates and cypresses, which were planned by Pierre Le Nôtre. Henri built the Pont Neuf, linking the new business and administrative centre to the Left Bank, and drove the Rue Dauphine through the alleys of the old city. Louis XIV had a passion for fortifications; Henri IV loved urban development. His two great squares, the Place Dauphine and the Place Royale (since known as the Place des Vosges) combined Italian elegance with the grouping of modest town houses, and were imitated in England around 1630 when Covent Garden was built. The projected Place de France designed like an open fan, with eight avenues leading off, each to be named after a province of France, was never completed. Henri's buildings combined grandiose ambition with business realism. The gallery of the Louvre housed the studios of the royal architects, painters and craftsmen; the arcades of the Place Royale had shops to attract foreign visitors, and the Place Dauphine contained a goldsmiths' quarter. Although the planning of the squares emanated from the court, the buildings were financed by the rich bureaucrats, and the fashionable homes of the *noblesse de robe* centred on the Place Royale. The new townscape both exemplified the support of the office-holders for the Bourbon dynasty and also advertised the resilient response of Paris to the lead given by Henri IV.

The literary world mirrored the new tranquillity. Paris bowed to the court poet, Malherbe, the critic of Ronsard and the advocate of control and restraint in style. His father, an office-holder in Caen, had turned from Calvinism to Catholicism and back again. But Malherbe, a conformist, thought that 'la religion des princes était la religion des honnêtes hommes' and believed in absolute monarchy. The influential Huguenot pamphlet, the *Vindiciae contra tyrannos*, had in 1579 advocated changing the captain when the ship was making for the rocks, but Malherbe held that mere passengers should not interfere. Yet the thick sediment of Catholic fanaticism was easily stirred both over the Huguenot question and over foreign policy. Catholic sentiment preached ideological alliances with the Habsburgs, thus opposing nationalist opinion, which remembered the support given to the League by Philip II, and considered Habsburg power still dangerous. The Peace of Vervins in 1598 had left almost intact the Habsburg rampart, which encircled the French frontiers from the Jura to the Channel, and thrust forward a salient in the north-east. Beauvais was still a fortified town; Paris was uncomfortably close to Spanish armies in the Netherlands. In 1610 Henri IV, allied to German Protestant princes, was preparing to use the treasure in the Bastille for war on the Rhine against the Habsburgs.

It can be argued that he chose his moment well, since conflicts in Vienna and Prague neutralized Imperial power, but Henri's posthumous reputation probably owes much to the accident that the war was never fought, for the king was assassinated on the eve of his departure from Paris. The years of peace had given only a veneer of prosperity. The Governor of Guyenne had warned Henri of general resentment against heavy taxation while Carew qualified his usual admiration when he said that 'concerning the common people, they hold it a true principle of state in France, that they must be kept low and out of heart by exactions and oppressions'. In his view the taxes were so heavy that 'they are scarce able to go or wag under them'. Carew was horrified by the price of highly taxed salt and infuriated by the duties paid by his Loire wine on its way to Paris. Another diplomat, Sir Dudley Carleton, while paying tribute in 1610 to the 'sumptuous buildings', the new roads and canals, yet deplored the 'poor face of the people and such extreme misery that happiness is only known by comparison'. War and heavier taxation as the century proceeded led to much greater suffering, and it was against an increasingly dark background of misery and degradation that the reign of Henri IV became in retrospect suffused in a golden light.

Louis XIII's minority, when a Médicis was again regent of France, showed not only the fragility of government in the absence of an effective king, but also how much had been accomplished. There were rebellions and constitutional friction, but the fabric of the Bourbon monarchy held. Marie de Médicis inherited her family taste for splendour, and deficits replaced Sully's balances. The court was dominated by favourites and tarnished by scandal, while pensions mounted, distributed according to whim and fear, not policy and prudence. The crown building programme concentrated on royal palaces. In the year after Henri's death the regent, anxious to emulate Catherine de Médicis who had possessed the Tuileries, sent to Florence for the plans of the Pitti palace as a model for the Luxembourg. Her architect, Salomon de Brosse, was the first since Delorme to concentrate on mass instead of decoration. But the interior, entrusted to Rubens, the greatest Baroque artist of the age, was lavishly ornate, and the gardens had elaborate fountains, served by the first aqueduct designed for this purpose seen in France, and for which the young king laid the foundation stone. Marie de Médicis combined extravagance with fashionable piety so that money was also poured out on paintings and chapels for religious orders in Paris. Moreover she abandoned the foreign policy of Henri IV, bowing to Catholic solidarity by marrying Louis XIII to the Spanish infanta, Anne of Austria, the daughter of Philip III.

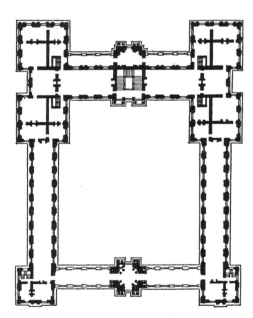

Marie de Médicis commissioned the Luxembourg palace from Salomon de Brosse in 1615. The plan was based on the traditional pattern of main block, two wings and a screen enclosing a court. The wing on the right housed the gallery for Rubens' great series of paintings

The Young Richelieu

Misgovernment and social tensions offered the Prince of Condé opportunities to attempt the role once played both by his own family and also by the Guises. The Huguenots had their fortified towns and feared aggressive Catholicism. Carew had thought that there was a danger that 'the husbandman, and the citizen and artificer, finding that they have no interest in the conservation of a

government, whereby they are oppressed, and that they receive of a monarchy nothing but *le fournir et le servir*, must needs be desirous of a change'. He considered that the towns, 'like the bondsmen of a galley', might rise again as in the time of the League. The *Parlements* had yielded reluctantly to Henri IV's authoritarianism, while the economic malaise of the nobles, a main cause of the anarchy of the later 16th century, still continued. Returns from estates were rising and dues in kind were a hedge against inflation, but the nobility were encumbered by debts incurred during the civil wars and still lived extravagantly. According to Loyseau, whose *Traité des Ordres* of 1610 provides the classic exposition of the structure of French society, a noble who engaged in sordid money making lost caste. Office-holding could have provided a supplementary source of revenue, but education as well as money was required for entry into the bureaucracy. In England the gentry swarmed into Oxford and Cambridge, stimulated by the hope of employment in the civil and diplomatic services, but the French squires stayed aloof from university education. The English ambassador in 1598 had sympathized with their plight, lamenting that France was governed by the 'pen-and-ink gentlemen; whilst the nobles themselves, lacking in education are given no employment'. The situation had not changed; debt forced the provincial squires to continue to sell land to merchants and office-holders, and they resented the weakening of their social and political supremacy.

These class antagonisms, accentuated by the introduction of the *paulette*, foiled the intrigues of Condé. Tocqueville held that the great crime of the monarchy lay in causing the divisions between the classes, but those divisions also preserved the monarchy. The force of Henri IV's boast that he had broken the links of clientage between the nobility and the office-holders was demonstrated in the Estates General of 1614, when the Estate of the Nobility both asked that a proportion of offices be allotted to them and demanded the abolition of the *paulette*. Concerted pressure was impossible: instead the crown was called in as arbiter. The ebb and flow of revolt in the next years showed the value of the *paulette* as a divisive agent, yet since moral denunciations of the sale of office made the crown uneasy, definitive re-establishment of the *paulette* did not take place until 1620. The grant was then made on conditions favourable to the crown, while preferential terms for holders of legal posts ensured that the monarchy could in future exploit jealousies within the ranks of the office-holders. While the crown raised from office-holders about 8% of the revenue under Henri IV, this rose to 38% between 1620 and 1624.

This last year saw Louis XIII showing judgement by allowing Richelieu to dominate the government, and it is worth pausing to consider the problems which faced the young Cardinal. Richelieu inherited chaos in the Treasury and graft in the provinces, for sale of office, though a political emollient, was an administrative irritant, since office-holders tended to be lax and dishonest. Besides, part of the attractions of office lay in procuring exemption from the *taille* or land-tax; this might take two or three generations but inevitably led to a heavier burden being placed on the peasantry. Richelieu's assumption of office coincided with the beginning of the era of peasant and urban revolts; like marsh gas, when snuffed out in one place they bubbled up in another. Finally, Catholic pietism was gaining ground against its various enemies: Gallicanism with its anti-papal doctrines, Huguenotism protected by the Edict of Nantes, and the sceptical tradition bequeathed by Montaigne. In 1623 the young and brilliant court poet, Théophile de Viau, suspected of atheism and hated by the Jesuits, was imprisoned in the cell once occupied by Ravaillac, the assassin of Henri IV, and burned in effigy on the charge of obscenity. In 1625 the Franciscan, Marin Mersenne, later the patron of science and mathematics, declaimed that there were fifty thousand atheists in Paris, while other preachers howled against insolent free-thinkers, who corrupted manners and morals.

Yet when Louis XIII died in 1643 this first part of the century was christened '*le siècle des saints*', for the Catholic movement produced Cardinal Bérulle, the promoter of reform among the secular clergy, St François de Sales, the writer of popular devotional manuals, and St Vincent de Paul, the apostle of charity and a champion of orthodoxy. Catholic pietism was also personi-

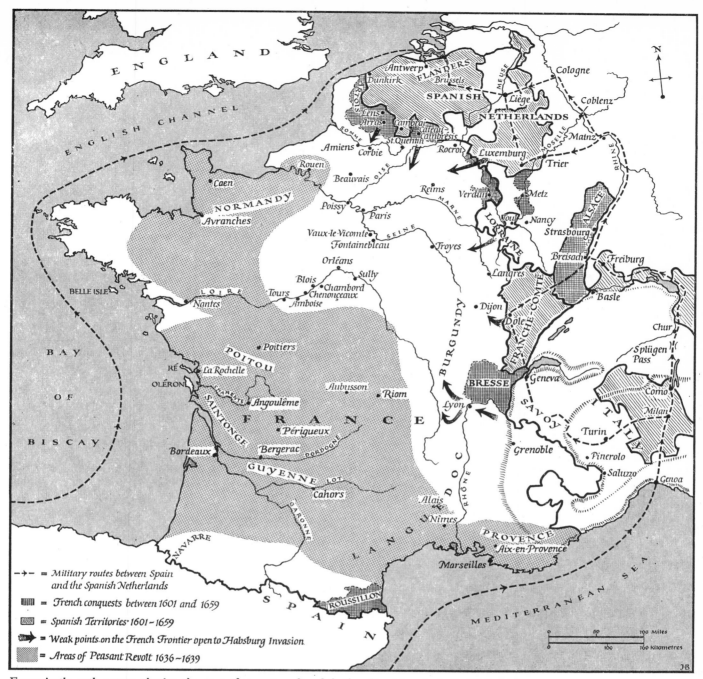

France in the 17th century, showing also areas of peasant revolt and the three Spanish routes to the Netherlands.

Legend:
- = Military routes between Spain and the Spanish Netherlands
- = French conquests between 1601 and 1659
- = Spanish Territories 1601–1659
- = Weak points on the French Frontier open to Habsburg Invasion
- = Areas of Peasant Revolt 1636–1639

fied in men such as Father Joseph, the aristocratic Capuchin, who led a mission to convert the Huguenots of Poitou and who sought to unite Catholic Europe in a crusade against the Turks. In 1624 the Catholic party was victorious at court. Louis XIII had just led a war of religion in the Loire valley, while the Jesuits had persuaded him that a Huguenot revolt in Béarn in 1620 presaged an international conspiracy against monarchs. As a result, the king both refused help to the Bohemian nobility in their revolt against the Emperor Ferdinand II and also persuaded the Protestant Union of German princes, to which Henri IV had given his patronage, to disarm at Ulm. The Austrian Habsburgs conquered Bohemia; the Spanish Habsburgs occupied the Rhenish Palatinate. The rampart running from Milan to the Netherlands had been strengthened, and the encirclement of France had been practically accomplished. The weakening of the French position as a result of Catholic influence on foreign policy presented Richelieu with what he considered his greatest problem. He always gave first priority to challenging the Habsburgs. Other problems had to be solved—or left unsolved—within this context.

Richelieu was a complex character. He was a worldly prelate, but yet possessed a piety which stemmed from his predilection

for obedience and submission. Yet when he put the interests of the state before those of the Church, he suffered from no guilt or conflict, for the monarchy had a charismatic aura and its divine institution was a fundamental of French political thought. Born in 1585, Richelieu's early memories were of his father's estates overrun by League troops in the pay of Spain. His reply to the Spanish occupation of the Palatinate was to try to seal the eastern passes of the Alps to the Spanish *tercios* by sending an expeditionary force to occupy the Grisons, the Swiss cantons which had been clients of Henri IV. The conquest of Bohemia foreshadowed Imperial domination of Germany and a subsidy was therefore given to Christian IV of Denmark, who was threatening an invasion in the north. But Richelieu overplayed his hand, for French finance could not sustain these gestures. The forces had to be withdrawn from the Grisons, making the moral clear; if Richelieu were to play the role of Henri IV he needed the sound financial basis which Sully had provided.

But the accumulated debt was now 52 million *livres* and the deficit ran at 11 million, while as much as 30% was asked on short-term loans. Richelieu's answers were not narrowly financial and administrative, since he set these problems in their general

Plus on a de moyens, plus on en veut auoir
Ce pauure apporte tout, bled, fruit, argent, salade
Ce gros Milord assis, prest a tout receuoir
Ne luy veut pas donner la douceur d'une œilla
                                              de

a la mouche
qui volle
il ne faut
point dais

Il faut
paier ou
agréer.

A tous
Seigneurs
tous
honneurs.

Maigre
comme un
leurier
dataché

Le Noble est l'araignée et
45 le Paisan la mouche.

Plus a le Diable
plus il en veut auoir
J. lagnid ex.

Oppression of the peasantry is the refrain of this proverb of Lagniet's, published 1657–63: 'This noble is the spider and the peasant the fly'. The verse drives home the maxim 'The more the Devil has the more he wants,' . . . 'This poor man brings everything, corn, fruit, money, vegetables; the fat milord sits ready to take everything, and does not even grant him the kindness of a glance'. The milord says, 'You must pay or serve' the peasant 'thin as a greyhound' says, 'To all masters, all honours'.

economic and social perspectives. Although he described the people as mules, useless if they were not made to work, he saw that high taxation was a disincentive and he contrasted low French productivity with the growth economy of the Dutch. And it is to Richelieu's credit that the *taille* was slightly reduced in 1626. The deficit coincided with the difference between what the Treasury should have received and what it did receive. Administrative reform could bridge this gap, and an attack was made on the Treasury, where accounts had often not been presented for years, while the profits made by provincial officeholders were investigated. Finally, court pensions and spending were slashed.

'To Check the Advance of Spanish Power'

An Assembly of Notables was called in 1626, which was informed of recent measures and harangued on the need for business recovery and an export drive. Richelieu's radical proposal was the abolition of the *paulette*, because it would provide an administrative tonic and also release capital for business investment. Merchants, as in other countries, ploughed back profits into land, which gave social status and safe returns, but in France the flight of capital from commerce and industry was given an additional incentive by the attractions of office. Yet although Richelieu appears as a progressive economist, his concern with the results of the sale of office arose also from his preoccupations with the restlessness of the nobility and from his sympathy with their economic plight.

Richelieu saw clearly how the court nobility mobilized local support, concealing factiousness behind the Huguenot flag and provincial separatism, or giving support to the reversionary interest of Gaston d'Orléans, the king's brother and heir presumptive. Richelieu was the son of a Poitevin noble who had incurred debt through trying and failing to obtain court office, and in his *Testament Politique* he deplored the fact that the nobles, rich only in courage and expected to give their lives for their country, had lost ground to the office-holders, the caterpillars of the commonwealth. He advocated court austerity not only for reasons of economy but also for its social effects, since he thought that once the courtiers spent less the provincial squires would follow suit. Secondly, if the *paulette* were abolished the price of office would fall and give a chance for the nobles to buy. But, as we have seen, education as well as money was needed to acquire office. Although Loyseau analyzed the social structure in formal terms, citing Aristotle's defence of rule by the nobility, he recognized that the rise of an educated bureaucracy had upset the natural order of the three estates. Richelieu was aware of this, and in his opinion merchants, anxious for their sons to acquire office, were responsible for the spread of colleges and the lowering of educational standards. He wanted less emphasis on the liberal arts and more on technological education. But in urging these reforms on the Assembly of Notables Richelieu showed naïveté, for half the members were office-holders. He showed his great strength as a politician, since he bowed to circumstance and concentrated on empirical solutions.

Arguments of power were always given priority by Richelieu. The last campaign against the Huguenots came in 1628, partly financed by sale of office and justified by the English alliance made by the Huguenot nobles. But the campaign also appeased the Catholic party, a necessary move for Richelieu who was contemplating action against the Habsburgs. The Peace of Alais in 1629 crushed the political power of the Huguenots but exacted a heavy economic toll. The pious Duke of Ventadour razed to the ground the château of Pradel, famous as the home of Olivier de Serres, who under the auspices of Henri IV had written the *Théâtre d'Agriculture*. The orchards he had planted were uprooted and the Duke pillaged and burned forty-seven villages around Nîmes. The textiles of Languedoc, of the greatest importance for the Levant trade, collapsed, as did the trade of La Rochelle, the biggest port of western France. Neither revived until Colbert in the 1660s applied artificial respiration.

In the year of the Peace of Alais Richelieu told the king that 'it must be our permanent aim to check the advance of Spanish power'. Yet he limited his objectives, for he did not advocate great territorial expansion, but merely wished to breach the Spanish rampart at strategic points. Gateways would be acquired for future offensives, but immediately Richelieu's policy was one of containment, though the line between the offensive and the defensive was necessarily blurred. Strasbourg would give an entry into Germany; Geneva and Neuchâtel would cut Spanish communications between Italy and Franche-Comté; Saluzzo and Pinerolo would threaten the recruiting centre in Milan. In 1630 Pinerolo, on the edge of the Alps, was captured from the Duke of Savoy. Richelieu, with his sense of the histrionic, saw this as the moment of decision. He wrote to Louis XIII: 'If it is decided to make peace, then this must be done promptly without losing a moment, while the king enjoys prestige. If the king decides on war, then all thoughts of tranquillity, economy and reform in internal affairs must be abandoned. If, on the other hand, peace is desired, then all thoughts of conquering Italy in the future must be abandoned'. Richelieu knew the risks which even limited operations carried, for he had stressed in 1629 that open war must be avoided as long as possible and that attacks on Spanish bastions must be conducted with the utmost discretion.

He recognized the social costs of war, but blandly remarked that war was one of the scourges which it had pleased God to inflict on men. Peasant and urban revolts were already occurring with depressing frequency, and he was aware of the financial and administrative problems. Higher taxation would intensify the threat of revolt without fully solving the problems of war finance, for taxes were collected slowly while military offensives and prompt payments of subsidies required immediate cash. The Spanish Habsburgs could borrow from Genoese bankers on the security of Peruvian silver; Gustavus Adolphus had both his copper mines and the customs dues of the Baltic ports. But since the collapse of Lyons in the mid-16th century France had no commercial loan-market. The crown had one advantage in the *rentes,* government bonds, issued under the guarantee of the City of Paris, which attracted the small investor, just as Bank loans did in England after 1694. Yet immediate funds could be raised only through the small circle of Paris financiers, who asked high interest rates and security on particular taxes. Another source of immediate money lay in creating more offices and in exacting forced loans and new charges from existing office-holders. Richelieu, who had denounced the *paulette,* made sale of office one of the main props of his war-finance and settled the system more firmly than ever upon society. The grip of the Parisian financiers upon the Treasury and their huge profits came to be detested, yet both they and the office-holders rendered vital services to the war. In 1638 a loan by a financial syndicate enabled Richelieu to subsidize the revolt of Portugal against Spain. And ironically Alsace was eventually gained through the loan of the banker, Herwarth, the descendant of an Augsburg émigré family, who bought up in 1639 the mercenary army of Christian of Saxe-Weimar on the security of a new block of offices put upon the market.

Richelieu's plans for even limited war raised acrid debate in 1630. The Catholic group, led by the Chancellor Marillac, opposed war. Marillac avoided the ideological argument, but pleaded financial stringency and emphasized political and economic unrest. The expedition against Pinerolo was a small affair in comparison with the proposed operations in Alsace and the subsidies to be paid to Sweden. Besides, it could be argued that Austrian power was already weakened by Richelieu's diplomatic triumph at Regensburg in 1630, when the Elector of Bavaria was persuaded to bring pressure on the Emperor to dismiss his ablest general, Wallenstein. But Richelieu held to the axiom that France must advance to the Rhine. In 1631 he was proved right, for Wallenstein was recalled, while Bavaria, far from leading a Catholic third party under French patronage, rapidly came to terms with the Emperor. When the initial victories of Gustavus Adolphus were countered by the subtle strategy of Wallenstein, the dual monarchy of the Habsburgs presented as great a threat as ever.

The Economy at breaking-point

Yet the internal state of France in 1630 weighted the debate heavily in Marillac's favour, especially by a coincidence which he could not have foreseen, for the decade which followed not only saw taxation practically quadrupled, but also witnessed a general stagnation of prices after an upward movement which had lasted a century. From 1640 prices began to fall, so that by ill-luck the moment at which Richelieu decided on war spelt for the peasant heavier taxation at a time when he began to get less for his produce. Even before 1630 the plight of the peasantry was marked. Sir Dudley Carleton told the House of Commons in 1626 how fortunate Englishmen were, for abroad (and in all probability he was referring to France) the peasants, wearing only wooden shoes and eating no meat, looked 'like so many ghosts and not men'. A generation later when John Locke travelled in France with the keen eye of a productivity expert and the kindly disposition of a liberal, he was shocked by the peasant diet of rye-bread and bean soup and by a poverty which made 'a distinction between flesh and fasting days' impossible. France was essentially a country of cereal production. The size of the population accentuated the fear of a bad harvest, so that more and more land was put under the plough. Locke was to be annoyed by the absence of milk, while Du Bellay's vision of waving wheat had turned into a nightmare problem in the time of Richelieu, for the absence of livestock and therefore of manure resulted in low yield. Malnutrition and starvation, when bread prices rose after a bad harvest, made the population susceptible to plague.

Ironically the first of a long series of catastrophic harvests, a feature of French agriculture until the early 18th century, occurred in 1630, which gives this year a claim on all counts to be a turning-point in the history of 17th century France. Plague had already appeared in Burgundy in 1626 and, travelling west and south, reached a peak in 1631, with sporadic outbreaks occurring until the next peak in 1652. These years saw the independent peasant proprietor reduced to the position of a labourer: houses and whole villages were abandoned, while shanty towns sprang up in the *faubourgs* of the cities. A bad harvest produced the conditions in which revolts incubated. High food prices cut back consumer demand: unemployment and starvation led to riots and repression: epidemics produced fumbling charity. Mortality figures, especially in the case of children, were horrifying, but nevertheless France presented the model of a Malthusian economy. Population was scythed periodically, yet still pressed on resources as a result of a failure of productivity. The falling population of Spain in this period is regarded as a pointer to and a cause of economic decline, but the large population of France, as of India today, was not a sign of a healthy economy.

Strained finance, internal tensions and armies lacking leadership, discipline and experience meant that Richelieu, far from enjoying triumphs, almost encountered defeat. The Swedes quickly marched off the maps they brought into Germany, but Richelieu had to negotiate for the occupation of Lorraine, while the penetration of Alsace was slow, complicated by the presence of both Habsburg and Swedish troops. Richelieu cautiously refused offensive alliances with the Dutch for the partition of the Southern Netherlands and with the Swedes for war in Germany, but Habsburg recovery after the battle of Nördlingen forced open war upon him in 1635. He had to try to hold Alsace and the north-east with armies for which the supply system was chaotic, and he wrote bitterly in the *Testament Politique* that 'history shows that far more armies have perished for lack of food and discipline than from the effect of enemy action, and I am a faithful witness to the fact that enterprises in my time have failed for these reasons only.' Desertion was prevalent; starving soldiers looted in Lorraine and Artois, while towns such as Cambrai refused to provide wheat, since their own supplies were made inadequate by the influx of refugees. The Flanders campaign was a failure, understandably since a desperate intendant reported a shortage of muskets and swords and an even greater shortage of boots. In 1636 an Imperial army advanced from Franche-Comté almost to Dijon, while Spanish forces from Flanders reached Corbie on the Somme. They were within striking distance of Paris and the resulting crisis can be paralleled to that produced when the Germans reached the Marne in 1914. Richelieu was lucky that over-extended communications led to both invasions petering out.

The Volcano Erupts

French military weakness was inevitable in the context of a strained economy and endemic revolt. The *taille* and the salt tax mounted, while the quartering of troops was a heavy burden in many areas. Villages on the route to the eastern front through Langres and Dijon disappeared never to be repopulated, and western France suffered when open war with Spain opened up a front on the Pyrenees. Retail taxes rained down, leading a Paris doctor to say: 'I am afraid that they will soon tax the beggars warming themselves in the sun and those who satisfy the needs of nature in the street.' Bitter resentment against the new taxes, farmed out to Parisian financiers, provoked provincial hatred for the capital. This was a feature of the great revolt of the *Croquants* in 1636, which started at a fair in Poitiers, where a man suspected of being the collector of a rumoured new tax was lynched. As in the Peasants' Revolt of 14th century England, the fiscal agents were the first victims of peasant atrocities. In a village in Saintonge a tax-collector's body was cut up and the little bits nailed to the doors of the houses. The rising of the *Croquants* was rightly considered by Richelieu 'one of the most important affairs of the kingdom', for it coincided with the Habsburg invasions. Fortunately the third prong of the attack, planned by Olivares to strike at Provence, was foiled by Catalan particularism.

France had become an active volcano; a second big eruption occurred in 1639 with the revolt of the *Nu-Pieds* in Normandy, a province which contributed a sixth of the taxation of France. The Treasurer, Bouthillier, thought that the foreign war might become a civil war, and looked to Richelieu for salvation. The Estates of Normandy had complained throughout the 1630s of deserted villages and of the plight of the tanning, cloth and linen industries ruined by taxation. Like the peasants of Poitou, they denounced the profits of the Paris tax-farmers and resented the exactions of the office-holders. They had cause, since the percentages charged on the tax collections could mount to 47% of the yield. Richelieu acted promptly: ten thousand troops marched in, while the Chancellor Séguier, in charge of judicial repression, was instructed to show no mercy. The revolt was less dangerous than that of the *Croquants*, for troops could be recalled to suppress it. In 1638 Breisach, the vital point on the Rhine, the junction of the two Spanish military routes over the Alps, was captured. When in 1639 the Dutch cut the sea passage between Spain and Flanders by the battle of the Downs the way was clear for a French offensive. The collapse of the Norman revolt enabled Richelieu to capture Arras in 1640; he could now negotiate from a position of strength.

Two questions arise from the history of the 1630s. First, were the peasant revolts merely protests against oppressive taxation and thus the more easily suppressed, or were they backed by other disaffected elements in society? Secondly, how did Richelieu transform weakness into strength? How did an administration which rested on office-holding become geared to war? Risings occurred in most of France, except for areas to the north-east and south-east of Paris, which were close to or in the fighting zones. Burgundy suffered heavily from the invasion of 1636, while

Lorraine experienced the prolonged horrors of war, depicted both in the despatches of the intendant, Vignier, and in the etchings of Callot, who lived in Nancy.

The intendants, on whom Richelieu relied to check disaffection, considered that although grinding poverty provided the background to the revolts, they were instigated by the bourgeoisie and by the nobility. In 1630 Marillac had warned Richelieu that the *Parlements* were unreliable, and the pressure of war soon impinged on all ranks of society. Forced loans and new creations depreciated the value of offices, and by 1640 the market was sated. The *Parlements*, notably in the *Pays d'Etats*, stiffly resisted policies which infringed privilege in the interests of more efficient taxation. Meanwhile estate returns were falling for both office-holders and nobles, partly because of stagnating prices, but more because of crown demands on the peasants. The *Parlement* of Rouen was suspended because its members were implicated in the revolt of the *Nu-Pieds*. In the towns the intendants could rely neither on the local authorities nor on the spineless bourgeois guards; in the countryside the nobility were often impervious to the appeals of governors and intendants. The intendant charged with suppressing the revolt of the *Croquants* preferred not to investigate the activities of the nobles, since it was more important that calm should be restored. But as the war proceeded the intendants found the collection of taxes increasingly impeded by the support or encouragement given by landlords to the peasants.

The Intendants: linch-pins of the state

The intendants became the linch-pins of Richelieu's administration. But how were they recruited and what were their powers? In 1630 Richelieu had considered administrative reform incompatible with war, and, as he foresaw, he was pushed into dependence on funds raised from office-holders and on loans from the tax-farmers. Inevitably immediate relief spelt subsequent emaciation of the revenues. Yet the war which made Richelieu renounce administrative reform stimulated an administrative revolution. Action was thrust upon Richelieu both because of the revolts and also because the Parisian bankers demanded better security and therefore more efficient taxation. Even so Richelieu had to find his administrators. His solution was provided by the legal dynasties of the *noblesse de robe* and he drew mainly upon Parisian families, whose rise, often involving four generations of effort, had been eased by their political loyalty to Henri IV. He recruited from the *maîtres de requêtes*, members of the Paris *Parlement* and the most important legal officers of the crown, whose writs controlled cases in which the monarchy had a special interest. The acquisition of this office was the decisive step for ambitious young men. In the 16th century *maîtres de requêtes* had been given roving commissions, but Richelieu gave the intendants, as they came to be called, longer tenure and wider powers. In 1637 they were entrusted with supervising the collection of the *taille* and with levying a forced loan in the towns. They worked either with the existing bureaucracy or through their own subordinates, but in 1642 they acquired overriding powers. This administrative revolution was bitterly resented and was a cause of the *Fronde* in 1648 when France again came near to civil war. Office-holders bewailed their empty titles, and a member of the *Parlement* of Paris then orated on the difference between thirty-five persons collecting the taxes and the employment of three thousand office-holders.

The intendants formed an élite; their offices were neither purchasable nor lucrative. They were recruited on grounds of merit and ability with an admixture of clientage. On leaving the elegance of Paris for the provincial backwoods they were tested in difficult and often disagreeable conditions. Only eighteen of Richelieu's forty-eight intendants failed to become members of the royal council. Despite the rigidity of the French social structure, with its sharply vertical as well as horizontal divisions, administrative talent was tapped and political loyalties were formed at the decisive moment. The successful recruitment of a new élite is comparatively rare. It had been achieved, though in a more favourable social environment, under Elizabeth I of England; and it was to be achieved again in 19th century England, when the intellectual aristocracy flooded into the professions and the

*Il a bien chault qui tout ſes habits porte
et neantmoins contre cẽ francs Narquois
du moindre hyuer la rigueur eſt trop forte
n'ayant aulx pieds que la paillieſt le bois*

A Jeuneſſe oyſiue vielleſſe penible

*pauureté n'eſt pas
vice*

rapport des gal

Il nont pas beſoin de fort hyuer

*quelque part qu'il alie il ſe promene
touſiours dans ſes bois*

On les entend de loing ils ont des ſabots chauſſez

' Il doit auoir bien chaud qui a tous ſes habitz ſur ſoy

Plague and famine set many of the poor wandering. This illustration from the Lagniet 'Proverbs' bears the legend, 'He who wears all his clothes at once must be very warm, yet the rigours of even the mildest winter prove too strong for these rogues since they wear nothing but straw and clogs on their feet'. 'Youth spent in idleness leads to a bitter old age' is countered by 'Povery is not vice'. The bowl is labelled 'Beggars' passport'.

reformed civil service. This Victorian intelligentsia formed almost as cohesive a group as had the *noblesse de robe*; both took pride in their tasks, responded to the call of duty, were consolidated by inter-marriage, and were content with a status below that of the territorial nobility. The English civil servants found their patron saints in Bentham and Chadwick: the intendants were equally dedicated, but learned their skills and loyalties from the Jesuits who controlled French education. Moreover the mould of political thought in Richelieu's time was, partly as a result of his own skilful shaping of propaganda, predominantly authoritarian, and to this intendants naturally adapted themselves.

They saw the needs of a state at war as paramount, but yet differed in their attitudes. Some were disciplinarians, regarding torture or despatch to the galleys as routine, but the consciences of others were pricked by contact with war and starvation. Nicolas de Corberon wanted taxation radically reformed; the piety of René d'Argenson was infused with mysticism, but he saw no disparity between his three aims, 'the glory of God, the service of his Majesty and the contentment of the Cardinal'. Even so his sympathy for the plight of the peasants led to the charge in 1649 that his leniency was responsible for rebellion in Guyenne. But although d'Argenson could on occasion protect the oppressed, his loyalty was unquestionable and his career epitomizes Richelieu's success in harnessing Catholic piety to the war against the Habsburgs. Father Joseph, too, remained the devout Capuchin while successfully conducting diplomacy in French interests. The Chan-

cellor Séguier demonstrated his piety by translating a mystical work by his father and by showing suspicion of the rationalism of Descartes, but he supported Richelieu's foreign policy and also its consequences when he was entrusted with crushing the revolt of the *Nu-Pieds*. Catholic piety was also deflected into charity. Louise de Marillac, whose family supplied the leaders of the extreme Catholic faction, was one of the many society ladies recruited by St Vincent de Paul for his order of the *Filles de Charité*.

Richelieu's administrative success lay in his deployment of the intendants and he achieved a psychological triumph when he united piety with patriotism, but he failed to reform the financial institutions. Clientage and personal power were too important to permit the reintroduction into the Treasury of the standards once enforced by Sully. Corruption and sycophancy resulted. The crusty Treasurer, Bullion, who made a huge fortune, was impervious to reproaches that military operations had failed through lack of funds. When he ultimately agreed in 1639 to introduce some reform and to stop the practice of burning records of payments this was because he wanted Richelieu's help in arranging a marriage between his son and a rich heiress. Visits to the Paris of the affluent office-holders, grasping financiers and opulent ministers by those from provinces afflicted by taxation, plague and starvation can be compared to journeys from the Russian steppes infected by peasant revolts to 18th century St Petersburg, adorned by the palaces of Rastrelli.

Architecture, for 'gods or kings'

Richelieu himself set the tone. He drew enormous wealth from his ecclesiastical revenues, but he also expressed his appreciation of the pensions and gifts showered on him by the king, and indeed his personal accounts were inextricably entangled with those of the Treasury. Lemercier, whose apprenticeship in Rome just preceded the victory of Baroque, gave French architecture its classical stamp. Extensions to the Louvre began in 1624; Louis XIII built a modest country château at St Germain-en-Laye, and gave Fontainebleau a new staircase and some painted ceilings. But the buildings of the Cardinal overshadowed those of the king, just as the recessive personality of the latter became pallid when dominated by the tense and compulsive energy of Richelieu. The great buildings of Richelieu coincide with the 1630s, the decade of war and heavy social costs, and express his political dominance. The first great dome, designed by Lemercier for the Sorbonne, appeared on the skyline of Paris. He was simultaneously engaged on the construction of the Palais Cardinal, which had Simon Vouet and Philippe de Champaigne as decorators. Corneille paid a tribute both to the palace and the metamorphosis of Paris when he wrote:

> *Et l'univers entier ne peut rien voir d'égal*
> *Aux superbes dehors du Palais Cardinal.*
> *Toute une ville entière, avec pompe bâtie,*
> *Semble d'un vieux fossé par miracle sortie,*
> *Et nous fait présumer à ses superbes toits,*
> *Que tous ses habitants sont des dieux ou des rois.*
>
> *(No sight throughout the world can equal*
> *The superb exterior of the Palais Cardinal.*
> *Here a whole town, built with pomp,*
> *Seems by a miracle to have risen from an old ditch,*
> *And its splendid roofs make us think*
> *That all its occupants are either gods or kings.)*

But some counted the cost of these aesthetic splendours. In 1636, the year of the revolt of the *Croquants*, malevolent verses expressed the hope that:

> *Ce superbe bâtiment*
> *Du faîte jusqu'au fondement*
> *Puisse tomber en décadence*
> *Et que le démon infernal*
> *Fasse, du Palais Cardinal,*
> *Le tombeau de son Eminence.*
>
> *(This superb building,*
> *From its roofs to its foundations will crumble,*
> *And that the infernal demon will turn the Palais Cardinal*
> *Into the tomb of his Eminence.)*

Richelieu was neighbour to the king in Paris; his country home at Rueil was close to St Germain. He crowned his astonishingly successful court career by building his resplendent palace of Richelieu, bigger and more sumptuous than the Luxembourg of Marie de Médicis, on the estate where his father had lived the pinched life of a country gentleman. Niches contained the busts of ancient Romans, symbols of the heroic view of the age, just as on the Parisian stage Corneille invoked the classical past as a model for the present. Obelisks and columns, ceilings and wall paintings commemorated triumphs such as the fall of La Rochelle, while Richelieu collected pictures not only by Renaissance artists but by contemporaries such as La Tour and Poussin. His answer to the poverty of Poitou was to build just beyond his palace gates the little town of Richelieu, designed on a grid pattern. The richly decorated houses on the main street were owned by Richelieu's clients, his doctor, royal councillors, including the Chancellor Séguier, and the financiers who both supported and preyed upon the regime. Richelieu's palace has been demolished, but his artificial town, lacking commercial roots, survives as it was planned, commemorating his political egotism. In the provincial capitals, and above all in Paris, the wealth of the rich bourgeoisie and office-holders was displayed in their town residences, beginning to be called *hôtels*, and in their country retreats. Lemercier did

not reign alone: he had a rival in Mansart, a subtler and more strictly classical architect. Mansart built for the king's brother the superlative wing of the palace at Blois, and for a Paris magistrate the elegant mansion of Maisons, now a jewel set in an undistinguished suburb, of which Voltaire wrote:

> *Simple en était la noble architecture;*
> *Chaque ornement en sa place arrêté*
> *Y semblait mis par la nécessité:*
> *L'art s'y cachait sous l'air de la nature,*
> *L'œil satisfait embrassait sa structure,*
> *Jamais surpris et toujours enchanté.*
>
> *(This noble piece of architecture was simple;*
> *Each ornament set in a fixed place*
> *Seemed placed there by necessity:*
> *Art was disguised as nature,*
> *And the satisfied eye, never surprised and always enchanted,*
> *Took in the whole structure.)*

Free Thought and Prudence

Classicism was triumphing in the arts with Mansart, Poussin and Corneille, but French thought still had a varied texture. France had no Inquisition and the Index was respected more in the breach than in the observance. The *Académie Française*, incorporated in 1635, achieved Richelieu's aim of linking literature to the state. But the danger of fossilized attitudes and deferential pliancy was recognized: attendance was poor and the members were rudely described by one critic as 'cette canaille qui combat la vérité pour du pain'. In contrast, the Paris salons scintillated with curiosity, showing zest for learning and respect for tolerance and combining the humanist traditions of Erasmus with the scepticism of Montaigne and the modernity of Galileo. The brothers Dupuy, members of the *noblesse de robe*, presided over one of the most distinguished and learned circles in Europe, attracting to their evenings those who sighed for the liberty of republican Venice and Holland and deplored political tyranny and monkish superstition. These sceptics were repelled by the credulity which produced belief in miracles and witchcraft; for them history and contemporary travel in America and Asia demonstrated the relativity of morals. They found more consolation in Seneca and Socrates than in the saints of the Church.

Science and mathematics especially attracted the intellectuals. In Provence among his eucalyptus trees, statuary and paintings lived the learned Peiresc, who gazed at Jupiter and made a map of the moon and who corresponded with such diverse personalities as Malherbe, Rubens and Galileo. Peiresc introduced Pierre Gassendi, a canon of the Church but also a sceptic and a mathematician, to the Dupuy circle. Mersenne, who had denounced atheism, became a distinguished mathematician, the friend of both Hobbes and Descartes. But just as Hobbes protected himself behind the laws of nature, so the French free-thinkers, especially after the condemnation of Galileo, prudently bowed to a faith which their reason condemned. Their negative attitude and a contempt for the multitude confined scepticism to a small circle. Gassendi, always careful to perform his religious offices, could not lead a religious revolution, but Descartes and Mersenne, who hated scepticism, bridged the gulf between science and religion. Yet Descartes thought it wise to leave Paris for Amsterdam and his *Discours de la Méthode* was published in Holland in 1637. The full title, stressing the importance of science and mathematics, advertised its modernity, while the contents contained the consoling doctrine of innate ideas. Another strand of intellectual independence was represented by the Jansenists, again mainly drawn from the *noblesse de robe*, and they too were an élite. The free-thinkers lived in libraries and salons: the Jansenists withdrew to Port-Royal outside Paris to avoid contamination by the world. Their strict morality and pessimistic theology deprived them of popular appeal. Corneille too, although portraying in heroic and tragic terms the conflict between the individual and the state, also deprecated the mob. Without any aid from Richelieu the French Leviathan drew strength from the fear of the state of nature.

Internal Strife: the Fronde

Richelieu had won on all fronts save the financial. But well before his death in 1642 he recognized the acute administrative and social tensions exacerbated by the war and accordingly opened peace talks. He could negotiate from strength, since the efficiency of the intendants had generated enough confidence among the Paris bankers to finance campaigns, while army reforms were about to result in the victory of Rocroi. France had faced risings, but Spain encountered revolutions in Portugal and Catalonia. Richelieu's posthumous triumph was the peace of Westphalia in 1648 by which, although Strasbourg, the gateway from Germany into France, remained a free city, the French frontiers advanced from the Meuse to the Rhine. Yet the year of the peace saw the outbreak of the Fronde which, lasting for five years, constituted the greatest crisis between the revolution of the League in 1588 and the revolution of 1789.

The Fronde was partly a revolt against a corrupt court, especially an Italianate court, for the extravagance and intrigue of Mazarin, Richelieu's successor—who had become a naturalized Frenchman in 1639—evoked the same xenophobia which the regencies of Catherine and Marie de Médicis had done. Richelieu had restricted his war aims, but Mazarin sought conquests in Italy and the absorption of Flanders. He ignored the warnings of Richelieu's intendants who found the extraction of taxes increasingly painful and difficult, especially since Mazarin laid new burdens on an exhausted country. The flags of victory in Notre-Dame were already drooping wearily when peace was made with Austria; yet Mazarin chose to continue war with Spain. Peripheral revolutions had weakened the Spanish monarchy since 1640; in 1648 Mazarin faced revolt in Paris itself.

The prolongation of the war, combined with the tactlessness and shortsightedness of Mazarin, caused the Fronde. Richelieu had irritated the older bureaucracy, but provincial discontent had remained uncoordinated. In January 1648 the *paulette* came up for renewal, and inevitably Mazarin tried to bleed the office-holders. But he also attacked the *noblesse de robe* in their main citadel when he proposed to create additional posts in the *Parlement* of Paris. He simultaneously reduced the investment income of the bourgeoisie when he juggled with government bonds, advertising the fraudulence of his rule by protecting the interests of court circles. The tensions, which Richelieu had controlled, snapped, and an attack was launched on the new agencies of government on which he had relied. The *Parlements* and the office-holders fought for power and profit but when they also assumed the role of protectors of the oppressed they were not necessarily hypocritical. Richelieu's intendants had often been stricken by conscience as they travelled over their provinces, and Catholic charity at this time was active. When members of the Paris *Parlement* deplored social suffering, saying that laurels produced no food, they were speaking in the context of the greatest economic crisis of the century. In the summer of 1648 the *Parlement* attacked arbitrary arrest, called for an investigation of Treasury corruption and demanded the summoning of a grand assembly to consider reform. Their immediate demands for the abolition of the intendants and a major reduction in the *taille* imperilled the conduct of the war.

The victory of Lens restored the initiative to Mazarin and the genial ghost of Henri IV came to his aid. Concessions to the office-holders blunted their anger, while the enmity of the nobility towards the bougeoisie precluded joint action. Moreover riots and barricades in Paris produced a reaction in favour of order. The civil wars of the 16th century had stimulated theories of resistance, but thereafter the doctrine of absolute monarchy had struck deep roots, fertilized by the propaganda of Richelieu. The king was held to owe mystical obligations to God alone, while monarchy was equated with sovereignty. Those who preferred more fashionable language were given the argument that sovereignty was as indivisible as a point in geometry. The Fronde saw the old distinction drawn between tyranny and absolute monarchy, but the main attack was launched against the rule of ministers. The Fronde had no religious backing; the Huguenots were quiescent, while the exclusive Jansenists could not play the popular role of the sects in the contemporary English revolution. The sceptics, who had sighed for freedom, either gave no lead or

escaped to enjoy the patronage of Queen Christina in Sweden. The Church preached submission, but its charitable organizations gave a practical response to the problem of poverty. The people of Paris paid the price when siege forced up food prices, while the peasantry in the surrounding areas suffered acutely when nobles without a cause but often in the pay of Spain marched and countermarched. The Fronde produced anarchy, but the League had been more dangerous because more liable to proliferate. The League had been an anti-monarchical movement, impregnated with religious fanaticism, and had also represented an attack on venal office-holding which the Valois had inaugurated and extended. In the Fronde the office-holders were merely asking—as they saw it—for a fair deal. Henri IV had given them too heavy a stake in the monarchy for them to risk revolution.

Besides there was only a thin social distinction between the new administrative monarchy of Richelieu, centred on the intendants and dependent on the Parisian bankers, and the older order resting on a venal bureaucracy. Richelieu's intendants were recruited from the *noblesse de robe*, while members of the Paris *Parlement* were often closely affiliated to the financiers and showed nervousness when in 1648 enquiries into loans and tax-farms were pressed. As a result the intendants crept back surreptitiously; their return signalized both more efficient tax collection and also the reopening of the Paris loan market. Yet continued corruption in the Treasury and high interest rates made it impossible to mount a major offensive. Mazarin gained a diplomatic success when he won the alliance of Cromwell's England, but Dunkirk was captured from the Spanish only to be ceded to the English. Yet the alliance paid dividends, for the Peace of the Pyrenees gave France final victory over Spain and the distant hope of absorbing the Spanish empire.

Louis XIV's Inheritance

The internal cost was an anaemic economy, a frightening mortality rate, and a depressed peasantry. Once the Fronde was over the profits of those with Treasury contacts continued as before. Fouquet, Mazarin's Treasurer, blazoned his gains when he built

Descartes' 'Discours de la Méthode', published in Leyden in 1637, laid the foundations for scientific enquiry. Here he explains diagrammatically how he produced the red band of a rainbow by substituting for a raindrop a large round glass container filled with water, through which the sun's rays were reflected and refracted (BCD) to appear red at E (observer's eye), as long as the line DE was at an angle of about 42° with the line EM (continuation of sun-eye line). At K a weaker red appears because there is more refraction through GHIK.

Vaux-le-Vicomte, which harmonized the skills of Louis Le Vau as architect, of Lebrun as interior decorator, and of Le Nôtre as landscape gardener. Mazarin quickly recouped his fortune, jeopardized during the Fronde. He was the great purchaser of Charles I's pictures sold by the Rump, and in his old age he shuffled around his magnificent library, gazed at his paintings, fingered his brocades, and sighed heavily at the thought that death would part him from these. He drew wealth from his benefices and from the state, for he was an astute speculator who drew profits from army contracts, accepted bribes from bankers and sold offices down to that of the Queen's laundress. The future of his possessions exercised him, but he accepted the advice of Colbert, his man-of-affairs, that he should prudently offer all to the young king, who in honour would refuse the legacy. After three agonizing days Louis XIV came to the decision which Colbert had predicted. Mazarin as a result could cling to life, neatly piling the pistoles for yet another gambling evening. He peremptorily dismissed a confessor who dared to suggest that he should reveal the sins he had committed in the management of the Treasury, telling this tactless priest that he had been summoned to talk of God alone.

But although Louis XIV refused Mazarin's personal legacy his inheritance seemed rich indeed. Mazarin passed on to him the intendants bequeathed by Richelieu; and he also handed on his personal assistant, Colbert, whom Louis had the wit to make Steward of France. Abroad the French monarchy had defeated the Habsburgs. Louis XIV could look forward to the Spanish succession and to achieving Ronsard's premature congratulation given to Henri II on the capture of Metz that:

Du Grand Rhin t'apparut l'Allemagne captive.

(From the great Rhine, a captive Germany appeared before you.)

At home the monarchy had surmounted the two great crises of the wars of religion and of the Fronde. Internal reforms, initiated by Colbert, were for a time to go far towards meeting the grievances which remained. Louis XIV was determined to rule, and he had the powerful encouragement of Bossuet, whose sermons equating monarchy with divinity went far beyond Du Bellay's boast made a century earlier:

Car rien n'est, après Dieu, si grand qu'un roi de France.

(None, after God, is as great as a King of France.)

France had been enriched by its great architects, town-planners, painters and writers. Yet, considered from the point of view of the country rather than of the court, a different aspect is revealed. The smiling countryside of the *Guide* of 1553 had seen both the miseries which Ronsard observed and those he had feared. The humanism of Du Bellay and the intellectual debates of the age of Richelieu were succeeded by the defensive irony of Molière, while Bossuet preached only too effectually the doctrine of the 'Christ empistollé' denounced by Ronsard a century earlier.

VII BRITAIN TRANSFORMED

Crown, conscience and Commonwealth

G. E. AYLMER

'The poorest he that is in England hath a life to live, as the greatest he, and therefore ... every man that is to live under a government ought first by his own consent to put himself under that government.'

COL. THOMAS RAINBOROUGH, at the Putney Debates, 1647

'Rebellion is but Warre renewed.'

THOMAS HOBBES, 'LEVIATHAN'

'This island,'

wrote the artist Peter Paul Rubens, 'seems to me worthy the consideration of a man of taste, not only because of the charm of the countryside and the beauty of the people, not only because of the outward show which appears to me most choice and to announce a people rich and happy in the bosom of peace, but also by the incredible quantity of excellent pictures, statues, and ancient inscriptions which are in this court.'

Rubens wrote in 1629, during the reign of Charles I; but the luxury of English court life that he noticed was one of the features which marked a difference between late Tudor and Stuart rule. Henry VIII had been a splendid patron, but Elizabeth preferred to save her own money and encourage her subjects to spend theirs on the entertainment of her court on its progresses through the countryside. James I, inheriting a prosperous England after the comparative poverty of his native Scotland, was encouraged by his favourites and his pleasure-loving Danish queen to entertain on a lavish scale. He promoted a distinctively 'court' art which had not existed under Elizabeth. His son Charles I, while drifting towards political disaster, excelled his father in taste, ambition and strength of artistic purpose and he initiated several projects that make his reign a cultural milestone. He began the royal collection of major continental paintings; he commissioned Inigo Jones to build the Queen's chapel at St James's; had the times been pro-

pitious he would have expanded his father's Banqueting House into a vast English equivalent of the Louvre; and he retained the services of Rubens when the latter came to London on a diplomatic mission in 1629, endowing the capital with its only Baroque masterpiece—the Banqueting House ceiling. This was completed in Brussels in 1634 (the sections of the canvas can be clearly seen since it has been cleaned), shipped to London the following year and installed by 1636.

The subject of the central panel (shown opposite) is the Apotheosis of James I. The king, leaving behind the symbols of imperial glory—the globe and the eagle—is raised by allegorical figures of Justice, Religion and Scriptural Truth to the blazing light of the Christian Heaven, where Victorious Peace and Legitimate War crown him with laurels.

Rubens goes on to qualify his description of the English people as 'rich and happy in the bosom of peace'. He notices the signs of economic malaise: 'both public and private interests are sold for cash'. But he had no suspicion of the social and religious upheavals that were to come within the next decade. His painting represents the high-watermark of the English monarchy, when the Divine Right of Kings was the most potent political philosophy. 'Kings are called gods by the prophetical King David', wrote James, 'because they sit upon God His throne in earth'.

Elizabeth ruled by a combination of diplomatic skill, good advice, ability to compromise and personal magnetism, in all of which – to varying degrees – her successors were deficient.

The queen's minister: William Cecil, Lord Burghley (*left*), served the queen ably for forty years. His advice was essentially cautious and conservative – restraint in financial affairs, safety in foreign policy, compromise with factions such as Puritanism at home. His son Robert Cecil became secretary in 1596, and it was he who masterminded the succession to James when Elizabeth died.

The queen's gift rewarded ministers out of the profits of administration. The officers of the Court of Wards and Liveries, shown here with Burghley presiding, reaped a large income from the wardship of rich orphans.

The queen's last favourite: when Robert Devereux, Earl of Essex (*centre left*) fell out of favour, it was more financial than political desperation that led to his downfall.

Ireland was exploited by her English landlords as a colony rather than responsibly administered. Richard Boyle, first Earl of Cork (*left*), was the most successful of the English adventurers who made fortunes there.

NON SINE SOLE
IRIS.

The Rainbow Portrait conveys something of Elizabeth's charisma. Although painted about 1600 when the queen was over seventy, it idealizes her as a beautiful young woman, one of the poetic commonplaces of the time being to pretend that she was immune to age. Her dress is an elaborate allegory; the eyes and ears mean that she sees and hears everything that takes place in her kingdom; the serpent on her left sleeve stands for wisdom; on each side of the serpent's head a small armillary sphere and a heart signify intelligence and prudence; and in her right hand she holds the rainbow, with the motto, 'No rainbow without the sun'. The style is that of the Flemish painter Marcus Gheeraerts.

The face of England in the early 17th century is portrayed with unusual freshness in these sketches made for the album of a Dutch student visiting London in 1614. *Above:* an impression of the cockpit of Whitehall, with James I among the spectators.

A carter and meat porter in the London streets. Note the corded bales in the cart with their customs mark.

Old London Bridge, seen from the east. On the left is the tower of the present Southwark Cathedral – below it can just be seen the heads of executed traitors stuck on poles – and at the other end St Paul's and the City churches.

By the Thames at Richmond a party of Morris dancers perform to be rewarded by a lady and gentleman who have descended from their carriage. A horse-ferry crosses the river behind them. The date is about 1620, the painter probably Flemish. Richmond Palace, in the distance, had been given by James to Prince Henry. Later in the century it fell into decay.

The nine-year-old Prince of Wales sheathes his sword after a successful stag-hunt. Prince Henry is accompanied here by his friend Sir John Harington, aged eleven. Both wear hunting costume and their family arms appear above them. The picture, painted in 1603, probably commemorates a royal visit to the Harington estate.

The belated English Renaissance in architecture, repeatedly heralded in Elizabeth's reign, only really arrived in that of her successor. The Tudor style was an idiosyncratic mixture of late Gothic and Renaissance motifs mostly derived from Flanders. It was not until the work of Inigo Jones, who had studied Italian Renaissance architecture at first hand, that England was able to appreciate what that style really meant.

Wollaton (*above*), begun in 1580 for Sir Francis Willoughby, Sheriff of Nottingham, has up-to-date details such as the coupled pilasters at the corners and the scroll pediments with miniature obelisks above the bays, and the plan is taken from a design published by Serlio. But the general character, with its large mullion-and-transome windows, is still traditional and the central upper storey is a conscious medieval revival. The long gallery of **Knole** (*below*), built for the Sackvilles, again shows classical features in the panelling.

The 'Laudian' porch (1637) of St Mary the Virgin, Oxford, was probably designed by Nicholas Stone. It is a curious example of Anglo-Flemish style, with a Gothic vault inside, but classically derived figures in the spandrels above the arch.

Inigo Jones' main source for the Queen's House at Greenwich (begun in 1616, completed in the 1630s) was the Italian architect Palladio, whose vocabulary he handled with a confidence and sureness of touch that remained unmatched in England for nearly a hundred years.

Traces of Rome and of Michelangelo can be seen in Nicholas Stone's monument to Francis Holles in Westminster Abbey (*right*). Holles died in 1622. Stone, who completed his training in Holland, worked closely with Jones. The pedestal is wholly in the classical tradition.

The weeping daughters of Sir Thomas Hawkins look back to medieval 'mourners', though the sculptor, Epiphanius Evesham, had practised in the Paris of Henri IV. The tomb is at Boughton-under-Blean in Kent, and dates from 1618.

The trial and execution of a king by his own subjects was an event without precedent, although many kings had been killed or murdered before. And it horrified the courts of Europe when the news became known. After his defeat in the first Civil War Charles surrendered to the Scots, who handed him over to Parliament early in 1647. In November he escaped, negotiated with the Scots and began the second Civil War, during which he was again defeated. Parliament was still ready to bring him back under suitable conditions, but the Army's patience had run out. In December 1648 Parliament was purged of its Presbyterian members, leaving only the Independents. A Court was set up which the king refused to recognize. He was found guilty 'of treasons, murders, rapines, burnings, spoils, desolations, damages and mischiefs to this nation, acted and committed in the said wars', and was beheaded outside the Banqueting House in Whitehall on January 30th 1649. The scene is shown here, with many inaccuracies, by a contemporary Flemish painter. In the top right-hand corner is a portrait of the executioner, who, it was absurdly rumoured abroad, was none other than the Lord General Fairfax. His true identity remains uncertain. At the bottom is a vignette of people dipping their handkerchiefs in the king's blood after his death.

The struggle between king and Parliament went back many years. Charles found it impossible to rule without Parliament, but when he did finally recall it, in 1640, it was dominated by his enemies, notably John Pym. Pym succeeded in removing from power two of the King's most powerful advisers, Archbishop Laud and the Earl of Strafford, whose execution in 1641 is shown here.

Civil war broke out in 1642. In October of that year came the first major battle, an indecisive one at Edgehill. In 1644 the royalists were heavily defeated at Marston Moor, and a year later more heavily still at Naseby (*below left*). Parliament appointed Sir Thomas Fairfax as its new Commander in Chief and Oliver Cromwell as Lieutenant General of the famous New Model Army.

Radical questioning of accepted attitudes and privileges, in politics as well as religion, grew up in the fervent atmosphere of the civil war. *Above:* John Lilburne, leader of the democratic 'Leveller' movement, and the most popular man in London, shown behind bars, from a Leveller pamphlet of 1646. Twice tried for his life, in 1649 and 1653; twice acquitted by London juries.

The Lord Protector, Cromwell, his sword impaling three crowns, tramples monstrous Faction and Error and the Whore of Babylon underfoot. On the right the three kingdoms of England, Scotland and Ireland offer him wreaths. The small scenes at the top and bottom exemplify proverbs on the theme of the peacemaker, and the dove carries aloft an olive branch – a pun on 'Oliver'.

The Rump Parliament – so-called because it was what was left after the Long Parliament, elected in 1640, had been purged of all but about 60 members – lasted until 1653 when Cromwell dissolved it, allegedly with the words 'Be gone, you rogues, you have sat long enough' – shown (*right*) in a satirical print. At the back Harrison pulls the Speaker from his chair. The strange birds and animals are symbolic (the owl, for instance, unable to see in spite of a candle and spectacles, the dog a derisive image of the British lion), while on the wall has been painted the legend 'This house is to let'.

The republican experiment ended soon after the death of Cromwell in 1658. A disunited country rejected his son and, with stringent safeguards, invited Charles II to return.

TERRAS ASTRAEA REDISIT

'Astraea revisits the earth' – an allegory of the return of peace, painted for Charles II's bedroom.

Crown, conscience and Commonwealth

G. E. AYLMER

Any historian who seeks to portray a past society in all its aspects is tempted to make the whole more than the sum of the parts. To catch the true character, to descry the real nature and quality of the age must be his aim. Yet this is an impossible ideal. In the century with which we are concerned in this chapter, England enjoyed what was probably the greatest flowering of literary talent and genius in all its history. The age saw notable, if less pre-eminent achievements in music, and in the visual and the applied arts. No historian has so far succeeded in explaining satisfactorily why this great cultural outpouring came when and how it did. In particular, the greatest of all epochs in English lyric and dramatic poetry occurred between the latter years of Elizabeth I and the end of the reign of James I. Sidney, Spenser, Marlowe, Campion, Donne, Webster, Herrick, Herbert, to name only a selection, were all born within the span of about forty years from the 1550s to 1590s and all produced their greatest works within about a fifty year period. Even without Shakespeare, the Elizabethan and Jacobean age would be glorious in the history of literature. With Shakespeare, and in prose with the King James or 'Authorized' version of the Bible, it has a quality almost without parallel, at least in modern western civilization. The historian of political, religious, social, or economic affairs can, at best, only suggest where his subject appears to have some bearing on the literature and the arts of the period.

Continuity and Change

In these respects too it was an age crowded alike with events of immediate drama, and with developments of momentous future consequence. The accession of Elizabeth I and her Church settlement; the trial and execution of Mary Queen of Scots; Francis Drake's circumnavigation, the defeat of the Spanish Armada; the union of the crowns of England and Scotland; the final English conquest of Ireland; the first British colonial settlements in the New World; the beginnings of trade with India; the deepening breach between Crown and Parliament under the early Stuart kings; the Scottish Covenant; the meeting of the Long Parliament; the fall and death of Strafford; the Civil War with the defeat of the king and his eventual execution; the period of republican rule first by what was left of the House of Commons, then by the Puritan 'saints', finally by Oliver Cromwell as Lord Protector; the victories over the Dutch and then over Spain; the collapse of Puritan and republican rule and the return of the monarch, House of Lords and Anglican Church—these are but some of the events of this turbulent and exciting century.

It would be easy to conclude from this that it was an age of rapid and fundamental change; in some respects it was. In religion, for instance, England broke decisively, if at first cautiously, from the papacy and the Roman communion within months of Elizabeth's accession. After the restoration of Charles II, the Church of England, which had been brought into being by the earlier transformation and had undergone such intervening vicissitudes, became irrevocably 'Anglican'; the uncompromising radical Protestants were henceforth permanently excluded from it. From the establishment of a Protestant English Church to the birth of modern Nonconformity there is indeed a momentous and lasting shift in the religious balance of power. The rise,

Queen Elizabeth, the symbol of her age for her subjects, is shown as the stately prince watching her hawks 'flee the hearone', a woodcut from George Turberville's 'Booke of Falconrie', 1575.

temporary victory and final defeat of the Puritans has left permanent marks on English life. The constitutional transformation, from the near absolutism of the Tudors to the semi-parliamentary, limited monarchy of the later Stuarts suggests almost as striking a contrast.

But if we look more carefully at England over this hundred years the evidence of underlying continuity is no less powerful. On the political scene we find a monarch who, through his Privy Council and other executive ministers, still ruled as well as reigned. In administration there was still very little of what we should call a modern civil service. For the most part officials did not think of themselves as public servants but as holders of a right, or a piece of property in their office. Financially they depended on fees and gratuities from users of their departments, or on perquisites and indirect gains from office, rather than on salaries paid by the state.

In local government also, the salient characteristic of the English system remained, under Charles II as it had been under Elizabeth I, rule by part-time amateurs, from the parish constable and churchwarden up to the J.P. and the Lord Lieutenant. Within a year of the Restoration there was once more no standing army—or virtually none. There was still only a tiny hereditary peerage, a much larger but still numerically small landed gentry class, and a tiny business élite of financiers and export-import merchants, almost all of whom were Londoners. Agriculture remained the basis of the economy. Commerce was important but not central. Industry typically was small-scale. The rate of economic growth can only be guessed. But in 1660 as in 1559 it was characteristic of what is now called a pre-industrial, or an 'under-developed' society. Population growth, although considerable compared with the post-Black Death era (1350–1450), was modest measured against the coming 'explosion' of 1750–1850. Indeed it was probably slower again by the mid-17th century than it had been under Elizabeth I and James I.

In 1660–2, as in 1559, a state Church prevailed with a semi-Calvinist theology, a semi-Catholic liturgy and ritual, and an episcopalian system of government. Here too there was continuity, as well as change.

The moralist, Bateman, attacked the seven deadly sins in contemporary guise in 'A cristall glasse of christian reformation', 1569. Here lechery is castigated; the banquet 'signifieth fleshly delight', the cup held by the harlot is 'horrour', her demon legs, destruction, 'the men fighting, murder: and hell the place for such offendors'

The Balance of Forces

Popular tradition celebrates 'good Queen Bess' as a great national heroine, and there are solid grounds for this. But the victory of 1588 and the splendours of the 'Elizabethan age' in literature and the arts must not obscure the desperate weakness of Elizabeth I, indeed of the whole Tudor system, during the first decade or so of her reign. Politically her problem was simple to see, yet difficult to solve. The effective authority of the crown had been on the increase from about 1470 to 1540. Edward IV, Richard III, Henry VII, Cardinal Wolsey, Thomas Cromwell and Henry VIII had created a state machine which, despite its limitations, was formidable compared with that at the disposal of the Lancastrians. The standards of law and order, and the pursuit of the 'common weal', if sadly inadequate to our eyes, marked an improvement on those of the 14th and 15th centuries. Then came the declining years of Elizabeth's father, lacking a minister of real ability and rashly committed to foreign war on two fronts. His debasement of the coinage to help finance these futile expeditions worsened an already dangerous economic situation. England's exports were damagingly over-dependent on the cloth market of Antwerp, western Europe's great entrepot. In the early 1550s inflation at home and dislocation abroad had led to the collapse of the export boom. Englishmen of enterprise began once more to look elsewhere, to Muscovy, the Baltic, the Mediterranean, the Levant, even further afield to the Indies, east or west. This was to be a continuing reaction to difficulties in European markets. Despite a renewed boom in cloth exports to north-west Europe after James I's peace with Spain in 1604, English merchants would never again feel justified in depending so much on markets so near home.

In government, the minority of Edward VI and the unpopular, ineffectual reign of Mary I had brought a real danger of collapse. If we look at later 16th century France we can see what England was spared. A combination of factious, over-mighty subjects and ideological divisions, might easily have undone all the work of the Yorkist and early Tudor monarchs. This is not to decry the contrary danger, of encroaching royal absolutism—certainly real enough in recent reigns. Yet in the 1550s the main danger lay on the other side. Feebleness and incompetence at the top, viciousness and irresponsibility a little further down, encouraged the recrudescence of the overmighty subject, even of dynastic and religious civil war. If Mary had lived another ten years, there would surely have been a major revolt, technically perhaps 'Protestant', like that of the Huguenots in France. Nor did

Elizabeth's accession remove these dangers. Had she married the wrong person—one is tempted to say, had she married at all—a similar crisis might well have been precipitated. Certainly had she died at any date before the early 1570s, perhaps before the mid-1580s, leaving her Catholic cousin Mary Stuart of Scotland as heir apparent, at the least a violent alteration of the succession by the Protestant nobility and gentry, at worst a civil war could scarcely have been averted. Elizabeth I gambled on her own survival. Fortunately, she won.

Yet the risks were great. The Tudors were an unhealthy stock, and the average expectation of life at that time was hardly more than thirty or thirty-five years. Was Elizabeth justified in the risks she took with her subjects' and her country's future? In fact she had no better alternative. To marry the wrong man; to marry and then fail to bear a legitimate male heir who would be of age at her death; to die in childbirth; to declare (as her subjects demanded) a remote but Protestant successor—all these courses were surely more dangerous than the gamble which she took on personal survival. In the detailed history of the reign the queen's many and varied 'courtships' are of considerable importance. On the long view Elizabeth's celibacy and survival were decisive for the future—and enormously beneficial to the country.

The Elizabethan Church settlement of 1559, like the queen's own life, secured the country against immediate internecine conflict. It too was a gamble—the choice of a lesser evil in the face of intolerable alternatives. No doubt there were advantages in unqualified submission to the papacy—and to her sister's husband, Philip of Spain. It would have led to the recognition of her mother's marriage, and of her own legitimacy. But in the circumstances of the time, such a solution was scarcely thinkable. More attractive perhaps was a qualified Catholicism: the anti-papal system of her father. But the hardening of the religious divisions between the 1530s and the 1550s made this impracticable even if she had desired it. The men of the 1530s were now dead or scattered. It would have meant relying on a few ageing trimmers and alienating both Papalists and Protestants. It has been forcibly argued that the queen's first Parliament pushed her into a more Protestant settlement than she wished. Yet why did Elizabeth choose councillors such as William Cecil and Nicholas Bacon, or prelates such as Matthew Parker and Edmund Grindal, if she wanted to stop short of a broadly 'Protestant' settlement? That her settlement was meant to be a compromise, to retain certain Catholic elements in the form of worship and the system of discipline is, however, unmistakable. And this was to be the cause of continuing dissension among the radical Protestants or 'Puritans', who complained that the queen took as permanent what they regarded only as a stepping-stone towards a complete 'reformation'. All through her reign, Elizabeth found herself in conflict with the Puritans, lay and ecclesiastical, inside Parliament and without; and the struggle overflowed from domestic into foreign affairs.

At the very beginning of the reign, English help for the Scottish Protestants, in their attempt to throw off French control, seemed—misleadingly—to indicate a united 'British' religious alliance. But Elizabeth sanctioned limited intervention for strategic and dynastic, not for ideological motives. Then came the queen's dangerous illness, to the great alarm of her Protestant subjects; and next, the flight of Mary Stuart from Scotland to England and her subsequent involvement in plots against her host and cousin, Elizabeth. Meanwhile more strictly ecclesiastical disputes, over issues such as vestments, had also arisen. These disputes, carried into Parliament, soon raised the further issues of parliamentary privilege and freedom of speech. Finally, as the danger of direct collision with Spain grew, through support for the Dutch rebels and the activities of the 'sea-dogs' like Hawkins and Drake, foreign policy again became a contentious issue. The queen opposed, some of her ministers and many M.P.s supported, an alliance based on a common ideology; she denied, they insisted, that in the face of Spanish power this was vital to the country's interests, indeed to survival.

On the Catholic side, Elizabeth's position remained precarious, as unsure as her own life—and assassination plots would soon be added to the hazards of illness and accident. Yet the virtual imprisonment of Mary in England, the failure of a conspiracy against Cecil from within the government, and of the rising of the northern Earls from without, the long delayed, damp squib of the pope's Bull of Excommunication and Deposition, and release from immediate threats of French and Spanish intervention, mark a turning point in the reign around 1568–72. Admittedly, there were many perils ahead. The result of the Armada campaign was by no means a foregone conclusion; nor was this the last serious threat of Spanish invasion. Nonetheless these years can be seen as the end of an apprenticeship: both of the queen and of her chief minister, William Cecil. Despite one crashing failure—their intervention in the French Civil War in 1562–3—these first twelve or fourteen years have an unsurpassed interest as a study in statecraft. Their outcome marks the triumph of sheer ability, favoured by good fortune, over fearsome difficulties and weaknesses.

Men round the Throne

Historians have seen another climacteric after the Armada in the 1590s. This is partly a matter of perspective. The queen's personal defects grew more pronounced with age. Her characteristic mixture of imperiousness and procrastination, of parsimony and vanity must have infuriated all those who suffered from its alternating gusts. She could still call on reserves of charm, as is shown in her famous 'Golden Speech' to the 1601 Parliament. But her greatest service had already been rendered, by having survived and by having avoided any fatal, irrevocable blunder. Nor can she be blamed too severely for impatience with some of her critics and opponents, or for suspicion of those who wanted a larger scale, more costly war in order to feed their own ambitions or to line their own pockets. In her government too, time brought its changes. Too much may perhaps be made of the conflict of generations. But there is an unmistakable contrast between the two Cecils. William Cecil, Lord Burghley, chief minister for most of the reign was in marked decline from about 1595 on; he died in 1598, and Robert later Earl of Salisbury, became Secretary in 1596, and in effect was chief minister from 1601. Simply to say that the younger Cecil was less scrupulous, or more corrupt, or had less caution and more unrestrained ambition than his father, is to deal in psychological clichés. Despite much successful research, there is a great deal we can never know about the characters of these statesmen, like those of the monarchs whom they served. More significant is the difference in their respective tasks. William Cecil's role was initially to consolidate his own position in his mistress' counsels—and her own on her throne in Europe. From the 1570s on, his outlook was essentially conservative, advising caution and restraint against military commitment abroad, and compromise with

rather than persecution of Puritans at home. Robert Cecil's task, on the other hand, was the reconstruction of an existing political system. His greatest achievement was the bloodless succession of James, the union of the two crowns, in 1603. But his role was the more difficult and his new master, though by no means in every way Elizabeth's inferior as a monarch, was ultimately harder to serve. Which Cecil was the more gifted statesman is an open, if not a meaningless question. William without doubt was the more successful.

Robert Devereux, second Earl of Essex, the queen's last favourite, provides a striking contrast too with her first favourite—his own step-father, Robert Dudley, Earl of Leicester. Although Leicester was to the end of his life an enigmatic and potentially menacing figure, with absurd and damaging military pretensions, in the last resort he was prepared to accept co-existence. As councillor, courtier, peer, he remained immensely wealthy and influential, even though another man enjoyed the queen's political confidence to a greater extent than he, and no man held the ultimate key to her affections or the entry to her marriage bed. Essex by contrast lacked this sense of limits: he was a character not of politics but of drama, even tragedy. Since he inspired the devotion of poets and dramatists, of Puritan divines, sea-captains and professional soldiers, his fall was more than the end merely of a worthless favourite, a greedy, over-ambitious nobleman.

Sir Walter Ralegh's career too illustrates the changed climate of the late Elizabethan world. Ralegh, like his contemporaries' hero Sir Philip Sidney, displayed that combination of qualities which the men and women of their time most admired—and which we have come to think of as characteristically Elizabethan. He and Sidney both enjoyed precarious royal favour, and jeopardized it, by marrying young ladies of the court. The nastiest side of Elizabeth's character surely came out in her jealousy of younger women, though in fairness her worst wrath was reserved for those who lost their virtue before marriage and thereby harmed the reputation of the court. When we look at the disreputable tone of her successor's entourage, and the political damage which this did him, we can see the queen's point. Ralegh and Sidney were both pre-eminent as men of action, as writers and intellectuals, and as socially accomplished courtiers. Both were involved in financial difficulties—the worst of Sidney's being posthumous.

Fortune-seekers

The financial difficulties of individuals also underline the weaknesses of government throughout the whole century. The grants of money or privilege, which leading political and court figures needed in order to compensate for the inadequacy of their official salaries (or fees from the crown) were inherently un-

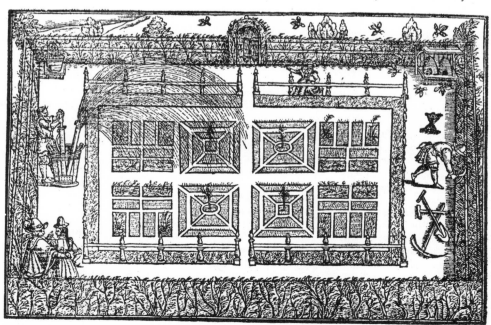

Classical authorities and a contemporary interest in scientific appliances are combined in this practical treatise 'The Gardeners Labyrinth', 1577, by 'Didymus Mountain' (alias Thomas Hill). This type of hedged-in formal knot-garden was popular with the Elizabethans as a sort of outdoor room. Here the author demonstrates 'the maner of watering with a Pumpe in a tubbe' to simulate rain.

satisfactory. Some, such as monopolies and 'farms' (or leases) of various branches of the revenue, were constitutionally objectionable to the Commons, who felt that the subject was milched for private rather than royal advantage. Moreover these grants (and pensions from the crown) were wholly dependent on continuing royal favour. Even outright grants of royal lands could be recalled in extreme cases. Different branches of the administration had their own characteristic rewards for those in the queen's service. The Cecils between them, through their mastership of the Court of Wards (from 1561 to 1612), controlled vast opportunities for patronage. Sidney, Essex, Ralegh were less fortunate, perhaps deservedly so.

The profits of war and colonization provided an alternative, if infinitely more hazardous, economic basis for political and courtly ambition. No successful English overseas colony was founded in Elizabeth's reign, and it is significant that the main promoters of these schemes were Ralegh and his stepbrother, Humphrey Gilbert, landless younger sons who lacked the luck or the genius of their Spanish prototypes, Hernán Cortez and Francisco Pizarro. In the following reigns colonization was found to require capital outlay, and therefore the backing of moneyed men. These were the merchants and financiers, of London and the other major seaports such as Bristol. It was not, on the whole, a quick or a sure way to riches, but a very slow means to eventual wealth both for individuals and for the nation. Privateering and licensed plunder of the Spanish American empire could of course yield fantastic profits. Yet the typically successful freebooter of the 1570s to 1600s was not the professional commander of genius, Francis Drake, still less the impoverished aristocrat or courtier, but the hard-headed mercantile type, whose returns bore a steadier, less sensational relation to his outlay. The profits of privateering may have helped to finance successful colonization in the next reign; but during the late 16th century the two seem more nearly alternatives, the one often militating against the other.

To all this there was one major exception. The prolonged and bloody destruction of an even semi-independent Celtic Ireland carried forward the frontier of English colonization. That frontier was not, of course, a neat continuous line, moving regularly forward. The advance was piecemeal, and in depth, as the expansion of the English 'Pale' into central Ireland (achieved in the 1550s), and the Elizabethan creation of frontier provinces in Munster and Connaught opened up large additional areas for settlement. Only Ulster remained virtually untouched until after the defeat and subsequent flight of the last and most nearly successful opponents of Tudor conquest: O'Neill and O'Donnell, the so-called 'earls' of Tyrone and Tyrconnel.

It was often the same Elizabethans who showed an interest in Virginia, the north-west passage or Guinea, and who had a stake, frequently as absentee landlords, in Ireland. From the time when Henry VIII abandoned his father's policy of indirect rule (through native or 'Anglo-Irish' magnates) and took the offensive against the Irish, right on to the settler revolt of 1780–82, Ireland was in one sense little more than a vast out-relief settlement for enterprising or indigent members of the English upper classes. The career of Richard Boyle, first and great Earl of Cork, who reputedly landed with a few pounds in 1588, and by the 1630s was the wealthiest man in Ireland (and one of the richest in the three kingdoms) indicates what fantastic opportunities were open to the right combination of talent, good fortune and total lack of scruple. That Cork's sons included Lord Broghill, a constructive 'moderate' statesman of the mid-17th century, and Robert Boyle, father of English chemistry—and perhaps the second greatest British scientist of his time—is a redeeming irony of history; but it can scarcely redeem their unattractive father.

Such opportunities, however, came to few, or perhaps there were few so well able to grasp them. Rather, historians have argued, the last years of the queen and perhaps even more of Lord Burghley, with the added stresses of war, economic difficulties and continued inflation, saw an intensification of the political and personal competition for the profits of office and court favour, together with a deterioration in official morality, and in the

standard of administrative probity. Certainly, if this view proves acceptable it is possible to make some kind of unity out of the 40 years or so from around 1588–90 to 1628–9. It is always unwise to try to characterize whole periods of history. There is nevertheless a sense in which the first 30 years from 1559 can be viewed as a time of recovery and consolidation, the next 40 as one of stress and doubt, and the last thirty odd from 1628–9 one of crisis and its temporary resolution.

This may appear to underestimate the importance of the great queen's death and the succession of James VI of Scotland as James I of England and Ireland. The achievements of the three great Tudors—Henry VII, Henry VIII and Elizabeth I—stand out in clear contrast to those of their Stuart successors. Nonetheless James' accession only accelerated the trends which were to lead to disaster for his son. This is true of the constitutional conflicts between Crown and Commons, the religious disputes between Anglicans and Puritans, and the economic problems of the monarchy and the propertied classes. New ideas and social forces were emerging which were to prove incompatible with the old hierarchic order, alike in church, state and civil society.

Parties and Power

The traditional view of English constitutional history is that Parliament had been increasing in strength steadily from 1529 to 1601, yet was still in basic harmony with the crown; and that it then made a sudden assertion of its strength in the face of James I's high-handed ineptitude. This view has now been substantially revised, in part because we know a good deal more about Elizabeth's earlier parliaments. Whether the first, that of 1559, forced a Protestant Church settlement on her may be left open. It is beyond dispute that in at least five other parliaments (those of 1566, 1571, 1572, 1584 and 1587) the Commons were prepared to challenge the queen on major issues, involving—as she saw it—essentials of her prerogative: religion, the succession, the boundaries of privilege and free speech, the security of the realm and of the queen's person. To bring in a bill to abolish the Prayer Book and the bishops, or to make the voting of subsidies conditional upon the queen promising to marry or on her naming a successor, was about as far as a strictly parliamentary challenge could go. One difference from the 17th century is that there does not seem to have been much continuity in this opposition. The ex- and future M.P.s appear to have had little organization between parliaments or even between sessions of the same parliament. Still less, (except for the so-called Bond of Association of 1584–5 aimed at Mary Stuart), do they seem to have contemplated any direct action outside the parliament in defiance of known royal wishes.

The attempts at a clandestine Presbyterian church system in the 1580s provide an exception to this. Some recent writers have seen in Puritan 'party' organization the forerunner of organized political opposition to the Stuarts. Too much should not be made of this. Although some of Elizabeth's most trusted and influential ministers were sympathetic to the Puritan cause, and afforded patronage and protection to Puritan ministers, it is far from clear that they approved, or were even aware, of these plans for a rival, anti-episcopal church. As the events of the 1640s were to show, there were always lay and clerical sides to English Puritanism. And the two could only remain in harmony so long as their 'party' was in opposition. Even the minority of M.P.s who supported the more far-reaching Presbyterian schemes, can hardly have wanted a 'Genevan' discipline—if indeed they knew what this might involve. The Puritan shadow-church was crushed, thanks to the vigilance and vigour of Elizabeth's later bishops, and the queen's unswerving support. Suppression left the movement leaderless. Puritans either conformed within the Church of England, or went outside it altogether and became 'separatists'. Meanwhile their one-time lay patrons and allies did little to help them. At the other extreme, because of the power of Spain, the irreconcilable Roman Catholics were potentially more dangerous. But, once again, the irreconcilable were a small minority. Just as there were conformist church-Puritans, so too there were church-Papists, many of them in high office and among the nobility.

Outside the anglicized Pale, the native Irish constantly rebelled in Elizabeth's reign. The O'Neill who became chief of Tyrone in 1567, and thus leader of the current Ulster rebellion, kneels in submission to Sir Henry Sidney, Lord Deputy of Ireland 1565–78. O'Neill's 'wild Irish' subjects are shown with their long hair and rug-mantles in this woodcut from Derrick's 'Image of Ireland', 1581.

However by the 1590s the Anglican *via media* had ceased to be a mere pragmatic compromise. The Church of England could claim to have steered England clear of religious war. It possessed a beautiful liturgy and a fine translation of the scriptures, as well, of course, as the many magnificent buildings which had survived the Reformation. Now in the person of the self-effacing Richard Hooker, it produced a major apologist. Hooker's work enables us, perhaps for the first time, to speak of an Anglican ideology. His main contribution to the religious debate was his distinction between 'essentials' on which men *must* agree, as a matter of faith imposed by duly constituted authority, and inessentials or 'things indifferent' on which legitimate divergencies of opinion were to be expected, some of which could indeed be tolerated, although on others outward conformity was demanded in the public interest. A man of genuine piety and devotion himself, the tendency of Hooker's writings was to produce a classic apology for an establishment—one might almost say for 'the establishment', against doctrinaires whether radical or reactionary. He offered to the Anglican leadership the theoretical foundation for a wide measure of unity, on a basis which would exclude only rigid separatist Puritans and diehard recusant Papists. If his successors, the bishops and leading divines of the 17th century mistook uniformity for unity, and so destroyed the basis of Protestant unity which the Elizabethan settlement and then Hooker had delineated with such masterly skill, the fault was theirs—and in the long run this was an immeasurable loss to the Church of England.

The rub of course with Hooker's thesis lies in deciding who is to define essentials and things indifferent, and to draw the boundary between them. To Elizabeth's last Archbishop, John Whitgift, and his chief agent in enforcing uniformity, Richard Bancroft (Bishop of London), essentials were one thing, to the Puritan leaders within the church they were quite another. When Bancroft succeeded Whitgift as primate and James failed—despite his initial inclinations—to assert his mediating authority at the time of the famous Hampton Court Conference of 1604, the policy of repression was reinforced. Again the great majority of Puritans, laymen and ministers alike, accepted the necessary minimum of discipline and conformity, and stayed inside the Church. Nor indeed need they have felt, until the reign of Charles, that its essentially Protestant character was in doubt. On the supposedly central Calvinist dogma of predestination, for instance, Whitgift was substantially at one with them to the end of his days. Further, James's second Archbishop, George Abbott (primate 1610–33) represented that characteristic Elizabethan mixture of episcopalian and Calvinist, of Anglican and Puritan. The Authorized Version of the Bible, while it drew heavily on Tyndale's and other 16th century translations, represents the successful cooperation of Anglicans and church Puritans. Never can a series of committees have produced a greater literary masterpiece, or a work of such spiritual power.

Work, Wages and Wealth

The 1590s were a time of general economic difficulties, when bad harvests spelt near famine for many. The Spanish War profited only a minority; normal overseas trade lost more than it gained. But this decade seems to have been a turning point in the history of the land-owning classes and to mark the beginning of an improvement in their fortunes. Since the early 16th century commodity prices and other costs, except that of labour, had on the whole been rising faster than rents. Tenant farmers and the self-employed stood to gain from this, landlords to lose. The attempts to restrain wages, achieved by a partnership of the royal Privy Council, Parliament, and the J.P.s enjoyed some success. It may be that wages lagged behind prices because, with population growing faster either than total national wealth, or—more particularly—than available food supplies, labour's bargaining position deteriorated. Real wages might have fallen in the 16th century, without any government action to prevent money wages rising. In the cheapness of labour and the continued buoyancy of agricultural prices lay the hope of better things for landlords. If they could bring rents into line with prices, or else revert to large-scale direct or 'demesne' farming (that is producing for the market themselves), they might well get the better of the inflation. There was indeed a massive increase in rents. Over the whole century or so c.1540–1640 rents probably rose at least as much as did the average level of all prices. From the 1590s to the 1630s, they seem to have risen much more

YOVTH
RECREATION
The English Gentleman
SPES IN CÆLIS
DISPOSITION.
ACQVAINTANCE
EDVCATION
MODERATION
VOCATION
PERFECTION
PES IN TERRIS.

Ro: Vaughan fecit

Richard Brathwait gives good advice to the country gentry (rather than those of the court, the theme of most courtesy books of the period) in 'The English Gentleman', first published in 1630 and dedicated to Wentworth (later Earl of Strafford). 'A Gentleman is a Man of himselfe, without the addition of either Taylor, Millener, Seamster or Haberdasher... A Crest displays his house, but his own actions expresse himselfe... Hee eyes the Court with a vertuous and noble contemplation... Hee lives in the Countrey without thought of oppression.'

On the engraved titlepage the ideal gentleman holds the rod symbolizing his office as J. P. with the tag 'Hope in Heaven, feet on the ground', and below his crest and motto 'I flourish with offshoots of good stock'. Also illustrated are Brathwait's 'sundry excellent rules'; for instance, on the left: Youth, the choice between 'Salvation through Virtue' and the siren with 'joyful voice, but eager for oblivion'; Education, with the seven liberal sciences, 'Breasts and rods', nourishment and correction. On the right: Recreation, hunting, 'Apollo does not always bend his bow'; Acquaintance, 'love for true worth never fails'; Perfection, 'a head breaking thorow a cloud, cloathed or impaled with sunbeames', with the motto 'This way leads to Heaven'.

steeply. Some families achieved recovery in this way; others by direct production for the market, whether of wool, cereals, meat, or dairy products. Moreover the burden of debts which many had incurred through the purchase of one-time Church property, either directly from the crown or indirectly from the original buyers, had now been successfully absorbed.

Certain sections of the landed classes, however, continued to live beyond their means. Those who indulged in the building and furnishing of the large and costly country houses which are such a feature of the period, those who aimed to marry their daughters above their own social level, those who wanted to cut a figure in the capital and at the royal court, in short to spend competitively on display and entertainment—these would be very fortunate to make ends meet on the profits of land alone. Those families lucky or prescient enough to have acquired valuable building sites in London, or to have coal and other mineral wealth under their land, were better placed, but even they could hardly manage the outlay for a London and court life without heavy borrowing.

William Cecil, for instance, had laid a sure foundation for the future of his family. His eldest son, the second Lord Burghley (and later first Earl of Exeter), could have lived very comfortably as a 'mere' landowner. In fact he aspired to a political career, though whether he made much out of it seems doubtful. By contrast, William Cecil's second son, Robert, would have had to be content with a relatively modest portion as a landowner. In fact he was trained by his father for a political career. By the time he died, as first Earl of Salisbury, Lord Treasurer, Master of the Wards, and principal Secretary of State in 1612, he displayed in an extreme form the lavish getting and spending of the ambitious courtier-peer. Families prepared to cut their coat according to their cloth could get along. Families on the make, who wanted to spend competitively as builders, courtiers, or political leaders could only prosper if the members achieved success as politicians or lawyers. For only then would their returns bear some correspondence to their outlay.

The career of a less admirable figure than Robert Cecil shows how this worked. Richard Weston, who ended his days as first

Earl of Portland and Lord Treasurer under Charles I had been a hanger-on at court enjoying minor perquisites and going on occasional diplomatic missions for many years before he obtained his first lucrative and influential post, as Chancellor of the Exchequer and Under-Treasurer. Portland died heavily in debt, despite having been one of the most lax, if not dishonest Lord Treasurers of his time. Thus the economic significance of office and royal favour for the upper sections of the landed class was of a circular nature. For those who aspired to office, office was normally essential. For a minority of the gentry, it provided the basis for a rapid increase in wealth, and a permanent improvement in family status and fortunes. For an unlucky minority the court was the road to ruin, either because they never obtained the necessary offices and other favours to make up for the expense of living in London and cutting a figure at court, or because political failure, defeat or death, cut them off prematurely.

If the aristocracy began to prosper anew in the new century, the crown did not. Admittedly, James I found himself on his accession about a year and a half's revenue in debt. But this, though inconvenient, was nothing unusual. What was more serious was that Elizabeth and her ministers had, inadvertently, allowed the crown's scope for financial manœuvre to be narrowed. Royal revenue could only be increased, if Parliament's help was not forthcoming, by raising the yield from monopolies and 'farms', from impositions (that is non-parliamentary additions to the customs duties), and from wardship. These were all areas where the crown was vulnerable to parliamentary attack. The Jacobean propertied classes would neither tax themselves more effectively, nor suffer the crown to do it for them. Herein lay a large part of the growing constitutional deadlock.

But when every excuse has been made for James I, it is hard to see that the financial situation of the monarchy was yet irreparable. The Irish were defeated in 1603; subsidies to France and soon to the United Provinces were no longer necessary. On the other hand, James had larger domestic expenses, with a wife and three children. The truth seems to be, that he had taken a considerable interest in government finance and administrative reform in Scotland, and had lived—more or less—within his frugal means. But he, and the numerous Scottish courtiers who came south with him, had a grossly exaggerated expectation of what the English crown was worth. A combination of prodigal expenditure and rising costs soon mortgaged his 'ordinary', non-parliamentary revenues, and the extravagance of life at court quickened the pace of competition to enter it.

It also quickened 'puritan' reaction. No doubt some Puritans had disapproved of Elizabeth's foreign policy as insufficiently radical. No doubt they had also disapproved of some of her suitors and favourites. But such disapproval, in her time, had not touched the centre of politics. Under James it did. His policy was not merely insufficiently anti-Spanish: it was positively pro-Spanish. His affections were not merely deplorable, even

perverse: he confused personal affection with the public interest. Elizabeth had never done this. No wonder James' parliaments were unforthcoming: so unforthcoming that all but the last, three out of four of them, were dissolved in an atmosphere of rage and frustration.

Ireland: Repression and Rebellion

How much significance in England's history, and in those of the sister kingdoms—should be ascribed to the union of the crowns in 1603?

The final defeat of the native Irish forces in the very month of Elizabeth's death was a coincidence. From then on Ireland remained at peace until the autumn of 1641, a longer interval than it had enjoyed at least since before 1540. As far as the native Celtic Irish were concerned it was a peace of exhaustion, not reconciliation. Yet the peoples of conquered colonial territories have sometimes prospered. Imperialism is often more damaging to the conquerors than to the conquered. Why then did the case of 17th century Ireland turn out to be hopeless? The difference of religion was not fundamental. A significant minority of the longer established settlers, the so-called 'old English', themselves were and remained Roman Catholics and could have provided a bridge between Celtic natives and English officials, but they failed to do so.

Until late in the 16th century the Irish language and Irish literary culture had actually been getting the better of English. But the new features of Tudor policy helped to reverse this. Conquest and direct rule over the whole island meant that English became throughout Ireland the language of law and government. To retain its property, a family had to negotiate in English. The Irish had also to conform to English ideas of land tenure. Royal wardship was extended to Ireland. Moreover many families' titles to their estates were open to challenge. If the screw was turned in the right places, this applied alike to the old Irish landed nobility, the semi-independent 'kings' of the Tuaths (the units of Celtic rule), to the long-established 'old English' settlers and to the 'new English', of whom the first Earl of Cork is the most noted instance. Thus the Irish upper class (both native and old English) was anglicized, or re-anglicized, as the price of survival. Moreover most of the dominant new English—high officials, lawyers and clergymen—tended to identify the native Gaelic culture of Ireland with a combination of the Scarlet Woman of Rome, economic stagnation, a barbarous way of life and treason against their rightful sovereign. In a sense they were right. Given the terms on which the English now wished to rule Ireland, there could be no compromise. And because the Irish *upper* classes were prepared to forego their language but saw their religion as a unifying element with their own tenants and dependants, who were in a more strict sense 'priest-ridden', it is understandable that the Catholic faith and not the Gaelic tongue and Irish literature became the battle ground of Saxon and Celt.

The native Irish were despised by the English as barbarous and priest-ridden. In this illustration from Derrick's 'Image of Irelande', the chieftain of the Mac Sweynes (sprung from 'Macke Swine ... which mai bee perceived by their hoggishe fashion') has laid aside his helmet of leather and iron to feast with his lady on the results of a cattle-raid (a common means of livelihood in Ireland as well as Scotland). 'Lacking pannes' the ox is cooked in its own hide; 'Fryer Smelfeast sneaking in' is given the best place, and the bard and harper complete the 'Irish myrth'.

Faced by this problem, successive English viceregal regimes oscillated between firmness and conciliation, alternately wooing and crushing the old English and the defeated native Irish. The colonization of Ulster (begun in 1610) resulted from the defeat and then the flight of the Celtic earls, O'Neill and O'Donnell. It was a blow primarily against the native Irish. By contrast the Commission on Defective Titles, the Irish Court of Wards, the use of the Court of Castle Chamber to impose political loyalty, and of the High Commission in Dublin to enforce Protestant ascendancy, and the treatment of the Catholic Church as a non-conformist sect, if not a subversive organization—all these measures were directed equally against the older established settlers and the native inhabitants.

The result of these inconsistencies was the renewed Irish rebellion of 1641. A tough 'forward' policy in Ulster and elsewhere (c.1610–1625) gave way to a conciliatory policy towards the old English (1625–9). Then came a sudden reversion to complete control by a new English group in 1629–32, and next the promise of a strong viceroy, above party divisions, in the person of Thomas Wentworth, later Earl of Strafford, who arrived in 1633. This was followed by growing resentment at Wentworth's increasing reversion to a tough, forward policy of further colonization, anglicization, and protestantization (1634–7). Finally the removal of his strong hand from Ireland in 1640 came at the very time when a now Puritan-dominated English parliament seemed to augur a renewal of persecution and confiscation, aimed perhaps at the extirpation alike of native landowner and Catholic priest.

The barbarities of the Irish Rebellion of 1641 (the first for nearly forty years) in which English Protestants were massacred, were never forgotten. Cromwell's brutal massacres at Drogheda and Wexford in 1649 were in part a revenge for these.

To the native Irish the rebellion was a renewal of the campaign for their rights, for their very being as a Celtic, Catholic people. For the old English it was a desperate dilemma. Some of them were forced into rebellion by the grasping and bigoted clique of new English who took over in Dublin after the collapse of the Wentworth regime. Others put loyalty to the king before fears for their Church and their property. By 1642, in effect, a three-cornered war was in progress between the 'Confederates', that is the native Irish together with some old English, the Royalists including some new and rather more old English, and the Parliamentarians, the remaining new English together with the Scottish settlers in Ulster. The tide of war finally turned in Parliament's favour only in 1647, and the final defeat of the Irish awaited the arrival of Cromwell and the main English army in 1649.

The crushing defeats and the massacres which followed, and the vast transplantation of the 1650s marked the elimination of Ireland as an independent national entity. The Gaelic educational structure was deliberately and wantonly destroyed. The Irish language became a heritage shared between a few exiles, largely religious seminarists, and the illiterate masses at home. Increasingly Ireland became divided between an upper crust of English Protestant officials and landowners, and a subject population of Irish Catholic peasants. Only Ulster and some of the towns

elsewhere constituted partial exceptions to this. The old English, saved by the Stuart restoration of 1660, survived till the Stuart débâcle of 1688. In the next century they would pay dearly for their Jacobitism, under the grinding severity of the penal laws. Such was the process which reduced Ireland, in the course of a century, from an equal kingdom into 'a kind of colony'—as Henry Cromwell put it in 1657.

Charles' attempt to impose the Anglican Prayer Book on the Scottish Kirk provoked a scene in 1637 in St Giles's, Edinburgh, when the Archbishop of St Andrew's used it: probably only one stool was thrown, which did not hit him. In 1639 war was declared.

Scotland: the neglected kingdom

The effect of the union of the crowns on Anglo-Scottish relations was equally unpredictable. A separate government was retained for Scotland, with its headquarters in Edinburgh. Between 1603 and 1641, James VI and Charles I each paid one visit to their northern kingdom. In short, the Stuart dynasty was so thoroughly anglicized that they became virtually strangers in their native land. This only became fully apparent with Charles. By the standards of his country and his time, James VI had been a remarkably successful king. He had repressed the over-mighty Scottish nobility, helped to bring about increased prosperity, improved law and order, and kept the Kirk at bay, so preventing a complete theocracy. If he could not, even by 1618—the high point of his achievement here—do more than temper the rigours of presbyterian Calvinism, he successfully retained a foothold for an episcopalian element in the Scottish Church.

Exactly why James and Charles neglected Scotland is a matter of surmise. James might reasonably have said that Scotland could take care of itself, that governing England was a full-time task, and that life in his southern kindom was more agreeable. Unfortunately he and Charles failed to govern England effectively despite their neglect of Scotland, while Charles resumed interference in his native country without his father's shrewdness and sense of limits. Whether the forces of the Covenant, those who came out in open resistance to Charles and his bishops from 1638 on, represented more than a militant, well-organized minority, remains arguable. Except in one or two areas, there was no corresponding royalist, anti-presbyterian (Catholic or episcopalian) minority to offer them effective opposition in support of the crown. A section at least of the nobility and the lairds had been alienated by Charles' threat to resume ex-church lands at the beginning of his reign. More Scottish peers were indignant at his reliance on bishops and courtiers in the administration, and at their own exclusion from office and favour. Others, including some nobles and lairds, a number of lawyers, many ministers of the Kirk, and a wide section of the middling orders of society, were genuinely affronted by Charles' apparent determination to Anglicize the Scottish Church, which became evident in 1637.

The problem of governing Scotland was to some extent a purely regional one: James VI sought the victory of lowland Scotland over the traditional Celtic culture of the Highlands and

Islands. As in Ireland, so in Scotland, the advance of royal government and of a uniform legal system spelt the conflict of two cultures. Lowland, or anglicized Scotland, which was also Protestant Scotland, embraced the border hills, the central basins of the Forth and the Clyde, the extreme south-western lowlands along the Solway, and modern Fife. Likewise the whole length of the narrow eastern coastal plain, from Dundee to Inverness (or at least to Elgin and Nairn), belonged to this modern world of commerce, law and order, and English speech. But for the purposes of religion, and the political allegiances which normally went with it, the Tay was more or less the effective boundary of the Lowlands and of Presbyterian support.

To this geographical division the great Campbell connection of Argyllshire and the south-western Islands was another notable exception. The chief of the clan Campbell, McCailen Mor, *alias* Archibald, eighth Earl and later first Marquess of Argyll (1639–61), was the personification of Calvinist resistance to Anglicanism. His family had served the Stuarts loyally in the task of pacifying and anglicizing the west of Scotland, because this had also served to advance their own fortunes. Yet ironically the Argyll following bore more resemblance to a semi-independent tribal unit than did those of many chiefs and lords who were on the other side in the Scottish conflicts from 1638 to 1746. James VI and his predecessors had broken the independent political power of the Highland and Island chiefs. But a major collision with the dominant groups in Lowland, anglicized Scotland (such as occurred in 1638–40) could only be met by alliance with the largely Catholic aristocracy of the north—anglicized in the case of the Gordons of Aberdeenshire, still Gaelic in the case of the Highlanders proper.

In Scotland the general course of events was similar to that in Ireland. First the Covenanters defeated the Stuarts and their supporters; then they were in turn defeated by the English Parliamentarian army and its few native allies. The result was the supremacy of the English throughout the British Isles. In Scotland, however, no colonization was attempted. At the most extreme extent of anglicization, under the shot-gun marriage of the Cromwellian union (1652–1660), the regime depended upon a combination of military occupation, and the conciliation of the Scots by firm, just government. For all the differences between the two countries, English and Lowland Scots had much in common: Cromwell, Monck and Broghill were in many respects only continuing the policies of James VI. Even their 'Puritanism' does not contradict this. For, like James in the face of the Kirk and its pretensions, all sensible lay rulers, including Oliver Cromwell, were first and foremost Erastians. Cromwellian Britain was puritan in the outlook of its rulers, but it was not ruled by churchmen.

In 1637 the Puritan propagandists, Prynne, Bastwick and Burton were savagely sentenced by the Star Chamber. In this attack on Laud of 1641 he is shown dining on his victims' ears, cut off in the pillory.

Constitutional Deadlock

By the late 1620s, England appears to have become ungovernable. This may seem paradoxical. Barring the constitutional deadlock, the country was probably as well governed as it had been under the Tudors. However, the system contained many grave weaknesses. Officials, dependent on the rewards and abuses of office, opposed reform within the administration. In the country, and in Parliament, there was suspicion of Stuart designs. Puritans—and not only Puritans—resented the Catholicizing tendency of the Church. Not least, the gentry disliked both the court and its fiscal machinations, while the common lawyers were jealous of the conciliar courts. Thus the whole regime became suspect and as tax-payers M.P.s were reluctant to contribute even to the legitimate costs of government. From 1624 to 1630 the crown faced about and pursued an 'Elizabethan' foreign policy: war with Spain and alliance with continental Protestants. But even the Spanish war did not find the Commons over-generous. They gave niggardly subsidies. They opposed alternative means of supply. In 1627, when the crown resorted to a forced loan—the largest ever attempted—a section of the gentry refused to pay. At one time 70-odd knights, esquires and gentlemen were under arrest for their refusal.

The years 1628–9 mark a political climax. Parliament attacked abuses such as unparliamentary taxation, wrongful arrest, forced loans, billeting of soldiers and martial law, and went on to arraign some of the high-churchmen whom the king supported. At first they avoided renewing the frontal attack on his favourite, George Villiers, Duke of Buckingham. If Charles I had been capable of the statesmanship of Elizabeth I something might still have been done. Sir Thomas Wentworth, the leader of the Commons, a

James' pro-Spanish policy, especially hateful to the Puritans, ended in 1623 when Buckingham and 'baby Charles' returned home from Madrid, spitefully revengeful against Spain after the failure of their blundering attempts to secure a Spanish match for Charles. In spite of the burst of national rejoicing at his return, the Commons were not over-generous with subsidies for the new policy.

This illustration for Vicars' 'Sight of the Transactions of these latter years', 1646, shows Puritan soldiers on their way north to fight the Scots in 1640, destroying 'Popish pictures', breaking down altar rails and restoring the communion table in the body of the church.

trenchant but constructive critic of misgovernment and a firm friend of strong, effective administration was a man of immense personal ambition. He crossed over into the king's service; and under more radical leadership, the Commons over-reached themselves during the next session early in 1629. These facts gave the king certain advantages; and with them he set out on a new course, the famous 'Eleven Years' Tyranny'—of rule without Parliament.

It is often suggested that Charles, through his two great ministers of the 1630s, Wentworth (later Earl of Strafford) and William Laud (Archbishop of Canterbury from 1633) was trying to achieve a radical shift in power and policy. However, Wentworth spent most of his time in the north of England and then in Ireland until the winter of 1639–40, and by then the time for any grand design was past; while he and Laud always had to share power with other factions in the king's counsels. Moreover Charles failed to grasp that a policy of indefinite non-parliamentary rule, because it required solvency, depended on peace. In 1639–40, he involved himself in war in Scotland. War forced him to return to Parliament, and the recall of Parliament in 1640 proved fatal not only to his own personal rule but ultimately to the whole Tudor system of conciliar government.

For the collision with the Scots, which necessitated meeting Parliament, Charles, Laud and Strafford were all responsible: Charles for his obstinacy and over-confidence; Laud for supporting advice; Wentworth because he misjudged almost every force at work. He underestimated the religious resistance in Scotland, supposed that his small Irish Army could play a decisive part in defeating it, and believed that the Parliament of England, like that of Ireland, could be alternately brow-beaten and bamboozled. These disastrous mistakes suggest that Wentworth's political judgment had been warped by the viceregal atmosphere of Dublin Castle. But even without these errors, it is questionable whether Charles' 'tyranny' could have lasted. Conceivably England might have developed a financially independent monarchy no longer restricted by Parliament or the common law. But equally there might well have been a rebellion at home. Charles had no troops in England, and the readiness with which most people stopped paying Ship Money in 1639–40 suggests an atmosphere of incipient revolt to which Hampden's famous case (1637–8) may be seen as a curtain-raiser. So perhaps the Scottish crisis was the occasion rather than the cause of Charles' downfall.

During its first session (1640–1) the Long Parliament dismantled first the personal rule of Charles I, then the machinery of the Tudor State. This in itself was a major and virtually bloodless revolution. But it left a political vacuum. The idea of ministerial responsibility to Parliament was formulated, if only in a fitful and fragmentary manner, but it was unacceptable alike to the king and to many M.P.s and others who had supported the reforms of 1640–1.

If Parliament had been united against Strafford in 1641, it was fairly evenly divided when civil war broke out in 1642, and many members would have preferred to remain neutral. This helps to explain the evenness of the contest, and something of its non-revolutionary character.

It also underlines the remarkable nature of John Pym's achievement. As the leading parliamentarian from November 1640 to his death three years later he has justly been described as the first man to have ruled England from the benches of the House of Commons. The absence of any memorial to Pym in the precincts of Westminster and Whitehall is truly astonishing, not least as both Charles I and Oliver Cromwell have been so honoured.

Civil war was not intended by those who brought about the changes in 1640–1. As far as we know, many of these reforms were carried unanimously. It was an accidental conflict, the result of fear and suspicion in a political vacuum. Men fought it reluctantly and repeatedly tried to end it on compromise terms. Eventually the issue could only be resolved by a decisive military outcome. Religion too was an issue; for some on both sides the crucial issue. But since the Erastian Puritanism of the victors was not so far away from the Anglicanism of the pre-Laudian regime, the compromises suggested there too might well have succeeded in an atmosphere freer of mutual fear and suspicion. Under duress, after his military defeat, Charles I was prepared on the face of it to sign away the Anglican church in England for a term of years, in Scotland for good and all. He believed that this could be effectively reversed in the fluid situation which existed and by exploiting the religious divisions among his opponents. Only at the last, when the bargain had patently fallen through did he stiffen his position and resolve to die for his conception of the Church.

Charles I in 1647 and his son in 1650 accepted the Covenant to obtain Scottish support. In this satire of 1651 'Jockey' turns the 'stone of all [Charles'] plots. For none turnes faster than the turne-coat Scots'; the Presbyter finds the King he made 'more obsequious than his Dad', but Charles thinks, 'You deep dissemblers, I know what you doe, and for revenges sake, I will dissemble too.'

Revolutionary forces: Cromwell and the Independents

The continuing constitutional deadlock is evident in the failure to reach a settlement with the king, after he had acknowledged military defeat in 1646. It is also shown in the parliamentary army's purges of the House of Commons in 1647 and again on a far more massive scale in December 1648. While the improvised wartime machinery of government, by committees in Westminster and the counties, was to last until Cromwell dissolved the Rump of the Long Parliament in 1653, in winning the war the parliamentarian cause had produced two revolutionary movements—themselves ultimately irreconcilable. The first, and in a

The Grandees (above, Fairfax and his officers in the General Council of the Army, September 1647) opposed the Levellers' demands in the Putney debates for something much nearer manhood suffrage. They feared that such men as these tradesmen of London (right), self-appointed preachers, would overturn the social system based on property rights. (13, 14)

sense the less radical, were the so-called Independents. The younger Sir Henry Vane was their most prominent, though far from most typical, parliamentary spokesman; Oliver Cromwell their military champion, and his son-in-law Henry Ireton their most accomplished theorist. They were not republicans on principle, or initially even by preference. The few outright believers in non-monarchical government won widespread support, especially in the army, as a result of Charles' undeniable responsibility for the Second Civil War of 1648. Only then did removal of the king come to be part of Independent policy. Even so, many leading Independents, especially those prominent in Parliament such as Vane himself, avoided being regicides. But they were realists. Until 1648 they were prepared to seek agreement with the king on the basis of a limited but powerful monarchy; after his execution in 1649 they sought to govern directly, as an oligarchy, combining legislative and executive powers. It is doubtful whether such a system could have worked with a normally elected parliament, not under military duress. As it was, elections for a new parliament proved at least as distasteful to contemplate in 1649–53 as they had been for Charles I after 1629. In solving the constitutional deadlock, by cutting off the king's head, the Independents had isolated themselves not only from previous royalists and neutrals but from many one-time parliamentarians. After 1648 the latter were in practice royalists, although they wanted the king, or later his son, back on their own terms, which included some kind of non-episcopalian, puritan church settlement.

Revolutionary forces: the Levellers

The second revolutionary movement which challenged the Independent leadership was that of the Levellers: a radical movement which seemed to many contemporaries to threaten upper-class control of the state. The Levellers did not operate like a modern party, even less like a modern revolutionary movement. They did not attempt to seize power themselves.

Instead they tried to persuade their one-time allies, the Independents in Parliament and the army leadership—the Grandees as Cromwell and Co. were called—to adopt their plan for a constitutional settlement. They demanded a more democratically elected parliament (on a franchise something like that which obtained in Britain from 1885 to 1918), and an executive separated from the legislature. On the selection, composition and powers of this executive the Levellers had less to say. Many of their other proposals reflected popular grievances of the middling and labouring classes in England, the views of sectarian Puritans, or the temporary interest of the army rank and file. The Levellers wrote and spoke fluently and persuasively, and they provide a historical link between the peasant and plebeian radicalism of earlier centuries and the popular movements of the late 18th and early 19th centuries. Many of their proposals were practicable as well as admirable, and could have been implemented by a strong government of sufficient goodwill and determination. Others, however, represented the sectional interests of the soldiers and of the small independent shopkeepers and artisans or of the middling peasantry, and were not necessarily any more 'progressive' or in accord with the general good than the policies for which Cromwell and Ireton, or even—in their better moments—the Stuarts stood.

Our knowledge of the Levellers and their views is remarkably full. They wrote in a time of unparalleled journalistic activity. Their leaders included several talented and attractive personalities. Moreover the meetings held in Putney church in the autumn of 1647 and at Whitehall in January 1649, found a masterly recorder in Fairfax's secretary William Clarke. They had against them in these debates an opponent of impressive skill and force in Henry Ireton. The text of the so-called Putney Debates, a record of the discussions in the General Council of the Army between the Grandees and the Agitators (as the soldiers' representatives were called), is the most remarkable single political document of the whole period. Even the original amended manu-

Non est potestas Super Terram quæ Compareretur ei Iob. 41. 24

LEVIATHAN
Or
THE MATTER, FORME
and POWER of A COMMON-
WEALTH ECCLESIASTICALL
and CIVIL.

By THOMAS HOBBES
of MALMESBVRY.

London
Printed for Andrew Crooke
1651.

Thomas Hobbes, who knew Ben Jonson, Galileo, Bacon, Mersenne, Descartes, and Harvey, published his 'Leviathan' in 1651; the titlepage sums up Hobbes' political philosophy. The multitude is embodied in the 'Leviathan', the absolute sovereign on whom individuals, contracting together for self-preservation, have conferred all their power, and to whom are given the attributes of both secular and ecclesiastical authority. Hobbes had fled to Paris on the impeachment of Strafford in November 1640, one of the first of a stream of Royalist refugees, including the Prince of Wales in 1646 to whom Hobbes taught mathematics. The 'Leviathan', however, horrified the exiles, and Hobbes' flight back to England in 1652 seemed to confirm suspicions that he had written it partly to ease his return. Nevertheless, it was also badly received in England. Charles forgave his old tutor on the Restoration, and Hobbes lived until 1679, protected by the king from the bishops and other would-be persecutors.

script versions of Queen Elizabeth's speeches, even the best of the parliamentary diaries must yield to it in vividness and interest. In brief, Ireton's argument was that by putting their claim to popular sovereignty on the basis of 'natural' right the Levellers placed all 'civil' rights in jeopardy, including that to property; he saw the sanctity of contract as a necessary basis for all law and government. Put more crudely, he and Cromwell maintained that political democracy would lead to economic levelling, if not to anarchy. This was made more plausible by the existence of a very small communist sect, the Diggers, who opposed Levellers and Independents alike.

'This mortal god'—the state

Ironically, the greatest and most radical political theorist of all was a supporter of unqualified absolutism, preferably an absolute hereditary monarchy. Thomas Hobbes published his masterpiece, *Leviathan*, under the Commonwealth in 1651. With ruthless logic he argued from the utter insecurity and misery of men in a 'state of nature', without government and so without law, to the necessity of their total submission to Leviathan, 'this mortal god'—or, as we should say, the state. Hobbes was disowned and denounced on all sides. Constitutional royalists and Anglicans abhorred his wholly secular premises; his neglect of divine-right legitimism pointed to the acceptance of any effective *de facto* government, such as Cromwell's .He was anathema to parliamentarians and common lawyers because of his unqualified denial that law was anything more than the edict of the state, that individuals had any absolute right to private property, and that there could be anything like a 'division of powers' or constitutional government. Hobbes demonstrated persuasively the perils of freedom, and after the turmoil of the 1640s–50s men did not care to be reminded of these, or not without appropriate religious edification. As with other original thinkers who have emphasized the darker side of man's nature, Hobbes had more influence on many of those who attacked him than they cared to admit.

His younger contemporary, the materialist philosopher James Harrington, admired Machiavelli and maintained that the distribution of landed property dictated the balance of political power. Unlike Hobbes, Harrington supported a republican constitution; he believed in 'checks and balances', the rule of law and a separation of powers. His great influence came in the next century, with Montesquieu and the American Constitution. Although politically suspect to royalists, Harrington's ideas were—correctly—regarded as intellectually and morally far less disturbing than those of Hobbes.

The challenge to accepted orthodoxies by political theorists was only part of a more general ferment of ideas. Although the main body of English Puritans were no more tolerant than their Anglican opponents, it was on the radical wing of the Puritan movement that the first coherent demands for full religious toleration and intellectual freedom were made. Ideas of equality, as between social classes, between religious groups, between the sexes and before the law, were all brought into popular currency by the turmoil of those years. Without the parliamentarian cause, oligarchic and in some ways conservative as it was, the popular challenge to hierarchy and to traditional values and authority is scarcely thinkable. Without the patronage of Cromwell, radical democratic ideas would never have found such free expression. Cromwell's own tolerance is indeed remarkable. Part of the tragedy of the 1650s is that the New Model Army, which had in 1645–49 been a finely tempered, yet (except towards the Irish) a remarkably humane revolutionary instrument, itself developed into a political and economic vested interest, and so became, in the end, a massive obstacle to constitutional settlement.

The political complexities of the Republic (1649–60), provide variations on the same underlying theme as the crises and conflicts of the 1620s–40s. The country remained ungovernable, save by use or at least threat of military force. There was still too little common ground, too little give and take, for government by consent to be possible. Ironically, after the semi-absolutist experiment of the 1630s, and the unicameral legislative sovereignty of 1649–53, Cromwell as Lord Protector (1653–8) made extraordinary efforts to gain acceptance as uncrowned constitutional monarch. He failed, but not for lack of trying. His weakness, like that of Charles I, was financial, and like Charles I he was driven to supply it by questionable means. Indeed, the taxes levied by him made the exactions of the previous monarchs look modest, and aroused no less resentment.

Taxation was only one cause of political dissension. First, Rump Parliament and Army became divided against each other. Then followed in 1653–4 the split between republicans and Cromwellians. At the same time radical sectaries were opposed by moderate Erastian Puritans, swordsmen by civilians. Only Cromwell himself could keep this regime from falling apart. The threat of anarchy to which this disunity pointed by the end of 1659, contributed much more to the return of king, church and House of Lords, than did the merits of the royalists and their cause. The settlement which followed in the 1660s was a temporary makeshift. The constitutional centre of gravity had shifted a long way towards Parliament but the final outcome remained in doubt until the further revolution of 1688–9. The divisions within the Protestant communion were to prove more lasting. Until 1689 there was no statutory toleration for those outside the state Church, while non-Anglicans were to remain second-class citizens until the 19th century.

Despite the republican collapse and the return of the old order in 1660, it would be wrong to underrate the importance of the Interregnum. The English ruling class—from the royal family down to the local county and civic oligarchies—had seen its power undermined and its existence threatened. A different set of men, from a lower social background, had seized power and had proved that they could govern the country. The English monarchy and nobility learnt some lessons from this. The fate of James II in 1688, abandoned by his one-time Tory supporters, and pushed out by his natural allies, the peers, is proof of this. James was hustled off the stage and his successors hastily installed—on conditions, unlike Charles II in 1660—so that a popular momentum for reform should not develop, as it had done in the long drawn-out agony of 1640–9.

Science and Society

In the world of thought and belief our century ends with the foundation of the Royal Society and the formal victory of the new science over Aristotle, scholasticism and acceptance of the Ancients as the measure of all things. It can be argued that British science suffered from this aristocratic embrace, and from the dilettante approach of the virtuoso. Yet the change over the century is remarkable. In 1559 it would have been risky to pro-

This engraving of 1647 shows a congregation, probably of Presbyterians (a plain church with the emphasis on the sermon), and also attacks Jesuits, Papists, Arminians and the various extreme sects with their 'mechanic' lay preachers; for instance, the 'Family of Love' are shown with typical virulence and misunderstanding, as naked and libertine.

mulgate the views of Copernicus in astronomy and almost unthinkable to question the authority of the Ancients in other fields. By the 1660s, thanks to the influence of the great continental scientists and to the achievements of native scientists, such as Gilbert, Napier, Harvey and Boyle, the whole attitude to hypothesis and experiment was different. By then Newton was about to embark on his most original and constructive work. How large a place England ought to have in the *European* story of the scientific revolution is a more difficult question. Nor is it easy to be sure how much the advance of science owed to the other elements in English life which have been emphasized in this chapter. The coincidence is there. Protestantism of an Erastian, reasonably flexible kind survived; the Stuarts were defeated by Parliament and the classes it represented; business enterprise was substantially released from monopolies and controls; and science flourished as it had not done before, and—as had not been the case earlier—more so in Britain than in most continental countries. The connection between these developments may not have been one of cause and effect operating only in one direction. How far did the other changes arise from those in the economy and the social structure of the country? The 'Price Revolution' had come to an end. Except for harvest fluctuations and wars, prices remained fairly stable from the 1640s to the 1740s. The rate of population growth seems to have slowed down, and as a result living standards may have been marginally improved. The country's foreign and colonial trade and its merchant shipping grew faster after 1660 than they had done before 1640. Yet in industry the period after the Restoration was perhaps less progressive than the 80 or so years before the Civil War. Commerce and manufacturing were freer from restraint and direction, but the economy as a whole may have been more sluggish, although in the long run the opportunities for economic advance and social mobility were now greater than they had been before 1640.

Here we can only speak of England. Ireland's position continued to be one of involuntary servitude punctuated by unsuccessful rebellion. In Scotland 1660 saw a more violent counter-revolution. For Scotland the Restoration was an intermediate stage in the process which was to culminate in the Act of Union, and the anglicization of the Highlands after Culloden. For England, however, the Restoration showed a way forward, acceptable to most of those who counted politically and in the long run flexible enough to be adapted to changing needs, without a repetition of the events of 1642–60.

The Poetry of Revolution

With the closing of the theatres by the Puritan Parliament in 1642 and the dispersal of the Cavalier poets by the civil war and royalist defeat, English literature may seem to pause, even to falter. This is to overlook much polemical writing of the 1640s and 50s, which possesses a vigour and plainness of style in refreshing contrast to much of the prose written under Elizabeth and James. Moreover the Carolean drama of the 1630s and 1640s was already the merest postscript to that of the great Jacobeans. The greatest poet of the mid-17th century was already at work in the 1630s. John Milton's preoccupation with religious and political issues from 1641 to 1658 interrupted his poetic output, but scarcely his development as a poet. By the end of the 1650s Andrew Marvell had written most of his finest poems, and John Dryden's poetical career was well launched. Milton's greatest epic poetry was to follow in the 1660s.

In architecture our century ends, as it had begun, with a revolution. The classical influences of the continental Renaissance

had first begun to replace the late Gothic style and manner of building in the 1550s, through a group of aristocratic patrons and designers associated with the Protestant leadership of Edward VI's reign. A fusion of these two traditions, a kind of English 'Mannerism' can be seen at its most successful in such varied Elizabethan and Jacobean country houses as Wollaton and Montacute. The besetting fault of this style was fussiness and over-elaboration. The second architectural revolution began in the 1610s and its initial phase was reasonably complete by 1660. This saw the successful adaptation of Palladio's simpler neo-classicism from Italy by Inigo Jones and his subsequent imitators. Jones was originally patronized by the royal court, but his influence survived his masters' defeat. By contrast, architecturally speaking 'Baroque' is little more than an interlude in early 17th century England. Laud's porch on St Mary's, the university church, and his Canterbury quadrangle in St John's College, Oxford, are among its few authentic manifestations. Some of the more elaborate funeral monuments of the period, seem better to deserve the name Baroque. Just as the High Renaissance was received late in England, so too was the Baroque. For a genuine English Baroque we have to await Vanbrugh and Hawksmoor at the turn of the 17th and 18th centuries. The genius of Wren which flowered during the intervening years, owed more to Jones and his native classical school than to direct continental influences.

In painting, one art form survived changes of regime and religious orthodoxy. Miniature painting blossomed with Nicholas Hilliard and Isaac Oliver at the court of Elizabeth, continued with John Hoskins during the reigns of James and Charles, and reached its climax with Samuel Cooper, a minor Cromwellian official who also enjoyed court patronage before and after the days of the Republic. Within the chosen limits of the miniature, Cooper achieved a perfection as exquisite as that of the great continental masters. One of the supreme epochs in European painting saw distinguished visitors at work in England—notably Rubens and Van Dyck—and two great connoisseur collectors—the Earl of Arundel and King Charles I—but no native artist of the first rank. Again in sculpture during the age of Bernini, it is the best practitioners of a secondary, almost an applied art—that is, sculptors of funeral monuments—who come to mind, such as Epiphanius Evesham and Nicholas Stone.

In music, few people still believe that all was glorious until the blight of Puritanism cast its deadening pall. Yet royal, aristocratic and clerical patronage was important. Between the age of William Byrd and the Elizabethan madrigal and that of Henry Purcell, only the beginnings of opera at Cromwell's court as Protector contradict the adverse view, or at best the portrait immortalized by Sir Walter Scott and Macaulay of the psalm-singing Puritans on the march.

With the return of the royal court and many of the aristocracy from exile in 1660, England moved nearer to the Continent in literature and the arts than she had been for many years. The new fashions in literature and the theatre, the new manners of London and the court (such as the wearing of wigs), indeed the whole social and political tone of the Restoration capital, brought England near to becoming a cultural satellite of Louis XIV's France. Audiences who preferred the tragedies of Dryden to those of Shakespeare, might well prefer the political system of Louis XIV to that of the Long Parliament. This tension underlay the Restoration of 1660, and is reflected in the second English revolution—of 1688/9—and the settlement which followed. Its outcome belongs to the story of Britain in the 18th century.

VIII SLAV NATIONS

Poland and the evolution of Russia

HENRY WILLETTS

'The Lord God sometimes waits till Poland's foes

hemming our wretched country in on every hand

have taken their pleasure of her, and cries at last:

Enough!'

ŁUKAZ OPALIŃSKI

On the eastern frontier of Christendom

lived the Slavs. Many groups had already succumbed to foreign rule. In the extreme north-west they were in process of assimilation by the Germans, in the centre they were governed by the Habsburgs, and further south by the Turks. Lithuania and Poland (populated mainly by Slavs) had been united in 1386, forming a dual monarchy which, in the middle of the 15th century, stretched from the Baltic to the Black Sea.

The other independent Slavonic state was Russia, whose development had been held back for two hundred years by the Tartars, Asiatic conquerors who compelled the Russians to pay tribute. In 1480, however, Ivan III, Grand Duke of Muscovy, threw off the 'Tartar yoke' and made Moscow the centre of a Russian state which in the next eighty years rapidly expanded both eastwards and westwards. In the west the Muscovite state came into conflict with Poland-Lithuania. Poles and Russians differed in language, culture and religion, Poland looking towards western Europe and Rome, Russia cherishing its Byzantine heritage and the Greek Orthodox Church. In the south, a Tartar remnant, the Khanate of the Crimea, plagued both nations.

The last of the ancient Jagiellonian line of Polish kings was Zygmunt August, known in the west as Sigismund Augustus.

He died in 1572 without an heir; whereupon the Polish gentry reasserted their traditional claim to elect the new king. In the elections of the following century, only members of European ruling houses were chosen; but the result was not satisfactory, for the foreign kings had their own dynastic interests which were often irrelevant to Poland. In 1573 the successful candidate was Henri duc d'Anjou, brother of Charles IX, King of France; but after a reign of five months, his brother having unexpectedly died, he succeeded as Henri III of France and surrendered his alien and elective for a native and hereditary crown.

The next choice was the Transylvanian prince Stefan Batory (opposite), who reigned in Poland from 1576 to 1586. He never troubled to learn the language of his new subjects, but devoted his energy and talents to their service. He won a series of brilliant victories against Russia, driving the armies of Ivan the Terrible back along the Baltic. When he died in 1586 he was preparing to lead an expedition against the Turks.

Although his main achievements were diplomatic and military, Stefan Batory continued the cultural integration of Poland into Renaissance Europe that had begun under his predecessors. He patronized the Jesuits, but was careful not to encourage religious discrimination or persecution.

STEPHANVS D
REX. POLON. X
AO. 1576

Elective kingship, as we have seen, was an ancient principle in Poland and remained theoretically valid even during the reign of the Jagiellonian kings. But when Zygmunt August died childless, the election of Henri de Valois was the first such occasion within living memory when the choice was really open. His successor was Stefan Batory, to be followed by Zygmunt III, of the Swedish royal family, the Vasas. He is shown here (*above*), presiding over the Diet. In spite of the elective system, clashes were still frequent between the magnates and the king.

SCHMOLEN SKA.

War with Russia smouldered all through the 17th century. In 1609 Zygmunt III, seeing the anarchy in Russia and fearful that Sweden would profit, declared war and marched on Russia. His main army was held at Smolensk, however, and was forced to conduct a siege (*above*) that lasted for nearly two years. Polish forces entered Moscow in the autumn of 1610 and Prince Władysław was proclaimed Tsar, but the campaign brought no permanent advantages.

To unite Poland with Sweden was the ambition of both Zygmunt III and his son Władysław IV, seen here (*left*) receiving Swedish envoys.

The last of the Vasas to sit on the Polish throne was Jan Kazimierz (*right*), Władysław's brother, who ruled from 1648 to 1668.

Zygmunt August, who ruled Poland for twenty-four years (1548–72), sought to create a single nation out of his diverse peoples. He united the Diets of Poland and Lithuania, and strengthened cultural links with the West.

Zygmunt III Vasa (*below*), a bigoted Catholic, reigned in Poland from 1587 to 1632. In 1594 he was crowned king of Sweden also, but dethroned in 1599. He never renounced his claims to the throne of Sweden, but was never able to enforce them.

Władysław IV (*left*) was the opposite of his morose father, cheerful, sociable and by temperament a soldier. But his difficulties were severe. He failed to strengthen the Polish position in the Baltic, suffered repeated incursions by Crimean Tartars against whom he had no effective defence, and postponed rather than solved the problem of Cossack autonomy in the Ukraine. He was succeeded by his brother Jan Kazimierz.

Jan Sobieski (*below*) was elected to the throne after Jan Kazimierz had retired to a monastery in 1668 and his successor had failed to quell the disorders which threatened the very existence of the state. He provided a strong leadership which was, for the first time since the death of Zygmunt August, uncomplicated by non-Polish ambitions. It was Sobieski who in 1683 led the coalition army that routed the Turks before Vienna.

The magnates and the gentry dominate the political history of Poland in the 17th century. These two vivid stucco reliefs from the church at Tarłów are part of a series showing Death coming to fetch men from various classes. The magnate (*left*) holds a legal document, the gentleman (*right*) is armed with knife, sword and whip. The magnates usually held the great offices of state which conferred membership of the Senate, while the gentry elected the Chamber of Deputies.

Trade flowed into Poland-Lithuania through the great port of Danzig, a strongly Protestant centre and formerly one of the cities of the Hanseatic League. This engraving (*below*) of 1687 shows the banking centre, the 'Arthushof'. *Right:* the town hall of Poznán.

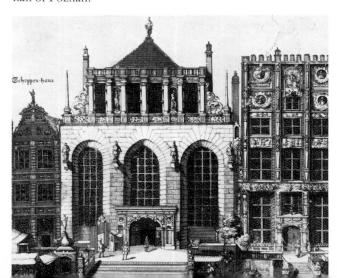

A prosperous burgher class was growing up in Poland as in the rest of Europe, but its wealth did not bring political influence. *Above:* the two houses built by Mikolaj Przybylo and his brother Krzysztof about 1615 at Kazimierz. The façade is covered in bas-reliefs including a giant St Christopher.

The king, though his real power was severely limited, enjoyed the traditional trappings of royalty. His castle at Cracow (*above*) had been built between 1502 and 1535 by Italian architects and contained splendid furnishings from Italy, France and Flanders.

Cracow, the old capital (*below*), grew up round the Wawel, the rocky hill on the right. Here was the king's castle and the Stanislaw Cathedral, where the Polish kings were crowned and buried from 1305 to 1764. In the foreground is the river Vistula and on the left the great church of the Virgin, with its uneven towers, and the 'Praetorium', or town-hall.

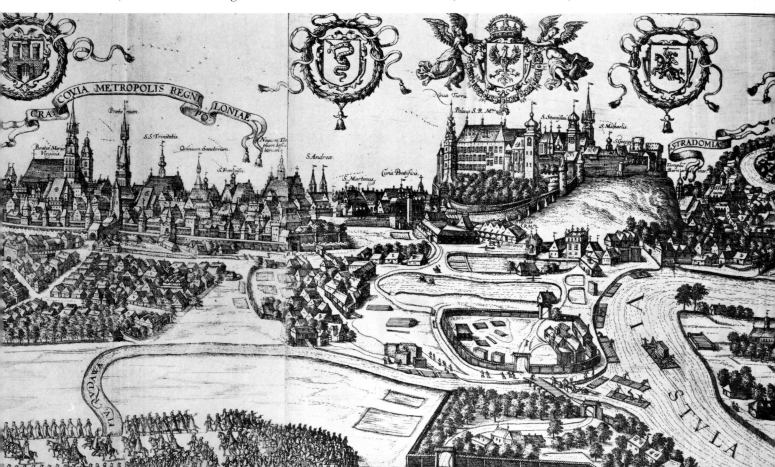

The 'Time of Troubles' followed the extinction of the old ruling house of Moscow. Three years before his death (1584) Ivan the Terrible had killed his eldest son in a fit of rage. His second son Fyodor proved unequal to the task of government (his favourite occupation was bell-ringing) and power passed into the hands of his brother-in-law Boris Godunov. When the Tsar's nine-year-old brother Dimitri was murdered in 1591, Boris was universally suspected. Whether he was really guilty or not is obscure, but when Fyodor himself died in 1598 it was Boris who, with boyar support, took the crown. The icon shown here (*right*) reconstructs the murder of Dimitri. A man claiming to be Dimitri (*above*) appeared in Poland in 1603 and gained the support of some magnates and the Jesuits. He invaded Russia and on the sudden death of Boris, was even elected Tsar.

The Grand Duchy of Moscow began to bring other Russian principalities under its sway during the period of Tartar domination. Ivan III (1465–1505) refused to pay tribute to the Tartars, conquered Moscow's leading rival Novgorod, and was the first Prince of Moscow to call himself 'Tsar'. His grandson, Ivan IV, called 'the Terrible' (*above*), who became Grand Duke at the age of three in 1533, built up the central authority against the nobles, or 'boyars'. He was violent and unbalanced, and his struggle with the boyars plunged Russia into a generation of bloodshed and hatred. But he added large tracts to his territory, and by consolidating his autocratic rule may have saved Russia from the fatal division of powers that ruined Poland.

In the great hall of the Kremlin 'the false Dimitri' is seen (*right*) giving audience to the Polish embassy in full state. But his rule was brief. In 1606 he was assassinated by the boyars, and for six years Russia was a prey to invasion and rebellion.

Anarchy was ended by a national rising which drove out the Poles. In February 1613 the Assembly of the Land elected a new Tsar: Mikhail Romanov (*right*). He was the first of the dynasty that reigned without interruption until 1917.

Russia still seemed remote from western Europe, though the Tsars employed western craftsmen and technicians. The Ambassador's Palace in Moscow (*above*, in a sketch of 1661) shows 'modern' features, such as the arcaded gallery, next to others purely Russian.

In the audience hall (*below*) ambassadors on a mission to Persia from the Duke of Holstein in 1634 are surrounded by the boyars in long robes and tall black fox fur hats.

Moscow expanded rapidly until 1700, when its growth was checked by Peter the Great's foundation of St Petersburg. The city clustered round the Kremlin, the triangular fortress overlooking the river. In the view *right*, showing Palm Sunday in what is now the Red Square, the golden spires and domes of its churches rise above the ramparts. On the left is St Basil's (wrongly labelled Kremlin) and in the centre the Redeemer Gate, built – in spite of its Russian appearance – by an Italian and an Englishman: the base by Marco Ruffo in 1491, the top by Christopher Galloway in 1624.

Boris Godunov (*left*) was an 'elected' Tsar, and to begin with popular, but his position was never really secure. He pursued a vigorous foreign policy and tried to build up the lesser gentry against the boyars.

The Church in Russia had always been closely bound to the State. But in 1653 the Patriarch Nikon (*right*) tried to assert the primacy of the Church over the State. He was dismissed by the Tsar, and defrocked. He also introduced 'reforms' based on the practice of the Eastern Orthodox churches which aroused fanatical opposition.

Overleaf: an icon of the Last Judgment, painted in Moscow in the 17th century, and reflecting both a mode of thought and an artistic style that had changed little in a thousand years.

Poland and
the evolution of Russia

HENRY WILLETTS

This crest of King Zygmunt August (Sigismund Augustus) with his initials 'S A' entwined round the Polish eagle, comes from the 1560 edition of 'Confessio Fidei Catholicae Christianae' by Cardinal Stanisław Hosius.

IN THE EARLY MIDDLE AGES Eastern and Western writers alike were awed by the numbers and the military prowess of the Slavs: 'a people so mighty and dreadful', according to the Arab historian Al-Bekri, 'that if they were not divided into a multitude of tribes and clans, no one in the world could withstand them'. By the middle of the 16th century most of the tribes and clans had been subjugated by other peoples. In the north-west corner of the Slav world German conquerors were rapidly assimilating the Slavs of the Elbe basin and the Baltic coast. In central and southern Europe the Slavs had passed under Hungarian or Ottoman rule. To protect their own interests against Habsburg and Ottoman encroachment the Venetians had occupied the maritime towns of Dalmatia. In the Balkans there was one irreducible Slav community—the tiny theocratic republic in the highlands of Montenegro. Apart from this, only two Slav states had retained their independence—Poland and Russia.

The Slavs and their Oppressors

Both had survived onslaughts from east and west. The greatest threat to Poland had come from the Teutonic Knights, who first securely established themselves in Eastern Europe in the 13th century. The ostensible purpose of these ex-crusaders was still the propagation of Christianity by the sword, but in reality they offered a lucrative career to many thousands of military adventurers, and acted as a spearhead of German expansion in the Baltic lands. The Teutonic Order and the fraternal order in Livonia, the Knights of the Sword, gradually made themselves masters of the Baltic coast from west of Danzig to Narva. Hopes of expansion into Christian Russia were dashed in 1242 when Prince Alexander Nevsky defeated the Knights of the Sword on Lake Peipus (the 'battle on the ice'). The 'crusaders' were more successful against Catholic Poland. In 1308 they answered a Polish call for help against Brandenburg and rewarded themselves by seizing the old Polish town of Danzig (Gdansk) and its hinterland. The foes who most excited their self-righteous cupidity were the heathen princes of Lithuania, who in the 14th century built their small country into a multi-national state, stretching from the Baltic to the Black Sea, and including not only the whole of White Russia and most of the Ukraine but some of the old Great Russian principates. The Teutonic threat to Poland and Lithuania brought about a dynastic union of the two countries (1386), and the consequent conversion of Lithuania's rulers to Christianity removed the pretext for further German expansion. The Knights endeavoured to disrupt the union, but at Grunwald in 1410 the Poles and Lithuanians, with some help from the Czechs, heavily defeated them. Their power steadily declined until Poland, by the Treaty of Thorn of 1466, regained its old Baltic territories. Danzig, Elbing, Marienburg and Thorn, which had grown into flourishing towns under German rule, were subjected to Polish rule and known thenceforward as 'Royal Prussia', but the Order continued to rule East Prussia from Königsberg as vassals of the Polish king. In 1525 the last Grand Master of the Order, Albrecht Hohenzollern, with the king's permission, converted his domain into a secular duchy.

While Poland was engaged with the crusaders, Russia had suffered a much more damaging experience. In the years 1237-41 the 'Mongols' of the Golden Horde, a vast predatory swarm led by Baty, a grandson of Jenghis Khan, swept through the Russian lands and reduced the squabbling princes to vassaldom. The Horde soon abandoned any attempt to rule Russia directly, but dominated it indirectly and exacted tribute for nearly 200 years. Rebellions were frequent, but it was not till 1480 that Ivan III, Grand Duke of Moscow, formally threw off the 'Mongol-Tartar yoke' and refused to pay further tribute. The 'gathering of the Russian lands' under Ivan III and his successors involved bloody subjection of other Russians by Moscow and the creation of an autocratic system which owed less to Russian tradition than to the example of the Tartars. The expansion of Moscow brought it into conflict with the Grand Duchy of Lithuania, which had profited from the Tartar conquest to incorporate 'Russian lands', and the remnants of the Golden Horde itself. In the first half of the 16th century, Moscow extended its boundaries in both directions, 'recovering' from the Lithuanians Smolensk, Bryansk, Chernigov and other territories (1500-37), and conquering the Tartar khanates on the Volga, Kazan (1552) and Astrakhan (1556).

Poland and Lithuania escaped direct conquest but they too were plagued for centuries by the most powerful of the Horde's successor states. This was the khanate of the Crimea, established in 1443, and from 1475 a vassal of Turkey. The extension of Turkish power along the Danube and around the northern shores of the Black Sea created great difficulties and dangers for Poland and Russia alike. Both were regularly savaged and bled by the Crimean Tartars, and both feared that energetic punitive action would bring Turkish reprisals. The Pope, the Emperor and the Venetian Republic frequently tried to enlist Poland and Russia in a crusade against the 'common foe of Christendom', but it was not until the late 17th century that the two countries fought together in an anti-Turkish coalition.

At the other end of Europe, the 16th century saw the rise of another formidable military power which affected the history of the two Slav states scarcely less than the Turks. This was Sweden, which in its drive to dominate the Baltic clashed both with Poland and with Russia. Sweden's aggrandizement helped to weaken Russia by barring its way to the Baltic and so at first benefited Poland. But at a later stage Sweden brought Poland to its knees, and Russia was able to detach much of the territory in dispute between itself and Poland long before, under Peter the Great, it expelled the Swedes from Ingria and Livonia.

In the second half of the 16th and first half of the 17th century, Poland and Russia were irreconcilable enemies. The hostility which sprang from territorial disputes was aggravated by social, cultural and religious incompatibilities. Poland was a feudal monarchy, European in culture, Catholic (or Protestant) in religion. Russia was a despotic land, only superficially influenced by Europe, Orthodox in religion, and indeed in the minds of its rulers the centre of the true Christian faith since the fall of Constantinople. Both countries in this period came close to national collapse, Russia in 1605–11, when Poland seemed likely to be the main agent and beneficiary of its destruction, Poland in the mid-1650s, when it found itself at war with Russia, Sweden, Brandenburg, Transylvania and its own rebel subjects in the Ukraine. But Russia struggled through its 'Time of Troubles' and in the following century matured into a great European power, while Poland never fully recovered from the 'Deluge', declined steadily into military impotence and international insignificance, and became at last the plaything of more successful neighbours. The weakness and misfortunes of Poland created the conditions for the ascent of Russia: Poland therefore will occupy the foreground in this account of the two states in the years 1548–1668.

The Multi-Nation of Zygmunt August

In the reign of Zygmunt August [Sigismund Augustus] (1548–72) Poland was a powerful, wealthy and enlightened country. The skill and courage of its incomparable cavalry impressed all Europe. Poland and Lithuania, through Danzig and Riga, were the main exporters of grain to the great markets at Amsterdam, and their trade not only enriched landlords but stimulated the growth of a thriving bourgeoisie. The privileged gentry were numerous, secure against challenge from below, and well educated by the standards of the time. Poland's cultural ties with western Europe, particularly with Italy, were close, and Poles responded eagerly to the influences of the Renaissance.

But the prosperity of the country rested on insecure political foundations. Poland-Lithuania was the second largest political unit in Europe. It was, however, a multinational country, in which the Poles were a minority. The Germans, dominant in the vassal dukedom of East Prussia and the semi-autonomous towns of Royal Prussia, were numerous also in most Polish cities. Lithuania, was inhabited mainly by White Russians and Ukrainians, who looked naturally towards Russia rather than Poland. This heterogeneous population was governed by a loosely organized feudal state, in which the king, the great landlords or magnates, and the gentry contended for mastery. Political disunity was aggravated by religious disunity: the state religion of Poland and Lithuania was Catholicism, but Protestantism made great inroads in both countries in the 16th century. East Prussia embraced Protestantism in 1525. The great majority of the White Russians and Ukrainians professed the Orthodox faith.

Zygmunt August took some steps towards integrating his multinational domains into a unitary state, and reinforcing the central power. His death in 1572, and the extinction of the Jagiellonian dynasty with him, interrupted this process and fatally enfeebled the monarchy as an institution just when it had laid the basis of possible strength.

In his endeavour to make Poland a Baltic power Zygmunt August sought to tighten his hold on the former lands of the Teutonic Order. A monetary union between Ducal and Royal Russia and Poland had been effected in 1528. In Royal Prussia, the middle gentry and the lesser burgesses looked to Poland for support against the magnates and the patricians of the great towns. In 1569 Zygmunt August ordered the electors of Royal

Prussia to send representatives to the Polish Diet, and the Prussian Diet became in effect a mere provincial Dietine. The province, however, retained its own treasury and its levies were not required to fight outside its borders. Albrecht Hohenzollern's change of religion had estranged him from his Catholic protectors, and he had acknowledged the king's right to arbitrate between himself and his subjects. But in 1563 Zygmunt August made the first of a series of mistakes when, to secure his rear during the Northern War, he accepted the Hohenzollerns of Brandenburg as co-vassals.

The fierce independence of the German patricians in the towns of Royal Prussia, which enjoyed a large measure of autonomy, created special problems. Danzig in particular, the main entrepot in Polish trade with the West, assumed the position of an independent maritime power. Thus in 1557 the patricians of Danzig declined to harbour a privateer fleet which was to be the nucleus of the Polish navy, and Zygmunt August yielded to their refusal. But in 1568, when they challenged the king's right to establish a maritime commission for the Baltic Sea, opened fire on his vessels, and shut their gate against his envoys, they found that they had overstepped the mark. In 1570 the king humbled the rebels and forced them to recognize his supreme authority in maritime questions. This important instrument was known after its author, the Bishop of Włocław, as the Karnkowski Statutes.

In these efforts to tie Royal Prussia more closely to the crown, Zygmunt August was supported by the Polish gentry. Still more popular with them was his master-stroke in revising the relationship between Poland and Lithuania. Since the dynastic union of 1386, Lithuania had its own representative bodies and organs of government, modelled on those of Poland, and pursued its own foreign policy, often to the embarrassment of the Poles. The need for concerted resistance to the growing Russian menace, and his failure to provide an heir, convinced Zygmunt August that a firmer union was necessary. Pressure for political fusion came from the Polish and Lithuanian gentry alike. The Poles wanted to sweep away the barriers, jealously maintained by the Lithuanian magnates, against colonization of the sparsely populated Ukraine, and the Lithuanian gentry hoped for emancipation from their oppressive aristocracy. Many of the great Lithuanian landowners resisted fusion, fearing Polish competition for offices of state, encroachment on their lands, and a reduction of their power over other classes. When the Polish and Lithuanian Diets met together at Lublin early in 1569, the Lithuanian magnates deplored the proposed unification as both precipitate and inequitable, and stalked out of the Diet in protest. But the king, with the connivance of the local gentry, transferred the Ukrainian provinces of Lithuania to the Polish crown. The Lithuanian magnates, terrified that their country thus reduced would be left to face Russia without Polish help, yielded and in July 1569 the Act of Union was formally adopted. Henceforward Poland and Lithuania would have a single Diet, elect its monarch jointly, and pursue a common foreign policy. Lithuania, however, retained its own great officers of state, its own treasury, its own military and administrative structure, and later acquired its own supreme civil court.

Threats to Poland

The achievement of Zygmunt August in reinforcing Polish dominion over Prussia and Lithuania was in large measure a by-product of his foreign policy. Unlike many of his predecessors he kept clear of unprofitable or dangerous foreign entanglements. In his relations with the Habsburgs he manoeuvred carefully. He concluded a vague alliance in 1549 against enemies domestic and foreign, and in 1553 he took to wife the Archduchess Catherine (to whom he quickly contracted a dynastically unfortunate aversion). On the other hand, he supported the anti-Habsburg faction in Hungary and resisted Habsburg attempts to embroil him with the Turks. Thus set free in the south, the king was able to concentrate his attention on the northern front, where dangers and opportunities were created by the decay of the Livonian Order and its quarrels with the Archbishop of Riga.

The main danger lay in the possibility that Russia might conquer Livonia and break through to the Baltic. This was now the dearest ambition of Ivan the Terrible, who had rejected advice to follow up the conquest of Kazan and Astrakhan with a cam-

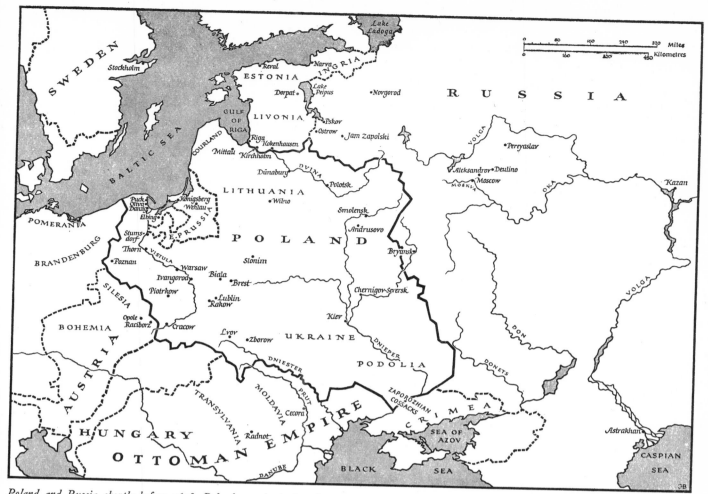

Poland and Russia shortly before 1648. Poland was destined to lose much of her conquered territory in the east, but gained Opole-Raciborz.

paign against the Crimea in favour of this apparently easier and certainly more profitable enterprise. Once entrenched in Livonia, the Tsar would have access to Western weapons and expertise; by control of Riga he would be able to block a third of the total Polish and Lithuanian grain export to the West; and he would be in a stronger position to prise away White Russia from its Lithuanian rulers. To forestall such disasters, Poland and Lithuania entered the Northern War of 1563–70, fighting first, till 1568, with Denmark against Russia and Sweden, and afterwards with Sweden against Russia and Denmark. All the contestants won prizes. Poland's share of Livonia included Riga and the vassal Duchy of Courland, but Ivan the Terrible kept Narva, Russia's first Baltic port, which he had seized in 1558, and also the strategically and commercially valuable town of Polotsk, which he had taken from the Lithuanians in 1563, while Sweden remained in possession of Reval and Estonia.

The Northern War precipitated important political changes in Poland. In the first decade of his reign Zygmunt August had resisted most of the demands of the embattled gentry for reform. By 1559 his relations with them had become so bad that he did not convene the Diet for three years in succession. But to obtain subsidies for the conquest of Livonia, and to reconcile the gentry of southern and western Poland to a costly undertaking which promised them no obvious benefit, he changed his tactics. He appeared before the Piotrkow Diet in 1562 demonstratively wearing Polish costume instead of his usual Italian finery, and made the first of a series of concessions which seemed to offer a prospect of durable cooperation between the king and the gentry in reinforcing the Polish state. Above all, he went some way towards satisfying the desire of the gentry for a fairer system of taxation by bringing under contribution crown lands in the possession of the magnates. He also trenched on the privileges of the spiritual lords and abolished ecclesiastical jurisdiction over the gentry. Finally, by annulling his father's harsh, though largely ineffectual, legislation against heretics he removed one of the most troublesome causes of national disunity.

Seen against the background of bitter political strife in the three preceding decades these were considerable achievements, but measured against the nation's needs they were small and precarious beginnings. The process of consolidation which Zygmunt August had begun would require stability of government, continuity of purpose, patient and tactful cooperation between king and subjects. Only a Poland firmly united under strong rulers could complete the assimilation of the non-Polish territories and face the dangers to which northward expansion must expose her. The death of Zygmunt August at this critical moment, and the failure of the Jagiellonian line, snapped the tenuous link between the crown and the gentry, undermined the authority of the monarchy and led ultimately to creeping political paralysis.

A Choice of Kings

The immediate problem was the succession to the throne. In 1538 the gentry had exacted from Zygmunt the Elder a reaffirmation of their ancient, but now almost outworn, right to elect the king by personal vote. Had Zygmunt August left a son, it is inconceivable that they would have looked any further in 1572; but as it was, the rank and file of the gentry saw an opportunity of asserting themselves. They were the king-makers, and they would make kings to suit themselves. From the beginning they hankered after a 'Piast'—a king of Polish stock; but a hundred years were to pass before that could be achieved. In 1572 the only viable candidates were foreign princes.

In choosing a king, two conditions weighed most heavily with the Electoral Diets: first, the new king must not be the tool of a foreign power; secondly, he must not be a threat to the privileges and the political supremacy of the gentry. The great European rivals, France and Austria, intrigued for control of Polish policy, and each had its supporters in Poland, recruited partly by massive bribery and partly by ideological attraction. But each also encountered strong opposition. To the gentry at large France was a horrid example of absolute government. But the Habsburgs were a nearer threat. They had thwarted Polish ambitions in central

Europe, incorporated ethnic Polish lands, and deprived the Hungarian gentry of their privileges. From the start, the mass of the electorate was determined that Poland should not suffer the fate of Bohemia and Hungary, and hatred of the Habsburgs was to remain a constant feature of Polish elections. In 1573 it gave the crown to Henri de Valois, brother of the French king. His reign, however, was short. He lived five months in Poland, received news of his brother's death, and slipped away to reign in France as Henri III.

After another troubled interregnum the gentry again imposed their candidate. Frustrating a senatorial attempt to foist the Emperor Maximilian on them, they declared for the Transylvanian Prince, Stefan Batory (1576-86). On Stefan's death, they elected the Swedish Prince, Sigismund Vasa, who reigned as Zygmunt III (1587-1632). He was a nephew of Zygmunt August and was expected to procure the transfer of Swedish-occupied Estonia to Poland. On this occasion, the thwarted Habsburg candidate, Archduke Maximilian, invaded Poland in the hope of rallying support, and even (unsuccessfully) assaulted Cracow. Zygmunt III was followed by two of his sons: first Władysław IV (1632-48), whose election was unopposed; then Jan Kazimierz (1648-68), whose only serious rival was his younger brother.

These elected kings of Poland struggled to strengthen the monarchy. Some of them were handicapped as foreigners. Stefan Batory never learned the language of his subjects, and Zygmunt III, though half Polish by birth, was in character and manner every inch a Swede. On the other hand his sons were no less Polish than Zygmunt August, and there were those who urged that they should be liberated from restrictions devised for 'foreign kings'. But foreign or not, they encountered the same resistance from the Polish gentry, who were stuck fast in their defensive stance, and in any initiative to strengthen and stabilize the central power, in any costly military enterprise, saw only dynastic ambition and tyrannical aspiration.

They had some justification for this view. Some of the kings undoubtedly sought to use Poland for their personal or dynastic ambitions. Stefan Batory dreamed of liberating the Danubian states from the Turks. The first two Vasas regarded Poland as a base for the recovery of the Swedish throne, from which Zygmunt III had been deposed in 1599, and their attempts to conquer Russia were involved in the crusade against their usurping Protestant cousins. Often, royal proposals for internal reform—pre-election to the throne, the replacement of subsidies voted *ad hoc* in the Diet by adequate regular taxation, the abandonment of the rule of unanimity in the Diet—were intended to reduce the king's dependence on the gentry and enable him to draw more heavily on the nation's resources for his own ends. But there was a tragic irony in the relationship between king and gentry. The interests of throne and nation coincided more fully and more often than the gentry were prepared to admit. Even the 'dynastic' foreign wars sometimes served national interests too. In the reinforcement of the monarchy lay Poland's only hope of escape from debilitating anarchy, and kings invested with fuller powers and assured of dynastic continuity would surely have been readier to sacrifice private interests to the needs of the nation.

War on three fronts

In the century between the death of Zygmunt August and the abdication of Jan Kazimierz, Poland's military commitments grew steadily, and greatly exceeded the resources of the crown. The period began with Stefan Batory's triumph over Ivan the Terrible, and closed with Poland's irremediable discomfiture at the hands of Sweden and Russia. Throughout, Poland was harassed by the depredations and the opportunism of the Crimean Tartars. Periodically, it was in danger of invasion by their mighty overlord the Sultan.

Ivan the Terrible had profited from Poland's disarray after the death of Zygmunt August, and before Stefan Batory was securely established, to annex Northern Livonia as far as the Dvina. King Stefan Batory easily rallied his subjects against this aggression, and, to make sure of a generous subsidy from the Diet, he set up in 1578 elected supreme civil courts for the gentry. To strengthen his position, he abandoned one of Zygmunt August's gains and

compounded one of his errors. The sullen Danzigers had declared themselves for the Habsburgs during the royal elections, and came out in open rebellion against the new king. Failing to reduce the city by siege and blockade, the king suspended the odious Karnkowski Statutes, receiving 200,000 złoty in compensation. To achieve this result, the Danzigers had used the good offices of envoys from the Princes of the Empire who wanted Poland to put the ailing Prussian Duke under the guardianship of the Elector of Brandenburg. For 200,000 guilders, Stefan accepted this arrangement, although it strengthened still further the hold of the Brandenburg Hohenzollerns on East Prussia. The proceeds from these transactions, both of which weakened the crown, went largely to finance the war with Russia.

That war opened with a series of successes. The loss of Polotsk (1579) and a Polish thrust against Pskov (1580-81), followed by Swedish occupation of Narva and Ivangorod, compelled Ivan the Terrible to accept the failure of his Baltic policy. Under the armistice of Jam Zapolski (1582) Russia evacuated the Livonian fortresses, without renouncing her claim to them, and gave up Polotsk, while Poland withdrew from Russian territory occupied during the campaign. Russia was thus driven back from the Baltic, at least for the time being. But there were qualifications to Poland's success. If Russia had been repelled, Sweden was now stronger. The price of success in Livonia had included setbacks to Poland's naval plans and her hopes of assimilating East Prussia. Stefan was accused of sacrificing vital Polish objectives to the interests of the Lithuanian and East Polish magnates, and his dealings with the gentry were made no easier by his failure to consult the Diet on his concessions to Danzig and the Hohenzollerns. For these reasons, after his initial military successes, he found gentry support for the war cooling. This became apparent in the last four years of his reign, when he laid plans for the conquest of Russia, as a base for an eventual assault on Turkey. His opportunity came on the death of Ivan the Terrible in 1584. Stefan then pronounced the Jam Zapolski Truce invalid and prepared for a renewal of war; but the Diet saw no advantage in this scheme and successfully obstructed it.

Stefan's successor, Zygmunt III, aroused greater opposition to his military plans. A Catholic zealot, an admirer and imitator of Philip II of Spain, he dreamed of subduing the enemies of the faith—Protestant, Orthodox or Moslem—by the sword. This brought him into conflict with the Turks, whom his immediate predecessors had handled with care, and into dependence on Papal and Habsburg diplomacy. Early in his reign, Zygmunt made his peace with the Habsburgs, who had tried to prevent his accession in Poland by force, forgave their supporters in Poland, resisted suggestions that Habsburg candidates for the Polish throne should be disqualified by law, himself married a Habsburg princess, and even contemplated resigning the throne of Poland to the Archduke Ernest.

This rapprochement with the Habsburgs alarmed the Turks, who declared war on Poland in 1590. The Diet supported Chancellor Zamoyski's projected campaign on the Danube, but the Turks were induced to withdraw their declaration by the English, who urged them not to disrupt Polish grain exports to the enemies of Spain. The Polish gentry, mobilised by Archbishop Karnkowski, thereupon assembled in an (unconstitutional) convention, and cancelled the subsidies voted by the preceding Diet, thus demonstrating that their readiness to defend the country against an imminent threat should not be misinterpreted as consent to military adventures. However, Polish-Turkish relations continued tense. A massive Cossack raid on the Crimea, organized in 1594 by Michał Jałowecki on orders from Rome and Vienna, might have ended in war with Turkey, and Chancellor Zamoyski himself in 1600 forcibly installed in Wallachia a *hospodar* unacceptable to the Turks.

Zamoyski's campaign swallowed up the subsidy voted by the Diet for defence against the Swedes. On his election as King of Poland, Zygmunt had undertaken to transfer Swedish Estonia to Poland. As King of Sweden, however, he hesitated to carry out this promise, of which he was constantly reminded. Only after his Swedish subjects had dethroned him in 1599 did he sign the transfer. The result was a Swedish invasion of Livonia in 1600. The

Swedes quickly advanced to the Dvina, though without taking Riga and Kokenhausen. The Polish counter-thrust developed slowly, hindered by inadequate funds, but the Lithuanian *hetman* (commander-in-chief) Chodkiewicz recovered territory as far as Dorpat in 1603, and thrashed a greatly superior Swedish force at Kircholm in 1605. Inconclusive fighting continued until 1609, when both sides were distracted by their involvement in the troubled affairs of Russia.

Russia: Internal Conflict, Foreign Intervention

Russia's 'Time of Troubles', following the extinction of the house of Rurik in 1598, whetted the appetites of Lithuanian and Eastern Polish magnates for territorial expansion, and of the Jesuits for spiritual conquest. In 1600, a mission, under the Lithuanian grandee, Lew Sapieha, sought the agreement of Tsar Boris Godunov to a union between the two countries on the death of either ruler, but obtained no more than a prolongation of the existing truce until 1622. Polish armed intervention in Russia began in 1604 with unofficial help from border magnates 'for the Pretender Dimitri. Chancellor Zamoyski called the enterprise 'a comedy of Plautus or Terence', but Zygmunt connived at it in the hope of disrupting the Russian state, and the Jesuits saw it as the first stage towards the enlistment of Poland and Russia in a great anti-Turkish crusade. 'The false Dimitri' was murdered in 1606, and succeeded by Tsar Vasili Shuisky. Both Poland and Sweden now intervened openly in Russia on opposite sides. *Hetman* Żółkiewski occupied most of western Russia, marched on Moscow, and induced the boyars to elect the Polish Prince Władysław as their tsar. The Swedes, called in by Shuisky for his own protection, contented themselves with reinforcing their conquests in Livonia by annexing adjacent areas of Russia. Polish aspirations went much further. Żółkiewski genuinely wished to install Władysław, while some of the king's advisers preferred a personal union under himself; but neither project had any real chance of success. Starved of money and reinforcements, the Poles in Moscow capitulated to the newly rallied Russian patriotic forces in 1612. In 1617, Żółkiewski and Prince Władysław mounted another attack, and reached Moscow, but once again inadequate support at home frustrated them, and a fourteen year's truce was concluded at Deulino in 1619, under which Poland retained the Smolensk and Seversk lands, and Władysław did not renounce his claim to the Russian throne.

By then, Poland was already at war again with the Swedes, who had made their own advantageous peace with Russia in 1617. In the Livonian war of 1617–22, Gustavus Adolphus was helped first by Poland's continuing involvement in Russia, and then by yet another crisis in Polish–Turkish relations provoked by the intrigues of Polish magnates in the Danubian principalities. The outcome of this was the disastrous Battle of Cecora on the Prut (1620) when *Hetman* Żółkiewski, intervening to protect the Moldavian *hospodar* against his overlord the Sultan, was killed and his army destroyed. Taking advantage of Poland's distractions, Gustavus Adolphus, after some setbacks, mastered the Livonian littoral, capturing Riga in September 1621. By the truce of Mittau, next year, the Poles remained in control of eastern Livonia, but the Swedes kept Riga and Parnau, and lay across the vital trade route from Lithuania and eastern Poland to the West.

Hostilities were renewed in 1625. This time the Swedes did not confine their activities to Livonia, and within a year had neutralized Ducal Prussia, seized most of Royal Prussia, and blockaded Danzig, where they imposed a 30% tax on all goods leaving or entering the port. Ruin stared the Polish gentry in the face, and for once they solidly supported the king. In spite of Austrian armed assistance, and minor victories on land and even on sea, Poland's strength was insufficient to prise the Baltic littoral from Sweden's grasp. Zygmunt was glad to accept the good offices of France, England and Holland, who wanted to draw Sweden into the war against the Habsburgs. Under the Truce of Altmark (1629), Sweden kept all Livonia as far as the Dvina, the Prussian ports except Danzig and Puck, and the right to exact dues from vessels trading into Danzig. These humiliating losses do not exhaust the tale of Poland's setbacks on the Baltic in this reign. In return for a subsidy from Brandenburg, and in order

The frontier city of Smolensk constantly changed hands during the 16th and 17th centuries. This woodcut from the 'Chronicles of Poland' of 1597 shows an earlier battle after Russia had 'recovered' it from Lithuania. In 1611 it was recaptured by the Poles, in 1654 lost again to the Russians.

to detach the new Elector George William from Sweden, Zygmunt in 1621 recognized the Elector's tutelage over Ducal Prussia. The fleet which Zygmunt had commissioned, not without some complaints from the Danzigers, was handed over to the king of Spain, only to fall into Swedish hands two years later.

A Warrior King

Władysław IV, who succeeded his father in 1632, was very different in character and outlook. Well-educated, at ease in society, a dashing and skilful soldier, tolerant if not indifferent in matters of religion, he enjoyed great popularity in the early years of his reign. He began with no grand design, but the legacy of the last reign determined the course of his policy. Polish troops still occupied Smolensk, and the Swedes were still on Polish soil in Royal Prussia. Władysław, in name, was Tsar of Russia and King of Sweden. The Russians, expecting, wrongly as it turned out, that Poland would be paralysed by a difficult interregnum, invested Smolensk. Władysław took the field himself, raised the siege and forced the Russian army to surrender. The Peace of Polyanovo (1634) confirmed the Deulino agreement of 1619, except that Władysław resigned his claim to the Russian throne.

The disappointed Russians relieved their feelings by executing their luckless generals, Shein and Izmailov. Władysław followed up this success with another, against Sweden. The death of Gustavus Adolphus at Lützen, and Sweden's defeat at Nördlingen, emboldened the Polish king to raise an army and a fleet in readiness for the expiry of the truce in 1635. The Diet might have denied him its support; but in fact the mediation of Sweden's apprehensive allies brought him important gains without a war. The truce of Stumsdorf (1635) put an end to Swedish occupation of Royal Prussia, and released Danzig from the heavy burdens which Sweden had imposed on it.

Władysław, however, made no progress towards overcoming Poland's chronic weakness on the Baltic. He used his fleet in an attempt to awe the Danzigers into paying him the dues which they had previously paid to the Swedes, but Danish intervention in support of the obdurate merchants forced him to settle for a lump sum. He was so discouraged that in 1641 he abandoned his naval plans and coastal fortifications in Royal Prussia. In preparation for war with Sweden, Władysław had brought Ducal Prussia under Polish administration, but after the truce of Stumsdorf he tamely restored the province to the Elector of Brandenburg.

Some historians have lamented Poland's failure to exploit the Thirty Years' War for her own ends, and in particular to recover Silesia. But insurmountable differences with Sweden made it impossible for Poland to enter the war against the Habsburgs and she obtained all she could reasonably expect from limited co-operation with them by regaining (in pawn) the principate of Opole-Raciborz (Polish from 1647 to 1666).

In the last three years of his reign Władysław lent a ready ear to the urgings of Austrian and Venetian diplomacy that he should join in an assault on Turkey. The prospect naturally appealed to him. Władisław was above all a soldier, but his military ambitions were cramped by the parsimony and suspicions of the Diet. In one direction, however, he might hope to wage war with support. The Crimean Tartars, vassals of the Sultan, made some thirty devastating incursions into Polish territory in the years 1576–1648, sometimes ranging as far as the Vistula in search of loot and captives for sale on the slave markets of Kaffa. The garrison army in the Ukraine, numbering between 2,000 and 4,000 was totally inadequate, and Poland was dependent on the dubious support of the Ukrainian Cossacks. *Hetman* Koniecpolski favoured a campaign against the Crimea, which might in any case have led to war with Turkey; but Władysław conceived the fantastic scheme of carrying the war direct to Constantinople. He sent agitators to the Balkans, sought an agreement with Persia, made an arrangement with Russia for joint action against the Tartars, and, aware that the Diet would not support him unless Poland were first attacked, inspired provocative raids on Tartar territory. His death in 1648 put a timely end to this programme. Poland would shortly have enemies enough about her ears, and could be thankful that she had not succeeded in provoking the Turks too far.

The Ukrainian Rebellion

The first in a series of blows which fatally sapped 17th century Poland was struck by the rebellious Cossacks of the Ukraine. Poland's relations with these turbulent frontiersmen had grown more and more difficult since the Union of Lublin. She used them, as Russia used the Don Cossacks, as a buffer between herself and the Tartars: and, like Russia, she was unable to control her fiercely independent auxiliaries. Attempts from 1572 onwards to limit the Cossack army by registering a small part of it, and treating the rest as ordinary peasants, sparked off rebellions. Polish troops might briefly subdue the rebels, but the Cossacks, based on their stronghold, the 'Sich' below the Dnieper rapids, repeatedly threw off Polish authority, and insisted that they were a self-governing 'army'. The influx of Polish colonists into the Ukraine after the Union of Lublin made the Ukrainian peasant and the rank and file Cossack natural allies. A further cause of unrest was the Union of Brest (1596), under which most of the Ukrainian bishops submitted to Papal authority, though their church retained the Eastern rite. The Ukrainians at large and the Cossacks rejected this 'Uniate' church, and rallied to the defence of Orthodoxy.

Władysław IV crushed a Cossack rebellion in 1637–38, set the number of registered Cossacks at 6,000 (less than a sixth of the whole 'army'), replaced their elected officers by Polish nominees, allowed them to reside only in districts well to the north of the rapids, and rebuilt the fort at Kodak, which was intended to cut off the Cossacks from Zaporozhe and the lower Dnieper. After this there was peace in the Ukraine for ten years, until in 1648 Bogdan Khmelnitsky, smarting under ill-treatment by a Polish magnate, raised the standard of revolt, was elected *hetman* and allied himself with the Crimean Khan. His initial intentions went no further than the annulment of the 1638 agreement and the restoration of Cossack privileges. The Poles replied by dispatching an army under *Hetman* Potocki, whom Khmelnitsky defeated and handed over to the Tartars as a prize. Władysław died at this point, and Khmelnitsky, although the whole Ukraine rose in support of him, held his hand in the hope of an understanding with the new king Jan Kazimierz, who was known to favour conciliation. The extremists however prevailed in Poland, and

committed their country to the complete reduction of the Ukraine.

In the struggle which followed, mischievous Tartars held the balance. In 1649, when Jan Kazimierz was in danger of a heavy defeat, the Khan took a Polish bribe and persuaded Khmelnitsky to the compromise agreement of Zborow, under which 40,000 Cossacks would be registered, the Uniate Church abolished, and the Metropolitan of Kiev admitted to the Polish Senate. These terms were unacceptable in Poland, and unsatisfactory to most of Khmelnitsky's supporters. The Poles entered the Ukraine in force in 1651, and when the Tartars, who had taken the field only reluctantly under Turkish pressure, deserted him Khmelnitsky had to accept the agreement of Biała Cerkiew, which reduced the Cossack register to 20,000. In 1653, the Polish army and the King himself were surrounded at Zwaniec, but the Tartars made a separate peace and left Khmelnitsky with no more than a renewal of the Zborow agreement.

In his quest for more reliable allies the Cossack leader had at various times offered the Ukrainian crown to the Prince of Transylvania, invited the King of Sweden to become his Protector, accepted a vassal's caftan from the Sultan, and reminded Tsar Aleksei that he was the heir of the Grand Princes of Kiev. After much hesitation, the Tsar agreed to 'take under his high hand *Hetman* Bogdan Khmelnitsky and the entire Zaporozhian Host with its lands and cities' and to make war on Poland. The Cossacks took the oath to their new master at Pereyaslav in 1654. They soon discovered the cost. The Tsar enlarged the register, and guaranteed the right of the host to elect its *hetman*; but he dispatched Russian governors to Ukrainian cities, garrisoned Kiev, supported the refusal of the Moscow Patriarch to recognize the autonomy of the Ukrainian Church, and ordered the Cossacks to reinforce his army in White Russia. To add to Bogdan's troubles, his submission to Russia swung the Tartars into an active alliance with Poland.

In 1654 the Russians made a direct attack on Poland. In the course of a furious onslaught they recovered Smolensk and captured and destroyed Wilno. In the Ukraine however, a Tartar diversion drew off the Cossack and Russian forces from Lvov, and even compelled Khmelnitsky to formal recognition of Jan Kazimierz as his king. In the summer of 1655 the struggle with Russia was interrupted by the Swedish invasion of Poland. Tsar Aleksei was not anxious to facilitate Sweden's aggrandizement, and in November 1656 he made a truce with the Poles, who (insincerely) agreed to accept him as their king on the death of Jan Kazimierz. Khmelnitsky died in 1657, and was replaced by the pro-Polish *Hetman* Vyhovski, who at Hadjach in 1658 brought the Ukraine into union with Poland as a semi-autonomous 'Ruthenian Principate', enjoying rights similar to those of Lithuania.

The Shadow of Partition

There remained the Swedes. Assisted by the treachery of demoralized magnates in western Poland and in Lithuania, they had quickly occupied the whole country and forced the king to take refuge in Silesia. Many Poles had been prepared to accept the dethronement of Jan Kazimierz as the price of peace, and some had even imagined that Sweden would then help them against the Cossacks. Charles X of Sweden had very different objectives. He intended to annex the coastal areas of Poland and make East Prussia a Swedish vassal state. But the depredations of his army soon provoked an upsurge of patriotic resistance, and by the end of 1656, despairing of holding down Poland alone, he devised a scheme of partition. Under the Treaty of Radnot, Poland was to be divided between Sweden, Brandenburg, George Rakoczy, the Cossacks, and the Lithuanian traitor Bogusław Radziwiłł.

But Poland was not yet to be partitioned. Rakoczy's invasion brough help from Austria, enabling Poland to recover Cracow. War with Denmark prevented Charles X from mounting a fresh campaign in Poland. Rakoczy, left to his own devices, was defeated at Czarny Ostrow (July 1657) and deposed by his overlord the Sultan on his return to Transylvania. In September, to detach Brandenburg from Sweden and to gratify the Habsburgs, Poland recognized the Elector's sovereignty in East Prussia (Treaty of Wehlau), retaining only the reversionary right should the Hohenzollern line fail. In the war with Sweden, Poland now cooperated with Denmark and her allies, sending Polish contingents to fight on Danish territory and in Western Pomerania. The war was concluded in 1660 by the Peace of Oliva. By it Poland gained no compensation for a ruinous war and the loss of East Prussia. She retained only the south eastern corner of Livonia, around Dünaburg; and Jan Kazimierz resigned his rights to the Swedish crown.

War between Poland and Russia broke out again in 1659, was waged actively until 1663, and formally terminated only in 1667. The military honours went to the Poles, who forced the Russian army in the Ukraine to capitulate at Cudnow in 1660, made the new (pro-Russian) *hetman*, Yuri Khmelnitsky, swear allegiance to Jan Kazimierz, and recovered Wilno in 1661. Neither side, however, had faith in its capacity to subdue the whole of the Ukraine, and both were alarmed by signs that Turkey was planning an invasion. They concluded a truce at Andrusovo in January 1667, under which Poland retained the right-bank Ukraine, except Kiev, which the Russians were to hold for two years. Russia received the lands beyond the Dnieper, kept Smolensk and Chernigov-Seversk, and in the event never relinquished Kiev.

When Jan Kazimierz abdicated to live out his days as Abbot of St Germain, near Paris, his country was sadly reduced. It had lost almost all of Livonia, its conquests in Russia, the Ukraine beyond the Dnieper, its sovereignty over East Prussia, a small portion of Royal Prussia surrendered to the Elector of Brandenburg in 1657, and even the principality of Opole-Raciborz. The material and demographic losses were enormous. In the third quarter of the 17th century nearly a third of the population perished or fled the country. Devastation, plague, famine and growing shortage of labour had reduced agricultural production. Invasion, blockade and civil war had damaged Polish trade, and falling grain prices on Western markets further reduced the national income. Some indication of Poland's increasing economic difficulties may be obtained from the figures for the export of grain through Danzig: 110,000 lasts in 1618, 35,000 in 1652, 21,000 (at most) in 1691.

Yet even under Jan Kazimierz the Poles had pulled themselves together with remarkable rapidity after the Swedish invasion and carried the war across the Baltic. They threw back the Russians in 1659-61. They could not keep the Turks from their own door, but in 1683, under Jan Sobieski, saved Vienna from them. Why was Poland capable of these astonishing exertions, but not of sustained self-defence? Part of the answer must be sought in the changing balance of forces between the Poles and their antagonists. But it must be recognized that Poland seldom used her strength effectively, and never to the full. Lacking a strong central government, and unable, for political rather than economic reasons to support a large standing army, the country was dangerously dependent on the ability and loyalty of great warlords, to whom it owed its victories as well as most of its humiliations. The impotence of the monarchy, the inflated power of the factious magnates, the fanatical resistance of the gentry to institutional change, resulted in civil anarchy and military inadequacy.

Failure to reform its antiquated and inefficient social and political structure was perhaps the main reason for the decline of Poland in the 17th century.

Liberty and Equality

In 16th and 17th century Polish usage 'the commonwealth' meant in effect 'the gentry'. Only they enjoyed political rights, and the virtues and defects of their institutions had an enormous influence on the fortunes of their country. Nowhere were the gentry a more numerous section of society than in Poland—nearly one tenth of the population belonged to this class at the end of the 16th century—and nowhere did they enjoy more extensive privileges. The common devotion of the gentry to their 'golden freedom' was a cohesive force in the domains of the Polish king: and it was also the fatal obstacle to effective unification under a strong central authority.

The power of the gentry derived from their role as soldiers and taxpayers. Try as they might, the Polish kings were never able to dispense with the gentry levy, still less with the subsidies, usually grudging and inadequate, voted by the Diet. For their part, the gentry were ready enough to shift some of the military and fiscal burden, but only with safeguards against damage to their own status. Their great victories in the struggle for privilege were won in national crises, when they could exploit the king's need, sometimes holding him to ransom with the threat of a military or fiscal strike. Few of them conceived of a national interest higher than that of their own class. They gloried in Polish freedom, and despised less happy lands where kings ruled absolutely or burgesses shared in government. The price of gentry freedom was exploitation of the peasant, denial of rights to burgesses and stunting of urban growth, and, in the end, surrender to an oligarchy of great territorial magnates.

There was no titular aristocracy in Poland proper until the 18th century. Legally the richest landowner and the ruined squire belonged to the same Estate and had equal rights. 'Our liberty', said the great Chancellor Jan Zamoyski, 'depends on this equality'. The gentry, in the name of this equality, hastily scotched an attempt by Władysław IV in 1637-38 to form an élite 'Order of the Immaculate Conception', which he hoped would also be the kernel of a royal party. But such legal equality did not prevent agglomerations of wealth and influence. Partly by intermarriage, and partly from gifts or nominally temporary grants from crown lands (which in the late 16th century covered one sixth of all the Polish territories), a few landlords built up huge estates. Although compelled by no law, the king usually chose his military commanders, ministers, counsellors and provincial governors from amongst these magnates or their *protégés*. To strengthen his own hand the king might favour a particular group of magnates against their rivals, or enrich and promote obscurer gentlemen. But since the highest appointments in the state were usually for life, rapid redistribution of influence was not possible. At any time in the second half of the 16th or in the 17th century a handful of families held between them most of the great offices under the crown and many of the richest ecclesiastical benefices.

The great officers of Church and State sat, *ex officio*, in the Senate, which shared, and sometimes overtopped, the power of the king. In 1501 the magnates tried to formalize the position of the Senate as the supreme power in the land. The middle and lesser gentry helped King Alexander to resist this demand. But for this support the gentry claimed their reward. They were granted privileges which were to be of the greatest importance in Polish history.

The gentry had already won extensive rights. They had secure hereditary tenure of their land and full jurisdiction over the peasants. A law of 1496 forbade any but the eldest son of a peasant family to leave his master's estate. Probably earlier, but certainly from 1493, local Dietines, which previously pronounced individually on new tax proposals, had begun to elect delegates to a national Diet, in which they could make concerted demands in the interests of their class at large. King Alexander used this national Diet to turn the tables on the ambitious magnates. Two bills in 1504 provided that the king could bestow or mortage royal land only with the Diet's approval, and that no one could hold several high offices simultaneously. In the event, these rules were ineffective, at least as a check on accretions of wealth and power. Of much greater practical significance was the enactment of 1505, the celebrated 'Nihil Novi', which guaranteed the gentry a share in legislation. Henceforward, only bills approved by the king, and by both houses of the Diet—the Senate, and the Chamber of Deputies elected by the gentry—acquired the force of law.

'The Execution of the Laws'

Under the last two Jagiellonian kings, the gentry pressed for what they called 'the execution of the laws'. The most popular objective of this 'executive movement' was a more equitable system of taxation. The gentry groaned against encroachments on the royal lands, which in the king's hands could replenish the treasury and ease their own burdens. More bitterly still, they resented the tax immunity of the Church, which exacted tithes from them and haled defaulters before ecclesiastical courts, drained money out of the country in the form of Peter's pence and tribute to the Pope, and contributed to the coffers of the state only an occasional *subsidium charitatis*.

The more far-sighted leaders and propagandists of the executive movement aimed at the reduction of sectional privileges generally and the reinforcement of the central state power. But the rank and file of their supporters aspired to extend their own rights while curtailing those of others. Already in 15th century Poland political writers had detected in the pretensions of the gentry a threat to strong and efficient government, and one of then, Philip Buonaccorsi ('Callimachus') had urged on the king heroic measures against his upstart subjects: he should curb the Diet, limit its activities, give public offices to burgesses, repeal some of the gentry's privileges, confiscate their land, or, best of all, kill off as many as possible on a disastrous campaign and poison the rest.

The ordinary Polish gentleman, even in the 16th century saw himself not as a revolutionary but as the champion of established and continually threatened institutions. All that he wanted was more effective guarantees of existing rights, strict enforcement of existing laws, and the correction of certain anomalies which might be rooted in tradition but were incompatible with his rights. Within the ranks of the gentry there was room for a wide variety of views, particularly concerning the role of the king and relations between church and state. A champion of gentry rights at the beginning of the 16th century, Stanisław Zaborowski, could identify his class with 'society', and insist that the king must always reckon with the wishes of those whose exclusive duty it was to defend the country, yet oppose the subordination of the church to the secular power and the use of its property for temporal purposes. Later in the century, the brilliant demagogue Stanisław Orzechowski, who considered Polish institutions perfect and the gentry the freest and most chivalrous of 'nations', evolved a model of government in which the king was reduced to a mere regulator of the commonwealth of the gentry, each of whom was absolute master of his own peasant 'subjects', while final authority was vested in the church. On the other hand, the greatest political thinker of the executive movement, Andrzej Frycz-Modrzewski, brought out its astute foe, the future Cardinal Hosius, in the improbable role of a defender of the gentry. In his *Commentaries on the Amendment of the Commonwealth* (1551–54) Modrzewski insisted that the law should be the same for all citizens. Hosius denounced this work as 'an insult to our mother country and especially to the gentry.' One of the leaders of the executive movement, Jakub Przyłuski, found it politic to abandon his plea for equal laws, which might alienate supporters in his fight against church privileges and for the reinforcement of the royal power. In the cross-currents within and around the executive movement we can discern the pattern of a future compromise between the gentry and other privileged groups.

The executive movement did not bring about a reform of Poland's political structure, as its more far-sighted leaders wished, but it greatly reinforced the prerogatives of the gentry. In 1538, a rebellion compelled Zygmunt the Elder to guarantee that on the death of his son, fraudulently pre-elected, the gentry would be able to exercise their traditional right of electing his successor. Zygmunt August in 1562 yielded to demands for an 'execution' of royal estates and an end to ecclesiastical jurisdiction over the gentry. The Diets of 1562–63 and 1564 ordered a general review of titles to royal lands and the restoration to the crown of estates illegally held. In the event, little of this land was in fact restored, but periodic visitations firmly established the tax obligations of the magnates, and a quarter of the sum thus raised was appropriated to the maintenance of a frontier force. In its attempts to make church property taxable on the same basis as that of laymen the executive party had no success. On the death of Zygmunt August in 1572 the gentry rallied to prevent the magnates and prelates from usuping the electoral function, and at Warsaw in 1573, made a compact ensuring religious toleration for all denominations. Fifty thousand gentlemen flocked to the Electoral Diet of April 1573, which chose Henry of Valois; but they also imposed stiff terms, including acceptance of a bill of rights for the gentry.

These 'Henrician Articles' guaranteed their accumulated privileges, bound the king to summon the Diet for six weeks every two years, forbade him to raise taxes or levies without its consent, forced on him a permanent advisory council of senators

The Pope and King Zygmunt August shown as the two props of Poland (again the eagle is entwined with S A) on the titlepage of Stanisław Orzechowski's 'Quincunx Poloniae', published in Cracow in 1564. Orzechowski devised a model of government by which the gentry formed the commonwealth, the king was a mere regulator, the Church the final authority.

(the 'residents'), reaffirmed the rule *de non praestanda oboedientia*, which released subjects from their oath of loyalty if the king broke contract with them, and committed the king to upholding the Warsaw declaration on religious freedom. Subsequent Polish kings had to swear to further stipulations embodying the Henrician Articles. The last great institutional innovation granted to the gentry was Stefan Batory's permission to elect supreme courts for civil cases affecting their own class.

'Gentry Democracy'

To many observers the hypertrophy of 'gentry democracy' seemed to be the main cause of Poland's political instability after the extinction of the Jagiellonian dynasty. The arrogant deputies, it was said, had 'taken everything upon themselves, as though the Republic must stand or fall according to their judgement'; 'the knightly order has transferred all authority and power to itself, leaving the senators only the name of eminence'. Poland was an 'ochlocratic' state, 'the worst and most turbulent of all, in which the laws have lost all force, all men govern and none obeys': the Chamber of Deputies made all the decisions, while the king and the senators 'drew pictures in dust'.

On the face of it, the gentry enjoyed enormous power. They could elect kings who would not threaten their privileges. They blocked all proposals of pre-election, the sole guarantee against the disorder of an interregnum. Nor was their right to renounce obedience an empty formula. In 1606, the Palatine of Cracow, Zebrzydowski, brought out in arms a faction amongst the gentry resentful of King Zygmunt's demands for a permanent defence subsidy, the establishment of a regular army, and the introduction of decision by majority vote in the Diet. Though defeated in battle, they were amnestied, and the king was compelled to reaffirm his adherence to the Henrician Articles. Such a rising, which the Polish kings regarded as treasonable, was to the gentry merely a general assembly in arms, the traditional means of defending their privileges, and they called it a *rokosz*, after the Field of Rakos, where the Hungarian gentry had held their own camp assemblies. Much more damaging than the Zebrzydowski episode was the *rokosz* led by *Hetman* Lubomirski in 1666, and supported largely by gentlemen who feared the 'absolutist' designs of Jan Kazimierz. Lubomirski defeated the King's forces in battle, and although his following melted away after Jan Kazimierz gave up his plan to appoint a successor, he was pardoned and retired unscathed into exile.

'*Rokosz*' was the supreme sanction which the gentry might occasionally invoke against the king. A more continuous and serious weapon was the power of the Diet to grant or withhold subsidies. No Polish king after Zygmunt August was assured for more than a year or two at a time of the means to finance his military commitments. The king was often compelled to contribute heavily from his own pocket to the maintenance of his armies. Shortage of funds checked the impetus of victorious armies, in Livonia under Stefan Batory, and in Russia under his successors. Unpaid soldiers sometimes resorted to mutiny, (characteristically dignified by the name of 'confederation'), and lived off the country until their demands were met. Even in face of the Swedish threat in 1626, the Diet found less than a quarter of what a contemporary expert estimated as the minimum defence requirement. Whenever a plea was made for a large regular army, and subsidies for its maintenance, the Diet feared that the king was designing a coup against their liberties. The gentry found relief for their consciences in the thought that they themselves were the surest defence of their country. But although the cavalry supplied by the gentry levy was a powerful striking force, it contributed little to routine defence of the frontiers and did not reduce the need for regular and well equipped artillery and infantry. Moreover, the gentry might 'vote with their feet' against campaigns which seemed to them unduly protracted or ambitious. The inadequacy of his regular forces increased the king's dependence on the magnates, some of whom raised private armies and, for certain purposes, on the undisciplined and demanding Cossacks.

The Structure of Power

The citadel of 'golden freedom' was the lower house of the Diet, the Chamber of Deputies. It would be difficult to devise a political body more apt for obstruction. The Dietines elected their representatives sometimes with a limited mandate and sometimes with plenary powers. Members of the king's party towards the end of the 16th century recommended that deputies should be required to report back to the Dietines, in which, as they hoped, the king might be able to assert his authority more easily. But no coherent code governing relations between Diet and Dietines, or the procedure of the Diet itself, was ever evolved. In the last quarter of the 16th century the Chamber of Deputies took its decisions by a majority, though in theory valid decisions required the consent, or at least the tacit acquiescence, of all deputies. In the course of the 17th century the rule of unanimity was more rigidly interpreted. It was accepted that any deputy could freely impose his veto, and that this not only ended the discussion in progress but nullified the decisions already taken at that session of the Diet. In the reigns of Stefan Batory and the first two Vasas the Diet had broken up without decision on at least eleven occasions. Of the 55 sessions between 1652 and 1764, 42 were to be disrupted by the *liberum veto*.

Deputy Sicinski in 1652 was the first to frustrate the work of the Diet by an individual veto. The Marshal (Speaker) of the Diet on this occasion, A. M. Fredro, later declared that the *liberum veto* was a necessary safeguard against the triumph of 'an ignorant majority over a wise minority'; but Sicinski had in fact acted on the instructions of a disgruntled magnate, Bogusław Radziwiłł. Ironically, this institutional safeguard of their privileges ended by

undermining the collective power of the gentry. Since the Diet was useless for positive purposes, policy was made by the Senate, or by a camarilla of great dignitaries. The king could act only in alliance with this or that magnate faction. Perceptive foreigners in the 17th century found that the land of 'gentry democracy' was in fact ruled by shifting combinations of quarrelsome oligarchs.

But there was no remedy. Proposals for procedural reform enraged the zealots of 'golden freedom', obsessed by fear of royal tyranny. Their political philosophy was summed up by the Dietine of Slonim in 1666: 'Since innovations more than anything harm the fatherland and undermine old rights, they should never be permitted.' For their part, the magnates were ardent converts to 'golden freedom', and conjured up the spectre of absolutism whenever some statesmanlike initiative threatened the anarchy on which they thrived.

Though they had great scope for obstruction, the 'power' of the gentry was almost wholly negative. As long ago as 1565, Andrzej Frycz Modrzewski and his group had suggested that the conduct of ministers and officials should be subject to review by elected 'instigators'. This and similar proposals had no result. The king often ignored his duty to act only with the 'knowledge and counsel' (not, of course, consent) of the 'residents', imposed on him by the Henrician Articles. Władysław IV enunciated in 1638 a principle on which most Polish kings acted as far as possible: 'Rights acquire force from use and observance, and lose it from disuse.' A wise Polish statesman, Jakub Zadzik, opposing in 1641 the Diet's demand for strict observance of the rules concerning 'residents', argued that 'they were old, and made for foreign kings.'

Land and Landlords

Changes in the economic and social condition of the gentry tightened the hold of the magnates over them. Even at the beginning of the 17th century there was not enough land to go round. Propagandists urged Poland to seek her own 'new world' in the East, and tempted the gentry with tales of Russia's latent wealth. Zygmunt Vasa and his son Władysław, however, won only fitful support for their schemes of conquest, and the colonization of the Ukraine brought new riches to the magnates rather than relief to the gentry. The devastations of war, the interruptions of trade by the struggle for the Baltic and the decline of grain prices on Western markets swelled the ranks of impoverished gentlemen. In large numbers they sought employment on the *latifundia* of the magnates, at their courts, in their private armies, or in local administrative posts which were in practice often in the gift of magnates. The great lords ruled their provinces like petty kings, flouting the rights of the gentry, packing the Dietines and dominating the sessions of the Diet, which the Lithuanian magnates in particular attended with great retinues, 'accoutred and arrayed, with banners and drums and bugles and horns.' Outbursts of resentment against domineering magnates were common. The rebellion of Zebrzydowski, and to some extent that of Lubomirski, were fuelled by the desperation of downtrodden gentlemen. Their sense of inferiority and impotence found expression in proverbs—'With a cap and a sop and some salt men take men in thrall'—and in verses like Wacław Potocki's musings on the Diet, where 'You may be a Cato in counsel or a Cicero in judgment', but 'a fly cannot be seen beside an eagle, nor a mouse beside a camel'.

While other European countries established effective centralized governments, reinforced by a rising merchant class, a strong regular army and a professional administration, Poland degenerated into a loose association of great lords. The royal court at Warsaw (after 1596) was less populous and magnificent than the palaces of some magnates. Poland lacked a strong administrative centre. The growth of the towns had long been hampered by discriminatory legislation and the autarkic policies of the great landowners. The ravages of invasion in the 1650s, and the unfavourable turn in the terms of trade, plunged the towns into a decline from which they began to recover only in the next century. The 17th century Polish gentleman asked nothing better than to laze peacefully on his estate, where he was proverbially 'as good as a voivode', hunting, carousing, and living on the backs

LITVANI

Peasants and townsfolk were oppressed and exploited by the gentry. Above, the lower classes of Lithuania as portrayed by an Italian in 1636.

of his 'subjects' (peasants). They gave him remarkably little trouble. *Jacqueries* were not unknown, but infrequent. This was not because the peasants' lot was enviable in the country which one foreign visitor called *infernus rusticorum*. From the middle of the 16th century landlords, to increase grain production for export, made ever greater demands on the labour of their subjects. Anzelm Gostomski, a writer on agrarian matters in the late 16th century, recommended a 4-day *corvée* and 6 days of labour on the manorial land was often exacted in the 17th century. Landlords also encroached more and more on peasant holdings. Grain was exported which should have filled Polish bellies. One cynic wondered whether the peasants 'prayed to God for Gustav' during the Swedish blockade, when they were able to feed 'like oxen in the spring'. Thoughtful Poles often rebuked the gentry for their ruthless exactions. The Synod of Cracow at the beginning of the century exhorted landlords not to bear too heavily on their 'subjects', 'lest seeing the misery of paupers the Lord God rise up in the fury of his wrath and avenge them'. Krzysztof Opalinski pleaded with his compatriots:

In God's name, men of Poland, are you mad?
All that you have—your wealth, your substance, all due services.
You have it from your subjects. Their hands feed you.
How then can you so cruelly misuse them?

Fears that the peasants might not wait for divine intervention but avenge themselves were particularly lively during the rebellion of Bogdan Khmelnitsky, of which Chancellor Albrecht Radziwiłł said that 'nowhere has there ever been such a savage rebellion', because 'nowhere are 'subjects' so oppressed as here'. But in Poland itself there were only sporadic and quickly suppressed outbursts.

Secure and all-powerful in his little domain, the Polish gentleman gratefully subsided into rusticity, ignoring the world outside until some upheaval in the state or some devastating foreign intrusion shocked him into remembrance of his civic and soldierly duties. In the 16th century Poles had thronged the halls of German and especially Italian universities. The 17th century gentleman by contrast was parochial, philistine. Foreign intrigues around the throne and the ruinous Swedish incursions fostered xenophobia. There were gentlemen—and gentlewomen—who grew rich by trade, sometimes infringing the regulation that they might export free of duty only their own produce. But the more conventional gentleman was innocent of such base skills and left them to despised middlemen. In office the gentry managed the state's interests as carelessly as their own estates. Some Polish historians have argued that the chronic shortage of public funds was in considerable measure due to wastefulness and peculation.

In literature and at their public gatherings the gentry were often rebuked for their frivolity, their laziness, their haughty

ignorance. 'No sooner built than neglected', wrote one sober poetaster, 'leaks in the roof, holes everywhere, today's palace is tomorrow's cowshed.' Archbishop Gembicki retailed to the Diet an anecdote according to which the Austrian archduke, reluctant to pay the cost of demolishing a superfluous fortress, had been advised to appoint a Polish commandant, who would ruin it for nothing. In a crisis, spokesmen of the gentry might deplore the shortcomings of their class, as at the Diet of Thorn (1626), when one of them absolved the king of blame for the easy advance of the Swedes—'Our own baseness is the reason'. But a mood of complacent self-congratulation was more normal. Poland was an island of freedom and chivalry in a world of savage tyrannies. Disorders in the state were the price of this unique freedom. King Władysław IV may have derived little comfort from Castellan Grodzicki's assurance (1639) that he was 'a king of kings', unlike the French king, whom the Emperor had rightly called a 'king of asses', but this was certainly the sentiment of the Polish gentry. And in the end, Providence, which had so lavishly blessed Poland, would save her from herself:

The Lord God sometimes waits till Poland's foes
Hemming our wretched country in on every hand
Have taken their pleasure of her, and cries at last:
Enough! Be still, ye Turks, Tartars be still!
God's Providence alone is over us, O Poles!

The Old and New Faiths

In the 16th century the 'executive movement' stimulated and in turn was strengthened by the advance of Protestantism. In the following century the collapse of the gentry as a coherent political force and the triumph of the Counter-Reformation were aspects of a single process.

Conflict with the Teutonic Order in the 15th century had strained Polish relations with the Order's patron, the Pope. Learned Poles had questioned the *raison d'être* of the Order, condemned the propagation of the faith by force as a crime against natural law, upheld the right of pagans to defend themselves against Christian aggressors, and justified defensive alliances between Christian and pagan rulers. One of them said the last word on conversion by the sword: 'The cruelty of hypocrites is worse than any other crime or sin'. Somewhat later, King Kazimierz the Great had to forbid the reading of a Papal bull anathematizing Christians who joined alliances against the Order. The conciliatory tactics of Popes who wished to enlist Poland in a crusade against the Turks served only to aggravate suspicion of Roman power politics. National resentment of Papal intrigue, Papal patronage and ecclesiastical extortion inside Poland found expression in the work of Jan Ostrorog, in which he urged the king to end juridical and financial dependence on Rome, recognize no superior but God, appoint his own bishops, and put an end to the abuses of 'crafty Italians' who traded on superstition to squeeze an enormous annual tribute from the 'once free realm of Poland'. Though the Catholic Church in Poland never lacked learned and pious prelates, the hierarchy at large showed greater zeal in protecting its worldly goods than in combating heresy. A common clerical attitude was summarized in the words ascribed to a Bishop of Cracow, 'Believe in Old Horny, but pay me my tithes'.

National grudges against Rome, resentment of ecclesiastical power and privileges, the influence of immigrant heretics from the Bohemian Hussites onwards and the ideas of Western humanists, with which many thousands of Poles made contact in Italian universities, all prepared the ground for Protestantism in Poland. King Zygmunt the Elder, himself a staunch Catholic, inadvertently gave great help to the Protestant cause. His compromise with Albrecht Hohenzollern was not only the first compact between Catholic and Protestant rulers, but made East Prussia a centre for the dissemination and inculcation of Lutheran ideas. Lutheranism spread rapidly in Prussia, and amongst the German communities in Polish towns, although the Polish gentry generally seem to have found it at once too German and insufficiently radical. In Greater Poland the Bohemian Brethren enjoyed the protection of such families as the Leszczynskis, Ostrorogs and Tomickis. Calvinism reached Poland in the 1540s and quickly captured several leading families in Little Poland and in Lithuania, including the mighty Radziwiłłs.

Few among these defectors from the established church were moved by deep theological considerations. They merely disapproved of superstitious accretions and sacerdotal pretensions. It thus seemed feasible to unite them for practical purposes. In the Diet Protestant deputies, amongst whom the Calvinists were the most numerous group, did form a firm alliance in defence of religious freedom. But the efforts of Jan Łaski, a favourite pupil of Erasmus, came to nothing. A union of the Calvinists and the Bohemian Brethren was achieved in 1555, but after six years it was disrupted by social discrepancies: the Calvinist leaders formally accepted the participation of burgesses and plebeians in church government, but in practice reserved a dominant position for the gentry, while the Bohemian Brethren clung to the democratic principles of their Czech founders. However, though organizational unity was unattainable, Protestants continued to make common cause against their persecutors, and doctrinal pronouncements were often tactfully worded so as to minimize sectarian barriers. Only one denomination was excluded, by common consent, from the charity of other Protestants. This was the group who were often misleadingly called Arians.

The ideology of the 'Arians' was an unstable mixture of Anabaptist traditions, disseminated mainly from Moravia, and critical revaluation of fundamental Christian doctrine. Its most influential exponents questioned the dogma of the Trinity, practised adult baptism, and demanded a return to the ideals of early Christianity in social life. The new movement won many supporters from amongst the Calvinists, especially after the burning of the anti-Trinitarian Servetus in Calvin's Geneva. Its appeal lay largely in its insistence on absolute freedom of conscience, and its rejection of authority in matters of religion. In 1562 the anti-Trinitarian minority broke away from the Calvinists and formed their own connection. They called themselves the Polish Brethren. This split was shortly followed by a division within the Polish Brethren themselves. The extremists preached community of goods, withdrew entirely from public life, and refused to bear arms. The moderates, who found this stance impractical, attracted more followers from amongst the gentry.

To other Protestants, who resisted the accusation that their beliefs threatened the established order, the Polish Brethren were a great embarrassment. Moreover, anti-Trinitarianism, in the eyes of its enemies, was hardly distinguishable from atheism, and there is no doubt that some of its adherents went on to question other traditional beliefs. The anonymous author of an ironical epitaph for Stefan Batory's Arian friend Kaspar Bekesz credited him with views which some of his co-religionists may have held:

I care not for my body, and for my soul still less:
I'm dead and she died with me, I cheerfully confess.
So I'll be spared the trouble that other men will have
Of finding each his soul again when they get up from the grave.

Orthodox Protestants were ready to exclude the Brethren from the benefits of religious toleration, but the leaders of the Catholic party at first blandly deprecated suggestions of discrimination against them, on the principle that *'bellum haereticorum—pax Ecclesiae.'*

The hierarchy had been forced into this negative stance by a succession of defeats in its struggle to suppress heresy. Zygmunt I issued a long series of savage edicts, ordering the destruction of heretical books (1530, 1532), forbidding Poles and Lithuanians to study at heretical seats of learning (1535, 1540), making deprivation of nobility the penalty for harbouring heretics (1541), and introducing capital punishment for the offences of trading in, owning, or merely reading heretical works (1544). The only effect of this legislation was to popularize Protestantism as an ideology of resistance to royal and ecclesiastical tyranny and to seal the alliance between the champions of religious freedom and the executive movement. The royal decrees, and the enactments of the Synod sanctioned by the king, clearly infringed the principle of 'nihil novi'. The consistories could not keep up with the proliferation of heresy, and the civil authorities were increasingly reluctant to act on ecclesiastical denunciations. To the gentry at

Catholicism was the state religion of Poland–Lithuania but there were strong bodies of Protestants. In this woodcut from Orzechowski's 'Chimaera', the soldier as the 'type of Christ' attacks the 'deadly sects' which bring discord to Poland; for example the 'Arian fox'.

large it was self-evident that their rights must include freedom of worship. Catholic gentlemen often joined with Protestants in resisting the execution of ecclesiastical sentences and in condemning punitive legislation at sessions of the Diet. The king had sanctioned the burning of heretics in 1523, but only one old woman, Melchiorowa Wejglowa, convicted in 1539 of showing Judaistic leanings, went to the stake. If she had been of gentle birth, the Bishop of Cracow would undoubtedly have spared her.

'A Diabolical Freedom of Conscience'

Though the most powerful of the prelates urged rigid application of the laws against heresy under Zygmunt I and in the early years of the following reign, more moderate counsels prevailed in some sections of the church. A movement for reform without estrangement from Rome grew up, inspired by the writings of Cracow humanists, notably Andrzej Frycz-Modrzewski, and with supporters ranging from the village priest irked by celibacy to the learned and patriotic bishop Jakub Uchanski, later Primate. Zygmunt August began his reign with a show of hostility to heretics, hoping to earn the blessing of the bishops on his unpopular marriage with Barbara Radziwiłł. But in 1555 he approved the dispatch to Rome of Stanisław Maciejowski, who sought the Pope's sanction for the celebration of mass in Polish, communion in two kinds, the marriage of the clergy, and the calling of a national synod with lay participation to settle problems of ecclesiastical jurisdiction. This last and most important request the Pope tactically conceded, but nothing came of it. The king had already (1552) under pressure from the Diet agreed to a suspension of ecclesiastical sentences against the gentry. In 1555 a resolution of the Diet, accepted by the King over the protests of the bishops, in effect legalized Protestantism.

After 1562 Zygmunt made further concessions to the dissenters as part of his peace settlement with the gentry. Protestant deputies dominated the proceedings of the Diet, with little opposition from their Catholic brothers, and with the support of all lay members of the Senate. The king accepted the argument that ecclesiastical sentences against the gentry infringed their constitutional rights, and ordered officers of the crown not to execute them. This enactment amounted to the repeal of the laws against heresy; but the church continued to prosecute those who did not pay tithes, and also crown officers who refused to carry out the sentence in such cases, until 1565 when the king declared all juridical acts of this kind null and void, thus abolishing for all time ecclesiastical jurisdiction over the Polish gentry.

The final triumph of the movement for religious freedom came in 1573, during the interregnum after the death of Zygmunt August, when all lay deputies to the Diet of Warsaw (and one bishop) signed the compact ensuring toleration of all dissidents. Poland had become, in theory at least, the most tolerant of Christian states, and her record in practice in the 16th and even in the 17th century compared favourably with that of more disciplined lands like England and France. But, in religion as in other matters, the nobles of Poland did not see the need for lesser men to enjoy the freedom which they claimed for themselves. The Declaration of Warsaw guaranteed to masters, lay and ecclesiastical, the right to punish rebellious servants as they saw fit, even if they made religion the excuse for disobedience. This clause was easily interpreted to mean *cuius regio, eius religio*, and greatly assisted the reconversion of Poland when the gentry began to fall away from Protestantism. The Calvinist gentry, to the horror of the Bohemian Brethren, practised forcible conversion of their 'subjects' from the start, while King Stefan Batory drove all inhabitants of crown lands in his possession back into the Catholic fold in 1579.

Protestantism reached the limits of its expansion in Poland by the end of the 16th century, when about 2,000 churches had been taken over and perhaps a sixth of the gentry converted. The proportion of conversions amongst burgesses was certainly higher. But, except in districts of Greater Poland bordering on Prussia, Protestantism struck only shallow roots amongst the peasants, who seem to have regarded religious and political controversy alike as pastimes for the nobility. Besides adapting Catholic churches the dissenters established new places of worship, such as the great temple at Cracow built with the consent of Zygmunt August in 1569. They set up excellent schools, among them the Lutheran gymnasia at Danzig (1558) and Thorn (1568) (with the University of Königsberg behind them), the gymnasium of the Bohemian Brethren at Leszno (1555), of which Jan Amos Komenski (Comenius) was to be the most eminent rector, and, most famous of all, the Arian Academy at Rakow (1602). Side by side with the flourishing Protestant communities, enjoying the patronage of rich landowners or bourgeois, there were many others, where the leading laymen were interested above all in a cheap church, and the ministers were 'the poorest, most exploited and plundered of men, for Papist tyranny has taken a large part of church incomes and the gentry the rest'. Such complaints were met with the retort that the ministers 'desire to rule over the gentry as the Pope and the bishops did in days gone by'.

Poland had become a land in which 'all things were permitted to all men' (Christian Francken), and a 'diabolical freedom of conscience' (Theodore Beza) reigned. Into this ecclesiastical anarchy the Counter-Reformation moved slowly and cautiously. Though the Protestants were numerically weak, their legal position was strong. True, tolerance rested only on the decisions under Zygmunt August suspending execution of ecclesiastical sentences, and on the Declaration of Warsaw: still firmer guarantees were sought in vain in the following half century. But in practice any frontal assault on religious freedom would have been resisted as an attack on the rights of the gentry. One Papal nuncio was warned by his superiors that 'the liberty which reigns in the country does not allow recourse to severe means of correction'.

The Catholic zealots could seldom bring administrative and judicial pressure to bear on dissenters, but some of them on occasions provoked mob violence. Protestant temples were destroyed in Cracow (during the interregnum of 1574 and again in 1591), Poznan (1616), Lublin (1627) and many lesser centres. Stefan Batory deplored such attempts to 'propagate the faith by violence fire and the sword, instead of instruction and good example', but Zygmunt III—'the Jesuit King'—was less fastidious. Wiser heads placed their hopes on propaganda and education. Cardinal Hosius, who played such a prominent part in the Council of Trent, made his greatest contributions to the Counter-Reformation at home in his polemical writings, particularly his much translated *Confessio Fidei Catholicae Christianae*, and by introducing the Jesuits to Poland in 1564. They founded a number of excellent schools, for clergy and for laymen, including the College at Wilno which became an Academy in 1579. Its first rector was the greatest luminary of the Society of Jesus in Poland, Piotr Skarga (1536–1612), whose polemic writings and *Sermons before the Diet* are regarded as masterpieces of Polish prose even by those who detest his views. Though he urged the fullest use of all legal means to contain Protestantism, he preferred persuasion to coercion. Political indiscipline and religious disunity were, in his view, twin evils, and the cure would be found in the moral regeneration of the gentry, who must abandon the 'abuse of freedom' against their ruler and their own 'subjects', rid themselves of idle fears that a stronger monarchy must be tyrannical, and recognize that the Catholic faith alone could maintain national harmony and integrity.

His hearers in the Diet may have been entertained but they were not persuaded. Many amongst them, Catholics as well as Protestants, felt that the nation's interests were best served by religious peace, and the Jesuits were doubtless right in supposing that tolerance often sprang from indifference to religion. In any case, the Polish gentry could feel no enthusiasm for a programme of national recovery which included the reinforcement of the throne. The regalist party always included prominent churchmen, but the Jesuits, and the shrewdest of the prelates, after the rebellion of Zebrzydowski, tactfully refrained from supporting the king against the gentry, and even paid lip service to 'golden freedom'.

The decline of the reformed churches in 17th century Poland was, with one exception, not the result of persecution. Large numbers of Polish gentlemen rejoined the Catholic church as light-heartedly as they had left it. The drift back into the fold was observable shortly after the king's acceptance of the Tridentine Decrees in 1569. (The Polish hierarchy accepted them only in 1577, with reservations safeguarding certain cherished abuses.) The patient indoctrination of the Jesuits, whose excellent schools were patronized even by dissenting parents, and the example of many great magnates, who saw no advantage in drifting on an ebbing tide farther and farther from their king and the mass of their compatriots, eased the advance of the Counter-Reformation. War with Protestant Sweden and Orthodox Russia intensified distaste for foreign creeds. As Poland was more and more heavily punished for its internal disarray, the gentry embraced more passionately the spectral unity which they found in common allegiance to the church of their ancestors. They solaced their wounded national pride with the claim that Poland was 'the bulwark of Christianity' against the infidel Turk.

They also, during and after the 'Deluge', looked for scapegoats. Amongst the Christians, the 'Arians' were most vulnerable. Their spokesmen, unlike the more cautious Lutherans and Calvinists, had called for the complete abandonment of state intervention in religion, condemning the use of force against the heterodox as the only real heresy. The extremists amongst them, who refused to hold office or bear arms or condone serfdom, seemed to threaten the bases of Polish society. King Jan Kazimierz, rallying the country to drive out the Swedes in 1656, solemnly vowed that when peace was restored he would endeavour 'together with all estates . . . to deliver the people of my kingdom from all oppression and injustice', and also that he would drive the Arians from Poland. The second of these promises he kept. The Diet of 1658 decreed the expulsion of the 'loathsome and crazy sect'. Those who chose exile rather than conversion emigrated mainly to Transylvania, Holland or Ducal Prussia. Less provocative dissenters continued to enjoy religious freedom, although the Diet of 1668, in breach of the Warsaw Declaration, tried to preclude further conversions, making renunciation of Catholicism punishable by execution and confiscation of property.

Russia: Strength and Weakness

Russia's advantages over Poland were partly geographical. The lands to the north of Moscow and as far as the Arctic coast were inhabited by Russians. To the east lay the thinly peopled expanses of the Middle Volga and Siberia, which the Moscovite state annexed with little difficulty, extending its territory to the Urals before the end of the 15th century and the Sea of Okhotsk in the middle of the 17th. Moscow had only two frontiers to defend: the western, against the Lithuanians, the Poles and occasionally the Swedes, and the southern, against the Crimean Tartars backed by their suzerain, the Sultan. These enemies might detach peripheral territories—as the Swedes took Novgorod, and the Poles Smolensk, during the 'Time of Troubles.' They might strike through to Moscow itself: the Tartars burnt the capital, and carried off 100,000 prisoners in 1571, and the Poles occupied it in 1610–12. But the remoteness of the Russian heartlands, their poverty, and poor communications, were powerful deterrents to invaders. None of Russia's enemies had the will or the resources to hold the country down for long.

Nor did Russia's neighbours often succeed in concerting their onslaughts, though all might try to take advantage of damage inflicted by any of their number. Sweden's differences with

Lithuania and Poland precluded cooperation against Russia, and an
attempt by Charles X to ally himself with the Sultan against both
Russia and Poland led nowhere. Russia and Poland each lived in
dread that the other would conclude an effective alliance with the
Crimean Khan, and perhaps with his overlord in Istanbul. But the
Tartars had little interest in conquest, and less in strengthening
either of their Northern neighbours. Intent only on plundering
and exortion, they could be bribed to change sides, as they did
more than once in the struggle between Poland and Bogdan
Khmelnitsky. At a price they would limit, but not suspend, their
depredations. Russia, painfully weakened by the 'Time of Troubles',
paid them blackmail to the tune of one million roubles in the
years 1613–50, in spite of which the Tartars sold some 200,000
Russians into slavery. As for the Turks, in the years when Russia
was most vulnerable they were preoccupied with the struggle for
the Eastern Mediterranean, wars against Persia and Austria, and
revolts within their empire, so that a major campaign against their
Northern neighbours was unthinkable. Even so, they set out in
1569 to seize Astrakhan, which would serve as a base for further
expansion along the Volga, and began digging a canal to link the
Don and the Volga as a preliminary. A fierce Russian attack
disrupted this work, and a mutiny amongst the janissaries put an
end to the enterprise.

In the 16th and 17th centuries Russia enjoyed some of the
advantages of backwardness. Less attractive to invaders than
Poland and Lithuania, it could also more quickly repair the
damage caused by war to its relatively primitive economy. After
1553, when Richard Chancellor opened up the Northern Sea
Route, Russian trade with the West was less subject to interruption
than that of Poland and Lithuania. Moreover, Russia's income
from trade was little affected by the fall in grain prices on Western
markets. Grain was, as yet, a minor item of export. Much more
valuable were timber, flax and hemp, in great demand with
English and Dutch shipbuilders, the magnificent furs, largely
collected in the form of tribute from the Siberian peoples, and the
luxury goods which Russia bought from China, Central Asia and
Persia, and resold in the West. The proceeds of foreign trade did
not, as in Poland and Lithuania, disappear into the pockets of
landlords, but helped to fill the coffers of the state, for the Tsar
held a monopoly of many commodities and treated merchants as
his servants.

Russia then, was apparently weaker and poorer than Poland,
but for strategic and economic reasons, more resilient. An
examination of Russian political institutions reveals a similar
contradiction between appearances and reality. Russia, buffeted
and lacerated by other powers, was also rent by grave internal
disorders. From the 1560s until the 1660s not a decade passed
without some destructive and bloody crisis. In 1564 Ivan the
Terrible 'abdicated', fled from the boyars, whom he suspected of
conspiring against him, to his forest stronghold of Aleksandorov,
declared some districts, some towns, and a section of Moscow
territory apart ('oprichnina') from the rest of his domains, the
'land' or ('zemshchina'). From the Tsar's enclaves his 'men apart'
('oprichniki'), dressed in black, riding black horses, and carrying
at their saddlebows besoms to symbolize their task of sweeping
treason from Russia, purged and plundered the 'land'. Thousands
of aristocrats lost their possessions and perished, thousands of
humble gentlemen as well as great lords were uprooted from their
estates and resettled in outlying areas.

In 1581 in a fit of rage Ivan slew his heir with his own hand, and
left at his death (1584) two sons, the sickly Fyodor, who succeeded
him and died childless in 1598, and the infant Dimitri, who
perished mysteriously in 1591. The extinction of the dynasty, and
the appearance of a pretender—the False Dimitri—shortly afterwards plunged the Moscovite state into chaos, aggravated as we
have seen by Polish and Swedish intervention. Marauding bands
scoured the countryside, and for a time the lawless Cossacks
swayed the destiny of Russia. In those years, hard pressed serfs
first took up arms against their masters, led by the ex-slave Ivan
Bolotnikov. Under the first Tsar of the Romanov dynasty, Mikhail
(1613–45), the restoration of order was a slow and painful
process. His successor had to put down alarming disturbances in
Moscow itself—the 'salt riots' of 1648 and the 'copper coin riots'

*The titlepage of the Slavonic Bible, 'Biblia Russica', of 1663. A cam-
paign to remedy ignorance and superstition among Russian's clergy had
been begun by the Patriarch Nikon 1654.*

of 1662. By a series of enactments from 1598 to 1649 the serfs
were reduced to the status of chattels, and their protest reached a
climax at the close of our period in a great peasant war against
Moscow led by rogue Cossacks under Stenka Razin (1670–71).

The Tsar, the Boyars and the Church

Yet none of these traumatic events weakened the central power in
Moscow for long: indeed, the ultimate effect of Ivan's reign of
terror and the Time of Troubles was to reinforce the autocratic
system. In the middle of the 16th century the Moscovite state had
certain feudal features. The Tsar ruled in conjunction with a
Council of Boyars, drawn from the descendants of the apanage
princes whose domains had been absorbed by Moscow, and from
old Moscovite boyar families. These great lords owned their lands
outright. They were appointed to offices in the state by the Tsar,
but distribution of office was governed by a strict code of precedence ('mestnichestvo'). Once the old apanage principates had
been brought under Moscovite rule, boyars could exercise their
old right to transfer their allegiance from one prince to another
only by deserting to Lithuania. This the Tsars regarded as treason,
but it was by no means sure in the reign of Ivan the Terrible that
the boyars took the same view. The purpose of Ivan's purge was
to destroy potential rivals, some of whom boasted descent from

an older branch of the dynasty, to free him from irksome and self-assertive counsellors, and to provide additional land for the gentry who were more docile servants of the crown. Ivan did not abolish the Boyars' Council or the code of precedence, but the great families, depleted by his blood-letting, and some of them compromised by collaboration with Poles or Swedes in the Time of Troubles, lost much of their political importance. The parvenu Romanovs accelerated this process by introducing their kin and other newcomers into the ranks of the boyars. In the 17th century the boyars became no more than higher civil servants, and the rules of precedence were finally abolished in 1682.

Ivan sought to broaden the base of his power by convening an Assembly of the Land in 1549, which met periodically thereafter until 1682. Its members included not only boyars and prelates but representatives of the gentry, the merchants (from 1566), and sometimes the free peasants. The usual reason for its convocation was the Tsar's need for advice on foreign policy, and financial support. Some foreign contemporaries saw the Assembly as an embryonic Estates General. In 1584 a precedent was established which seemed to promise a great extension of its powers. Ivan the Terrible left no will, and the Assembly met to confirm the succession of his son Fyodor. In 1598 the Assembly elected Boris Godunov, and in 1613 Mikhail Romanov to the throne. In the difficult early years of Mikhail's reign it was in permanent session. But the Estates, even in those critical years, were too deeply divided by conflicts of interest to transform the Assembly into a constitutionally guaranteed representative body. The gentry, merchants and the free peasants all looked to the Tsar for favours at the expense of other classes. No single class was strong enough to dominate. The one attempt to determine constitutionally the rights, composition and periodicity of the Assembly, the Buturlin project of 1634, came to nothing. Under Tsar Aleksei the Assembly was convened infrequently, and the last Assembly of 1682, which enthroned the infant who was to become Peter the Great, was a random gathering of persons who happened to be in Moscow.

Thus the autocracy was never for long hampered by aristocratic or representative institutions. Ideological justifications of the Tsar's unlimited rights over his subjects were elaborated from the reign of Ivan III onwards. That monarch adopted the title of Tsar ('Caesar') to indicate that he was in some sense the successor of the Byzantine Emperors. The legendary descent of the ruling house from a brother of the Emperor Augustus, the imperial and religious responsibilities of Moscow ('the Third Rome') as the only independent Orthodox state, and Ivan III's connection by marriage with the last Byzantine Emperor, were all invoked to legitimize the principal of autocracy. Ivan the Terrible, in his correspondence with his former adviser and general, Prince Kurbsky, who took refuge from his wrath in Lithuania, argued that the greatest of his subjects were slaves commanded by religion to submit even when their divinely appointed sovereign was unjust. The awe which Russians felt for the old royal house helped the Romanovs, a family of relatively humble descent, to establish themselves on the throne. Mikhail's grandfather was the brother of Ivan the Terrible's first wife, and Mikhail soon improved on this tenuous relationship by describing Ivan himself as 'my grandfather'. Although the Assembly in 1613 determined the succession only as far as Mikhail's immediate heir Aleksei, like Ivan, he could regard Russia as the inalienable estate of his family.

The Orthodox Church, which had preserved Russia's consciousness of national unity in the Mongol period, and aided the rulers of Moscow in 'regathering the Russian lands', did much to further the consolidation of the autocracy. The supremacy of the Moscow Metropolitan in the Russian Church was finally ensured by the establishment of the Patriarchate in 1589. The secular and ecclesiastical rulers of Moscow had a common interest in the centralization of authority, and in general cooperated against centrifugal elements in church and state. At times, the primate pitted his authority against that of the Tsar. Thus, the Metropolitan Filip Kolychev tried to restrain Ivan the Terrible at the height of his murderous frenzy. The father of Mikhail Romanov, the Archbishop Filaret (Fyodor) was raised to the Patriarchate in 1619, given the title Great Lord, usually reserved to the Tsar, and

in effect ruled Russia for 14 years. Basing himself on this precedent, one of Filaret's successors, the Patriarch Nikon, attempted to assert the authority of the church over the secular power. But the Tsar always held the master hand: the hierarchy at large would never support the primate against him. Filip was deposed, and later murdered by the *oprichnik* Skuratov. Nikon was deposed, unfrocked and imprisoned.

The Russian church was not free from rivalries between prelates, or from disputes of principle, as for instance the prolonged quarrel between the wealthy hierarchs and the followers of Nil Sorsky (died 1508), who taught that churchmen should shun wealth and power for a life of ascetic contemplation. Victory in these controversies was determined by the Tsar, and his support bound the dominant faction still more closely to him. Heresies of Judaistic or Protestant origin sprang up sporadically in the late 15th and the 16th centuries, but were savagely exterminated before they could infect more than a handful of Russians. The great schism in the reign of Tsar Aleksei, caused by Nikon's reform of ritual and religious books, which the Tsar approved, estranged many millions from the official church, but not a single bishop joined them, and ruthless persecution made the 'Old Belief' a church of peasants and merchants. The servility of the hierarchy as a whole to the Tsar would make it possible for Peter the Great to abolish the Patriarchate and govern the church through a department of state.

How great then was the contrast between the powers of the Russian Tsar and those of the Polish king. The Tsar was never effectively limited by aristocratic or representative institutions, the king was their prisoner. The Tsar recognized no earthly superior or partner, and Ivan the Terrible could speak scornfully not only of Polish kings chosen by their subjects, but even of Queen Elizabeth I, who shared her power with certain 'peasant traders'. The Polish king was forced to pardon and compromise with rebels, the Tsar could destroy great men, not because they *had* rebelled, but because they might reasonably be expected to do so. Polish magnates could with impunity pursue their own foreign policy and endanger the state with military adventures on their own account: the rulers of Russia executed in 1634 the boyars Izmailov and Shein, who failed to capture Smolensk. In Poland, religious disunity helped to undermine the king's authority: in Russia an authoritarian church propped the autocracy.

In the 16th and 17th centuries the leaders of the Orthodox Christians under Turkish rule began to look to Moscow for alms, for protection, and perhaps for deliverance. They eagerly supported the Tsar's policies, encouraging for instance the 'reunion' of the Ukraine with Moscow, and enthusiastically anathematizing the awkward Patriarch Nikon. It was not, however, the Orthodox alone who placed their hopes on Russia. This account of the two great Slav states, Catholic Poland declining from its golden age and Orthodox Russia on the eve of its ascent to greatness, may suitably end with a mention of the first propagandist of Panslavism who was born neither in Russia nor in Poland, but was familiar with both. The Croatian Catholic priest George Krizhanich, a servant of the Roman Congregation de Propaganda Fide, went to Russia in 1659, not to proselytize but to serve the only country which, in his view, could unite all the Slavs—including the Poles —and save them from the Turks and Germans. Tsar Aleksei rewarded him with 15 years of exile in Siberia, where however he was able to work in comfort, devising a new common Slav language, and writing treatises in which he anticipated part of Peter the Great's programme of reforms. Though Russia seemed to him in many respects barbarous and backward, he believed that the autocratic principle guaranteed its future greatness. In relation to the feeble Russian state of his time his ideas appear ridiculous, but Krizhanich had accurately weighed the prospects of Poland and Russia. Released by the studious and pious Tsar Fyodor Alekseievich, he left Russia, still convinced that in its growing strength lay the great hope for all Slavs. In the meantime, he hurried to join in a holding action against the most aggressive enemy of Slavdom, the Turks. In 1683 this first apostle of Panslavism joined the army of the new native king of Poland, Jan Sobieski, and perished during the relief of Vienna.

Select Bibliography

I The Baroque Century

Boas, M. *The Scientific Renaissance 1450–1630* (London, 1962)

Boehmer, H. *Die Jesuiten: eine historische Skizze* (Leipzig, 1907); French translation: *Les Jésuites*, G. Monod (Paris, 1910)

Choisy, E. *L'état chrétien calviniste à Genève au temps de Théodore de Bèze* (Paris, 1902)

Hall, A. R. *From Galileo to Newton, 1630–1720* (London, 1963)

Haskell, F. *Patrons and Painters: a Study in the Relations between Italian Art and Society in the Age of the Baroque* (London, 1963)

Lecky, W. E. H. *The History of the Rise and Influence of the Spirit of Rationalism in Europe* 2 vols (London, 1910)

Male, E. *L'art religieux du XVIIe siècle* (Paris, 1951)

Monter, W. *Calvin's Geneva* (New York, 1967)

Mousnier, R. *Histoire Générale des Civilisations, vol. IV: Les XVIe et XVIIe siècles* (Paris, 1954)

Pagel, W. *Paracelsus* (Basel, New York, 1958)

Pattison, M. *Isaac Casaubon 1559–1614* (Oxford, 1875) *Essays* (Oxford, 1889)

Popkin, R. H. *The History of Scepticism from Erasmus to Descartes* (Assen, Netherlands, 1960)

Romano, R. 'Tra XVI e XVII secolo: una crisi economica 1619–1622' in *Rivista Storica Italiana* (Turin, 1962) 'Encore la crise de 1619–1622' in *Annales, Economies, Sociétés, Civilisations* (Paris, 1964)

Rubens, P. P. *Letters*, ed. R. Sanders Magurn (Harvard, 1955)

Symonds, J. A. *Renaissance in Italy* vol. II: *The Catholic Reaction* (London, 1886)

Trevor-Roper, H. R. *Religion, the Reformation and Social Change* (London, 1967)

Wittkower, R. *Art and Architecture in Italy 1600–1750* (London, Baltimore, 1958)

Yates, F. *Giordano Bruno and the Hermetic Tradition* (London, 1964)

II Spain's dominion

Bataillon, M. *Erasme et l'Espagne* (Paris, 1937)

Bennassar, B. *Valladolid au siècle d'or* (Paris, 1967)

Braudel, F. *La Méditerranée et le monde méditerranéen à l'époque de Philippe II* (Paris, 1966)

Dominguez Ortiz, A. *La Sociedad Española en el Siglo XVII* (Madrid, 1964–8)

Elliott, J. H. *Imperial Spain 1469–1716* (London, 1963)

Hamilton, B. *Political Thought in Sixteenth Century Spain* (Oxford, 1963)

Kamen, H. *The Spanish Inquisition* (London, 1965)

Kubler, G. and Soria, M. *Art and Architecture in Spain and Portugal and their American Dominions 1500–1800* (London, 1964)

Lynch, J. *Spain under the Habsburgs*, vol. 1: *Empire and Absolutism 1516–1598* (Oxford, 1964)

Merriman, R. B. *The Rise of the Spanish Empire* 4 vols (New York, 1962)

Vicens Vives, J. (ed.) *Historia Social y Económica de España y América* vol. III (Barcelona, 1957)

III The divided Netherlands

Blok, P. J. *A History of the People of the Netherlands* (New York, London, 1907)

Boxer, C. R. *The Dutch Seaborne Empire* (London, 1965)

Bromley, J. S. and Kossmann, E. H. (eds) *Britain and the Netherlands* 2 vols (Oxford 1959–1962)

Clark, G. *The Birth of the Dutch Republic* (British Academy, London, 1946)

Dorsten, A. van *Poets, Patrons and Professors* (Oxford, Leiden, 1962)

Edmundson, G. *Anglo-Dutch Rivalry* (Oxford, 1911)

Geyl, P. *The Revolt of the Netherlands* (London, 1932) *The Netherlands Divided 1609–1648*, English translation: S. T. Bindoff (London, 1936) *History of the Low Countries: Episodes and Problems* (London, New York, 1964)

Motley, J. L. *The Rise of the Dutch Republic* 3 vols (New York, 1856) *The United Netherlands* 4 vols (London, 1860–1867)

IV Peace in Germany

Abel, W. *Geschichte der deutschen Landwirtschaft vom frühen Mittelalter bis zum 19. Jahrhundert* (Stuttgart, 1962)

Carsten, F. L. *Princes and Parliaments in Germany from the XV to the XVIII century* (Oxford, 1959)

Gothein, E. 'Staat und Gesellschaft des Zeitalters der Gegenreformation' in *Der Staat* (Berlin, 1908)

Hohlbaum, C.; Lau, F.; Stein, J. (eds) *Das Buch Weinsberg. Kölner Denkwürdigkeiten aus dem 16. Jahrhundert* 5 vols (Bonn, 1886–1926)

Janssen, J. *History of the German People at the Close of the Middle Ages* 16 vols (London, 1896–1925)

Lütge, F. 'Die wirtschaftliche Lage Deutschlands vor Ausbruch des Dreißigjährigen Krieges' in *Studien zur Sozial- und Wirtschaftsgeschichte. Gesammelte Abhandlungen* (Munich, 1963)

Müller, K. *Kirchengeschichte, 1550–1618* (Berlin, Leipzig, 1912)

Paulsen, F. *Geschichte des gelehrten Unterrichtes an den deutschen Schulen und Universitäten vom Ausgang des Mittelalters bis zur Gegenwart* 2 vols (Leipzig, 1919–1921)

Ritter, M. *Deutsche Geschichte im Zeitalter der Gegenreformation und des Dreissigjährigen Krieges 1555–1648* 3 vols (Stuttgart, Berlin, 1889–1908)

Schultz, A. 'Das häusliche Leben der europäischen Kulturvölker vom Mittelalter bis zur zweiten Hälfte des 18. Jahrhunderts' in *Handbuch der mittelalterlichen und neueren Geschichte* (Munich, Berlin, 1903)

Soldan, W. G.; Heppe, H.; Bauer, M. *Geschichte der Hexenprozesse* (Munich, 1912)

Zeeden, E. W. *Die Entstehung der Konfessionen, Grundlagen und Formen der Konfessionbildung im Zeitalter der Glaubenskämpfe* (Vienna, 1965)

Pauw F. de *Grotius and the Law of the Sea* (Brussels, 1965)

Renier, G. *The Dutch Nation* (The Hague, 1944)

Zimmerman, L. *Der ökonomische Staat Landgraf Wilhelms IV von Hessen* (Marburg, 1933–34)

V Thirty Years' War

Albrecht, D. 'Die Auswärtige Politik Maximilians von Bayern, 1618–1635' in *Schriftenreihe der Historischen Kommission bei der Bayerischen Akademie der Wissenschaften* 6 vols (Göttingen, 1962) *Richelieu, Gustav Adolf und das Reich* (Munich, 1959)

Burckhardt, C. *Richelieu* 2 vols (Munich, 1965); English translation: E. and W. Muir (New York, 1964)

Delbrück, H. *Geschichte der Kriegskunst* 4 vols (Berlin, 1920)

Dickmann, F. *Der Westfälische Frieden* (Münster, 1959)

Dominguez Ortiz, A. *Politica y Hacienda de Felipe IV* (Madrid, 1960)

Essen van der A. *Le Cardinal-Infant et la politique européenne de l'Espagne, 1609–1641* (Louvain, 1944)

Franz, G. *Der Dreissig jährige Krieg und das deutsche Volk, Untersuchungen zur Bevölkerungs- und Agrargeschichte* (Stuttgart, 1961)

Houtte van, J. A. (ed.) *Algemene Geschiedenis der Nederlanden* (Utrecht, 1953)

Jessen, J. *Der Dreissig jährige Krieg in Augenzeugenberichten* (Düsseldorf, 1964)

Jones, J. R. *Britain and Europe in the 17th century* (London, 1966)

Ranke von, L. *Geschichte Wallensteins* (Leipzig, 1910)

Redlich, F. *The German Military Enterpriser and his Workforce* (Wiesbaden, 1964)

Roberts, M. *Gustavus Adolphus* 2 vols (London, 1953–58)

Seppelt, F. X. *Geschichte der Päpste* 5 vols (Munich, 1959)

Steinberg, S. H. *The Thirty Years' War and the Conflict for European Hegemony, 1600–1660* (London, 1966)

Sturmberger, H. *Der Aufstand in Böhmen* (Munich, 1959)

Trevor-Roper, H. R. 'The General Crisis of the 17th century' in *Past and Present* vol. 16 (London, 1959)

'Discussion' ... in *Past and Present* vol 18 (London, 1960)

VILLARI, R. *La rivolta antispagnola a Napoli* (Bari, 1967)

WADDINGTON, A. *La république des Provinces-Unies, la France et les Pays-Bas Espagnols de 1630 à 1650* 2 vols (Paris, 1895–97)

WEDGWOOD, C. V. *The Thirty Years' War* (London, 1967)

VI France: monarchy and people

BLUNT, A. *Art and Architecture in France 1500–1700* (London, 1953)

CHAMPION, P. *Ronsard et son Temps* (Paris, 1925)

CROZET, R. *La vie artistique en France au XVIIe siècle (1598–1661): Les artistes et la société* (Paris, 1954)

LE ROY LADURIE, E. *Les paysans du Languedoc* (Paris, 1966)

MOUSNIER, R. *L'assassinat d'Henri IV* (Paris, 1964)
Fureurs paysannes: les paysans dans les révoltes du XVIIe siècle – France, Russie, Chine – (Paris, 1967)
Lettres et mémoires adressés au Chancelier Séguier 1633–1649, 2 vols (Paris, 1964)

PAGES, G. *La guerre de Trente Ans* (Paris, 1939)
Naissance du Grand Siècle: la France de Henri IV à Louis XIV, 1598–1661 (Paris, 1948)

PORCHNEV, B. *Les soulèvements populaires en France de 1623 à 1648* (Paris, 1963)

ROMIER, L. *Le royaume de Catherine de Médicis* 2 vols (Paris, 1925)

SÉE, E. *Les idées politiques en France au XVIIe siècle* (Paris, 1923)

TAPIÉ, V. L. *La France de Louis XIII et de Richelieu* (Paris, 1952)

VII Britain transformed

ASHLEY, M. *The Greatness of Oliver Cromwell* (London, 1957)

BECKETT, J. *The Making of Modern Ireland* (London 1966)

BRUNTON, D.; PENNINGTON, D. H. *Members of the Long Parliament* (London, 1954)

COLLINSON, P. *The Elizabethan Puritan Movement* (London, 1967)

DONALDSON, G. *Scotland: James V to James VII* (Edinburgh, London, 1965)

FIRTH, C. H. *Oliver Cromwell* (New York, Oxford, 1953)

HALLER, W. *The Rise of Puritanism* (New York, 1938)
Liberty and Reformation (New York, 1955)

HEXTER, J. H. *Re-appraisals in History* (London, 1961)

HILL, C. *Society and Puritanism in Pre-Revolutionary England* (London, 1964)

HURSTFIELD, J. *The Queen's Wards: wardships and marriage under Elizabeth I* (London, 1958)

JORDAN, W. K. *Philanthropy in England* (London, 1959)

KEARNEY, H. F. *Strafford in Ireland* (Manchester, 1959)

MATHEW, D. *The Age of Charles I* (London, 1951)

McGRATH, P. *Papist and Puritan under Elizabeth I* (London, 1967)

NEALE, J. E. *Queen Elizabeth* (London, 1952)
The Elizabethan House of Commons (London, 1949)
Elizabeth I and her Parliaments 2 vols (London, 1953)
Essays in Elizabethan History (London, 1958)

PRESTWICH, M. *Lionel Cranfield* (Oxford, 1966)

QUINN, D. B. *Ralegh and the British Empire* (London, 1947)

RAMSEY, P. *Tudor Economic Problems* (London, 1963)

ROOTS, I. *The Great Rebellion* (London, 1966)

ROWSE, A. L. *The England of Elizabeth* (London, 1964)

STONE, L. *The Crisis of the Aristocracy* (Oxford, 1965)

TAWNEY, R. H. *Business and Politics under James I* (Cambridge, 1958)

TREVOR-ROPER, H. R. *Archbishop Laud 1573–1645* (London, New York, 1965)

WEDGWOOD C. V. *Strafford, a Revaluation* (London, 1961)
The King's Peace (London, 1955)
The King's War (London, 1958)
The Trial of Charles I (London, 1967)

WILLIAMSON, J. A. *Hawkins of Plymouth* (London, 1949)

WILLSON, D. H. *James VI and I* (London, 1963)

WILSON, C. *England's Apprenticeship* (London, 1965)

WOODHOUSE, A. S. P. *Puritanism and Liberty* (London, 1950)

WORMALD, B. H. G. *Clarendon* (Cambridge, 1951)

WOOLRYCH, A. *Battles of the English Civil War* (London, 1961)

WRIGHT, L. B. *Colonial Civilisation of North America* (London, 1949) or *The Atlantic Frontier* (New York, 1959)

VIII Slav nations

Poland

CHRZANOWSKI, I.; KOT, S. *Humanizm i Reformacja w Polsce* (Lwow, 1927)

CZAPLIŃSKY, W. O. *Polsce siedemnastoiwecznej* (Warsaw, 1966)

GRZYBOWSKI, K. *Teoria reprezentacji w Polsce epoki Odrodzenia* (Warsaw, 1959)

ŁOWMIAŃSKI, H. (ed.) *Historia Polski* vol. I, part 2 (Warsaw, 1958)

REDDAWAY, W. F. (ed.) *The Cambridge History of Poland*, Vol. I (Cambridge, 1950)

TAZBIR, J. *Swit i zmierzch polskiej reformacji* (Warsaw, 1956)
'La tolérance religieuse en Pologne aux XVIe et XVIIe siècles' in *La Pologne au XIIe Congrès International des Sciences Historiques* (Warsaw, 1965)

WYCZAŃSKI, A. *Polska-Rzecza Pospolita Szlachecka* (Warsaw, 1965)

Russia and Ukraine

DRUZHININ, N.; PAVLENKO, N.; CHEREPNIN, N. (eds) *Russkii Absolyutizm* (Moscow, 1964)

FLORINSKY, M. T. *Russia: a History and an Interpretation* (London, New York, 1959)

HRUSHEVSKY, M. S. *A History of the Ukraine* (Yale, 1941)

NASONOV, A.; CHEREPNIN, N.; ZIMIN, A. (eds) *Ocherki po istorii SSSR, konets XVIv nachalo XVIIv* (Moscow, 1955)

NOVOSELSKY, A.; USTYUGOV, N. (eds) *Ocherkipo istorii SSSR-XVIIv* (Moscow, 1955)

PLATONOV, S. F. *Lektsii po russkoi istorii* (St Petersburg, 1910) or *History of Russia* (London, 1925)

KLIUCHEVSKY, V. O. *A History of Russia* (New York, 1960)

In addition, the publishers would like to acknowledge the following works, which have been particularly useful in obtaining information about the pictures and in compiling the captions:

ALPATOV, M. W.; DACENKO, O. *Art Treasures of Russia* (Thames and Hudson, London, 1968)

BELLER, E. A. *Propaganda in Germany during the Thirty Years' War* (Princeton, University Press, 1940)
Caricatures of the Winter King of Bohemia (Oxford University Press, 1928)

BERTRAM, A. *The Life of Sir Peter-Paul Rubens* (Peter Davies, London, 1928)

BLUNT, A. *Art and Architecture in France 1500–1700* (Penguin Books, London, 1953)

GRIMMELSHAUSEN, J. C. *Hans von Simplicius Simplicissimus*, English transl. by Wallich (New English Library, London 1962)

NEVINSON, J. L. 'Sketches of 17th Century London: a Student's Album' in *Country Life*, vol. CXLII (London, 1967)

SUMMERSON, J. *Architecture in Britain 1530–1830* (Penguin Books, London, 1953)

TAESCHNER, F. *Alt-Stambuler Hof und Volksleben* (Heinz Lafaire, Hanover, 1925)

WATERHOUSE, E. *Painting in Britain 1530–1790* (Penguin Books, London, 1953)

WILENSKI, R. H. *Flemish Painters* (Faber and Faber, London, 1960)

List and Sources of Illustrations

Pictures are listed spread by spread, from top left to bottom right

I The Baroque Century

11 ● Detail showing pope from Palestrina's *Missarum Liber Primus*, 1572 edition

13 ● *Cathedra Petri* by Gianlorenzo Bernini; 1657–66. St Peter's, Rome. Photo *Scala*

14–15 ● View of St Peter's with Bernini's colonnade, and view of Piazza Navona with S. Agnese. Engravings by Lieven Cruyl from *Descriptio faciei variorum locorum .. urbis Romae*, 1694. British Museum, London. Photo *John Freeman*

● Façade of S. Ivo from Piazza di S. Eustachio 1664, engraving by Lieven Cruyl. Courtesy Anton Schroll Verlag. Photo *John Freeman*

16–17 ● Detail from *Carnival in Venice* by Joseph Heintz II; mid 17th C. Doria Pamphili Gallery, Rome. Photo *De Antonis*

● Detail from *The Forum, Rome* by Paul Brill; mid-16th C. Doria Pamphili Gallery, Rome. Photo *Georgina Masson*

18–19 ● *Urban VIII in the Gesù* by Andrea Sacchi; second quarter of 17th C. Palazzo Barberini, Rome. Photo *Scala*

● Louvain, church of St Michael by Willem van Hees (Hesius); 1650. Photo *ACL*

● Service in Reformed church in Nuremberg; 17th C. *Germanisches Nationalmuseum, Nuremberg*

20–21 ● Detail from *The Charlatan Toothpuller* by Theodor Rombouts; first half of 17th C. Prado, Madrid. Photo *Mas*

● Ivory anatomical figure; Italian, late 16th C. *Wellcome Historical Medical Museum and Library, London*

● Detail from *Anatomy lesson of Dr Tulp* by Rembrandt; 1632. *Mauritshuis, The Hague*

22–23 ● Portrait of Galileo by Justus Sustermans; c. 1636. Uffizi, Florence. Photo *Mansell Collection*

● Observing the moon, from Joannes Hevelius' *Selenographia*, 1647. British Museum, London. Photo *R. B. Fleming*

● Calculating machine invented by Blaise Pascal, and presented to Chancellor Séguier who in 1647 had obtained for him a patent. Paper pasted inside lid reads 'Illustrissimo Integerrimo Francia Cancellario D. D. Petro Séguier. Blasius Pascal Patricius Avernus Inventor'. Capacity is 999,999 livres 19 sous 11 deniers. *Photo Musée des Techniques – C N A M Paris*

● Harmony of the universe, from Johann Kepler's *Prodromus dissertationum cosmographicarum*, 1621. British Museum, London. Photo *R. B. Fleming*

● Portrait of Tycho Brahe by Michiels Mierevelt; second half of 16th C. Courtesy of the Royal Society London. Photo *John Freeman*

● Stellaborg, Tycho Brahe's observatory on island of Hveen, Denmark. Coloured engraving from Johann Blaeu's *Atlas Major*, 1662. British Museum, London. Photo *John Freeman*

24 ● *René de Laudonnière with King Athore at Ribaut's column* by Jacques Le Moyne de Morgues; 1564. *New York Public Library, Bequest of James Hazen Hyde*

● *Encounter with eskimos*, watercolour after John White; c. 1610. British Museum, London. Photo *R. B. Fleming*

● *Red Indian in St James's Park*; c. 1616 coloured drawing added to the autograph album of Michael van Meer, compiled during visit to London 1614–15. *University Library, Edinburgh*

25 ● Scene of war, from Daniel Sudermann's *Schöne auserlesene Figuren*, 1628

27 ● Detail from engravings of Madrid by F. B. Werner, engraved by Martin Englebrecht. Among buildings shown are 1. Royal Palace; 2. Treasury; 4. Church of Sto Domingo; 6. Jesuit Church; 7. Church of S Francisco el Grande; 8. Hospital; 9. Convent of Franciscan Recollects; 11. Church of Sta Barbara; 12. Church of S Jerónimo el Real; 13 and 14. Hospitals; 15. Church of S Blas

29 ● Palestrina presenting his mass to Pope Julius III, from titlepage of his *Missarum Liber primus*, Rome 1572 (first edition 1554)

31 ● Map showing religious divisions along the Rhine at beginning of Thirty Years' War

32 ● Beast of the Apocalypse, from titlepage of Cotterius' (Matthieu de la Cottière) *Apocalypseos Domini Nostri*, Sedan 1625

33 ● Zabbatai Zevi in Smyrna in 1666, from *Two Journeys to Jerusalem*, 1685

34 ● *Christianopolis*, from Johann Andreae's *Reipublicae Christianopolitanae Descriptio*, 1619

II Spain's dominion

35 ● Spaniard, woodcut from Hans Weigel's *Trachtenbuch*, Nuremberg 1577

37 ● *Modello* for the *Adoration of the Name of Jesus*, by El Greco; c. 1578. Courtesy Trustees of the National Gallery, London. Photo *John Webb*

38–39 ● Painting of Escorial; anon. 17th C. Escorial, Madrid. Photo *Mas*

● Portrait of Miguel de Cervantes by Juan de Jauregui; 1600. Instituto Valencia de Don Juan, Madrid. Photo *Mas*

● Detail of portrait of Lope de Vega by Caxés; early 17th C. Collection Lázaro, Madrid. Photo *Mas*

● Detail of the *Calling of St Matthew* by Juan de Pareja; 1661. Prado, Madrid. Photo *Mas*

● Detail of portrait of Philip III on horseback by Diego Velásquez; 1628–35. Prado, Madrid. Photo *Mansell Collection*

40–41 ● *Battle of Lepanto*, by A. Vicentino; late 16th C. Palazzo Ducale, Venice. Photo *Scala*

● Detail of design for tapestry of Armada; anon, late 16th C. *National Maritime Museum, Greenwich*

42–43 ● Detail of portrait of St Ignatius Loyola, attributed to Juan de Roelas; c. 1622. Museo Provincial, Seville. Photo *Mas*

● Portrait of St Francis Xavier; Japanese, early 17th C. Kobe Museum of Nanban Art, Kobe City. Photo *courtesy George Rainbird*

● Portrait of St Teresa of Avila by Fray Juan de la Miseria; 1576. Convento de Carmelitas Descalzas de Sta Teresa, Seville. Photo *Mas*

● Sketch entitled *The Expulsion of the Moriscos*, by Vicente Carducci (Carducho); after 1609. Prado, Madrid. Photo *Mas*

● *The Miracle of St Hugo* by Francisco Zurbarán; c. 1633. Museo de Sevilla. Photo *Anderson*

● Seville: Alcázar, courtyard; 1350–69 (restored)

● Toledo: Sta Maria de la Blanca; 13th C.

44–45 ● Portrait of Cardinal Fernando Niño de Guevara, Grand Inquisitor, by El Greco; c. 1600. Metropolitan Museum of Art, New York, Bequest of Mrs H. O. Havermeyer, 1929. The H. O. Havermeyer Collection

● Detail of *Dead Christ* by Gregorio Fernández, painted wood; 1614. Capuchin Monastery, El Pardo. Photo *Paul Pietzsch, courtesy Editorial Noguer*

● Central detail of *Auto-de-fé en la plaza mayor de Madrid*, by Francisco Ricci (Rizi); 1681. Prado, Madrid. Photo *Mas*

46–47 ● *Deer Hunt* by Juan Bautista del Mazo; 1665. Prado, Madrid. Photo *Mas*

● Detail of *Las Meniñas (Maids of Honour)* by Diego Velásquez; 1656. Madrid, Prado. Photo *Mas*

● Detail of *Don Baltasar Carlos in the Riding School* attributed to Diego Velásquez; c. 1634. *Wallace Collection, London (Crown Copyright)*

● Detail of *El Estamento Real* by Sariñena, *administrador* and *contador*; 1592. Palacio de la Generalidad, Valencia. Photo *Mas*

● Detail of carved altarpiece of S. Severo, Councillors of Barcelona listening to sermon of S. Severo; 1681. Cathedral, Barcelona. Photo *Mas*

48 ● *Las Lanzas (Surrender of Breda)* by Diego Velásquez; c. 1634–35. Prado, Madrid. Photo *Scala*

● Detail of portrait of Don Gaspar de Guzmán, Count Duke of Olivares, by Diego Velásquez; c. 1634. Metropolitan Museum of Art, New York, Fletcher Fund, 1952

49 ● Don Quixote and Sancho Panza from titlepage of Cervantes' *Don Quixote de la Mancha*, Lisbon, 1605

50 ● Detail of Spanish siege of Valenciennes 1567 from Famianus Strada's *De Bello Belgico*, 1651 edition

51 ● Engraving of *L'Ordine tenuta dell' Armata*, Rome, 1571

53 ● Engraving of the siege of Malta, Rome, 1565

54 ● Drawing of Castrovirreina in Peru from Poma de Ayala's *Nueva crónica*, 1613. MS GKS 2232. Royal Library, Copenhagen

57 ● Map of Spain in the 17th C.

58 ● Black Knight, detail of titlepage of Thomas Middleton's *A Game at Chaess*, ?1625

59 ● View of Granada with *Moriscos* from Georg Braun and Frans Hogenberg's *Civitates orbis terrarum*, 1572–1618

60 ● Titlepage of *El Fuero Privi-*

233

● *Charles X Gustavus at Battle of Ifverös, 1658* by Johann-Philip Lemke; second half of 17th C. Drottningholm Castle. Photo *Nationalmuseum, Stockholm*

128–129 ● *Officer dictating letter while trumpeter waits* by Gerard Ter Borch; ?c. 1650–60. Courtesy Trustees of the National Gallery, London. Photo *John Webb*

● *Siege of Ostend 1601–4* attributed to Sebastian Vrancx; first half of 17th C. Prado, Madrid. Photo *Mas*

● *Troops at the siege of Aire-sur-la-Lys 1641* by Pieter Snayers; 1653. Prado, Madrid. Photo *Mas*

130–131 ● Cannon, engraving from Johann Jacobi von Wallhausen's *Archiley Kriegskunst*, 1617. British Museum, London. Photo *R. B. Fleming*

● Lancer, Cuirassier and Harquebusier, engravings from Lodovico Melzo's *Regole militari . . . della cavalleria*, Antwerp 1611. British Museum, London. Photo *R. B. Fleming*

● Pikeman, Musketeer and Caliverman, engravings from Jacob de Geyn's *Exercise of Arms*, The Hague 1607 (published in 5 languages almost simultaneously: Dutch, English, German, French and Danish). British Museum, London. Photo *R. B. Fleming*

● Troops quartered in village, engraving from Lodovico Melzo's *Regole militari . . . della cavalleria*, 1611. British Museum, London. Photo *R. B. Fleming*

132 ● Detail from *Ratification of the Treaty of Münster* by Gerard Ter Borch; 1648. Courtesy Trustees of the National Gallery, London. Photo *Eileen Tweedy*

133 ● Broadsheet of 1627 prophesying hard times

135 ● Lucky-dip of Europe: broadsheet, second quarter 17th C.

137 ● Map of Germany in 1648. Base map from *Atlas of World History*, copyright 1965 by Rand McNally and Co. Chicago, Illinois

138 ● Laplander, Liyonian and Scot in Gustavus Adolphus' army. Broadsheet c. 1630

141 ● Proclamation of John Duke of Braganza as King of Portugal, 1640. Detail from engraving showing events in the Portuguese revolt

143 ● Trumpeting the peace through Europe, broadsheet 1648

VI France: monarchy and people

147 ● French peasant, woodcut from Hans Weigel's *Trachtenbuch*, Nuremberg 1577

149 ● Detail from *Peasant Family* by Louis le Nain; c. 1645–48. Louvre, Paris. Photo *Giraudon*

150–151 ● *Procession of the League*, Place du Grève, Paris, 14 May 1590; French School, late 16th C. Musée Carnavalet, Paris. Photo *Giraudon*

● *Ball given at the court of Henri III in honour of the marriage of the Duc de Joyeuse*; French School, late 16th C. Paris, Louvre. Photo *Giraudon*

● Detail of posthumous drawing of the Coligny brothers by Marc Duval; c. 1579. *Bibliothèque Nationale, Paris*

152–153 ● Portrait of Henri IV; French School, late 16th C. Musée de Peinture de Grenoble. Photo *Giraudon*

● Detail of portrait of Cardinal Richelieu by Philippe de Champaigne; c. 1640. Courtesy Trustees of the National Gallery, London. Photo *John Webb*

● Detail of portrait of Chancellor Séguier by Charles Lebrun; 1661. Louvre, Paris. Photo *courtesy Kindler Verlag*

● *Henri IV entrusting the Regency to the Queen*, from the *Life of Marie de Médicis* series by Peter Paul Rubens; 1622–25. Louvre, Paris. Photo *Giraudon*

154–155 ● Paris: Place Dauphine, engraving from Claude Châtillon's *Topographie française*, 1641. British Museum, London. Photo *John Freeman*

● Paris: Place des Vosges; 1605–1612. Photo *courtesy French Government Tourist Office*

● Paris: Place de France, engraving from Claude Châtillon's *Topographie française*, 1641. British Museum, London. Photo *John Freeman*

● Paris: exterior of church of the Sorbonne, designed by Jacques Lemercier; 1635–42. Photo *Giraudon*

● Paris: Louvre, Pavillon de l'Horloge, designed by Jacques Lemercier; 1624–54. Photo *Andrew Ritchie, courtesy Courtauld Institute of Art, University of London*

156–157 ● *Peasants' Meal* by Louis le Nain; 1642. Louvre, Paris. Photo *Giraudon*

● Detail of *St Vincent de Paul and the Filles de Charité*; French School, ?early 18th C. Musée de l'Assistance Publique, Paris

● Detail of *Ex voto* by Philippe de Champaigne; 1662. Louvre, Paris. Photo *courtesy Kindler Verlag*

● *Convent of Port-Royal* by Madeleine de Boulogne; c. 1700 Musée de Versailles. Photo *Giraudon*

158–159 ● Detail of *Beggars at a Doorway*; School of Le Nain, c. 1640–60. *Metropolitan Museum of Art, New York, Purchase, 1871*

● Infirmary of the *Hôpital de la charité* in Paris, engraving by Abraham Bosse; ?1635. Bibliothèque Nationale, Paris. Photo *Giraudon*

● Rapine by soldiers and peasants' revenge, two etchings from the series *Les Misères et les Mal-heurs de la Guerre* by Jacques Callot, 1633. British Museum, London. Photo *John Freeman*

● Detail of *Winter*, engraving by Abraham Bosse; ?1635. Bibliothèque Nationale, Paris. Photo *Giraudon*

● Detail of *Gallery of the Palais Royal*, engraving by Abraham Bosse; ?1640. Musée Carnavalet, Paris. Photo *Giraudon*

● Portrait of Cardinal Mazarin in his gallery, engraving by Robert Nanteuil; 1659. Bibliothèque Nationale, Paris. Photo *Giraudon*

160 ● Vaux-le-Vicomte, Seine-et-Marne: aerial view of château and gardens, designed by Louis Le Vau and André Le Nôtre; 1657–61. Photo *Diapofilm*

● Detail of *Duc d'Anjou being received into the Order of the Holy Spirit 1654* by Philippe de Champaigne, Louis XIV; c. 1665. Musée de Peinture de Grenoble

● Detail of portrait of Nicolas Fouquet; French School, mid 17th C. Musée de Versailles. Photo *Giraudon*

161 ● Scene from *ballet de cour*, from Jean Dorat's *Magnificentissimj spectaculi*, 1573

162 ● Massacre of Vassy from Jacques Perrissin and Jean Tortorel's illustrations of *Evènements remarquables, 1559–70*

163 ● Spanish charlatan from the *Satire Ménippée*, 1595 edition

● League satire on Henri III after the murder of the Guises; 1588. Bibliothèque Nationale, Paris

164 ● Section of the façade of the hôtel de Sully from Jean Marot's *Recueil des plans, profils et élévations*, ?1676

165 ● Engraving after Jean Toutin, decorative ornament for jewellery with goldsmith at work, 1619. British Museum, London

166 ● Paris: plan of the Luxembourg Palace, designed by Salomon de Brosse; 1615. From Anthony Blunt's *Art and Architecture in France 1500–1700*, 1953

167 ● Map of France in the 17th C, adapted from Roland Mousnier's *Les XVIᵉ et XVIIᵉ Siècles*, 1953, and Boris Porchnev's *Les Soulèvements populaires en France de 1623 à 1648*, 1963

168 ● *The noble is the spider and the peasant the fly*, from J. Lagniet's *Recueil de Proverbes*, 1657–63

171 ● *He who wears all his clothes at once must be warm*, from J. Lagniet's *Recueil de Proverbes*, 1657–63

173 ● Diagram of light refraction from René Descartes' *Discours de la methode pour bien conduire sa raison, & chercher la verité dans les sciences*, Leiden 1637

VII Britain transformed

175 ● English nobleman, woodcut from Hans Weigel's *Trachtenbuch*, Nuremberg 1577

177 ● Apotheosis of James I (centre panel of ceiling) by Peter Paul Rubens; 1634. Banqueting House, Whitehall. Photo *Ministry of Public Buildings and Works (Crown Copyright)*

178–179 ● Portrait of William Cecil, Lord Burghley, attributed to Marcus Gheeraerts II; late 16th C. Hatfield House, Herts. Reproduced by permission of the Marquess of Salisbury, K. G. Photo *Courtauld Institute of Art, University of London*

● Portrait of Robert Devereux, Earl of Essex; anon, 1597. *National Portrait Gallery, London*

● Miniature called Richard Boyle Earl of Cork; attributed to Isaac Oliver, c. 1610–15. *National Portrait Gallery, London*

● *Session of the Court of Wards and Liveries*; anon, c. 1585. Goodwood, Chichester. Courtesy Trustees of the Goodwood Collection. Photo *Eileen Tweedy*

● 'Rainbow portrait' of Elizabeth I; style of Marcus Gheeraerts II, c. 1600. Hatfield House, Herts. Reproduced by permission of the Marquess of Salisbury, K. G. Photo *Courtauld Institute of Art, University of London*

180–181 ● Coloured drawings of a cockpit, a carter and market porter, London Bridge, from the autograph album of Michael van Meer; 1614–15. *University Library, Edinburgh*

● *View of Richmond Palace*; Flemish School, ?1620s. Reproduced by permission of the Syndics of the Fitzwilliam Museum, Cambridge

● *Henry Frederick, Prince of Wales and Sir John Harinton*; Flemish School, 1603. Metropolitan Museum of Art, New York, Pulitzer Fund

182–183 ● Wollaton, Nottinghamshire: east front of the Hall; 1580–88. Photo *A. F. Kersting*

● Knole House, Kent: Long Gallery; 1605. Photo *Edwin Smith*

● Oxford; south porch of St Mary the Virgin; 1637. Photo *A. F. Kersting*

● Greenwich: north façade of Queen's House, designed by Inigo Jones; 1616–17, 1629–35. Photo *C. J. Bassham*

● Detail of monument to Sir Thomas Hawkins, by Epiphanius Evesham, right-hand front panel, weeping daughters; 1618. Church of SS Peter, Paul and Barnabas, Boughton-under-Blean, Kent. Photo *National Monuments Record, London*

● Holles monument by Nicholas Stone; c. 1625. Westminster Abbey, London. Photo *A. F. Kersting*

184–185 ● *Execution of Charles I* by Weesop; 1649. On loan to the Scottish National Portrait Gallery, Edinburgh. Courtesy Lord Primrose. Photo *Tom Scott*

186–187 ● Execution of Thomas Wentworth, Earl of Strafford, etching by Wenceslaus Hollar; 1641. British Museum, London. Photo *John Freeman*

● Battle of Naseby, engraving from Joshua Sprigge's *Anglia Rediviva*, 1647. British Museum, London. Photo *R. B. Fleming*

● Portrait of John Lilburne, engraving by George Glover (State II, bars added), for Richard Overton's *A remonstrance of many learned citizens and other free-born people of England*, 1646. British Museum, London. Photo *R. B. Fleming*

● Oliver Cromwell trampling faction and error, engraving by William Faithorne for *The Embleme of England's Distractions*, 1658. Photo *Mansell Collection*

● Satirical Dutch print of Crom-

Index